# MUSLIM LAWS, POLITICS AND SOCIETY IN MODERN NATION STATES

*For My Family*

# Muslim Laws, Politics and Society in Modern Nation States

## Dynamic Legal Pluralisms in England, Turkey and Pakistan

IHSAN YILMAZ
*SOAS, University of London, UK*

ASHGATE

Published by
Ashgate Publishing Limited
Gower House
Croft Road
Aldershot
Hants GU11 3HR
England

Ashgate Publishing Company
Suite 420
101 Cherry Street
Burlington, VT 05401-4405
USA

Ashgate website: http://www.ashgate.com

**British Library Cataloguing in Publication Data**
Yilmaz, Ihsan
Muslim laws, politics and society in modern nation states : dynamic legal pluralisms in England, Turkey and Pakistan
1. Customary law (Islamic law) 2. Customary law (Islamic law) - Case studies 3. Legal polycentricity 4. Legal polycentricity - England 5. Legal polycentricity - Turkey 6. Legal polycentricity - Pakistan 7. Legal polycentricity - Case studies
I. Title
340.5'9

**Library of Congress Cataloging-in-Publication Data**
Yilmaz, Ihsan, 1971-
Muslim laws, politics and society in modern nation states : dynamic legal pluralisms in England, Turkey and Pakistan / by Ihsan Yilmaz.
p. cm.
Includes bibliographical references and index.
ISBN 0-7546-4389-1
1. Islamic law--England. 2. Islamic law--Turkey. 3. Islamic law--Pakistan. 4. Sociological jurisprudence. 5. Islam and politics. I. Title.

KBP173.25.Y55 2004
340'.115--dc22

2004018317

ISBN 0 7546 4389 1

Printed and bound in Great Britain by MPG Books Ltd, Bodmin, Cornwall

# Contents

# List of Tables

# Acknowledgements

I am indebted to other writers, academics and colleagues whose footprints I followed during my long journey while writing this book. I have been indebted to too many friends to be capable of identifying all my obligations. But I would especially like to thank Professor Menski of SOAS for all the invaluable help, advice and support he has given me. I gratefully acknowledge his intellectual feedback to this book. I am grateful to Assoc. Prof Dr. Hasan Selçuk for his vision and efforts to send me to the UK for a PhD.

This book mainly draws from my PhD thesis (SOAS, 1996-1998) and my previously published papers: 'Marriage Solemnization among Turks in Britain: Emergence of the Hybrid Anglo-Muslim Turkish Law'. In: *Journal of Muslim Minority Affairs*. Spring 2004. V. 24 N.1; '*Ijtihad* and *Tajdid* by Conduct: Gülen and His Movement'. In: John Esposito and Hakan Yavuz (eds) *Turkish Islam and the secular state: The Gulen movement.* New York: Syracuse U Press. 2003. 208-237; 'Non-Recognition of Post-Modern Turkish Socio-Legal Reality and Predicament of Women'. In: *British Journal of Middle Eastern Studies*. 2003. Vol. 30 No. 1. 25-41; 'Instrumentalist Use of Secular Law in Turkey and the Emergence of Unofficial Turkish Muslim Law'. *The Middle East Journal*. Winter 2002. Vol. 56 No. 1. 113-131; 'Dynamic Legal Pluralism in England: The Challenge of Postmodern Muslim Legality to Legal Modernity'. In: *Journal of Ethnic and Migration Studies*. Spring 2002. Vol. 28 No. 2. 343-354; 'Law as Chameleon: The Question of Incorporation of Muslim Personal Law into the English Law'. In: *Journal of Muslim Minority Affairs*. Fall 2001. Vol. 21 No. 2. 297-308; 'Is Having A Personal Law System A Solution? Towards A Supra-Modern Law'. In: *Journal for Islamic Studies*. 2001. Vol. 20. 99-124; 'Muslim Law in Britain, Reflections in the Socio-Legal Sphere and Differential Legal Treatment'. In: *Journal of Muslim Minority Affairs*. Fall 2000. Vol. 20 No. 2. 353-360.

I owe a lot to the constructive criticisms of the anonymous peer-reviewers of these journals and of Ashgate Publishing. I learnt a lot from them. I also have to thank Alison Kirk of Ashgate who showed interest in this book, encouraged me to finish it as soon as possible and swiftly responded to my queries. Last but not least my special thanks goes to my family, my parents, my best friend and wife Arzu for their dauntless and unfailing support and to my little daughter Büşra whose time I stole when writing this book. Needless to say, any errors remain, of course, mine alone.

# List of Abbreviations

| | |
|---|---|
| AC | Appeal Cases |
| ALD | *All Legal Decisions* |
| All ER | *All England Law Reports* |
| ALRC | Australian Law Reform Commission |
| AUHF | Ankara Üniversitesi Hukuk Fakültesi |
| BAAKB | Başbakanlık Aile Araştırma Kurumu Başkanlığı |
| BMMT | *Büyük Millet Meclisi Tutanakları* |
| CA | Court of Appeal |
| CCME | Churches' Committee for Migrants in Europe |
| CCMWE | Churches' Committee for Migrants in Western Europe |
| Ch | *Law Reports: Chancery Division 1991-* |
| Ch. D | Chancery Division |
| CLC | *Civil Law Cases (Pakistan)* |
| CLR | *Criminal Law Reports* |
| CRE | Commission for Racial Equality |
| Crim LC | *Criminal Law Journal* |
| Crim LR | *Criminal Law Reports* |
| CrLJ | *Criminal Law Journal* |
| CrLR | *Criminal Law Reports* |
| CSIC-MR | The Centre for the Study of Islam and Christian-Muslim Relations |
| ECHR | European Convention of Human Rights |
| Fam Law | Family Law (England) |
| FCR | *Family Court Reports* |
| FLR | *Family Law Reports (England)* |
| FSC | Federal Shariat Court |

| | |
|---|---|
| HL | House of Lords |
| HMSO | Her Majesty's Stationery Office |
| HUNEE | Hacettepe Üniversitesi Nüfus Etüdleri Enstitüsü |
| ICE | Islamic Council of Europe |
| ISC | Islamic Shari'a Council of Britain |
| IUHF | Istanbul Üniversitesi Hukuk Fakültesi |
| Kar | Karachi |
| KB | King's Bench |
| Lah | Lahore |
| MEB | Milli Eğitim Bakanlığı (Turkey) |
| MFLO | Muslim Family Laws Ordinance, 1961 |
| MLD | *Monthly Legal Digest (Pakistan)* |
| MPDG | Ministry of Planning and Development, Government of Pakistan |
| MRG | Minority Rights Group |
| NLJ | *National Law Journal* |
| NLR | *National Law Reporter (Pakistan)* |
| P CrLJ | *Pakistan Criminal Law Journal* |
| PLD | *All Pakistan Legal Decisions* |
| PWRC | Pakistan Women's Rights Committee |
| QB | Queen's Bench |
| SC | Supreme Court |
| SCMR | *Supreme Court Monthly Review (Pakistan)* |
| SIS | State Institute of Statistics Prime Ministry of Turkey |
| SOAS | School of Oriental and African Studies |
| Sol Jo | *Solicitor's Journal* |
| SPO | State Planning Organisation Prime Ministry of Turkey |
| TCB | Türkiye Cumhuriyeti Basbakanlık |
| TCC | Turkish Criminal Code |
| TRSRG | The Radical Statistics Race Group |

| | |
|---|---|
| TRT | The Runnymede Trust |
| UCL | University College London |
| UKACIA | The United Kingdom Action Committee of Islamic Affairs |
| UMO | Union of Muslim Organisations (of UK and Eire) |
| UP | University Press |
| WLR | *Weekly Law Reports (England)* |
| WP | West Pakistan |
| Y21HD | Yargıtay 21. Hukuk Dairesi |
| Y2HD | Yargıtay 2. Hukuk Dairesi |
| Y4CD | Yargıtay 4. Ceza Dairesi |
| YHGK | Yargıtay Hukuk Genel Kurulu |
| YIBK | Yargıtay Içtihadları Birleştirme Kararı |
| YKD | *Yargıtay Kararları Dergisi* |

# Glossary

| | |
|---|---|
| Ar | Arabic |
| Fr | French |
| Ger | German |
| Heb | Hebrew |
| San | Sanskrit |
| Tur | Turkish |
| Ur | Urdu |

| | |
|---|---|
| adat, adah (Ar) | tradition, custom |
| Adil düzen (Tur) | just system |
| al-maqasid al-Shari'a (Ar) | purposes of *Shari'a* |
| Angrezi (Ur) | English |
| Angrezi shariat (Ur) | English *Shari'a* |
| aql (Ar) | reason |
| asr al-darura (Ar) | time of necessity |
| batil (Ar) | that which is false in doctrine, void |
| beth din (Heb) | house of religion. The highest office of Jewish religious authority |
| biradari (Ur) | brotherhood, group relationship, caste, fraternity, patrilineal kinship group |
| dar al-ahd (Ar) | country of treaty, covenant |
| dar al-aman (Ar) | country of security |
| dar al-darura (Ar) | country of necessity. See *darura* |
| dar al-harb, dar'ul harb (Ar) | country of war. The country of non-believers |
| dar al-hizmet (Tur) | country of service to spread Islam |

| | |
|---|---|
| dar al-Islam (Ar) | country of Islam |
| dar as-sulh (Ar) | country of truce |
| dar-al-dawah (Ar) | country of invitation to Islam, mission |
| darura (Ar) | compulsion. An extreme situation where one is allowed to do things which are otherwise forbidden in Islam |
| desh pardesh (Ur) | a home away from home |
| Dharma (San) | duty, doing the right thing at the right time |
| dhimmi, zimmi (Ar) | a free non-Muslim subject living in a Muslim country who, in return for paying a fixed poll and land tax, enjoys protection and safety. Belongs to a specific *millet* |
| din (Ar) | religion |
| din wa dawla (Ar) | religion and state |
| düğün (Tur) | traditional wedding celebration |
| fatwa (Ar) | juristic opinion. A religious or judicial decree, pronounced either by a *khalifa, mufti,* or *kadi* |
| fiqh (Ar) | works on Muslim law, Muslim canonical jurisprudence. Body of rules gradually developed from interpretations of the *Shari'a* |
| furu al-fiqh (Ar) | substantive law |
| Gemeinschaft (Ger) | community |
| get (Heb) | Jewish divorce document similar to Muslim pronouncement of unilateral divorce (*talaq*) by the husband. Yet in this case, husband's decision to divorce should be written and delivered to the wife |
| gizli (Tur) | hidden, secret |
| hadd (Ar) | limit. The limits which have been defined in the *Qur'an* or in the *Hadith*. Punishments for offences which are |

| | |
|---|---|
| | defined in *Shari'a* |
| hadith (Ar) | collections of traditions or records of what the Prophet of Islam did, what he enjoined, and that which was done in his presence and which he did not forbid |
| halal (Ar, Ur) | that which is permissible under *Shari'a*. Opposite of *haram* |
| Hanafi (Ar) | one of the four classical *fiqh* schools of *Sunni* Muslim law, founded by *Imam*-i-Azam Abu Hanifa |
| Hanbali (Ar) | one of the four classical *fiqh* schools of the *Sunni* Muslim law, founded by *Imam* Ahmad Ibn Hanbal |
| haram (Ar) | that which is forbidden in Islam. Opposite of *halal* |
| harem (Tur) | a separated place in a Muslim house where only women live. In Ottoman palaces, the female relatives of the sultan, other staff and female servants used to live in *harem*s |
| hodood (Ar) | plural of *hadd* |
| ibadat (Ar) | religious observations |
| iddah (Ar) | a period of time corresponding to 3 consecutive menstrual periods. The standard period of time during which a women should not remarry after the divorce or death of her husband |
| ijma (Ar) | consensus |
| ijtihad (Ar) | exposition of the laws, juristic exposition. Independent reasoning or judgement. The logical deduction on a legal or theological question by an expert whose qualifications are defined by the *Shari'a* and *fiqh* |
| ikhtilaf (Ar) | tolerated diversity of opinions |
| ikrah (Ar) | duress, compulsion, cohesion. A state of affairs where there is a fear or threat of injury to a person's property or honour |

| | |
|---|---|
| imam (Ar) | one whose leadership or example is to be followed. The one who leads the prayer |
| imam nikahı (Tur) | religious marriage ceremony conducted by an *imam* |
| istihsan (Ar) | the principle of *Hanafi* jurisprudence that in cases not regulated by the *Qur'an*, *Sunna* or *ijma*, equitable considerations may override strict *qiyas* |
| istishab (Ar) | presumption of continuity |
| istislah (Ar) | the principle that consideration of public interest may be a critierion for the elaboration of legal rules |
| izzat (Ar, Ur) | honour, pride |
| kadi, qadi (Ar) | a judge of Muslim canonical law, and in Ottoman history, governor of a *kaza* |
| kaza (Tur) | in Ottoman times, a district town |
| khalifa (Ar) | caliph |
| khilafa (Ar) | caliphate |
| khul, khula, khul' (Ar) | release from the marriage tie at the instance of the wife, for consideration of the husband |
| Lebenswelt (Ger) | life-world |
| Leitmotiv (Ger) | something that appears repeatedly and is seen to be of important interest |
| madhhab (Ar) | school of law |
| mahr (Ar) | dower. An amount of money or property settled or paid by the husband to his wife as an incident of the marriage. Without *mahr* marriage is not legal |
| Majalla, Mecelle (Tur) | the Ottoman code of civil law issued between 1869 and 1876 |
| mal (Ar) | property |
| Maliki (Ar) | one of the four classical *fiqh* schools of *Sunni* Muslim law. Founded by *Imam* Malik |

| | |
|---|---|
| maslaha (Ar) | public interest, public welfare |
| Medina (Ar) | city in Saudi Arabia to which the prophet of Islam moved from his own city, Mecca, and where he founded the very first Muslim state |
| millet (Ar) | a religious community, nation, living in a Muslim country, entitled to be ruled in their personal matters in accordance with their religious laws |
| muamalat (Ar) | social transactions |
| mubaraat, mubar'at (Ar) | mutual discharge. Divorce by mutual consent of the husband and wife |
| mufti (Ar) | official expounder of Muslim law. Legal consultant qualified to pronounce a *fatwa* |
| muhtar (Tur) | village headman |
| mujtahid (Ar) | jurist capable of making *ijtihad* |
| mujtahid-i mutlaq (Ar) | absolute *mujtahid* |
| mursal (Ar) | not textually specified |
| nafs (Ar) | person |
| nasl (Ar) | offspring |
| nikah (Ar, Tur) | literally 'conjunction'. Marriage |
| nikahnama (Ur) | marriage contract |
| Nizam-i-Islam (Ar) | Islamic system. Slogan coined by the traditional religious figures in Pakistan in their struggle against Zulfikar Ali Butto's administration |
| panchayat (Ur) | village tribunal. Council of village elders where disputes are settled which has popular roots in the Indian subcontinent |
| pardah, purdah (Ur) | veil. Seclusion of women |
| qiyas (Ar) | analogical deduction |
| Qur'an, Quran, Kuran (Ar) | holy book of Islam |
| resmi (Tur) | official |
| ric'i talaq (Ar, Tur) | revocable *talaq* |

| | |
|---|---|
| Şeyh-ul-Islam (Tur) | the highest Islamic authority in Ottoman State, this came next to the Grand Vizier in governmental importance |
| Shafii (Ar) | one of the four classical *fiqh* schools of the *Sunni* Muslim law. Founded by *Imam Shafi'i* |
| shari'a, shariat, shariah (Ar) | path. The divinely ordained law. The Muslim canonical law. The body of sacred law of Islam, embodied in the *Qur'an*, the *Sunna,* the *hadith*, and the *fiqh* |
| Shi'te, Shia (Ar) | followers. An Islamic sect that regards Ali (the fourth caliph of Islam) and his descendants as the rightful successors of the prophet and disregard the first three caliphs |
| sujet de droits (Fr) | an individual subject to more than one laws |
| Sunna, Sunnah (Ar) | custom. A path, a manner of life. The traditions which record either the sayings or doings of the Prophet of Islam |
| Sunni (Ar) | literally, one on the path. The largest sect of Muslims who, unlike *Shia*s, acknowledge the first 4 caliphs as the rightful successors of the prophet. They belong to the four classical school of jurisprudence, *Hanafi, Shafi'i, Maliki, Hanbali* |
| syyed (Ar) | descendant of the prophet |
| tajdid (Ar) | renewal |
| takhayyur (Ar) | a selection from various juristic opinions, eclecticism |
| takhyir (Ar) | selection |
| talaq (Ar) | the pronouncement of divorce by husband |
| talaq al-ahsan (Ar) | single pronouncement of divorce during the period of *tuhr* and abstention from sexual intercourse during her *iddah*. This |

| | |
|---|---|
| | type of divorce is revocable during *iddah* |
| talaq al-bida, bidah, bid'a (Ar) | divorce in a single pronouncement |
| talaq al-hasan (Ar) | a procedure of divorce, stretching over three months. This is where there are three pronouncements of divorce during three *tuhr*s. Before the third pronouncement divorce is revocable |
| talaq al-Sunna (Ar) | a name for *talaq-al-hasan* and *talaq-al-ahsan* |
| talaq-i-tawfiz (Ar) | delegation of the right of divorce by the husband. A form of divorce where the woman exercises the right of divorce delegated to her by the man while signing the marriage contract or later |
| talfiq (Ar) | piecing together |
| Tanzimat (Tur) | name of the nineteenth century period of Ottoman reforms that began in 1839 and extended to the enactment of the first Ottoman Constitution in 1876 |
| taqlid (Ar) | imitation |
| tarjih (Ar) | preference |
| tasnif (Ar) | classification |
| tuhr (Ar) | when a woman is not menstruating. The period of purity |
| ummah (Ar) | nation. The universal Muslim community |
| urf (Ar) | literally 'what is known' about a thing, and thus loosely encompasses custom and tradition |
| usul al-fiqh (Ar) | sources of law |
| Wahabi (Ar) | an Islamic *maddhab*, commonly practised in Saudi Arabia |
| wakil, vakil (Ar) | proxy |
| watta-satta (Ur) | exchange marriage |
| Weltanschauung (Ger) | worldview |
| zina (Ar) | the offence of illicit sexual relations |

# Table of Cases

*England*



*Pakistan*

*Turkey*

# Table of Statutes

*Other*

# Chapter 1

# Law, Politics and Society in the Post-Modern Condition

One of the most crucial legal and sociological issues of the modern age is how far and with what consequences law could be used in the process of the deliberate forming of society. In this regard, the modern nation-state law has often been employed as a modernizing agent or as an instrument of modernization. The law is expected to act as an agent of change and development. Almost all modern nation-states have steadily tried to use law as a tool of social engineering and as a mode of organizing beliefs and values to shape and to uniformize their societies in the modern era.

Post-modernity provides a philosophical frame or paradigm in which modernity is critically examined, using primarily the techniques of 'deconstruction' developed by hermeneutics and social linguistics.[1] Post-modernity can be seen as a multifocal symbol, which in its most generalized usage challenges the assumption of universality inherent in the legitimating discourses of modernity such as secularism, rationality, social stratification, urbanization and industrialization. There are various façades of post-modernity: Indeterminacy, fragmentation, irony, the fictionalization of identity, carnivalization, decanonization and hybridization (Hassan 1985: 119).

For Lyotard (1984: xxv), post-modern society is characterized by a disbelief in the availability of a privileged metanarrative or the ultimate discourse of the universal 'truth'. Instead, legitimization becomes plural, local and inherent within a specific context. Post-modern theory distrusts all attempts to create general, large-scale totalizing theories in order to explain social phenomena (Douzinas et al 1991: x). In the post-modern age, unitary theories of progress are increasingly being questioned. Objective 'truth' has been replaced by the plurality of viewpoints. Relative truths are on the stage. This undermines the existence of social life as a contained and integrated totality, a unified system of meaning. As a result of this mentality, the particular, the multiple and the heterogeneous are acknowledged and legitimized. In the post-modern condition, what one sees is a proliferation of social codes relating to ethnicity, gender, culture and religion. As a result, a field of stylistic and discursive heterogeneity has emerged. This age is characterized by diversity and cultural relativity.

[1] See in detail Connor (1991); Hollinger (1994); Tester (1993); Touraine (1992); Rosenau (1992); Foucault (1986; 1987; 1988; 1992; 1994).

Post-modern scholars have argued that knowledge claims can only ever be partial and local, as post-modernity implies a mistrust of the metanarratives of modernity (Lyotard 1984: 82). It is accepted that differences do not go away. Thus, post-modernism represents a radical potential in the attempt to formulate a defence of difference, while toleration gains importance (Rosenau 1992: 98; Bauman 1992: 2-23, 30-36). Post-moderns advocate that 'every culture... is equivalent to every other one' (Wagner 1995: 55).

Legal modernity is challenged in this age as well. It is being recognized that social space is not a normative vacuum. Local laws, along with local cultures and identities, are preserved. Thus, totality in the legal arena is questioned. Post-modern analyses of law and social movements have assaulted the claims of universal theories.

Legal pluralism is a key concept in a post-modern view of law. This broader conception of law indicates a more complex relation between law and society. Law is conceptualized as more plural, not located entirely in the state. This legally plural notion of law in which state law is only one of many levels does not give any privilege to centrality. While the legal officials and legal scholars assume the state monopoly of legal production, research on legal pluralism maintains the existence and circulation of a society of different legal systems, the state legal systems being only one of them. The whole structure of law of a people is not limited to the monistic system of state law. The whole structure of law as an aspect of culture should include all regulations which the people concerned observe as law in their cultural tradition, including value systems. An increase in attention to discourse, narrativity, and language along with legal culture, legal ideology, and legal consciousness could be observed in the post-modern condition. Faith in the progressive possibilities of law has been shaken. A new agenda about justice in today's world of discursive power and decentred subjectivities emerged in which no group is authorized to construct a vision of a socially just world.

There are crosscutting ties that are maintained by individuals on various levels in the post-modern condition. These ties do not replace territorially-based communities or bureaucratically organized formal organizations, but are superimposed on them. The self-identified and reflexive post-modern navigator is in continual dialogue with formal organizations and with ethno-religious communities whose boundaries are not necessarily defined by geography. The boundaries of a society or of a community no longer correspond with the modern nation-state's political borders. In that condition, 'the local' does not remain local since in the multicultural context of a country, ethnic or religious groups may appear as relatively isolated minorities, but when expanded into the global framework, their relationships must be understood as part of a transnational network (McLelland and Richmond 1994: 665).[2]

[2] So far as the Muslim minorities and their laws including their customs are concerned, this phenomenon is of paramount importance, since Muslims and Muslim law issues have started to frequently occupy the global public sphere. Although they might be minorities in some non-Muslim States, at the same time, they are a part of a transnational universal

Law is a socio-cultural construct and not an Austinian political one, thus, legal pluralism or legal post-modernity always co-exist with multicultural reality. In the socio-legal sphere, which consists of numerous semi-autonomous fields, law both helps to constitute social interaction and is itself constructed by social action where there is a continual dialogue between small, local narratives and totalizing metanarratives. Muslims have become the main players of this post-modern process.

Muslims not only have challenged the presumptions of legal modernity but have also shown that 'they can become citizens while at the same time retaining their Muslim identity' (King 1995: 112). They are not lost between cultures. They skilfully navigate across different cultures. In the normative space they reach the same end as 'skilful legal navigators': They apply relevant law in relevant contextual situations aiming to meet demands of different overlapping normative orderings. This phenomenon is a post-modern response to legal modernity. It reminds us again that legal modernity has limits and that legal post modernity is a reality. People retain their Muslim law in even secular and modern contexts in a post-modern way although uniform legal systems try to transform society through law, aiming for homogenization.

This book identifies Muslims' current socio-legal situation and their legal attitudes from different perspectives. The main aim of this study is to analyze the conflict between the assumptions of modern legal systems and plural legal realities. While there is a reconstruction of unofficial Muslim laws in the modern and officially uniform secular legal systems of England and Turkey, in the case of Pakistan, where Islamic laws are recognized to a great extent, legal reform attempts in the areas of Muslim family law by the Islamic Pakistani state have so far not been successful and have led to intense clashes. The study shows that Muslims in these countries react to the modern frameworks of legal systems and do not abandon their locally formulated and interpreted Muslim laws. State formulations and interpretations of Islamic law, as in the case of Pakistan, or its more or less total disregard, as in the cases of Britain and Turkey, lead people to reconstruct their own unofficial Muslim laws.

In these three scenarios, modern legal systems try to impose official laws, yet face the resistance of unofficial Muslim laws. The study argues that Muslims recreate, reconstruct, redefine and restructure their Muslim laws as unofficial laws even within a secular or modern framework and thus undermine and obstruct, in various ways, the claim of official law to be the unique regulator of human behaviour in any given social field. The main objective of the study is to show that there will always be dynamic legal pluralism stemming from unofficial Muslim laws.

In the case of Britain, it seems that the Muslim minority has not abandoned its adherence to customary laws and has reconstructed it in a new form. This study shows the same phenomenon in Turkey as well. In Turkey, at least some segments

---

*ummah* with 'transnational universal' laws which clash, encounter and interact with modern nation-state laws.

of the Muslim population have reacted negatively to the official, modern, and supposedly entirely secular legal system and are instead following Islamic rules. In Pakistan, again the traditional population has reacted to the modern legal system, which clashes with traditional local understandings and applications of Islam, even though the modern legal system claims to be Islamic.

Thus, in all three manifestations, Muslims are affected by official laws while at the same time maintaining their Muslim laws and local customary practices. Consequently, unofficial laws are reconstructed. In the English and Turkish cases, the net result is reconstruction of adapted Muslim unofficial laws. It is very clear that this evolution of Muslim laws is a direct consequence of interactions between specific groups of Muslims and the modern legal systems in which they live. As a result of this interaction, new hybrid laws have reconstructed. When official law cannot solve or does not recognize the problems of Muslim communities, people invent their own laws and find solutions to their problems even in a secular framework.

In addition, this study argues that in all cases, the official law is undermined. Recognizing that law has limits, modern legal systems, on some points, make some concessions; they are forced to accommodate more diversity and to make further readjustments over time.

The study also elaborates on the question of what would be a proper response from the side of both modern legal systems and Muslims to the challenge of post-modern legality. In that context, the question whether a Muslim personal law system can and needs to be introduced in Britain and Turkey will be examined. On this issue, the current situation of Pakistani Muslim law, and problems and issues in the Pakistani personal law system, are matters of considerable relevance and shed important light on the debates in Britain and Turkey. The case of Pakistan shows most clearly that whether one introduces a personal law system (and gives recognition to Muslim family law) or not, legal diversity and legal pluralism will not be overcome.

This study first attempts to depict a clear picture of the operation of law in society with special reference to legal pluralism studies. The study also endeavours to apply the theories of legal pluralism to the practical sphere of Muslims, Muslim laws and legal postulates. Thus, it portrays the Muslim dimension of jurisprudence or legal philosophy studies vis-à-vis legal pluralism. Muslim legal pluralism can exist at four different levels: Individual, communal, national, cross-national or global. Firstly, legal pluralism emerges at the individual level of the Muslim. Secondly, one sees legal pluralism at the community level. Thirdly, legal pluralism is an issue at stake on a national level within the borders of a country. Fourthly, legal pluralism emerges as a cross-national or global phenomenon as a result of the notion of universal *ummah*.

The literature as discussed in chapter 2 confirms a general principle that there is an inseparable and dynamic interrelationship between law and culture, as law is a cultural construct. The whole picture of law as it operates in society is composed of three levels: Official laws, unofficial laws, and legal postulates, since law must be understood as a cultural construct involving ideas, structures, processes, and practices. Law exists at every level of society, sometimes as state law, sometimes as norms or rules of conduct, and it usually conveys a cultural and historical meaning. People may be born into a particular culture and brought up to uphold certain values, but in the process of interacting with structures, they also create, continue, and constitute those structures. Law is a process shaped by rules and a cultural logic that is called a 'legal postulate'. The socio-legal sphere is not a normative vacuum and the operation of law is constantly under the influence of legal postulates that exist in this sphere. Individuals and communities deal with socio-legal issues under the influence of legal postulates. These postulates could be religious, ethnic, racial, political and economical. Here, unofficial law is not only indigenous law, but might be of several types as can be seen in the cases of England (ethnic minority laws and customs), Turkey (Muslim local law and customs) and Pakistan (local Muslim laws and customs other than the 'Islamic law' of the state). Law can evolve in expected and unexpected ways, through many small institutional changes and through people interacting at the borders of law who create new normative patterns and semi-autonomous spheres. The maintenance of law is a dynamic process of constant struggle and readjustment. Law has a tendency to intrude into all types of relationships, interacting with them, and changing itself until both become altered. As a result, a reconstruction process emerges in which laws change and adapt.

Legal pluralism is not only an issue for traditional societies, but also a concern for contemporary ones, as virtually every society is, in a sense, multicultural. Thus, dynamic legal pluralisms have come into operation as ubiquitous phenomena of the post-modern age. As a consequence of the interconnectedness of social orders, there is a mutually constitutive relation between official law and unofficial law(s). Dynamic legal pluralism is a direct result of the relationship between official law and society. It is not an issue of domination but constitutive of social life. Both official law and semi-autonomous social fields are composed by their interrelations to one another.

In the process of the active interaction between official and unofficial laws, official law may use the symbols of the unofficial law. On the other side of the fence, however, unofficial law may use the symbols and meanings of the state system, too. As a result of this mutual influence, while unofficial law may transform the meaning and effect of official law, the character of unofficial law may be affected at the same time in unanticipated ways by developments in the official law.

Whilst unofficial law may actively resist the demands of a modern official legal system, it may also actively incorporate the rules of the official law into its own rule system. In this process, unofficial law is open-ended, responsive to and grounded in social relations, albeit continually subject to normalization and partial termination. In the post-modern condition, 'there is a continual dialogue between small, local narratives and totalizing metanarratives' (McLellan and Richmond 1994: 668). A reconstruction of unofficial laws takes place as merely another swing in the pendulum towards increasing complexity in the dialogue. The post-modern stage of legal development is one of plurality rather than facile uniformity. In addition, at this stage, one can even talk about utopian legal subjectivity; a transformation 'from the law-abiding citizen to the law-inventing citizen' (Santos 1995: 573). This legal subjectivity is facilitated by 'an interplay of synchronic and diachronic perspectives that continually construct and reconstruct identity' (McLellan and Richmond 1994: 669). Individuals in the post-modern arena would become subject to more than one law and might, in some cases, be diametrically opposing as *sujets de droits*. However, they would overcome this challenge as skilful legal navigators and, in a way, would manipulate the laws and combine and amalgamate different types of normative orderings. They are the main actors of a post-modern scene in which new laws are continuously invented. It would appear that law, be it official or unofficial, would thence be continually constructed and reconstructed.

It is plausible to argue, then, that this phenomenon is ubiquitous and may be the case for Muslims as well, as they have become important main players in the post-modern process. This study asks whether dynamic Muslim legal pluralism, as a glocal phenomenon, is on the stage, and whether the reconstruction of unofficial Muslim laws is a mundane reality of everyday life that challenges legal modernity. It is also analyzed in the subsequent chapters whether Muslims recreate, redefine and reconstruct their laws and customs as 'skilled legal navigators', and, in the case of family law issues, if they develop strategies to satisfy the requirements of both official legal systems of modern nation-states and their 'Muslim law'.

The study consists of eight chapters. Following this introduction, the second chapter undertakes five major functions: Firstly, it briefly discusses the definition of law as a socio-cultural construct. Then, it analyzes legal modernity, the limits of law and the interaction between official and unofficial laws. Thirdly, it focuses on the theories of legal pluralism in some detail. In this context, a survey of legal pluralism studies is provided and classifications of legal pluralism are discussed. Fourthly, this chapter tries to find a formulation of the operation of law in society, while combining the theories of post-modernity and studies of legal pluralism. It, then develops an analytical tool to observe dynamic legal pluralism. Fifthly, still remaining at a theoretical level, the chapter elaborates on local, ethnic, and religious laws in a dynamic legal pluralist context. The following chapters are based on this theoretical framework.

The third chapter is another theoretical analysis: Muslim legal pluralisms in the post-modern age. It first looks at the traditional Muslim legal plurality or internal Muslim legal pluralism. In this context, the concepts of *Shari'a*, *fiqh* and *ijtihad* are defined and discussed. Almost 90 percent of all Muslims all over the world are *Sunni* Muslims. *Shia* Muslims who are seen as heteredox by the majority are mostly concentrated in Iran and Iraq. There are also some small *Shia* minorities in Turkey and Pakistan but the great majority of Muslims who live in all the three countries studied here are *Sunni* and almost 90 percent of these *Sunni* Muslims follow *Hanafi* school of jurisprudence (*madhhab*), which is one of the four mainstream legal schools, others being *Shafii*, *Maliki* and *Hanbali*. These are all traditional[3] schools

[3] Some literature refers to these schools as 'classical' rather than traditional. They are synonyms in this context. I will use these terms interchangeably in this study.

that developed in the second and third centuries of Islam. Each of these four schools recognize each other as legitimate. *Shias* have their own legal schools as well. Because the majority of people in this study are interested in *Hanafi* Muslims, where a specific *madhhab* is not mentioned it means that it is either a general rule agreed upon by all *madhhabs* or a *Hanafi* rule.

After discussing internal Muslim legal pluralism from theoretical and historical perspectives, the book looks at the internal Muslim legal pluralism in this age, focusing on the phenomena of neo-*ijtihad* and surfing on the inter-*madhhab*-net in *asr al-darura*. This chapter then proceeds to elaborate on external Muslim legal pluralism(s) which emerge as a result of the co-existence of official secular nation-state laws and unofficial Muslim laws.

It is not an aim of this book to critically analyze Islamic law and its classic, traditional, folk, and local manifestations vis-à-vis modernity, modern life, gender issues and so on. This would fall within the ambit of an entirely different study. This study envisages observing these different manifestations as they are and tries to look at the issues from different perspectives including Muslims' own perspectives.

The fourth, fifth and sixth chapters analyse the English, Turkish and Pakistani legal systems respectively. In all these three chapters, a historical background of Muslims, Muslim laws and nation-state laws is provided. These chapters analyze the monopoly claims of nation-state laws in the socio-legal domain and test these claims with empirical evidence vis-à-vis arranged marriages, solemnization of marriage (*nikah*), age of marriage, polygamy and divorce.

In the fourth chapter, a historical background of the Muslim presence in Britain is provided. The current situation and settlement patterns of British Muslims have a substantial effect on the recreation and reproduction of the British Islamic identity. Having studied this, the fourth chapter then concentrates on the nature of the modern English legal system and attempts to analyze its interaction with ethnic minority laws and customs. The claim of the system to be uniform and the issues of assimilation, integration and adaptation are discussed. Muslim responses to non-recognition of their unofficial laws and reconstruction of Muslim laws are analyzed as a mixture of formal and informal methods developed by Muslims settled in Britain.

The fifth chapter first provides the historical background of the official version of law in Turkey. After a brief elaboration of the history of political and legal modernization and secularization developments, the chapter then analyzes the nature of the secular, modern Turkish legal system. Again the emphasis is on family law. This chapter examines continuity and change of the Islamic rules regarding marriage and divorce. With regard to this evidence, the study researches various aspects of the relationship between official law and the Muslim majority. In conclusion, the reconstruction of unofficial Turkish Muslim law and responses to this new hybrid law are discussed.

The sixth chapter concentrates on the case of Pakistan where the state's incapacity to regulate family issues in circumstances of local resistance results in a limits of law situation characterized by dynamic legal pluralism. This chapter provides a crucial perspective to debates on personal law systems in Britain and Turkey. The Pakistani case is of utmost importance, showing that even in a personal law system; state interference within family law issues causes problems and does not successfully overcome the complication and existence of legal pluralism.

In a nutshell, these three cases suggest that the understanding, philosophy, basis and shape of state legal systems may have to be modified to take account of the continuing existence of groups within society with different goals, cultures, and living patterns than those defined by the dominant ideology of modern nation-state law. Legal pluralism is an intractable fact already within Islamic laws. As this study demonstrates, the interaction between Muslim laws and modern state laws increases legal pluralism, rather than resulting in the effective super-imposition of modernizing and uniformizing official laws.

The seventh chapter provides a summary of the findings and elaborates on the consequences of the post-modern Muslim legal pluralism: differential legal treatment, 'illegitimate' children, abuse of *nikah*, limping marriages, hidden (*gizli*) *nikah*, super-hybridity and post-modern hyper-fragmentation. This chapter shows that an equitable positive discrimination is needed to protect the vulnerable members of the society: ethnic and religious minorities, children and women.

The concluding chapter speculates on the future and after discussing the issues of neo-*ijtihad* and supramodern legality elaborates on possible responses (official and unofficial) to the challenge of dynamic Muslim legal pluralism. In this regard, legal uniformity, official legal pluralism, neo-*ijtihad*, Muslim alternative dispute resolution, official *ijtihad* committees, faith-based movement leaders to implement neo-*ijtihad* and supramodern state laws are discussed as possible answers.

Our discussions on supra modern legality are deliberately vague as the book shows law is culture-specific and also situation-specific. Thus, its operation would differ from one context to another. To offer a standard and a specific model to meet the challenge of dynamic legal pluralism in the post-modern condition does not seem possible. All one can do here is to offer a new, if not concrete, understanding of a theoretical legal system for the future of laws and dynamic legal pluralism. Supra-modern understanding is neither a full defence of modernity nor a complete acceptance of post-modernity, but a new approach that recognizes the significance of the points raised by the debates, and argues for an integrated theory which envisages that various types of laws interact in a harmonious way, that the state law is subject to legal postulates, and recognizes this officially and that state law is in charge of the legal processes as the ultimate referee. Thus, the problems and the opportunity to solve them would change from country to country but also a possible supra-modern model from a country or locality to another would and should change. Put differently, supra-modernity is a new socio-legal mentality not a concrete model and it is flexible enough to adapt itself to changing locality. It is this flexibility that qualifies it to be 'universal'.

# Chapter 2

# Dynamic Legal Pluralism

This chapter elaborates on the socio-legal reality of legal pluralism in modern legal systems. It provides a theoretical discussion that is supported by observational data. The major task of this chapter, therefore, is to develop a model of the operation of law in society that will enable us to classify legal pluralism studies, to pursue the manifold facets of the interaction between official and unofficial laws, and to encompass Muslim legal pluralism in post-modern age.

This chapter, first, addresses the question of legal pluralism and aims to provide a descriptive theory, as discussions and acceptance of the reality of legal pluralism have been hindered by some basic conceptual difficulties.

## Law as a Socio-Cultural Construct and Legal Pluralism

In this study, the operation of law in modern societies is discussed in the context of a cultural understanding of law, as it is widely believed that culture has a role of communication between the individual and social structures.[1]

At this point the definition of law gains importance. Austinian, legal positivist understanding simply puts it that 'law is the command of the sovereign'. But this is a very much state-centred approach. And it is known that law extends beyond the state such as religious laws or trans-national laws. Indeed, there is no agreed universal definition of law. A quick survey on the legal literature suggests that 'there are, generally speaking, basically two approaches to conceptualising law, focusing either on justice and morality, or on rules and regulations' (Menski 2000: 55). Law is not limited to acts, rules, administrative orders, courts decisions and so on. Law must be understood as cognitive and normative orders generated and maintained in a social field such as a village, an ethnic/religious/cultural community, an association, a state or a trans-national community. The term 'law' could refer to any set of observed social norms (Woodman 2000: 4). A globally-focused understanding of law is aware that:

- Law is a universal phenomenon but manifests itself in many different ways;
- It does not only take different forms but has also different sources;

[1] In this study, Geertz's (1973: 89) definition of culture is employed: A historically transmitted pattern of meanings embodied in symbols. a system of inherited conceptions expressed in symbolic form by means of which men communicate, perpetuate and develop their knowledge of and attitudes towards life.

- These sources are, in essence, the state, society and religion that compete and interact in various ways, so that any given body of rules may contain components of these three elements (Menski 2000: 60).

Even though there is no precise universal definition of 'law' and it seems that to formulate one is no more possible than finding the Holy Grail (Rosen 1989: 5), problems of definition do not prevent scholars from focusing on legal studies. In the same vein, the lack of a succinct definition of legal pluralism, which is criticized by Tamanaha (1993), does not negate the fact that descriptive study of law with regard to its operation in society should deal with the factual phenomenon of legal pluralism in which different regulatory orders dynamically interact. As Rosen (1999: 95) puts, legal pluralism should be seen 'as an analytical tool rather than as theory or an explanation. Just as a microscope does not explain anything about microbes, legal pluralism does not explain the subject of its concern. Rather, it lets us see what is there; in this case, a living, seething field in which law shows itself to be a process of regularizing relationships – a process that involves competing approaches which may be bound together by their reliance on common cultural orientations'.

Since this study focuses on the position of Muslim law and customs in three different modern nation-states, the emphasis on the unavoidable intermingling between culture and law gains greater importance when it is accepted that 'Islamic law represents an order which governs all spheres of life, in which... even the rules of protocol and etiquette are of a legal nature' (Hoffman 1993: 126). Indeed, this is vital, if one is to get beyond the narrow range of descriptions of state-law-society relations and solutions derived from colonial models which do not mention strong legal pluralism 'at home'. Moreover, one cannot construct a theory of the operation of law by solely regarding state law and its limited allowances for other legal systems. It is also important to understand the current social situation to which the official law reacts, although the response of the state is only one of many dynamic factors. It is necessary, therefore, to distinguish and identify different types and classifications of legal pluralism (McLachlan 1988: 58).

Advancing an argument through the theoretical space provided by 'new' legal pluralism, this chapter tries to explore the co-existence of different modes of law and their articulation. Legal pluralism must be envisaged as a factual description of the operation of several legal regulations that attempt to achieve justice by responding to cultural and legal diversity in society. It is the central theme of this study that recalcitrant legal pluralism is a feature of law in every society if it is understood as a cultural construct. Especially when it comes to Muslim law, which is one of the main concerns of the present study, legal pluralism is an undeniable factual situation whether the law of the state is secular, laicist or Islamic.

Before elaborating on legal pluralism in the post-modern age, the paradigm of legal modernity needs to be discussed in order to obtain a deeper insight into legal pluralism studies. This task includes presenting a map of legal modernity which covers legal positivism and legal centralism as this understanding of law has been the major hindrance to accurate observation. It has 'made it all too easy to fall into the prevalent assumption that legal reality, at least in "modern" legal systems, more or less approximates to the claim made on behalf of the state' (Griffiths 1986a: 4).

## Legal Modernity, Modernization and Limits of Law

Modernity is related to every dimension and aspect of life and has had substantial impacts in the legal field. With the advent of nation-states, legal modernity has found a 'Lebenswelt'. Nation-states which were founded on an imperial heritage tried to centralize and uniformize their legal systems, which eventually became the ultimate goal in the legal arena.

In all three cases studied here, the British, Turkish, and Pakistani states are under the influence of legal modernity and their legal systems have been structured accordingly. They aim to control and shape society by employing social engineering through law. However, there are certain limits to law. There are challenges and resistance to uniformity and the centralizing aims of modern nation-states. The experiences of these three countries have provided three different manifestations of the same phenomenon.

The characteristics of legal modernity have been listed by Galanter (1966: 154-156) as follows:

1. *Uniformity* of rules and their application. Modern law consists of rules that do not vary from one application to another.
2. *Transactional basis* for rights and duties. People's obligations to each other come from agreements freely negotiated between them, not from unchanging obligations based on personal or group identity. Legal rights and duties are not determined by factors such as age, religion or sex which are unrelated to transactions.
3. *Universalism*. Legal decisions, once made, are kept uniform rather than altered from case to case. Application of law is reproducible and predictable.
4. *Hierarchical administrative system*. Authority is distributed downward from higher officials to lower ones. This system is also uniform and predictable.
5. *Bureaucracy*. This means impersonal procedures and the use of written rules and records. The system operates impersonally.
6. *Rationality*. Understandable rules are designed to achieve clearly stated goals using demonstrably effective methods.
7. *Professionals*. The system is run by full-time staff with demonstrated qualifications.
8. *Lawyers*. The system includes specially trained persons who act as mediators between the specialists of the system and laypersons who must deal with the system.
9. *Changeability*. The rules and procedures can be modified for the purposes of achieving stated goals. There is no sacred fixity, the system is amenable and contains regular methods which are controlled by the state for revising rules and procedures.
10. *Politicality*. Modern law exists to serve the purposes of the state. The state enjoys a monopoly over disputes.

11. *Separateness* from other governmental functions. The judiciary is differentiated in personnel and technique. Legislative, judicial, and executive powers are separate and distinct.

Theoretical foundations of this centralist and uniformist approach have roots in legal positivism, which constitutes one major theme of legal modernity.

Legal modernity has several aspects. It is composed of legal positivism, legal centralism, instrumentalism use of law for social engineering purposes, and nation-state paradigm. The doctrinal study of law, in other words black-letter law, formalism or legal positivism, evaluates legal rules and cases as the universe (Fitzpatrick 1992a: 3). This is a 'view that sees law as becoming the predominant factor in the co-ordination and regulation of the complex of subsystems that establish modern societies' (Hunt 1992a: 30). Legal positivism or analytical school of law seeks to study law as an observable and empirical fact. This legal conception sees law as a distinct, uniform, coherent, autonomous, exclusive, and systematic hierarchical ordering of normative propositions. The state is the unique raison d'être of law. There is a sine qua non connection between state and law. Legal positivists insist on an analytical separation of law from morality thus do not deal with 'what law ought to be', instead they focus on 'what law is'. They have a so-called value-free approach to law.

In legal modernity, the territorial nation-state, rather than mankind, is adopted as the new point of reference for law (Sack 1986: 5).[2] Laws are applied over wider spatial, ethnic, religious and class areas; personal law is no longer an issue at stake, territorial laws replaced personal laws, special laws are replaced by general ones, customary ones by statute laws. Individual rights and responsibilities have taken the place of corporate rights and responsibilities. Secular motives and techniques have superseded religious sanctions and inspiration. Law making and applying are now the responsibility of certain professions and operate in the name of central national power (Galanter 1966: 153-154). This central national power tolerates no rivals by means of law in its sovereignty and uniform law is seen as a 'condition of progress toward modern nationhood' (Griffiths 1986a: 8).

Hart (1961) reaffirmed the positivist equation of law with official authority and formal pre-set meaning (see Fitzpatrick 1992a: 4). Dworkin (1986) challenged the rule-based paradigm, arguing that the most important issue in law is the interpretation of rules, not the rules themselves. However, only appellant judges have access in to this realm, not social scientists or laymen, (Tie 1999: 9). In Dworkin's analysis (1986), although law is bound to interpretations, at the end it 'has acquired a singular voice and posited identity distinct from the diversity of interpretation' (Fitzpatrick 1992a: 5).

The ideological role of law is of central importance in legal modernity. Law can be used as an instrument of social control, and as a mode of organizing beliefs and values. Law is viewed in legal modernity in utilitarian terms as a tool, 'an amoral and infinitely plastic device of government' (Cotterell 1989: 124). According to this instrumentalist mentality 'all legal goals consist of specific end

---

[2] See also in detail with several references, Kidder (1983: 185-208).

results realizable at some particular moment in time' (Summers 1977: 122). Instrumentalists take the social space between legislator and subject implicitly as a normative vacuum. In other words, they implicitly assume that the legislator is more or less autonomous from the social context in which the rule is to have its effects, the subjects of the rule are atomistic individuals and the legislator's command is uninfluenced by the social medium (Griffiths 1986a: 34).

The notion of legal centralism represents another characteristic of legal modernity. Legal centralism is an idea in which 'state agencies occupy the centre of legal life, and stand in a relationship of hierarchic control to other normative orderings, and in which indigenous law is consequently overlooked' (Galanter 1985: 67).

This mentality is reflected in the idea and definition of law. This 'is an ideology, a mixture of assertions about how the world ought to be and a prioiri assumptions about how it actually and even necessarily is. Legal centralism has long been the major obstacle to the development of a descriptive theory of law' (Griffiths 1986a: 3).

As a recent comparative study puts it, an absolutist and centralized legalism still prevails in the legal world (Legrand 1996: 240). Assimilationist assumptions of development and modernity underlie such conceptualizations: Until the heterogeneous structures have been smelted into a homogeneous population which modern states are likely to enjoy, allowances can be made while unification remains as a unique goal (Griffiths 1986a: 7-8). Put differently, positivist and centralist understandings of law may allow other forms of normative orderings with a hope for state-centred homogeneity.

Much of the legal literature seems to suggest that 'progress' towards legal modernity can be achieved in three different ways. In the first situation, the uniform law of a modern state can be imported into a developing country, and this imported or transplanted law supersedes all local laws.[3] As a second strategy, one or another system of local law, an amalgam, or a 'restatement' with varying mixtures of colonial or foreign law can be adopted as the uniform national law.[4] Thirdly, 'the general law of the colonial and post-colonial period can oust the indigenous legal orders after a period in which it has accorded them recognition' (Griffiths 1986a: 41).[5] In all those three conditions, it is taken for granted that local laws would recede and finally disappear.

This is not the place to attempt any general critique of legal positivism and legal centralism. The aim here is to stress that in practice the claims of legal modernity do not fully work and official state law has limits, a situation which feeds legal pluralism.[6] Thus, social engineering through law is not a simple but rather a highly contentious matter. Despite the claims of legal modernity, socio-

---

[3] Hooker (1975: 360-409) gives the examples of Turkey, Thailand, and Ethiopia for this type of modernization and unification.

[4] Griffiths (1986a: 41-42) pinpoints that European codification is a good example of that type of unification.

[5] Soviet policy in Central Asia was regarded in that context by Hooker (1975: 427-443).

[6] On limits of law, Allott's (1980) study provides a comprehensive and detailed analysis.

legal studies have repeatedly discovered that there are alternative normative orderings in society and that resistance to official law is always an issue at stake. As one writer comments, 'the "reach" of state power and state law is subject to specific conditions and always falls short of its ideological pretensions' (Hunt 1992b: 59).

Some problems emerge during modernization: The lack of power behind modernization programmes can cause failure, there may be a difference between reality and over-ambitious aims, insufficient knowledge of reality or ignorance of it, the lack of exploration of the possible consequences, and the neglect of social phenomena, cultural conditions, religious and customary traditions (Kulcsar 1987: 81).[7] At times state law can be seen as unnecessary, avoidable, and remediable by the people or society. Laws do not work effectively if they are not congruent with their social context. It is evident that no law can ultimately compel action. All the law can do is 'try to induce someone, by order or by persuasion or by suggestion, to a certain course of action' (Allott 1980: 45-46).

Legal instrumentalism has been heavily criticized by a number of scholars. They emphasized the limits to the capacity of law in transforming social life (see for example Allott 1980). Moore's (1973) semi-autonomous model is another effort to explain this phenomenon. With her theory, she tried to explicate why new laws legislated to effectuate direct change did not necessarily do so as anticipated. To her, the social space between legislator and subject is not a normative vacuum. Although the state has the power to use physical force, it does not mean that there are no other agencies and modes of inducing compliance.[8] In other words, even though the formal legal institutions enjoy a kind of monopoly in terms of the legitimate use of power, there are some other forms of effective coercion or effective inducement. Between the individual and political body there are various interposed social fields to which the individual belongs. These social fields have their own rules and the means of coercing or inducing compliance (Moore 1973: 723; 1978: 56). She puts that '(t)he social reality is a peculiar mix of action congruent with rules (and there may be numerous conflicting or competing rule-orders) and other action that is choice-making, discretionary, manipulative' (Moore 1978: 3).

In all communities a number of modes of normative orderings co-exist with the official law. Local law, custom and ethnic minority laws can be cited as some of the major factors that influence and impede the effectiveness of law in modern societies. These factors are the sources of incoherence, multiple legal authorities and interpretations, local interests and local concerns. There is usually a continuous competition between these normative systems for the allegiance of those to whom they are addressed. They also affect the degree of respect for the official lawmaker, other than being a source of justification for popular resistance. However,

---

[7] In this regard it is argued that 'the abstracted nature of legal discourse has the potential to implicate law in the perpetuation of social inequality by failing to adequately confront such sources of injustice in the multi-faceted and internally-differentiated forms that they take in actuality', Tie (1999: 7).

[8] See also in detail, Pospisil (1971: 193-232).

resistance is not a static process. If administrative measures are undertaken without ambiguity as to their objectives, they can cause extensive changes in behaviour and attitudes of people, regardless of previous resistance (Podgorecki 1974: 252). There is always a possibility of interaction between the official law and other unofficial normative orderings. In other words, '(r)esistance is always about establishing alternatives... it is an intrinsically creative process' (Ballard 1992: 485).

In sum, official laws are not always absolutely effective. Official law alone cannot deal with social problems and it has a limited capacity to enforce social change. States should acknowledge that there are limits and resistance to official laws in the community where their sovereignty is not absolute and that legal pluralism is a fact. However, this does not mean that unofficial laws always exist in direct opposition to the official law. The process is more complex and dynamic.

Following these discussions about legal modernity, the limits of law, and the co-existence of official and unofficial laws, it is necessary to elaborate on the earlier and more recent studies of legal pluralism and the phenomenon of 'dynamic legal pluralism' with a special emphasis on Muslim laws and customs in the post-modern age.

## Dynamic Legal Pluralism in the Age of Post-Modernity

All human societies are heterogeneous on many levels. Said differently, societies are inherently plural. A plural society is formed by cultural diversity and social multiplicity or heterogeneity, arising from different groups of people. In this type of society, other than political, cultural, religious or structural pluralism, the issue of legal pluralism arises where normative heterogeneity is an undeniable social fact.

### *Definition of Legal Pluralism*

Legal pluralism 'is not a technical term with a precise, conventional meaning' (Sack 1986: 1).[9] Rather, it is a description of a factual situation which emerges when different modes of normative orderings overlap in their application in a certain society or community. However, it provides a more adequate description of the role and operation of law in our age.

Vanderlinden defines legal pluralism as 'the existence within a particular society of different legal mechanisms applying to identical situations' (Vanderlinden 1971: 19 quoted in Woodman 1999: 4). Hooker (1975: 6) defines this as 'the situation in which two or more laws interact'.

Griffiths' definition of legal pluralism is, based on Moore's (1978) definition, 'the presence in a social field of more than one legal order', or is a 'state of affairs, for any social field, in which behaviour pursuant to more than one legal order occurs' (Griffiths 1986a: 129). These legal orders do not belong to a single system

[9] In that regard see for a vigorous critique, Tamanaha (1993).

(Griffiths 1986a: 8). Conflicting interactions of differing realms of official and unofficial laws create a kind of legal pluralism. Legal pluralism is an attribute of a social field and not only of a 'law' or of a 'legal system'. Within any field, laws of various provenances may be operative. If in a social field more than one source of 'law', or more than one 'legal order' are observable, then one can say that the social order of that field exhibits legal pluralism. In the condition of legal pluralism, law and legal institutions are not all subsumable within one system but have their sources in the self-regulatory activities of all the multifarious social fields present. These activities may support, complement, ignore or frustrate one another. Van den Bergh (1992: 451-454) views 'pluralism not as a situation but as a process that develops over time, a complex pattern of continuous interactions' (Jones and Gnanapala 2000: 95).

Griffiths (1986a: 5) classifies two types of legal pluralism: Strong and weak. On weak legal pluralism, he writes that 'a legal system is 'pluralistic' when the sovereign (implicitly) commands (or the grundnorm validates, and so on) different bodies of law for different groups in the population. In general the groups concerned are defined in terms of features such as ethnicity, religion, nationality or geography, and legal pluralism is justified as a technique of governance on pragmatic grounds' (Griffiths 1986a: 5).

Merry (1988: 869) equates 'strong' with 'new' legal pluralism which identifies the theories that take into account plural legal realities including those in the West, and 'classical' legal pluralism with 'weak' (Merry 1988: 869). Having already criticized Merry, Benda-Beckmann (1988: 900) suggests the terms 'early' and 'late' discoveries of legal pluralism. Fitzpatrick (1983b: 47), on the other hand, calls the latter a 'rediscovery' of legal pluralism. Vanderlinden (1989: 153) has conceptualized the term 'relative legal pluralism' instead of 'weak' legal pluralism. In this kind of legal pluralism, there is a single sovereign power. Claims of uniformity are still at stake. Even though there are different legal orders, in Moore's (1978) terms they are only semi-autonomous. These different bodies of law are applied to different pillars of society. Thus, they exist in several sub-categories: Native law, religious law, customary law, and personal law. In this understanding of pluralism, to reach real uniformity of the legal system is still an aim that needs to be achieved as soon as circumstances permit. Until then the sovereign will implicitly continue to command different bodies of law for different groups or communities.

There are two forms of weak legal pluralism. One is vertical with hierarchically arranged higher and lower legal systems or cultures as in the United States with federated component states (Chiba 1989: 36). The other type of weak legal pluralism is horizontal 'where the sub-cultures or subsystems have equal status or legitimacy' (Friedman 1977: 71). In history, it is possible to find some examples of this legal pluralism. It was an ancient, pre-modern system in the Indian subcontinent. The *millet* (nation, religious denomination) system is also another example of weak legal pluralism, applied by the Ottomans in earlier times. Islamic law was not applied to non-Muslims except in cases where non-Muslims came into litigation with Muslims or where both parties agreed to be judged by Islamic law when their own religious laws were insufficient. It was left to the non-

Muslims to use their own laws and institutions to regulate behaviour and conflicts under the leaders of their religion. Divisions of society into communities along religious lines formed the *millet* system. Different denominations dealt with the ruling power through their *millet* leaders.[10]

This system also came into prominence in India as an officially recognized way of dealing with diversity, first under Muslim then under the British rule. Pakistan, as a result, has that type of legal system which is now called a personal law system. In England, some Muslim groups have been campaigning to establish a personal system in order to regulate their family issues autonomously according to Muslim law.[11]

In 'strong' legal pluralism not all law is state law nor administered by state institutions, and law is therefore neither systematic nor uniform (Griffiths 1986a: 5). It is rather the coexistence of legal orders in a social setting which do not belong to a single system (Griffiths 1986a: 8). Most importantly, this empirical existence is not dependent on its recognition by the state (Griffiths 1986a: 17).

Woodman (1999: 5) states that many instances given in the earlier studies of legal pluralism 'fall into two general categories. The first consists of those instances in which there are two bodies of norms within the law of a state'. He calls this state law pluralism. In the second category 'the elements are, respectively, the law of the state, and normative orders not directly associated with the state' (Woodman 1999: 5). He refers to this type of legal pluralism as deep legal pluralism (Woodman 1999: 5). He argues that 'the only difference between the two types of legal pluralism is that the different bodies of law in state law pluralism are branches of one larger body of norms, whereas in the case of deep legal pluralism state law and the other law or laws have separate and distinct sources of content and legitimacy' (Woodman 1999: 10). He further refines his concepts and puts that '(l)ike state law, a developed body of customary law or a religious law may contain different sets of norms to regulate different sub-categories within one class of situations. The first type of legal pluralism should be regarded not as state law pluralism alone, but as pluralism internal to any legal order. It is referred to here as internal legal pluralism, state law pluralism being a subtype' (Woodman 1999: 10-11).

In order to analyze the socio-legal reality, one should look for a descriptive conceptualization of legal pluralism as well as establishing a descriptive conception of the operation of law in society. Indeed, there has been a constant effort to reach this aim which has paved the way for legal pluralism studies.

---

[10] Ottomans espoused 'the religious traditions of the Middle East and Balkans and codified them into laws. Each religious group was named as a *millet* (literally 'nation'). The *millet*s were in charge of the education, welfare, and personal law of their members. Their leaders represented the needs of their people to the sultan's government. Sometimes, as was the case with the Greek Orthodox, the place of the *millet* was specifically recognized by law. Other *millet*s, such as the Jews, were simply recognized by tradition. As the centuries passed, more sects were officially recognized…but the *millet* system was an essential element of Ottoman government from an early date. Even before individual *millet*s were officially recognized, they had a de facto separate existence', McCarthy (1997: 128).

[11] On Canada see McLellan and Richmond (1994).

*Early Studies of Legal Pluralism*

Mauss (1906), Ehrlich (1913), Llewellyn and Hoebel (1941), Gurvitch (1947), Weber (1954), Malinowski (1926; 1959), Nader (1965), Bohannan (1967a; 1967b), Vanderlinden (1971), Gilissen (1971a), Pospisil (1971), and Hooker (1975) contributed to the notion of legal pluralism in earlier times. Mauss (1906) found at least two legal systems which operated simultaneously among the Eskimos. Malinowski (1926; 1959) discovered the same phenomenon among the Trobrianders. Later, Hooker (1975) produced a comprehensive study of state-centred legal pluralism which, according to him, was the result of 'transfer of whole legal systems across boundaries' in Asia, Africa, and the Middle East (1975: 1).

Eugen Ehrlich (1913) refused the traditional orthodox view of law and did not accept the monopoly of the state on law. He provided a descriptive theory of legal pluralism. Accordingly, 'the people's behaviour is not necessarily ordered by the all-comprising state law, but primarily by the "inner ordering of associations", namely what Ehrlich terms "living law"' (Pospisil 1971: 103). Living law is 'the law which dominates life itself even though it has not been posited in legal propositions' (Ehrlich 1936: 493). The effectiveness of state law depends on it being in accord with this living law (see in detail Ehrlich 1913; 1936). However, as Fitzpatrick (1983b: 46) puts it, Ehrlich (1913; 1936) does not answer the question of what would happen if associations or bodies of living law were in conflict and what the outcome of such interactions between them would be. How does one explain the original effectiveness and the influence that state law sometimes seems to have on living law? In addition, Griffiths (1986a: 27-28) criticizes Ehrlich as being too state-centred (Griffiths 1986a: 27-28). Two other earlier studies in the field, Vanderlinden (1971) and Gilissen (1971a), have been criticized by Griffiths (1986a: 10-14) on the same grounds.[12]

Llewellyn and Hoebel (1941) tried to conceptualize what they call the 'multiplicity of legal systems' within a geographically delimited society.[13] They explicitly emphasize the relationship between society's law and subgroups' legal systems. According to them, even in the most homogeneous societies there may be several operating legal systems (Llewellyn and Hoebel 1941: 28; see also Nader and Metzger 1963: 584).

Bohannan (1967b), like Ehrlich (1913; 1936), sees state law as secondary or derivative. He developed the idea of 'differing realms of law' to illuminate the relationship between customs and law (Bohannan 1967b: 50). He is concerned with the institutionalization of norms into custom, and of custom into law. He has also been criticized by some scholars since his approach 'fails to take account of the difference in content of 'institutionalized' norms, and by the use of the term institutionalization avoids an analysis of the process' (Woodman 1985: 214).

Pospisil (1971) refines earlier considerations of legal pluralism. He argues that

---

[12] For an analysis and a detailed critique of Vanderlinden (1971) and Gilissen's (1971a) studies see Griffiths (1986a: 10-14).

[13] Llewellyn and Hoebel (1941) conceptualized law as essentially problem-solving.

every society has more than one legal organization. He criticizes Llewellyn and Hoebel (1941) in failing to conceptualize multiple legal systems within a given society and linking them to the societal structure. He, then, conceptualizes the rules generated at the margins of interacting social groups as a multiplicity of legal systems within one society. He contests the adequacy of seeing law and society in terms of interacting individuals and the state. To him society is made up of a collection of subgroups with their own legal systems which are in some respects necessarily different from those of other groups (Pospisil 1971: 100-102, 107). Although Pospisil's contribution to the notion is an original one, it is unsatisfactory, as every subgroup has its own legal system which may be ranked. His conceptualization wrongly implies that legal systems can always be ranked (McLachlan 1988: 53; Mehdi 1994: 50).

Another legal pluralist, Smith (1974: 128), takes 'corporations' as the 'sociological framework' of society. Corporations in a given society, according to Smith, might lead to a kind of legal pluralism. These corporations could be based on a variety of principles of membership. Smith (1974), like Pospisil (1971), locates all other corporate groups on the basis of their relationships to the central power or arena. Moreover, it is restricted only to formal corporations (Griffiths 1986a: 21).

There are several shortcomings of these 'classical' legal pluralism theories. They describe a static legal pluralism but do not explain it in terms of the dynamic interaction between legal orders (Fitzpatrick 1983a: 162). Also, Griffiths (1986a: 35) argues that such theories have paid little attention to the relations between non-state 'semi-autonomous social fields'. Further, they do not propose any general theory of the operation of law in society (McLachlan 1988: 54).

The modern founders of legal sociology such as Gurvitch, Weber, Ehrlich and others mentioned above were all concerned with legal pluralism in a certain sense. They envisage all societies as composed of groups with law-creating capacities. Yet they do not pay much attention to interactions between the laws of different social groups and institutions in society and do not address the question of how the legally pluralistic structure of a society can be captured in a descriptive conception.

Thus, although the above elaboration of early or classical legal pluralism studies might help us to understand legal pluralism in the post-modern age, they are not enough to analyze the operation of law in society and to describe the reconstruction of unofficial Muslim laws and Muslim legal pluralism today. Generally speaking, 'new' legal pluralism studies might serve us better in formulating an analytical scheme for our purposes.

### *Legal Pluralism in the Age of Post-Modernity*

The early twentieth century studies of legal pluralism in Asia, Africa, and the Pacific that were examined above deal with what is called 'classical legal pluralism' (Merry 1988: 872). These earlier studies tended to mix up the factual situation of legal pluralism with the state's responses to it. As a matter of fact, classical theories of legal pluralism have only centred on non-western situations. Chiba (1989: 4) argues that 'legal pluralism must be questioned and discussed not limited to non-western society but extended to Western society as well'. Indeed, as Griffiths (1986a: 2) puts it, 'unofficial laws can be found within the most sophisticated polity as well as the less developed'.

In the course of previous decades, studies on a 'new legal pluralism' emerged with which Chiba would be satisfied (see in detail Merry 1988).[14] The main concern has shifted from legal pluralism studies of traditional[15] societies to the pluralistic qualities of law in capitalist, urban, industrial and modern societies. New legal pluralism theories have started to take into account Western plural realities (Merry 1988: 869). Jones and Gnanapala (2000: 93) underline that '(s)cholars have attempted to interpret obligation patterns of subgroups in industrialized societies in terms of pluralism. The idea is itself not new, but has never been encouraged by lawyers, especially in Western Europe, where the predominant view is that different legal systems cannot co-exist within the one-nation-state structure'.

In the new legal pluralism, the main focus has switched from examining the effect of law on society or the effect of society on law to conceptualizing a complex and interactive relationship between official and unofficial forms of ordering (Merry 1988: 873). Another major shift can be observed where academics have started to be critical of the dispute paradigm since it has become too normative and positivistic (Merry 1988: 890; Griffiths 1986b; Starr and Collier 1987: 367). They have now started to examine day-to-day peaceful living in addition to rare moments of trouble.

Moore (1973; 1978), Forer (1979), Engel (1984, 1987), Galanter (1981), Greenhouse (1982) in the United States of America, Henry (1983, 1985), Sugarman (1983a), Arthurs (1985) and Fitzpatrick (1983a, 1983b) in Britain, Auerbach (1983), Santos (1987; 1995), Griffiths (1985a; 1985b; 1986a; 1986b), Chiba (1986a; 1986b; 1989; 1993), and Merry (1988) are some academics who tried to explore and formulate concepts of legal pluralism in modern, capitalist societies. New legal pluralists have also rejected official law 'centredness of traditional studies of legal phenomena, arguing not all law takes place in the courts' (Merry 1988: 874).

For Habermas (1976: 76-77), capitalist societies are dependent on areas of cultural tradition. The expansion of state activity penetrates these areas of cultural tradition, destroying their independent integrity. However, these areas cannot be taken over, manipulated and maintained by the state alone (Habermas 1976: 71).

14 Merry's distinction between 'classical' and 'new' pluralism was criticized by Benda-Beckmann (1988) as artificial and misleading. He proposes 'early' and 'late' discoveries of plural normative orders, Benda-Beckmann (1988: 900).

15 There is a vigorous debate about the dichotomy of traditional/modern societies. The terms 'traditional' and 'modern' are part of a value-laden system in common parlance, where 'traditional' stands for the irrational, non-scientific world view, and 'modern' for everything opposite. Classifications of 'the First World and the Third World' or the term 'underdeveloped countries', are also used to identify this dichotomy. But they are not value-free either. For practical purposes I use the term 'traditional', despite the debates, as there is no perfect alternative. Thus, in this study, 'traditional' refers to taking the attitude that one is doing things in the way in which they have always been done. Then, 'modern' becomes identified with a different view of the past, see Rippin (1993: 6).

Central governments try to invade the social field by means of legislation. Nevertheless, 'innovative legislation or other attempts to direct change often fail to achieve their intended purposes... The social arrangements are often effectively stronger than the new laws' (Moore 1978: 58).

The notion of 'semi-autonomous social field' was developed by Moore (1978) in order to describe multiple systems of ordering in complex societies. She underlines that the assumptions of legal modernity do not fully work: 'Ordinary experience indicates that law and legal institutions can only effect a degree of intentional control of society, greater at some times and less at others, or with more regard to some matters than others' (Moore 1978: 126). The semi-autonomous social fields have rule-making capacities, and the means to induce or coerce compliance (Moore 1978: 55-56).

In the theory of semi-autonomous social fields, different laws exist together. They mutually interact. They do not necessarily reinforce or conflict with each other. The semi-autonomous social field is not related to only one social group. It makes no claim about the nature and origin of the orders. Furthermore, it does not find any conclusion of the nature and the influence between the normative orders. An official legal system penetrates the semi-autonomous social field but cannot dominate it. Resistance and autonomy are always issues at stake. Yet as Rosen (1999: 91) argues in line with Griffiths (1986) that 'an emphasis on semi-autonomous legal fields still assumes that each such field gains much of its form and content from its interaction with, even its repugnance of, state-centered law. By contrast, a cultural emphasis finds among different domains a process by which commonsense orientations are adopted, rejected, transformed, or reversed – but in every way gaining legitimacy and justification for their powers and their results by virtue of their engagement with these resonant orientations'.

Geertz (1973; 1983) initially developed this study of law as a system of meanings, a cultural Code for interpreting the world. For him (1973; 1983: 232-233) legal pluralism is an interpretive phenomenon which is richly evocative of cultural diversity. He argued that law is 'a species of social imagination' (Geertz 1983: 232). He says that 'law is about meaning not about machinery' (Geertz 1983: 232). Simply put, law is local knowledge (Gerber 1994: 5). Rather than paying attention to relations of power or to the political economy, Geertz (1973) pays attention to history and context (Merry 1988: 886). To put it differently, his approach is part of a hermeneutic project which stresses that words are keys to understanding the social institutions and cultural formulations that surround them and give them meaning (Geertz 1983: 187). Social action largely consists of the meaning-oriented behaviour of actors. Everybody interprets the world from within group-informed perspectives (Rosen 1989: 5).

In hermeneutic or interpretive understanding, the total picture consists of several local expressions of legal sensibilities and the diversity and intermingling of these is not likely to end but may increase (Merry 1988: 887). Interpretivists keep on arguing that 'coherence cannot be the major test of validity for a cultural description' (Geertz 1973: 17), since 'there is nothing so coherent as a paranoid's delusion or a swindler's story' (Geertz 1973: 18). To them 'it is indeed possible to formulate a study of law as culture and culture as integral to law' (Rosen 1989:

xv), as 'there must be a logically meaningful relation between law and the society surrounding it' (Gerber 1994: 5).[16]

Vanderlinden (1989) seems to support the same argument. Legal pluralism in his view is 'the condition of the person who, in his daily life, is confronted in his behaviour with various, possibly conflicting, regulatory orders, be they legal or non-legal, emanating from the various social networks of which he is, voluntarily or not, a member' (Vanderlinden 1989: 153-154). To him two major arguments should be borne in mind pertaining to legal pluralism: 'on the one hand, the necessity, for legal pluralism to exist, of more than a single legal order meeting at the level of a '*sujet de droits*'; on the other the non-existence of pluralism when considered from the point of view of a specific legal system and not from the standpoint of the individual' (Vanderlinden 1989: 157).

Santos (1987; 1995) also worked on these themes of legal pluralism, arguing that legal pluralism is a cornerstone in the post-modern view of law (Merry 1988: 887). He sees legal pluralism as a conception of different legal spaces superimposed, interpenetrated, and mixed in people's minds as much as in their actions. He stresses on the phenomenology of diverse legal orders[17] converging in the mind of the individual. He argues that 'different forms of law create different legal objects upon eventually the same social objects. They use different criteria to determine the meaningful details and the relevant features of the activity to be regulated... they create different legal realities' (Santos 1987: 278). Legal life is constituted by an intersection of legal orders, that is interlegality, the phenomenological counterpart of legal pluralism (Santos 1987: 297-298).

### *An Analytical Tool to Observe Law in Operation in Society*

Another scholar who espouses the idea of law that cannot be separated from its social and cultural context is Chiba (1986a; 1986b; 1989; 1993). He tries to develop a speculative theory of cross-national legal pluralism which conceives law as a cultural construct. To him, law is inseparably rooted in society so as to be approachable by sociological methods. In his reading, law is understood as an aspect of the total culture of a people: 'A true legal pluralist may be required to observe and analyze culture in law on the basis common to that of the specialist of culture' (Chiba 1989: 3).

Chiba (1986a: 4) asserts that, 'the whole structure of law of a people is not limited to the monistic system of state law... (but) is plural, consisting of different

[16] Rosen underlines that the courts do not make arbitrary decisions, that they do not dispense what Weber called 'qadi justice', even though the judge has a great deal of discretion, Rosen (1980: 1). He puts it that 'the regularity lies in the fit between the decisions of the Muslim judge and the cultural concepts and social relations to which they are inextricably tied', Rosen (1989 : 18).

[17] Weber underlines that psychological as well as physical coercion may underlie a legal order: 'A 'legal order' shall rather be said to exist wherever coercive means, of a physical or psychological kind, are available; i.e., wherever they are at the disposal of one or more persons who hold themselves ready to use them for this purpose in the case of certain events', Weber (1954: 17), quoted in Rosen (1999: 90).

systems of law interacting with one another harmoniously or conflictingly'. In other words, his 'objective is, whether expressed as legal culture or legal pluralism, the working whole structure of law of a people, constituted not of a single system of state law, but rather a complex of various systems of law called customary, religious, local, primitive, tribal or whatever, on the one hand, and many ideational factors specifically relevant to the function of the law, such as ideas, values, beliefs, philosophies, attitudes and so forth, on the other' (Chiba 1989: 173).

He looks for an analytical scheme to observe and analyze the whole structure of law of a people as a phase of their culture and as a result of the struggles between received law and indigenous culture. He wants 'to operationally define the analytical tool concepts applicable to the existing legal pluralism in the world and to construct the general theory of legal pluralism with those concepts' (Chiba 1989: 3). He tries to formulate 'a conceptual scheme capable of being utilized as an analytical tool to accurately observe and elucidate that working whole structure of law of a people, Western as well as non-Western' (Chiba 1989: 173).

His initial scheme of a three-level layer of law in 1986 differentiated the whole structure of law into three levels consisting of official law, unofficial law and legal postulates. Stated summarily, official law is the legal system sanctioned by the legitimate authority of a state. Other types of law, such as religious law, family law, local law, ethnic law and so forth, may be classified as official law if they are officially authorized or sanctioned by the state and functioning in consonance with the state law.

Unofficial law is the legal system not officially sanctioned by any legitimate authority, but sanctioned in practice by the general consensus of a certain group of people, whether within or beyond the bounds of a state. The unofficial law is 'limited to one with some distinctive influences upon the effectiveness of the official law, supplementing, opposing, modifying or even undermining the official law' (Chiba 1989: 173). The third level is legal postulate.

A legal postulate is a value principle or value system which is specifically connected to a particular official or unofficial law, which acts to find, justify and orient the latter, thereby determining the relationship between unofficial and official law (Chiba 1986a: 6). A legal postulate is 'constituted of established legal ideas, religious precepts and teachings, social and cultural postulates related to fundamental social structure, or political ideologies often closely connected with economic policies' (Chiba 1989: 173). He applied his hypothetical conceptual scheme in six countries, Japan, Thailand, India, Egypt, Iran and Sri Lanka. The data from these countries verified his scheme and he then added another concept to the initial scheme, which dealt with the interaction between received law and indigenous law (Chiba 1989: 7-8).

In 1989, Chiba (1989: 177) goes further and attempts 'a synthetic reformulation of the conceptual schemes to obtain a useful analytical tool for legal culture, or legal pluralism, in the contemporary world, both non-Western and Western'. His revised scheme is called the three dichotomies of law. The first dichotomy comprises, in relation to the different modes of the authority of legal sanction, official law vs. unofficial law, terms which are defined respectively (Chiba 1989: 177). The second dichotomy is the contrast of positive rules or legal rules, with postulative values or legal postulates. While legal rules tend to be easily isolated from the rest of the cultural formalities, legal postulates are by and large difficult to isolate, with the exception of those specifically conceptualized, such as justice, equity, natural law in Western law, *Dharma* in Hindu law, and Heaven in traditional Chinese law. The legal rules and legal postulates coexist and co-function interactingly (Chiba 1989: 178).

In Chiba's terminology, 'identity postulate' is the most fundamental legal postulate of a people 'which enables a people to maintain their cultural identity in law' (Chiba 1986b: 45). It enables 'people to choose official or unofficial law alternatively so as to adapt themselves to changing circumstances while maintaining their individuality and identity' (Chiba 1986b: 43). This postulate 'is an attribute which is indispensable to every system of law which wants to remain culturally independent' (Chiba 1986b: 46).

Later, he refined his concept of 'legal-postulates' a little bit further in the light of the criticism that his 'category of unofficial law seems to be identified primarily by a tendency to have an effect on official law' (Woodman 1992: 145),[18] and suggested that a legal postulate is 'a value principle or system which (is) specifically connected with and work(s) to justify a particular official or unofficial law' (Chiba 1993: 203). His 'main point is that these 'legal postulates' influence the way in which official and unofficial law develop in practice, thus illustrating the point that the actual, living law is culture-specific and diverse, rather than value-free and uniform' (Jones and Gnanapala 2000: 96).

Chiba's third dichotomy relates to the different origins of law in society: indigenous law, broadly defined as 'law originated in the native culture of a people' versus transplanted law, broadly defined as 'state law of a non-Western country transplanted from Western countries' (Chiba 1989: 179).

He concludes that 'the law of an individual country may be accurately observed and analyzed in its working whole structure by the above analytical tool scheme of the three dichotomies of law. In other words, it may be elucidated as comprising different types of official law and unofficial law, each of which is constituted of legal rules and legal postulates as well as of indigenous law and transplanted law, received or imposed. The combination of the three dichotomies in reality vary (sic) country to country' (Chiba 1989: 179).

There are some flaws in Chiba's global theory. He seems to take people as a homogeneous group, excluding the fact that they consist of various communities with different cultural backgrounds. He also reduces interaction to a straightforward link between official and unofficial law, although in reality different unofficial laws interact among themselves as well. Moreover, he seems to conceive unofficial laws as the indigenous law of a people and official law as received law, yet in reality, as this study attempts to show, there are many variations of these two types of law. He also evaluates unofficial law on the basis of its impact on the official law. At first sight, one would be under the impression

[18] Indeed, in 1986, Chiba (1986a: 6) was suggesting that 'Unofficial law is here limited to those unofficial practices which have a distinct influence upon the effectiveness of official law'.

that if unofficial law has no impact on the operation of official law, then there would be no need to study it. However, unofficial law would still be there whether it exerts an influence on the operation of official law or not, and so needs to be studied as a factual phenomenon. His use of the concept of 'legitimacy' is also confusing. It gives the impression that legitimacy is directly related to state but not to society.

It also seems that his third dichotomy (indigenous law versus received law) is not really a separate dichotomy. If indigenous law is sanctioned by the official law it becomes official law, if not, then it becomes unofficial law. It is the same with transplanted law. If state transplants a law and sanctions it, it becomes official law. As in the case of England, if some immigrant communities carry their laws with them to their new country and if these laws are recognized by the lex loci, they also become part of official law. If they are simply seen as customs and are not recognized then they are unofficial laws. It should also be borne in mind that Chiba's model might not work in some legal systems, such as in ancient Hindu society that one can not observe official law as there is not any political power making or enforcing laws.

Nevertheless, Chiba's analytical scheme of the 'three dichotomies of law and interaction between laws' still provides a useful yardstick in understanding the operation of law in society despite the certain modifications that need to be made to it and the above-mentioned criticisms that should be borne in mind when making use of it, as it is clearly the most advanced analytical scheme ever accomplished. Thus, a modified version of Chiba's model will be an essential analytical tool for this study.

Thus, I argue that Chiba's model needs to be modified in the light of these points. In this case, then, law is composed of two dichotomies: official law versus unofficial law and legal rules versus legal postulates.

Since unofficial laws and official laws are interactive phenomena, it is evident that each in significant ways takes meaning from the other (Chiba 1989: 207; Moore 1978; Fitzpatrick 1983b: 45; 1986; Silbey 1992: 43). This is a highly dynamic process (Santos 1987: 298) since along with the changing nature of official laws, unofficial laws 'are not steel frames for social action', too (Burman 1988: 152). As a result of this mutual interaction of the control forms, both official and unofficial laws are recreated and reconstructed through discursive practices (Silbey 1992: 43).

Six different relationships can be identified between official state law and unofficial laws. First, state law can destroy local informal social controls through the introduction of new concepts and by introducing new 'legal' solutions to problems of social life.

Second, at the opposite extreme, local law can continue to flourish, with most members of the groups recognizing its authority and considering official state law as irrelevant to their lives. In between these opposites are a number of possibilities.

Third, local law and state law may co-exist so that disputants can use state law as an alternative to local law. Disputants could manipulate a system to their advantage.

Fourth, state law can delineate new areas of official social control by encroaching and moving through legislation into areas previously unregulated by state law.

Fifth, state law may 'codify' previously unwritten social controls or local law, raising this local law to the status of official law, and by using these new laws in official courts.

Sixth, state law may make provision to use people with status within the community who are considered to be knowledgeable on unofficial custom law as 'expert witnesses' in official state courts (Starr 1985: 124).

In addition to these six possible types of interaction between official and unofficial laws, there might also be interactions between and within unofficial laws itself.

Legal postulates are the main actors in the interactive processes between different types of laws in the socio-legal sphere. Since law is a cultural construct, these socio-cultural parameters fill the vacuum in the socio-legal sphere and govern the complex relations between individual, community, informal and formal institutions. They determine the nature of these interactive processes of legal pluralism.

It needs to be firmly emphasized that, in view of interaction of legal orders, official and unofficial laws are not two different and completely separate legal fields. It is rather a kind of cohabitation of interactive laws, operating in the context of 'dynamic legal pluralism'. I use the term 'dynamic legal pluralism' to denote 'strong' or 'deep' legal pluralism in order to put an emphasis on the dynamic interactions between official laws, unofficial laws and legal postulates in the continuous reconstruction and hybridization processes within a given socio-legal sphere.

Dynamic legal pluralism is an everyday reality of the post-modern condition. From the individual level to the global, many laws, be they official or not, cohabit and interact.

New hybrid official and unofficial laws are continuously being constructed either by states or skilful legal navigators in this post-modern climate of dynamic legal pluralism.

In sum, I argue that the whole picture of law as it operates in society is composed of two dichotomies:

- Official law versus unofficial laws.
- Legal rules versus legal postulates.

And, there is a constant reconstruction of hybrid unofficial laws as a result of dynamic interactions within the context of 'dynamic legal pluralism'. In these processes official laws change as well responding to socio-legal realities.

## Local Laws in a 'Dynamic' Legal Pluralist Context

There are a number of factors which might lead to a legal pluralist situation.

Resistance from the periphery or challenge of the 'local' is one of them. As a result of the diverse nature of human societies coupled with the fact that 'the role and importance of the law are inseparable from its connections to a wide range of social and cultural practices' (Rosen 1989: xv), normative orderings also differ. In the modern nation-state era, unification and homogenization attempts of states have clashed in legal terms with the heterogeneous structures of societies in legal terms. Local differences, ethnic diversities, indigenous normative orderings and religious laws are rivals of the official state laws. Islam has a special place in this contested issue because of the close connection between Islamic law and culture. In Muslim practice, 'cultural assumption, legal approach, and substantive law are all deeply entwined' (Rosen 1989: 44).

Since our study deals with the interactions between modern state law and unofficial Muslim laws and customs, it is necessary to first look at the theoretical dimension of the general relations between modern-state law and traditional local laws and customs. Following this, this study analyses the relations and interactions between the modern state law and the laws and customs of ethnic minorities in order to illuminate the position of Muslim laws and customs in England vis-à-vis the official legal system. Thirdly, a discussion about legal transplantation and its consequences regarding the emergence of legal pluralism will follow.

In modern states, as discussed previously, unification of laws is a paramount objective. In modern legal systems, there has been a strong tendency to replace the traditional local laws by one uniform modern state law.

In modern thinking, it is widely believed that 'traditional law does not serve as an instrument of change' (Kulcsar 1987: 40). Traditional law is a scape-goat that is accused of keeping people from acting in compliance with the development aims of the state (Benda-Beckmann 1989: 140). In contrast, modern state law is believed to change societies. Nevertheless, tradition can make some modifications over time (Shils 1972: 26-31).

As seen above, mainstream Western legal theory confines the concept of 'law' to modern state law. Local or folk law is disregarded. Folk law is supposed to exist outside of official legal systems. Although the term 'folk law' has a number of synonyms[19] there is no agreed universal definition.

One of the most prominent fundamentals of folk law is custom. It is, most of the time, the backbone of the local, folk or unofficial law. Custom has regularity like law. It also defines relationships. Both custom and law are sanctioned. Law is distinguished from custom, according to Hoebel (1954: 276), merely in that law endows certain individuals with the privilege of applying the sanction of physical coercion. Indeed, law for Austin is a command made by a sovereign and backed by the threat of an evil if disobeyed, namely a sanction. Hence the term 'the imperative theory of law' is used to describe Austin's doctrine. However, in contrast to these writers' assumptions of seeing custom as an unchanging

[19] For example: people's law, customary law, unofficial law, native law, native law and customs, native customary law, primitive law, folk law, informal law, living law, positive morality, non-state law, non-government law, autogeneous regulation, native justice, vernacular law, indigenous law and autochthonous law.

phenomenon, there is a plethora of evidence that custom is also dynamic and does not simply disappear (Merry 1988: 875).[20] As already argued by Sumner (1906), lawways cannot change folkways. There are legal systems penetrated by legal modernity where a modern legal system would seem not to have displaced a persisting custom, a custom which yet retains a powerful, even definitive influence on the system. Custom actively resists legal modernity creatively in many aspects (Fitzpatrick 1986: 67). According to this view, official law, in other words, has to operate 'in the shadow of indigenous ordering' (Galanter 1981: 23).

At times the term 'custom' is belittled as being very old and being supported by less social pressure than other official law rules (Allott 1980: 50). Accordingly, if a norm is applied in the courts or is a product of the legislative process, in other words if it is official, it is law. Otherwise it is custom. Customs generally are evaluated as lacking many of the necessary requirements of an effective legal system: They are not fixed and certain, they are not sharp and precise in their application, and they are not effectively complied with because there are no effective sanctions (Allott 1980: 55). Allot rejects the proposition that 'customary laws were, and necessarily are by their nature, static' (Allott 1980: 60). On the issue of effectiveness of law, he states that '(e)ffectiveness of law is measured by compliance with it' (Allott 1980: 62). He then asks that after comparing degrees of compliance to customary laws and modern Western laws, is it possible to say that there is less compliance in the former than the latter? (Allott 1980: 62-66).

Conflicts of laws between dominant groups and subordinate groups, such as between religious, ethnic or cultural minorities and the official law can be easily observed in modern societies (Merry 1988: 872). Indeed, there are several reports and existing research studies on self-regulation within religious groups and ethnic minority communities (Galanter 1981: 22).

As a result of the existence of ethnic minority laws and/or customs, interactions, clashes, concessions and complements between the official and unofficial laws emerge. In other words, official and unofficial laws meet and interact. Although one cannot argue in the same strength that customs also resist and interact, since people do not abandon them as well, in reality they are almost as effective as laws. The conflict between modern life, modern law, legal customs and customary law is solved, to paraphrase Ballard (1994a), by 'skilled cultural navigators' 'under the nature of living conditions of everyday life, in keeping with the nature of living conditions, with neglect, disregard, or re-interpretation' (Kulcsar 1987: 113).

At times, any group aspiring to state power attacks the old social order and attempts to use its own system of legal rules and principles first. To this end, laws are sometimes transplanted from another culture or other cultures by voluntary reception. In some other cases, laws are transplanted by involuntary imposition (Chiba 1986b: 40).[21]

---

[20] See in detail, Sumner (1906); Colson (1976); Fitzpatrick (1980); Chanock (1985); Starr and Collier (1987).

[21] Allott (1980) prefers to use the term 'translocation' instead of 'transplantation'. On the issue of transplantation, see also in detail Kidder (1979); Watson (1974; 1976; 1977; 1993; 1995; 1996.)

However, as Chiba (1989: 39) underlines, 'conflicts and accommodation between the received model and the indigenous model cannot be avoided from a cultural point of view'. Theoretically, it is widely thought that the received model in a way disregards or overcomes the local law(s) (Chiba 1989: 39). However, according to Hooker (1975: 362), 'the issue of policy, whether a legal policy or a national policy development, does not necessarily determine the content and effectiveness of any law'. Transplanted law should fit into the domestic socio-political context to be successful (Watson 1976: 81).[22]

A state can undertake the process of legal importation as a result of fundamental revolution and, under that upheaval, may adamantly attempt to establish a completely clean and blank legal sheet (Hooker 1975: 360). The élite of a given country may decide to transplant a law or a legal system entirely to procure the social transformation of society. As indicated above, in legal modernity, it is believed that in order to establish a modern uniform system, uniform law of a modern state is imported and this imported or transplanted law is expected to supersede all local laws. To reach this goal, the élite can impose radically new patterns of behaviour by opting for transplanted law, using law to reconstruct society and its social relations.[23]

However, it is possible that there may be a number of competing norms in the countries that transplanted their official law from abroad, usually from Western countries. *Shari'a* and dharma can be given as examples of norms competing against the state law. They are deep-rooted traditions which have developed approving 'postulates', in Chiba's terms, among their followers. Although they may be regarded by orthodox jurisprudence as simple customs and practices, these religious precepts and ethical imperatives influence both official and unofficial law (Chiba 1989: 125). Put differently, transplanted state law does not exist as a separate system but coexists with unofficial laws peacefully or conflictingly (Chiba 1989: 54). As a result, in some cases, a radical reform attempt in the legal arena may well fall far short of bringing the assumed crucial transformation.

Correlated to its position in a legal system, religion, most of the time, influences the society and the operation of the official law. It might also be a cause of resistance to modern state law since although secular and modern law claims monopoly in the legal field and restricts religion to the private sphere; religious laws are evident phenomena in both the private and public domain. As Chiba (1986, 1989, 1993) clearly shows, the official constitutional separation of religion and state is both supplemented and undermined by unofficial legal postulates requiring various forms of religious observance (Woodman 1992: 143). It is quite probable that there may be a number of co-existing and competing norms in the countries that transplanted their official law from abroad, usually from western

[22] See also in detail Allott (1980: 99-120).

[23] It must also be stated at this point that, in this age, a new dimension of transplantation has emerged. Laws of ethnic minorities have been unofficially transplanted by these migrant groups from their countries of origin to their new environments, causing a new type of legal pluralism.

countries.[24]

Transplanted state law does not exist as a separate system but coexists with unofficial laws peacefully or conflictingly. As a result, in some cases, a radical reform attempt in the legal arena may well fall far short of bringing the assumed crucial transformation.

Although *Shari'a* may be regarded by orthodox jurisprudence as simply customs and practices, these religious precepts and ethical imperatives influence official law, unofficial law and society, paving the way for dynamic Muslim legal pluralisms. Now, in the next chapter, internal and external Muslim legal pluralisms are analyzed from a theoretical point of view.

---

[24] In England, legal transplantation has not happened at the state level, but in this case Muslims carried their transnational Muslim laws with them to England to the effect of creating a new legal pluralism, see Pearl and Menski 1998.

# Chapter 3

# Muslim Legal Pluralisms

Internal plurality of Muslim laws (internal Muslim legal pluralism) has always been the case. In this age, as a result of losing its official status in many countries, Muslim law is also a source of another Muslim legal pluralism, external legal pluralism that this study mainly focuses on.

Muslim law is a repertoire of precedents, cases and general principles, along with a body of well-developed hermeneutical techniques (Al-Azmeh 1996: 12). There is a kind of plurality of Muslim laws and customs. This is mainly due to three separate reasons. Firstly, there are the main four schools of law (*madhhabs*) and other sects which have slightly different views on certain non-fundamental practices of Islam; secondly, written law (high Islam) does not completely coincide with people's practices (custom, *urf*, *adat*); and thirdly, there are some differences between the state's Islam and folk Islam or local Islam. From a legal pluralist viewpoint, Muslim law is not only the law stated in the Muslim law books but also what Muslim people apply in everyday life. The legal system is diffuse, lacking coherence in codes and enforcement and entailing a multiplicity of authorities and sources of law (Gerber 1994: 180). Thus, different changes have come into existence in a variety of contexts, and this has caused an internal Muslim legal pluralism.

In this age, as a result of losing its official status in many countries, Muslim law is also a source of another Muslim legal pluralism, external legal pluralism that this study mainly focuses on. Thus, this chapter puts the spotlight on the theoretical foundations and dynamics of this external Muslim legal pluralism.

Our theoretical discussion in chapter 2 showed that, in the socio-legal sphere, there are always 3 actors: Society, religion and state. In Chiba's terminology, official laws, unofficial laws and legal postulates always co-exist and dynamically interact in the socio-legal arena. Thus, this chapter looks also at the Muslim nation-states and their official laws (Islamic or secular) and unofficial Muslim law relations.

## Internal Muslim Legal Pluralism

Some scholars have asserted that the different perceptions of Islam throughout the world in various local contexts have led to different 'Islams' since 'considerable disagreements are apparent over what the fundamentals of Islam are and how they should be interpreted' (King 1995b: 3).[1] As one writer emphasizes, 'there are as many Islams as there are situations that sustain it. European Islam in its various forms and places is no exception' (Al-Azmeh 1996: 1). Whilst it is clearly observable that there may be different interpretations of Islamic doctrines, it is not entirely correct that this reaches as far as to the claim that differences of opinion relate to the fundamentals of Islam. Indeed, if anything the differences are usually more concentrated on the periphery issues of Islam and at times mainly within a degree of flexibility allowed by Islam itself. Matters of difference on more fundamental issues are usually based on different interpretations of the sources of Islam and are not as widespread as one may expect it to be for a religion with over a billion adherents. However, it is an obvious fact to the naked eye and perception that Islam has been interpreted and practised differently in different environments and obtained a slightly different unique taste and ethos in different settings. Iranian Islam contrasts strongly with Turkish Islam in the sense that the latter provides more emphasis on the spiritual, Sufi, man-God relationship side of Islam with particular sensitivity to tolerance and open-mindedness whereas Iranian Islam appears to be more rigid and robust and more concentrated on sanctions and man-state relationship of Islam.

### *Shari'a, Fiqh and Ijtihad*

*Shari'a* is the divine law whose principles are embedded in the *Qur'an* and *Sunna*. It is a territory of considerable textual complexity, for there is no simple set of rules that constituted the *Shari'a*, but rather a body of texts, including the *Qur'an*, *hadith*, and legal texts of various genres that supply the authoritative base for Islamic legal thought and practice. Muslims' concern about knowing God's Will in order to implement it produced classical Muslim law. The science of Muslim jurisprudence within the first two centuries of Islam devised both the sources of law (*usul al-fiqh*) and substantive law itself (*furu al-fiqh*) (Esposito 2001: 9).

*Fiqh* is the product of human understanding, which sought to interpret and apply the *Shari'a* in space-time (Esposito 1980: 240). When faced with new situations or problems, scholars sought a similar situation in the *Qur'an* and *Sunna*. The key is the discovery of the effective cause or reason behind a *Shari'a* rule. If questions arose about the meaning of a *Qur'an*ic text or tradition or if revelation and early Muslim practice were silent, jurists applied their own reasoning (*ijtihad*) to interpret the law (Esposito 1998: 83).[2] *Ijtihad* is not a source of law. It is an activity, a struggle, and a process to discover the law from the texts and to apply it to the set of facts awaiting decision. *Ijtihad* is not permitted on a clear and unambiguous matter and rule in the *Qur'an*ic text.

There are five layers of juristic activity as identified by Hallaq (2001: 22-23). First is *ijtihad* that is the province of only the highest ranked and most able jurists. Second, is *takhrij* that is a creative activity which involves a limited version of

---

[1] See also Bistolfi and Zabbal (1995); Eickelman (1982: 1); Kepel (1995b); Peach and Glebe (1995: 27); Scantlebury (1995: 427); Nielsen (1987a: 385).

[2] See also in detail Nyazee (1995: 47-50); Hallaq (2001).

*ijtihad* whereby the jurist confronts the views/*ijtihad*s of other jurists not the revealed texts. Third is *tarjih*, that is the act of choosing one decision or interpretation over another in a thorough sound reasoning and is 'responsible for determining the authoritativeness of the *madhhab* (juristic school) at any stage of its history'. The fourth layer, *taqlid*, is an act of imitation, the simple following of the *ijtihad*s of jurists. The fifth is *tasnif*, that is the writing and classifying of *ijtihad*s and is the activity of author jurists which characterizes all ranks and types of jurists except for the lowest and least knowledgeable.

The *Qur'an* and *Sunna* are the two most important and primary authorities and sources of Islam. The other instruments that are referred to as sources are consensus (*ijma*)[3] and analogy (*qiyas*).[4] While the *Qur'an* contains prescriptions about matters that would rank as legal in the narrow sense of the term, these injunctions comprise only about 300 out of the 6000 or so verses. Other verses are mainly about the belief, essentials of the faith, historical lessons, general directives as to what the aims and aspirations of Muslims should be; that is the 'ought' of the religious ethics of Islam (Esposito 2001: 3). *Qur'an*ic values were interpreted, applied, explained, practiced and concretized by the *Sunna* of the Prophet, which is the second material source of Islamic law (Esposito 2001: 5).

Although jurists generally agree on the four sources of the *Shari'a*, namely the *Qur'an*, the *Sunna*, *qiyas* (analogy) and *ijma* (consensus), they differ widely in their interpretations of the texts, in the value they attached to *qiyas* and in their definition of *ijma* (Nasir 1990: 7). The definition of *ijma* as given by *Shafii* includes the agreement of the entire Muslim community (*ummah*). Considering the difficulty of arriving at such an agreement, the view of *Shafii* is opposed by others while Ghazzali's *modus vivendi* confines unanimity of the community to the fundamentals, leaving matters of detail to the agreement of the scholars.

There are also several kinds of controversial legal reasoning and procedures on which there is no agreement among the jurists as to their validity; that being public benefit (*istislah* / *maslaha*),[5] necessity (*darura*), custom (*urf*, *adat*), presumption of

---

[3] The unanimous agreement of the jurists of a particular age on a specific issue.

[4] *Qiyas* is defined as establishing the relevance of a ruling in one case because of a similarity in the attribute (reason or cause) upon which the ruling was based.

[5] *Maslaha* is based on the belief that God's purpose in the *Shari'a* (*al-maqasid al-Shari'a*) is the promotion of human welfare (public interest). It is accepted as a source of law, provided that the case is suitable and relevant to either a universal legal principle or specific textual evidence. Although not textually specified (*mursal*), public interests (*al masalih al-mursalah*) can be served by determining what is in a person's or the community's best interest in a case and rendering a judgment that will promote it. In classical Muslim jurisprudence, this concept 'is not simply utilitarian; it did not develop as free-wheeling practice, but rather as a discipline of law with definite limits within which it was to function. The case involved must be one that concerns social transactions (*muamalat*), rather than religious observances (*ibadat*), and the determination of public interest must be in harmony with the spirit of the *Shariah*' (Esposito 2001: 9). Imam Malik who approved the idea of public interest as the source of law by formulating the theory of al-masalih al-mursalah attached three conditions to its adoption: first, the case under review should be one pertaining to matters of transactions so that interests involved in it may be considered upon

continuity (*istishab*)[6] and juristic preference (*istihsan*).[7] Traditional Muslim jurisprudence employs these legal instruments where the primary sources are silent (Moosa 1999: 163).

*Ijtihad* is a very important aspect of Islam regarding its dynamism. The mechanism of *ijtihad* allows Islam to dynamically develop itself within practical life in accordance with changing conditions in different contexts. It is like a self-repair system, although it is not about repairing but about developing practical aspects of Islam. As Moosa (1999: 162-163) writes: '(t)extbooks, legal opinions, and scholarly discourse that have been preserved indicate that the law responded to very real conditions and addressed the needs of the societies it served. Legal theory, as a metatheory, reflected contemporary sociopolitical realities. Even a law colored by religious imperatives had a functional sociology and anthropology. Of course, in order to survive Islamic law continuously made itself relevant to the societies it served. This is achieved by means of internal dynamism and regular synthesis between norms and changing social realities'.

Muslim jurists and Islamic legal culture not only experienced legal change but were also aware of change as a distinct feature of the law. As Hallaq (2001: 166) emphasizes, Muslim jurists were acutely aware of both the occurrence of, and the need for, change in the law, and they articulated this awareness through such maxims as 'the *fatwa* changes with changing times' ('*taghayyur al-fatwa bi-taghayyur al-azman*', or as is put in *Majalla* '*ezmanın tağayyuru ile ahkam dahi tebeddül eder*') or through the explicit notion that the law is subject to modification according to the changing of the times or to the changing conditions of society. Gerber (1994) shows in the Ottoman context that internal Muslim pluralism and dynamic legal change were everyday realities of life. In terms of Geertzian law-as-local-knowledge, 'it is misleading to assume that Islam everywhere was the same; even within the subcultures of Islam, changes over time are to be expected' (Gerber 1994: 59).

Over time, certain *ijtihad*s were accepted by more and more *fiqh* scholars, and thereby some endured the test of time, while others disappeared. Consensus (*ijma*) contributed to the creation of a relatively fixed body of laws or legal schools, namely *madhhab*s. Legal developments in the formative period of *fiqh* took place via the *madhhab* traditions, whereby jurists of different pedigrees operated within the broad interpretive frameworks of *madhhab* founders (Moosa 1999: 163). The *madhhab* tradition 'also developed a formidable and sophisticated intellectual and legal edifice. The coherence and continuity of this legal tradition was mainly

---

grounds of reason. The case should not be one relating to *ibadat*. Second, that the interest should be in harmony with *Shari'a* and should not be in conflict with any of its sources. Third, that the interest should be of the essential and necessary, and not of the perfectionist, (luxury) type. The essential type includes the preservation of religion, life, reason, off-spring, and property. The necessary type appertained to the betterment of living, Muslehuddin (1974: 53-54).

[6] *Istishab* is a principle of equity which refers to the presumption in the law that conditions known to exist in the past continue to exist or remain valid until proven otherwise.

[7] Where strict analogical reasoning leads to an unnecessarily harsh result, *istihsan* is exercised to achieve equity.

secured by a systematic methodology that favored adherence to the interpretive framework of the founders of the law schools' (Moosa 1999: 164).

The term, *madhhab*, acquired different meanings throughout history (Hallaq 2001: 155). Its earliest use was merely to signify the opinion(s) of the jurist. The term later acquired a more technical meaning to refer to the totality of the corpus juris belonging to a leading *mujtahid*, whether or not he was a founder of a school. It also meant the doctrine adopted by a *madhhab* founder and by those of his followers. Then, it was used to mean a corporate entity in the sense of an integral school to which individual jurists considered themselves to belong (Hallaq 2001: 155). Although there were many *madhhab*s, only four remain for practical terms in the *Sunni* jurisprudential realm: *Hanafi*, Maliki, *Shafii*, and *Hanbali*. *Shias* also have their own *madhhabs*.

After the tenth century the dynamism of Muslim jurisprudence was lost and the interaction of *usul al fiqh* was stifled due to a number of reasons. 'A series of events – debates about whether or not the door of *ijtihad* had closed, growing political fragmentation and decay, assimilated customs contrary to *Qur'anic* spirit, and finally the Mongol invasions of the thirteenth century – all played a part in halting creative legal activity' (Esposito 2001: 10). The interaction between *ijtihad* and *ijma* was dynamic: A fresh *ijtihad* of a scholar was either accepted or rejected by the community. There had been a free-market mechanism, as it were.[8] In the civil realm, new 'products' (*ijtihad*s) were being supplied by the *mujtahid*s and if it caught on it would remain on the shelves, if not it would be discarded. However, in the twelfth century, a majority of *Hanafi* scholars argued that the elaboration of law was essentially complete; the independent *ijtihad* was no longer needed and they encouraged jurists instead to follow, or imitate (*taqlid*), the established authoritative doctrines of *Hanafi madhhab*. The *Hanbali* and a minority of *Shafii* jurists continued to practice *ijtihad* (Esposito 2001: 10).

### *Neo-ijtihad*

For some time until the eighteenth and nineteenth centuries, *fiqh* functioned effectively without wishing to freeze it into a utopian past, it has been observed that certain events coinciding with the emergence of modernity disrupted its continuity. The most notable of these was the advent of the West/modernity and the displacement of the traditional Muslim educational systems. The juggernaut of modernity also dramatically influenced the cumulative social, cultural, and economic systems of the Muslim people. All spheres of life including the laws were affected (Moosa 1999: 164). The adoption of new bureaucratic processes in line with legal modernity, transformed conceptions of time, space, property, work, identity, marriage, body, and the state (Moosa 1999: 166). Coupled with the inability of Muslim jurists and lawyers (*fuqaha*) to renew the *fiqh* in accordance with the changing realities of the socio-cultural lives of Muslims, western modernity limited the role of Muslim law. In some countries such as Turkey, it was

[8] On juristic authority in Islamic law and the diversity of schools, see in detail Weiss (1998: 113-144).

gradually removed from the public life and was totally abolished in 1926. In many, it is only limited to family law issues. Even, on these matters, *fiqh* has to obey legal modernity. The modern nation-state decides centrally and for everybody which opinion is to be followed; it codifies it and makes it valid, rendering other opinions invalid.

Especially after the decline of Muslim power and advance of the West and its hegemony, Muslim advocates of renewal (*tajdid*)[9] and reformers have argued for a return to the right to exercise *ijtihad* to facilitate reinterpretation and renew the Islamic heritage. Most of these responses in the late nineteenth and early twentieth centuries to the impact of the West on Muslim societies resulted in substantial attempts to reinterpret Islam to meet the changing circumstances of Muslim life. Moosa (1999: 164) gives us a succinct picture of what has been happening:

> In recent years there has been an ongoing debate among scholars as to whether *ijtihad* had ceased in the *Sunni* legal tradition and, if so, for what reasons and by whose authority. The main reason provided for its discontinuity was that jurists capable of doing comprehensive *ijtihad* were no longer to be found. However, *ijtihad* of a lesser kind was still theoretically and practically possible. Modern Muslim reformers have spiritedly argued for the reintroduction of *ijtihad* into the fibre of Muslim intellectual life. Some traditionalist quarters, especially religious scholars in the Indo-Pakistani subcontinent, Turkey, and the Muslim republics of Central Asia still believe that a regime of *taqlid* is a necessary and a worthwhile methodology not to be abandoned. Other traditionalists in Egypt, Saudi Arabia, and elsewhere in the Middle East will either approve of *ijtihad* with some caution or allow it without restraint. Needless to say, the issue remains the subject of great controversy.

The purpose of *ijtihad* was a return to a purified Islam by weeding out those un-Islamic beliefs and practices that had infiltrated the law and life of Muslims. For modernists, revivalists and Muslim activists, *ijtihad* is a prerequisite for the survival of Islam in a modern world (Vikor 1995). They stress the dynamism, flexibility, and adaptability that characterized the early development of Islam. They

---

[9] Muslims are not happy with the term 'reform' as it has connotations to Christianity and its reform which was a radical departure from the past. For an example see Eickelman (1998). They rather prefer the term '*tajdid*' (renewal). This term is also supported by the *hadith* literature. In a *hadith* reported in Abu Davud, Hakim, Beyhaki and Tabarani, the Prophet is reported to have said that every century a renewer (*mujaddid*) will come and renew the religion. In Ottoman times, in addition to Said Halim, Ismail Hakkı, Mehmet Akif, Hamdi Yazır, and some other Ottoman intellectuals defended the idea and necessity of renewal and *takhayyur*, see Karaman (1996: 539); Karaman elsewhere lists Leknevi, Mercani, Kadri Pasha, Sıddık Hasan Han, Ömer Hilmi, Cevdet Pasha, Azimabadi, Abduh, Kasimi, Hudari, Ali Haydar Efendi, Rashid Rida, Hamdi Yazır, Hayri Effendi, Seyyid Bey, Manastırlı Ismail Hakkı, Izmirli Ismail Hakkı, Ahmed Hamdi, Ömer Nasuhi, Hallah, Ashur, Sherwani, Sibai, Udeh, Ebu Zahra, Yusuf Musa, el-Hafif, Senhuri, Zerkaa, Medkur, Mahmesani, Muhammed Hamidullah, Maududi, Nadwi, Abdulaziz Amir, Shalabi, Shahate, Zaydan, Sayis, Shaltut, Sabik and Qaradawi as scholars who defended new *ijtihad*, employed *takhayyur* and exercised *ijtihad*, see in detail Karaman (1999: 327-332).

argued for internal renewal through *ijtihad* and selective adaptation (Islamization) of western ideas and technology. Several leading modernist Muslim scholars have sought to demonstrate a clearer understanding of the complex origins and development of the *Shari'a* that provides grounds for ongoing reinterpretation and renewal to meet the needs of changing Muslim societies. The purpose of reinterpretation was not to formulate new answers but to rediscover forgotten guidelines from the past.[10] These pragmatic efforts have resulted in the emergence of a utilitarian approach to the traditional jurisprudence that certain legal concepts and instruments are selectively and arbitrarily taken from the traditional *fiqh* for their practical implications and then given a new function and value. Ceaseless invocation of the legal instruments of *darura* (necessity) and *maslaha* (public interest) is an example of this pragmatic attitude. These two instruments are very prominent in the present Muslim jurisprudential discourse but had a limited place in traditional *fiqh*. This new approach can be characterized as making constant reference to the primary sources, whilst avoiding blind acceptance of the inherited juridical legacy with a claim to the right to interpret the sources (Moosa 1999: 167).

In view of the important function given to the concept of *darura* in the modern Muslim discourse, it is worth while to make a number of observations on the point. *Darura* is a comprehensive concept that covers all *fiqh* rulings (Zuhayli 1997: 4-326). This concept developed within Islamic jurisprudence, facilitates and allows for actions which are normally forbidden in Islam. Its existence can lift a prohibition or a compulsory act. When there is *darura*, a *mufti* may issue a *fatwa* in accordance with the ruling of a given *mujtahid* most suitable for the circumstance at hand.

To decide if *darura* exists is not arbitrary. There are certain borderlines and conditions to decide if it is really the case.[11] If a vital interest needs to be protected, this condition is called *darura*. Vital interests as usually listed in *usul al-fiqh* literature may be related to the following: religion (*din*), person (*nafs*), offspring (*nasl*), property (*mal*), or reason (*aql*). In such contexts there is a well-known legal

[10] The three key authors in the making of a generic reform, al-Afghani who was a major catalyst for Islamic reform, Abduh and Rida were all active in restating motifs of the Enlightenment, Romanticism and Positivism. They all believed that the restoration of Islamic vitality required the reconstruction of the sources of Islamic law. Al-Afghani was the leading figure for such a reform and reason that began under the impact of the West. Following Abduh, Rida relied on the Maliki principle of the public interest or general welfare, *maslaha*. In classical Islamic jurisprudence this was only a subsidiary legal principle used in deducing new laws by analogy from the *Qur'an* and *Sunna*. Rida also relied on *Hanbali* law and Ibn Taymiyya. He argued as Ibn Taymiyya that laws regarding social affairs are not immune from change. Abduh, Rida and their Salafiyyah movement espoused the view that those injunctions of *Qur'an* and *Sunna* which governed social relations (*muamalat*) were revealed for the promotion of human welfare. They espoused the view that where social needs were not covered by specific *Shari'a* texts. reason might be used to interpret the law in light of the public interest, Esposito (1982: 242).

[11] See in detail Zuhayli (1997: 4-326-330).

maxim stating that 'Necessity lifts prohibition' (*al-darura tubihu l-mahzurat*).[12] A strict definition of *darura* allows that a primary necessity is one of an emergency nature, where one's life or circumstance is threatened. An exception made to protect a 'vital interest' cannot exceed the minimum necessary to obviate harm to that interest. If there is no permissible alternative, *darura* exists. On this, Muslehuddin (1975: 63) writes that: '(b)y 'necessity' it is usually meant something more pressing than 'need' and which, if not fulfilled, will lead to serious results. Hunger for instance, if not satisfied may result in death. Therefore, the rule of necessity and need is not a free licence but subjected to certain limitations'.

He further writes that a distinction must be drawn between necessity and need as argued by Ibn Qayyim. According to Ibn Qayyim, 'what is prohibited as a preventive measure becomes permissible in view of the public needs but what is forbidden with a definite purpose cannot be permissible unless there is necessity for it' (Muslehuddin 1975: 63). The condition of *darura* must be existent at the present time; a future possible *darura* condition has no legal weight (Zuhayli 1997: 4-327). The distinction between necessity and need must be observed in deciding cases. As the Articles 22 and 23 of *Majalla* puts it, necessity is estimated by the proximity in time of the occurring of the eventuality which causes concern. Whatever is permissible owing to some excuse ceases to be so with the disappearance of that excuse (Muslehuddin 1975: 63).

The reaction to the westernizing of Islam and Muslim society led to the formation of modern Islamic societies or organizations, such as the Muslim Brotherhood and the Jamaat-i-Islami that combined religious ideology and activism (Esposito 1999: 125-126). While pre-modern revivalist movements were primarily internally motivated, Islamic modernism was a response both to continued internal weaknesses and to the external political and religio-cultural threat of colonialism. Like Muslim revivalists and modernists, Jamaat-i Islami and Muslim Brotherhood rejected *taqlid* and upheld the right of *ijtihad*. Although they advocated change through *ijtihad* they tended to accept past practice and undertake change only in those areas not already covered by Islamic law.[13]

At this point, Bediuzzaman Said Nursi's (1873-1960) approach is very original and reflects 'the middle way'; in his opinion 'the door to *ijtihad* is open but there are six obstacles which block up the way to it' (Nursi 1997: 154). In sum, his points of arguments against the practice of *ijtihad* are: the increase of innovations in the Muslim world; the essentials of religion being in danger; the lack of the environmental conditions in raising *mujtahid*s; the very nature of *ijtihad* requiring it not to be forced upon but being the process of a natural course of events; the distance from the age of bliss; the domination of the Western civilization and atheistic philosophy over the minds of Muslims; increased difficulties in making livelihood which may sway ones reasoning and acceptance of *ijtihad* based on non-legitimate other considerations; questions of *fiqh* not being decided so much by reliance on reason (*illa'*); the diminishing concern for the hereafter and the

[12] This legal maxim is also the 21st article of *Majalla*.

[13] The literature on the need and urgency of *ijtihad* is now very rich, see for example Ziadeh (1995: 48-50); Ahmed (1992).

resultant ease on the conscience for those who practice and follow *ijtihad* and the misunderstanding of the principles of *darura* (Nursi 1997: 154-162). In his view, because of these conditions, many Muslims are inclined to take advantage of *darura*, which could possibly be against the spirit of *Shari'a.*[14]

*Asr al-Darura and Surfing on the inter-Madhhab-net*

In modern times, one motivation for rethinking on *ijtihad* was the situation of Muslims in non-Muslim territories. The juristic discourse on Muslim minorities with regard to whether or not Muslims may reside in a non-Muslim territory and under what circumstances, the relationships of these Muslims to *dar al-Islam* and the ethical and legal duties that these Muslims owe to the Muslim law and to their host non-Muslim polity have been debated since the eighth century. Indeed, the juristic discourse on the issue has not been dogmatic (see in detail Fadl 1994: 141-187; see also Masud 1989: 118-128). Other than the mutually exclusive concepts of *dar al-harb* and *dar al-Islam*, the persistent existence of Muslim minorities voluntarily residing outside *dar al-Islam* challenged this dichotomous view. In that regard, Islamic jurisprudence has developed several mechanisms and concepts that facilitate compromise, such as duress (*ikrah*), necessity (*darura*), and public welfare (*maslaha*). As a result, an understanding of *dar al-ahd* (country of treaty, covenant), *dar al-aman* (country of security), *dar al-sulh* (country of truce), and *dar al-darura* (country of necessity) have come to be recognized as situations and environments in which Muslims may live in non-Muslim territories. Perhaps, in modern times, it is more precise to speak of '*asr al-darura*' (time of necessity) instead of *dar-al darura*, since for Muslims, to a great extent, living under *darura* conditions has become the norm in the global village and is more associated with the *Zeitgeist* other than the geographical locality of one's residence. The phenomenon of *darura* is not specific to non-Muslim countries as the juggernauts of globalization, capitalism, and modernity are everywhere. Indeed, Zaki Badawi argues that Muslims are in minority in most countries as the concept 'minority' in Islamic jurisprudence is related to power to implement *Shari'a* in a given polity.[15] In the same vein, the concepts of *dar al-harb* and *dar-al Islam* are related to political power to implement *Shari'a* not to the number of Muslims.

The atmosphere of renewal, necessity and emphasis on the need for new *ijtihad* in *asr al-darura* paved the way for the revival of *takhayyur* and its wide usage in different contexts by individuals and institutions both in official and unofficial realms. *Takhayyur* has originally been the right of an individual Muslim to select and follow the teaching of a *madhhab* other than his or her own with regard to a particular issue (Coulson 1964: 135).

It is originally an act of *taqlid*. Under *darura*, an individual could *taqlid* minority interpretations or another *madhhab*'s view to resolve a particular problem. In other words, under *darura*, a Muslim is allowed to apply *takhayyur* or

[14] On Nursi's views on *ijtihad* see also Baktir (1998); Sanu (1998).

[15] Badawi (2000). In the same vein, the concepts of *dar al-harb* and *dar-al Islam* are related to political power to implement *Shari'a* not to numbers of Muslims.

to surf on 'the inter-*madhhab*-net'.

The inter-*madhhab*-net is composed of and maintained by the following:

- Intra-*madhhab* texts. These are traditional books of particular *madhhab*s, citing different views within the particular *madhhab*. For each issue, authors cite views of different scholars of the same *madhhab* one by one, from the strongest to the weakest. For instance, for the *Hanafi madhhab*, the view of Abu Hanifa is cited first, then Abu Yusuf, then Muhammad al-Shaybani, then Zufar, and then others. The reader is advised to follow the strongest view, yet it is lawful to navigate across the intra-*madhhab* net by following the view of another. Any view can be selected. It is possible that in the near future these texts will be available on the Internet and on DVD-ROMs for ease of reference and selection.
- Inter-*madhhab* texts. These texts are formatted in the same way as those discussed above; however, here the views of the four major *madhhab*s on a given topic are cited for contrast and comparison. In some cases, they offer a fifth *madhhab* (*Shia Jafari madhhab*).[16] As with the intra-*madhhab* example, readers may navigate across the different views by adopting one approach from one *madhhab* and another from another *madhhab*. Again, in the near future these texts will most likely be available in electronic form (see also Hassan 1997: 90).
- New inter-*madhhab fatwa* books.[17] Contemporary Muslim thinkers are continuing the traditional attitude of considering legal diversity as a source of richness rather than difficulty (Beşer 1991: 10). They reaffirm the traditional idea that dissension or legitimate diversity of legal opinions (*ikhtilaf*) is in fact a benefit to the Muslim community, demonstrating flexibility in the *Shari'a*. It is often reiterated that the *ikhtilaf* or diversity of *madhhab*s is bliss (Karaman 1992: 80; Beyanuni 1989). Thus many scholars today, in their books on contemporary issues, give *fatwa*s based on views of different *madhhab*s. Although they do mainly follow one particular *madhhab*, they employ *takhayyur* when necessary and thereby reach a conclusion on a given subject. In sum, these authors use the aforementioned texts but they navigate on behalf of the reader and come up with an answer. In some cases, they produce more than one answer and leave it to the individual to navigate across these re-produced *fatwa*s.
- Newspaper inter-*madhhab fatwa* columns. This is almost identical to the inter-*madhhab fatwa* books but here the medium is a newspaper. For instance, a close look at some Turkish dailies, such as *Zaman*, *Yeni Şafak*, *Vakit*, *Milli Gazete*, Türkiye and so on, shows that the columnists take a positive attitude to *takhayyur* and that they cite different views and opinions of *madhhab*s and scholars when dealing with a particular issue.

---

[16] Zuhayli (1997) is an example to this approach.

[17] For examples of such books in Turkish, see Kurucan (1998); Beşer (1991).

- Radio-TV programs. In addition to newspapers and journals, with the advancement and spread of telecommunication, radio stations and television channels have their own *mufti*s and question-answer programs. In Turkey a number of private TV channels broadcast such programs (see also Messick 1996, 310-320).
- Inter-*madhhab fatwa*s in cyberspace. This is no different from inter-*madhhab fatwa* books or newspaper columns, yet in this case cyberspace is the medium.[18]

Modern-day Muslim scholars are of the opinion that under *darura*, inter-*madhhab* surfing is permissible (*halal*).[19] However, a majority of them emphasizes that surfing is only *halal* if there is a condition of *darura*.[20] Injunctions of Islam are related to a great extent to the consciousness and psychology of the individual. This is even so more in secular environments, where Islamic laws are not enforced by the state. Thus, psychology is not a minor issue and must be thoroughly taken into account especially in the context of inter *madhhab* surfing when peace of mind of the navigator may be disturbed.

Initially, the concept of *takhayyur* was limited to adoption of variant opinions within a particular *madhhab*, or to the introduction of the dominant doctrine of another *Sunni madhhab*.[21] Later, justification for reform was based on any opinion of any jurist regardless of *madhhab*. Occasionally the doctrine of one school or

---

[18] For the effects of recent technologies on the transformation of Muslim concepts. see Mandaville (1999).

[19] See for instance, Beşer (1991: 8, 10); Kurucan (1998: 8); Sa'ban (1996: 450); Hassan (1997: 345-347).

[20] Karaman (1999: 327-332); Karaman (1985a: 345); Zuhayli (1997: 1: 10-11; 1: 53); Beşer (1991: 7, 8, 265, 266); Sa'ban (1996: 450, 451); Gülen (1995: 295-286, 288, 309).

[21] In the case of divergence of opinions among the *Hanafi* jurists, the preference was made traditionally according to the following hierarchy: In the case of disagreement between Abu Hanifa and his students, the opinion of Abu Hanifa was to be preferred, however, if the disagreement is about an adjudicative matter, then the opinion of Abu Yusuf is preferred because Abu Yusuf had worked himself as a *qadi* (judge). In the case of disagreement between Abu Hanifa and his students Abu Yusuf and Muhammad (who were called *Imamayn* 'the two *Imams*'), if their disagreement emanated from the fact of being lived in different ages, then the opinions of *Imamayn* are preferred because they lived later in time to Abu Hanifa, so that they might have had a better insight to the needs of the time. If Abu Hanifa did not have a known opinion about a given case, then the opinion of Abu Yusuf, and if Abu Yusuf also did not have a reported opinion, then the opinion of *Imam* Muhammad, and if none of those three had an opinion, then the opinions of *Imam* Zufar and Hasan ibn Ziyad were considered as a ground for a judgment. Nevertheless, if a judge has sufficient knowledge that enables him to make a choice among different opinions of the jurists or if he has strong evidence in favour of the opinion he preferred, even if that opinion is weak, then he is not obliged to follow that hierarchy.

jurist is combined with another (*talfiq*).[22] Family law reform is based on three legal mechanisms: *siyasah shar'iyyah* (government according to the *Shari'a*), *ijtihad* and especially *takhayyur*, which has been the most notable basis for reforms in the family law field (Anderson 1976: 48). This right of individual Muslims has been adopted in Muslim countries in draft legislation to justify the selection of one legal doctrine from among divergent opinions of the four *Sunni madhhabs*. This usage of *takhayyur* in fact departed from traditional understanding in which *takhayyur* was the right of the individual Muslim in a specific case and not that of a government in legislating change for all Muslims.

The *Majalla* is the first example of official institutional navigation across official and unofficial laws. The Majalla codified the official *Hanafi* law that in the *Majalla* there are certain rules derived not from the consensus of *Hanafi* law, but rather from divergent opinions from the *Hanafi* traditions in it. A *takhayyur* was made from existing rules. The substance of the *Majalla* was collected only from the opinions of the most eminent *Hanafi* school jurists, and in case of disagreement among them, the closest opinion to the primary sources of Islamic law and the most suitable to the present needs of the society were preferred.

Then, the application of this kind of navigation was extended and consolidated in the Ottoman Family Laws Ordinance (OFLO) (*Hukuk-u Aile Kararnamesi*) of 1917. This was an eclectic law which reflected and amalgamated the views of different *madhhabs*. The Ottoman Family Laws Ordinance (OFLO) of 1917 is the first official Muslim law whose provisions have been derived from Islamic law without conformity to any particular *madhhab*.[23]

After the Ottoman legislation, many Muslim modern-nation states applied this method of navigation of the various *madhhabs*, differing in their style and extent from one country to another. The Muslim Family Laws Ordinance of Pakistan (MFLO 1961) is another example of this.

A close scrutiny of contemporary literature on Islamic jurisprudence and *fiqh* will show that one can now see many examples of *fatwas*[24] based on *takhayyur* and

---

[22] For the purposes of this study, I am not dealing with the notion of *talfiq* that advocates amalgamation of *madhhabs* and hybridization. On this, especially, Rida wrote extensively, see in detail Rida (1974).

[23] This law tried to give marriage a more official character by stating that the unilateral *talaq* in the presence of two witnesses did not suffice to terminate a marriage. The law required the presence of a judge or a deputy. Moreover, every marriage and divorce had to be legally organized according to state procedures. The law also granted a wife two new grounds of divorce. Rights of petitions for divorce to Muslim wives did not exist in the *Hanafi* law and the law based these reforms on *Hanbali* and *Maliki* law and on the minority *Hanafi* opinion. For the first time age limits for marriage were set. The OFLO of 1917 prescribed a minimum age of 9 for women and 10 for men. It restricted the right of husbands to polygamy. The first wife was given the right to divorce her husband if he wanted to take a second wife. The new law also allowed women, at the time of betrothal, to write into the marriage contract that if the husband takes another wife, her marriage would be immediately null and void, see Karaman (1992: 77); see also Tucker (1999).

[24] The *fatwa* is a legal opinion given by a professional jurist (*mufti*) that is a specifically Islamic legal institution playing a certain role in the adjudication process of every subculture

suggestions for its usage.[25] In the socio-legal sphere, this legitimization has important reflections; by employing *takhayyur*, Muslim individuals, institutions and states navigate across official and unofficial laws.

Classical Muslim jurisprudence has provided room for choosing minority interpretations or another *madhhab*'s view to resolve a particular problem under the heading of *takhayyur*, *takhyir* or *tarjih*; that is eclecticism, selection or preference, respectively, from among the opinions of the different schools of law or the views of individual scholars within the schools (Coulson 1964: 135). *Takhayyur* refers to the right of an individual Muslim to select and follow the teaching of a *madhhab* other than his own.

The dissolution of *madhhab* boundaries justified by a modified understanding of *takhayyur* can be observed in the legislative attempts of some Muslim countries to modernize their societies by restructuring Muslim laws. The *takhayyur* right of individual Muslims was adopted in Muslim countries in drafting legislation to justify the selection of one legal doctrine from among divergent opinions of the four *Sunni madhhab*s, and it has been the most notable basis for reforms, especially in the field of family law (Anderson 1976, 48; Pearl and Menski 1998, 19-20).[26] This use of *takhayyur* departs from the traditional understanding in which *takhayyur* was the right of the individual Muslim in a specific case and not that of a government in legislating changes for all Muslims.

Preliminary observations and anecdotal evidence, as will be seen below, suggest that today both the official and unofficial realm employ *takhayyur*. A close scrutiny of contemporary literature on Islamic jurisprudence and *fiqh* also shows many examples of *takhayyur*, of *fatwa*s based on *takhayyur*, and suggestions for its

---

in Islam (Gerber 1994: 79). He further explains that Islamic legal production can be arranged along a continuum, or hierarchy, from the theoretical to the practical. The highest level is occupied by jurist (*mujtahid-ı mutlaq*, absolute *mujtahıd*); the lowest level is occupied by the qadi, or judge, whose legal role is to pronounce on what the law has to say concerning an actual human situation. The mufti stands between them and is probably somewhat nearer to the jurist. He relates not to people and their specific questions but to theoretical problems posed to him, his role being to state the position of Islamic law concerning such issues. It was mainly through the work of the *mufti*s that legal change was accommodated into the *Shari'a* (Gerber 1994: 79-80).

[25] For legitimacy of *takhayyur*, see Karaman (1992: 79; 1999: 339, 346, 341); Sa'ban (1996: 443). In the cyberspace, questions on *takhayyur* also frequently take place. see for example. http://Sunna.org/msaec/articles/madhhab_issues.htm.

[26] As noted above, Ottoman Family Laws Ordinance (OFLO) (*Hukuk-u Aile Kararnamesi*) of 1917 is the first official Muslim law whose provisions were derived from Islamic law without conformity to any particular *madhhab*. In the Pakistani context, the Muslim Family Laws Ordinance (MFLO) of 1961 is another example. However, tensions between traditionalists, who believe that the reforms militate against the basic tenets of Islam, and modernists, linger on regarding many legal issues. The MFLO is a particularly clear example of this controversy. The official law is widely perceived as being different from religious law and not accepted as the just law. This led to 'civil disobedience', which rendered the official law ineffective. There is, now, an observable gap between state law and popular practice.

usage.[27]

In conclusion, internal plurality of Muslim laws (internal Muslim legal pluralism) has always been the case. In this age, as a result of losing its official status in many countries, Muslim law is also a source of another Muslim legal pluralism; external legal pluralism that this study mainly focuses on. Now, the theoretical foundations and dynamics of this legal pluralism will be discussed.

## External Muslim Legal Pluralism(s)

In addition to state-Islam relationships in Muslim countries, the very same issue is also a major concern for non-Muslim countries, especially in the West. For the purposes of this study, which attempts to analyze the position of Muslims, their laws and customs in modern nation-states, it is necessary to first elaborate on the position of Muslim minorities, their Muslim laws and non-Muslim nation-state relations according to the different schools of Islam. Muslim law is always a source of legal pluralism in non-Muslim environments since the Muslim mind and conscience is always under the influence of Islamic principles, laws and customs wherever one is. Muslim minorities' legal situation and their responsibilities and duties according to Muslim law should be discussed so that it can be understood how Muslim minds are influenced in terms of religious law and ethics, which have a lot to do with Muslims' daily life wherever they may be. But before doing so, the importance of *Shari'a* in the Muslim mind, and the Muslim individual's universal responsibilities under the *Shari'a* law need to be outlined, in order to fathom the actual position of Muslim law in non-Muslim societies irrespective of nation-states' claims.

### *Shari'a and Muslim Individuals in Asr al-Darura*

Islam 'demands full allegiance from a person, once he has chosen freely to embrace it' (Kettani 1990: 226). Juristic discourse has asserted that Muslims should maintain a separate identity as a minority (Fadl 1994: 179). Where *Shari'a* law conflicts with the secular laws of nation-states, 'it is divine law which must prevail', according to the Muslim mentality and way of thinking (King 1995b: 3). The general principle that God's law must prevail appears in specific directives to Muslims not only in the West but also in their nation-states, 'to contest, defend and protect themselves against 'rational' and secular authority' (King 1995b: 4). Indeed, the impact of the juristic discourse can be seen in *Shari'a*'s 'potential of being a powerful resource for a reassertion of Islamic identity' (Nielsen 1987b: 17).

As a result, many Muslims in Muslim and non-Muslim countries remain 'concerned to relate themselves to the *Shari'a* rather than to such legislation of

---

[27] For legitimacy of *takhayyur*, see Karaman (1992, 79); Karaman (1999, 327-332, 339, 346, 341); Sa'ban (1996, 443). In cyberspace, there are also frequently questions on *takhayyur*, see, for example, http://www.Sunna.org/msaec/articles/madhhab_issues.htm.

particular countries' (Nielsen 1987b: 17), especially in cases pertaining to 'the laws relating to marriage and divorce, and to inheritance and other matters of property' (Lewis 1994: 15; Speelman 1995: 73). Some Muslim scholars have argued that '...Muslims residing in non-Muslim territories need their own judges to adjudicate conflicts and resolve disputes. That these judges are appointed by non-Muslims is regrettable but necessary' (Fadl 1994: 151). They recommend Muslims to organize themselves, and to elect their leaders and judges in order to preserve their identity. They have put much emphasis not only on dispute situations but also on family and daily life since to them 'absorption usually comes through mixed marriages, abandoning Muslim names' (Masud 1989: 125).

State-religion-Muslim relations in non-Muslim countries are not succinctly defined in Islamic jurisprudence. There is no precedent in Islamic history nor any previous discussion in Islamic legal literature regarding Muslim minority communities formed by voluntary migration from Muslim lands to predominantly Christian countries (Lewis 1994: 16). However, some jurists argue that 'if the holy law is still maintained and enforced, even under infidel authority, that country may still be considered, for legal purposes, as part of the House of Islam... Jurists give primary importance to the laws relating to marriage and divorce, and to inheritance and other matters of property' (Lewis 1994: 15).

Indeed, Muslims have come face-to-face with a number of difficulties in the West arising from the conflicts between their Muslim family law and Western legal systems (see for instance Poulter 1997). The '(r)eligious freedom does not extend to the granting of legal protection to religious (Muslim) codes of family law' (Nielsen 1987b: 22) in the West. For instance, some offensive and problematic cases emerged when a Muslim father discovered 'that his children by a second wife are not considered his legal offspring' (Speelman 1995: 74).[28]

As is emphasized above, the juristic discourse on Muslim minorities with regard to whether or not Muslims may reside in non-Muslim territory and under what circumstances, the relationships of these Muslims to *dar al-Islam* and the ethical and legal duties that these Muslims owe to the Muslim law and to their host non-Muslim polity have been debated since the eighth century (see in detail Fadl 1994). 'The history of the juristic discourse on the problem of Muslim minorities is the history of an attempt to reconcile the demands of theory with the challenges of history' (Fadl 1994: 142). In the practical sphere as well as in theoretical considerations, most Muslim community leaders in Europe today regard the old concepts of *dar al-harb* and *dar al-Islam* as outmoded and mostly irrelevant in the present-day context (Nielsen 1987b: 19; Sherwani 1988: 186). However, there is no concession or compromise about Muslim family life. All scholars have reached a consensus that Muslims are permitted to stay in such societies or states if they

[28] I met such a father who was the chief actor of the frequently referred to case of Radwan v Radwan. He had eight children by an English wife, after twenty years or more of marriage, the wife decided to divorce her husband and it turned out to be that the children were illegitimate in the eyes of the English law. It took the father years (and a substantial amount of money) to refute that their marriage was void ab initio in order to get his children to be recognized as legitimate. See Radwan v Radwan (No. 2) (1972) 3 All ER 1026.

can preserve their identity, uphold their religion, and protect their family (Shadid and van Koningsveld 1996a: 103), showing that '(a)lthough people may try to live in accordance with a religious dogma, they always will interpret it in ways that are socially and culturally specific' (Fadl 1994: 181).

*Religion, Secular Law, and Muslim Laws*

In the era of modern nation-states, the difference between secularism and religious faith or practice is real and profound. The struggle between them in the modern world cannot be ignored or easily explained. While secularism believes that the world may be understood entirely in its own terms (Breiner 1995b: 92), religions provide some other-worldly answers which, according to secularism, are considered irrational. Modern states advocate the idea of a separate autonomy of the state which may dominate religion but cannot be dominated by it. Secularism in the West suggests that religion should limit its concern to God and the sacred duties of life (Ben-Yunusa 1995: 78). The main aim of secularism is to eliminate the dominance of religion in human but particularly in political and legal affairs, by providing a system according to which people's religion would develop on a purely human, social and intellectual basis (Ben-Yunusa 1995: 81-82). In effect, this means that religion is allocated only a private space, while law occupies public space. However, in the legal field, it is a fact that so-called uniform, secular legal systems are neither uniform nor truly secular. As seen above, law is always culture specific, and legal systems are always influenced by non-legal factors, including legal concepts. Some scholars argue that secularism aims to establish a functional relationship between different sectors of society. To them, secularism and secular societies allow for new and different ideas to come in and thus facilitate contact with other societies and their value systems. This approach enables individuals to participate actively in running the affairs of a state without having their religious inclinations distract them from serving their nation and discharging their duty to develop it, though they are free to practise their religion after office hours (Ben-Yunusa 1995: 78-79). Stated summarily, secularism has attempted to construct a platform for human development based on a kind of moral independence from religious doctrines, influence and worship.

Post-enlightenment rationality, which has characterized the mode of thinking of modern society's functional systems, 'threatened to isolate and marginalize religious organizations... Within legal and political discourses decreasing emphasis tended to be placed on the "truth" of one religion over another' (King 1995c: 106). In the political arena, in some countries, e.g. India, secularism has been espoused by a government that is independent of any religious function or organization, meaning that no religion is recognized or adopted as a state religion (Ben-Yunusa 1995: 79). The role of religion in modern society has been restricted largely to that of a 'helping hand' (King 1995c: 105). This idea has formulated religion in terms of its responsibility for the moral health of the nation (King 1995c: 106). In the legal field, secularism opposes and rejects the idea that religion has any bearing on the source of legal systems (Ben-Yunusa 1995: 79). When the modernizing elite are trying to build a nation or to modernize an existing one, they ultimately attempt to secularize the legal system. According to them, law should not be open to any influence and interest aspiring from any other world but the tangible, apparent and non-controversial (Allott 1980: 176-179). Indeed, legal systems of the nation-states purport to be based on scientific rationality as the dominant determiner of truth and a notion of justice which is determined by secular laws (King 1995b: 2). Laws are obeyed in modern nation-states, because they have been passed by the state legislature, generated by the secular courts, or recognized by the state as applying (King 1995b: 1).

Correlated to its position in a legal system, religion contrary to secular opinion, usually, influences the operation of law, either positively or negatively. It might also be a cause of resistance to modern state law as, although secular and modern law claims monopoly in the legal field and restricts religion to the private sphere, religious laws are evident phenomena in both the private and public domain. As Chiba (1989) clearly shows, the official constitutional separation of religion and state is both supplemented and undermined by unofficial legal postulates requiring various forms of religious observance (Woodman 1988c: 143).

As a result of the existence and survival of religious law in the era of modern nation-states, interactions and relations between these are unavoidable. There are several possible relationships that currently exist between state and religion. A state may adopt an official religion such as in Pakistan, or it may follow the model of an established church that recognizes freedom of religion to a certain extent, as in England. In another model, state may be neutral or may have no official religion, like Turkey. Another model is the separation of the church from the state as in the United States of America. States may have agreements with the church or protect legally-recognized religious groups. Finally, there is also the *millet* model in which a state recognizes a number of religious communities and allows them to follow their personal religious law in issues such as family law (Hamilton 1995: 3-4).

Under the influences of modernization, the value of Islam as the main symbol of state or collective identity is decreasing. For many groups and individuals Islam has been replaced as an identity symbol by other ideologies (Shadid and van Koningsveld 1991c: 235). On the other hand, one of the most striking consequences of this assumed process of rejection is the re-emergence of religion as a symbol of identity, a phenomenon often labelled as the 'ethniciziation' of minority religions (Shadid and Koningsveld 1991c: 236).

The Austinian understanding of law as the command of the sovereign is the major theme in the socio-legal field. In the modern age, governments that call themselves Islamic are legislating and co-operating in attempts to codify Islamic law, whereas legislation and codification were traditionally anathema (Nielsen 1995a: 31). The quest for modernity is the *leitmotif* of many developing countries. In these countries, most of the time, Muslim law is usually perceived as conflicting with modernity. As a result, for the sake of modernization, Islam has been disregarded in the field of legislation. As a result of the Western domination over Muslim countries, traditional Islamic systems are replaced by systems modelled on European experiences (Nielsen 1995a: 30). This is the case in almost every Muslim country, but most obviously in Pakistan, 'even when the political élite avows purportedly Islamic principles... they act in ways which are readily identifiable with more secular motivations' (Piscatori 1991: 148).

In the light of these theoretical discussions on dynamic legal pluralism and internal and external Muslim legal pluralisms, the book now proceeds to analyze three different cases (British, Turkish and Pakistani) to see if and to what extent theory is substantiated by empirical findings.

# Chapter 4

# Muslim Legal Pluralism in England

Muslim law in Britain exists both on an official level where recognition is given by the legal system and on an unofficial level where the official legal system refuses its recognition. The present chapter analyses the foundations of dynamic Muslim legal pluralism in England by taking into consideration Muslims' perceptions and their manipulation of the official and unofficial laws. One can speak of legal pluralism in the English context since unofficial laws find ways to survive in an alien milieu whether the official law recognizes their existence or not. In that context, the Islamic law being unincorporated, the Muslims keep control over their own law without any outside interference. At the same time the Muslims use those aspects of the official law which benefit and assist them in maintaining their unofficial law. On the other hand, both official law and unofficial Muslim law make some adjustments and modifications.

This chapter analyzes the English legal system vis-à-vis the reconstruction of unofficial Muslim laws. After establishing a historical background of the Muslim presence in Britain, this chapter discusses the settlement patterns of Muslims, which have crucial impacts on the reconstruction of a new Islamic identity in an alien milieu. In the long run, this process has caused the reconstruction of Muslim laws and customs. Having emphasized this, the chapter then proceeds to discuss the uniformity claims of the English legal system and its expected assimilation of ethnic minorities in terms of legal issues. Despite the claims and expectations of the legal system, diversity in the legal arena is a fact; ethnic minorities are not eager to abandon their traditional and religious laws and customs. As a result, although haphazardly, the legal system has made some concessions and recognized some of these regulatory norms. The overall situation, however, has appeared to be that as far as the Muslim laws and customs are concerned, there is a differential legal treatment at the expense of Muslims when it is compared with the recognition given to other ethnic minorities. This situation naturally has many crucial consequences. There are a number of Muslim responses to this situation which will also be discussed in this chapter. It may well be said that the reconstruction of Muslim laws in England is a post-modern response to legal modernity.

### Purported Legal Uniformity in England and Expected Assimilation

As discussed above, the very idea of uniformity of laws has been propagated as an integral aspect of legal modernity. Coupled with a legal centralist understanding, the uniformist idea of a legal system is a core part of the modern English legal system. In this legally positivist system, all other mechanisms of social existencies in a given society, such as family or religion, are hierarchically subordinate to the law. As a modern legal system, the English legal system asserts itself as supreme uniform and centralist; applicable to everybody without exception. Therefore, in England, the legal system is the one and only official legal system, and other systems of law have prima facie no place in it except to the extent that the official legal system may recognize their rules. However, this purported uniformity of English law is increasingly being questioned. As will be seen below, official law maintains uniformity only at a formal level whilst in reality there exists legal plurality.

As Nielsen (1992: 164) puts it, because of the power relationships, western societies have always expected the Muslim minority to carry the weight of adapting. In modern societies where uniformity of the legal system is claimed, ethnic minorities are expected to conform to social and legal patterns of the dominant majority. The legal system expects adherence to the mainstream culture. It is widely believed that settlers from abroad should conform to the norms of those societies in which they have decided to settle. This is an ideology that assumes that it is in the best interest of the ethnic minority population to be like the majority; ethnic identities should be confined to the private realm (Parekh 1990: 67; see also Barot 1991: 196).[1]

A policy of assimilation entails the 'absorption' of the minorities into the mainstream culture of the majority community. Minorities are required to surrender the distinctive characteristics of their separate social identities and blend into wider surrounding society (Poulter 1998: 12-13). It is taken for granted that the majority's culture is superior to that of minorities and that it is desirable to have a homogenous society through 'acculturation' at the expense of minorities. The acceptance of the minorities by the majority and by the state as full members of society is made conditional upon the abandonment of their differences. Poulter (1998: 13) underlines that 'many white people in Britain still consider assimilation through "adaptation" to be a moral obligation on the part of migrants and their descendants and their descendant today is apparent from the frequently heard utterance of the old adage – "When in Rome, do as the Romans do"'.

In the understanding of legal modernity and legal centralism, a number of tools should be employed to assimilate the 'others'. Education is one such tool. In the case of instrumentalism, law can be used to assimilate people and adapt them to the majority. However, the challenge of multiculturalism is seen as a crucial hindrance to the assimilationist policies of modern societies, including England.

## Recognition of the Ethnic Minority 'Laws' by the English Legal System

Religious groupings, particularly in the post-modern age, have emerged almost everywhere as a basis of the refusal to assimilate. Ethnic minorities have been

[1] In that context, Poulter (1996: 10) even ventures to say that some 'customs' of ethnic minorities are 'unnecessarily restrictive'.

developing avoidance and resistance strategies. Moreover, in reaction, they have been trying to re-assert their identities. These minorities have refused to be assimilated and have in fact become more ethnic and more distinctive through their attempts to resist assimilation.

Thus, the purported uniformity of the English legal system too is challenged by the very diverse customs and laws of ethnic minorities. It is abundantly obvious that new forms of ethnic minority laws are now operating in the country. Although the uniform English law remains the official law of the country, it is not the only one which uniquely governs and regulates all sides of familial relationships and other legal relations.

As seen above, there is a dynamic interaction between official and unofficial laws whatever the context may be. This is of relevance for England and ethnic minority customs and laws as well. In contrast to purported uniformity and expected assimilation of the legal system, diversity of laws is a reality in England today. At times the legal system comes face-to-face with the recognition demands of ethnic minority customs and laws that have not been abandoned. Muslim laws and customs which are the unofficial normative orderings of the country's largest minority and the second largest religion in terms of number of adherents, are of much concern in this regard. The wish of ethnic minorities in Britain to continue to adhere to their own customs and personal laws has been one of the most difficult challenges for the English law. The English legal system's approach to these customs and laws has crucial implications and consequences.

Confusion about the definition of 'ethnicity' or 'ethnic minority' causes some problems, especially for Muslims since both the general public and the authorities define minority communities according to a variety of social variables, not according to religious criteria (Jansen 1994: 41).[2] In the current English vernacular, the term 'ethnicity' has no agreed meaning. Very often it is understood as either a synonym or a euphemism for 'race'. Paradoxically, however, on the basis of the questions in the 1991 Census (and also in the 2001 Census), ethnicity is seen 'as membership of or affiliation to a culturally distinctive community of some sort, while race is best understood as referring in some way ... to a person's distinctive biological inheritance' (Ballard and Kalra 1993: 3-4). On the other hand, a catch-all category is not sufficient to distinguish non European whites from persons of other ethnic or racial backgrounds or from religions other than the religion of the majority (Ballard and Kalra 1993: 3-4).

Especially with regards to marriage, the law reflects Christian ideals and traditions, it is not truly secular. Thus, 'parties whose religious traditions conflict with Christian traditions may find, not only that their marriages will not be recognised, but they are liable to criminal prosecution... tolerance of different religious traditions is limited to those practices acceptable to a western, Christian

[2] For instance in France, it is asserted by the official authority that there is no Muslim community, but Muslim individuals, see in detail Roy (1994: 55, 57, 61). The French notion does not acknowledge the existence of ethnic groups in the public arena; it recognizes the rights of individuals to declare specific adherences only in their private lives, on condition that their expression is not to the detriment of law and order, Rachedi (1994: 68).

state' (Hamilton 1995: 80).

There are also inconsistencies in English law's approach to the recognition of religion and religious practice. Although Sikhs are not a separate racial group and rather a separate religion, they are recognized as a separate ethnic group by the official legal system within the ambit of the Race Relations Acts.[3] As a result, Sikhs, like Jews, are provided with greater protection against discrimination and inadvertently are entitled to more rights than those similar religious adherents who are not deemed to be a racial group. Muslims, are one such example of those who closely resemble the Sikhs as a group of adherents but for some reason are not considered to be classed and categorized as being an ethnic group and as a direct result are left outside the terms of the existing anti-discrimination legislation (Modood 1994: 14; see also Modood 1993: 513-519). In Mandla v Dowell-Lee, the House of Lords defined seven criteria by which, according to the Race Relations Act 1976, a group of people could be regarded as an ethnic group. There are two essential criteria: a long shared history and a cultural tradition of its own. While the criteria of 'race', 'colour', and 'ethnic characteristics' have been written into the Race Relations Act 1976 – but not religion – they have not been defined clearly. The entire system of recognition is haphazard and contradictory. The race relations law is based on discretionary distinctions. The judiciary has been given wide discretionary power to deal with issues as they arise, haphazardly. Thus, for instance, while the Sikhs, clearly a religious group; have won 'ethnic minority status', the larger religious groups of Muslims and Hindus have been refused such recognition (Jones and Gnanapala 2000: 244-245). The courts and 'judiciary have been illogical and inconsistent in their application of the criteria developed to establish the ambit of "racial group"' (Jones and Gnanapala 2000: 244).

Religion is not explicitly within the wording of the statute, it is among the non-essential criteria of the common law. Per se it does not qualify a group to be classed an ethnic group. According to this, Muslims in Britain are not an ethnic group but the Whites, Gypsies, Sikhs and Jews are. As far as Muslims (unlike Sikhs and Jews) are concerned, the unifying religion is ignored.

However, as Poulter (1997: 64) emphasizes 'the most important characteristics of the minority communities today are not so much the (predominantly) brown or black skins of their members but their adherence to certain customs, traditions, religious beliefs and value systems which are greatly at variance from those of the majority white community'.

Even though 'English law has shown a marked reluctance to accept concepts of legal pluralism' (Jones and Gnanapala 2000: 244), there are some older observable elements of legal recognition granted to ethnic minorities in Britain. One can find a number of concessions afforded to ethnic or religious minorities in the history of English law. For example, in the field of family law, as a result of these concessions and recognitions, there is neither a uniform procedure in English law for marriages nor a uniform tradition (Bradney 1993: 43). Jews and Quakers have had their marriage rites protected on a statutory basis since 1753, with Lord

[3] Mandla v Dowell-Lee (1982) 3 All ER 1108 (CA) and Mandla v Dowell-Lee (1983) 1 All ER 1062 (HL).

Hardwicke's Marriage Act, and they are exempt from the rules concerning the solemnization and registering of their marriages which are regulated by the Marriage Acts, 1949-1996. Jews and Quakers do not have to celebrate their marriages in the day-time and in a registered building (Bradney 1993: 42). They do not require the presence of any official appointed by or notified to the state authorities; and the form of the wedding merely has to follow the customs of the Society of Friends or the tradition of the Jews in this respect.[4] They might register their marriage after it takes place. However, these exemptions for non-Anglican beliefs have not been granted to other ethnic minority groups in the country (Bradney 1993: 42).

As Hamilton's (1995) study has skilfully confirmed, the English legal system gradually introduced more and more official legal recognition to the religious minorities during the 19th and early 20th centuries. The same concessions, however, have not automatically been granted to new ethnic minorities. Nevertheless, English law has partially adjusted itself to the new socio-legal reality if not fully and in a way which coheres with its past practice on this matter. Rather than outlawing important Asian customary rituals, some have been officially endorsed. There are a number of examples of this development. It was held in a case that it is only after registration and the respective religious ceremony that an Asian marriage achieves full legal validity. Although this was a Sikh case, it can be applied to Muslims.[5] It was held in this case that 'in order fully to marry according to Sikh religion and practice, it is necessary to have not only a civil ceremony in a register office but also a Sikh religious ceremony in a Sikh temple'.[6]

The Children Act, 1989 imposes a new obligation upon all local authorities and voluntary organizations to give due consideration to the racial, cultural and religious background of any child whom they are looking after in making any decision about the child's future.[7]

With the Marriage (Registration of Buildings) Act, 1990, separate building requirements which had been a significant impediment to certification and thus to reconciling the civil and religious forms of marriage were abolished to the effect that one obstruction was removed to help people to jointly celebrate a religious and civil marriage (Bradney 1993: 41).

On the matter of English laws recognition to religious practice and how this can to some extent be considered discriminatory in not being a comprehensive approach to all religions, one may refer to section 53 of the Shops Act, 1950 which exempts Jews from the need to close shops on Sundays as long as they do so on Saturday. Other examples of the English law's recognition of religious duty

[4] Marriage Act 1949, ss 26(1), 35(4), 43(3), 75(1)(a).

[5] Kaur v Singh (1972) 1 All ER 292.

[6] Kaur v Singh, at 293. There are some other cases that took into account the cultural and religious background of the parties. See, for example, R v Bibi (1980) 1 WLR 1193, R v Bailey (1967) Crim LR 42, CA; Malik v British Home Stores (1980) unreported, discussed in Poulter (1986: 264). Bakhitiari v Zoological Society of London (1991) 141 NLJ 55; Re J (a minor) (adoption: non-patrial) (1998) 1 FCR 125.

[7] Section 22(5) (c); section 61(3) (c).

includes s. 1(2) of the Slaughter of Poultry Act, 1967 and s. 36(3) of the Slaughterhouses Act, 1979, which allows for Jews and Muslims to slaughter poultry and animals in abattoirs according to their traditional methods. The Sikhs are exempted from wearing crash helmets provided they are wearing turbans.[8] The law on carrying knives in public places contained in the Criminal Justice Act, 1988 exempts those carrying them for religious reasons.[9] Also, it was decided in Mandla v Dowell-Lee that Sikh school children could wear their special garments and turbans in school.[10] The Education Reform Act 1988 states that religious needs and practices of religions other than Christianity must be taken into account when providing for the educational needs of the school children.[11]

One of the major predicaments of the English legal system pertaining to recognition of ethnic minority laws and customs is its piecemeal and ad hoc character. It does not have a uniform, systematic, coherent and objective recognition system (Hamilton 1995: 38). The English legal system has not found it necessary to define 'customary law' as an abstract concept. It has reacted to a wide range of customary values haphazardly (McLachlan 1988: 84). In the final analysis, generally speaking, 'the interpretation and application of law as it applies to ethnic minority groups has been quite restrictive, with little or no accommodation of the value system of such groups and, to apply Chiba's illuminating term, their "legal postulates"' (Jones and Gnanapala 2000: 243).

It is evident that the protection of the law is not extended even equally to all ethnic minorities. Thus, it would not be wrong to argue that '(t)o describe the law as being neutral to matters of religion when it is concerned with family life is... inaccurate or, at least unhelpful' (Bradney 1993: 51). The legal system in spite of the all claims and assumptions plainly discriminates between different kinds of religions (Bradney 1993: 42). Poulter (1998: 205) concurs with Bradney: 'Whereas in the eighteenth century the privileges accorded to Jews and Quakers reflected religious toleration, in the twentieth century they symbolize religious discrimination… There is no good reason why some religious minorities should be exempt from the normal legal requirements, but not others.'

This might easily cause differential treatment to the different ethnic minorities that can possibly undermine the respect for the lawmaker. As a result, as far as Muslim law as a religious law is concerned, it can have the status of moral but not legal rules, in civil as well as in public law. In that context, the Runnymede Trust published detailed research, which has recently given the impetus to the relatively new term 'Islamophobia' (TRT 1997). In this study, the Commission on British Muslims and Islamophobia states that it is a serious anomaly, in view of case law to the effect that members of Judaism and Sikhism are fully protected under the Race Relations Act, and that no such protection exists for members of other faiths.

[8] Road Traffic Act, 1988, s 16(2); Employment Act, 1989, ss 11-12.

[9] Section 139 (5) (b).

[10] Mandla v Dowell-Lee (1983) 2 AC 548.

[11] Section 8(3); see now Education Act, 1996, s 375(3). See also the decision by the Department of Education to accord grant maintained status to Muslim schools, *Times Educational Supplement*, 16 January 1998.

Now possible and actual Muslim responses to this situation will be analyzed. Before doing this, the reconstruction of Muslim identity in Britain will be analyzed.

## Reconstruction of Muslim Identity

Britain is both de facto and de jure a multi-ethnic, multi-religious, multi-communal and multi-racial society. Through its Race Relations Acts of 1965, 1968, 1976 and 2001, the state has actively recognized this reality. Britain has also 'become a much more overtly poly-ethnic society. Inspired as they are by cultural, religious and linguistic traditions whose roots lie far beyond the boundaries of Europe, the new minorities have significantly expanded the range of diversities covered by local British lifestyles' (Ballard 1994: 1).

As a result, a very diverse 'post-modern' picture has emerged. In that picture, one can easily identify the active resistance of these groups to the assimilation expectations of the legal system. The various ethnic minorities of England have actively developed strategies of resistance to 'English hegemony' which are mainly religiously inspired (Ballard 1992: 486, 491). This post-modern phenomenon is very observable among British Muslims. Instead of assimilation or adaptation along expected lines, they have re-ordered their lives 'on their own terms' (Ballard 1994a: 8).

### *Historical Background*

Ethnic minority groups in Britain are diverse. They originate mainly from different parts of the former British colonial world. While primary immigration movements were effectively stopped by the mid-1960s, family reunification and natural growth have created communities that today form over six per cent of the population of England and about one and a half percent in Scotland and Wales (Modood 1994: 1). Muslims constitute a substantial part of these minority groups and Islam is now the second religion of the country in terms of the number of adherents.

The Muslim presence in England goes back three hundred years to the activities of the East India Company. Sailors were recruited from the Indian subcontinent into the merchant navy. These men were present in Britain's ports. At the beginning of the Second World War, seamen from South Asia constituted almost 20 per cent of the merchant navy. Another group came from Yemen after the opening of the Suez Canal after the 1870s. They now had settlements in London, Cardiff, Liverpool, South Shields, Hull and Sheffield together with Muslims of other backgrounds including British converts (Lewis 1994a: 11; Nielsen 1988: 53).

After the Second World War, as a result of Britain suffering from an acute shortage of labour, immigration from different parts of the world further served the growth of Islam in Britain. Immigration from Pakistan during the 1960s and early 1970s was added to other immigrations of Muslims from Cyprus, East and West Africa, the West Indies, Guyana, India and later Bangladesh. In addition there were some immigrant groups from the Middle East (Nielsen 1988: 53).

Earlier migration movements to Britain were for economic reasons. Immigrants intended to live temporarily and then to return home. Nevertheless, as Ballard (1994a: 12) asserts, 'the longer they stayed, the more rooted and at ease they felt in their new British environment'.

Multiplication and consolidation of the Muslim presence in Britain is evidenced by the rising curve of mosque registrations. Many Muslims in the West now emphasize the maintenance of their social and cultural identity by increasing the visibility of themselves and their infrastructure in the encompassing society (Shadid and van Koningsveld 1991a: 11). Ansari (2002: 6) notes that '(b)y the mid-1990s, there were at least 839 mosques and a further 950 Muslim organisations'.

*Current Situation and Settlement Patterns of Muslims*

There are around 2 million Muslims in the country (Ansari 2002: 7). Muslims with origins in Bangladesh, India and Pakistan constitute approximately 80 per cent of this figure. The rest are either from the Arab world, Malaysia, Turkey, Cyprus, or East and West Africa. There is a majority South Asian representation of Muslims in Great Britain who are 'likely to dominate the public face of British Islam' (Lewis 1994a: 16; Peach and Glebe 1995: 35). However, despite the diversities and differences in the perception of Islam, Muslims' Islamic background remains a common-identity symbol that differentiates them from the surrounding society (Shadid and van Koningsveld 1991a: 17). Muslim ethnic identity in Britain is constructed on a cultural rather than racial basis.

Muslim communities are not evenly distributed across the country. 60 per cent of British Muslims live in the south-east, mainly in Greater London (Ansari 2002: 7). Immigrants arrived as connected individuals. They came in cascading chains along increasingly well-worn paths of kinship and friendship. This phenomenon has had an impact on patterns of settlement (Ballard 1994a: 11). As a result of this process of 'chain migration', it has become possible for Muslims to reconstruct their traditional milieus in Britain (Shaw 1988: 22). This can even be labelled as a kind of 'village transplantation'. As a matter of fact, one's former geographical location formed a much stronger point of settlement in Britain. Hence, for instance, Punjabis are predominant in Birmingham, Mirpuris in Bradford, Gujaratis in Leicester and Sylhetis in East London (Wahhab 1989: 7; see also now Ansari 2002: 7).

With their highly localized settlements, they live in Britain, but in reality in their own world, over which they have a much larger extent of daily control. Under these circumstances, there is always a tendency to avoid officialdom and to set up internal regulatory frameworks. Indeed, some situations arise where communities ignore the state law and do what they have always done.

*Reconstruction of Islamic Identity*

It has become clearly evident that as a result of the process of chain migration – migrants have been drawn from particular villages – which has important implications for the subsequent development of Muslim communities in Britain, its settlement patterns, its social structure and its members' attitudes towards life in this new country (Shaw 1988: 28).

After the collapse of the 'myth of return' (Anwar 1979), Muslims started to rebuild their religious institutions 'to safeguard Islam from the growing secularisation of British society' (Joly 1989: 32). Put differently, as the prospect of return became less realistic, vigorous desires to practise Islam in Britain intensified (Wolffe 1994: 156). It has become clearly evident that the process of chain migration has had important implications for the subsequent development of Muslim communities in Britain and their members' attitudes towards life in this new country (Shaw 1988: 28). The emergence of a distinctive Muslim identity is also an inevitable product of the secular social environment (King 1995b: 7). As seen above, there is no doubt that Islam is a binding force for most Muslims in their daily lives as an all-encompassing regulatory system that claims to be a total way of life.[12] This also continues to be the case with the British Muslims as the tables below show:

**Table 4.1 'Religion is very important to how I live my life', by proportion of life spent in UK and by age at entry into UK**

| | Pakistani | Bangladeshi |
|---|---|---|
| Born in Britain | 57 | 50 |
| 67-100% in Britain | 67 | 62 |
| 34-66% in Britain | 80 | 80 |
| 1-33% in Britain | 88 | 86 |
| Entered Britain before 16 | 69 | 74 |
| Entered Britain after 16 | 83 | 81 |

*Source*: Modood et al (1997: 306).

**Table 4.2 Muslim visits to mosque, by gender and age**

| | 16-34 | 35-49 | 50+ |
|---|---|---|---|
| **Men** | | | |
| Once a week or more | 65 | 83 | 78 |
| Never | 5 | 2 | 5 |
| **Women** | | | |
| Once a week or more | 48 | 46 | 67 |
| Never | 32 | 29 | 12 |

*Source*: Modood et al (1997: 304).

Thus Muslims, along with other 'new' minorities, are committed to cultural and religious reconstruction (Ballard 1994a: 2). Muslim identity in Britain 'is actively

[12] See also in detail Anwar (1979: 158-169); McDermott and Ahsan (1980: 7).

produced, reproduced, and transformed, through a series of social processes' (Kahani-Hopkins and Hopkins 2002: 288). In that respect Islamic teaching has been fortified by some other factors such as the need of Muslims to find a sense of identity and dignity in the face of the racist and post-colonialist mentalities widespread among 'whites' (Raza 1991: 104-107; see also Wolffe 1994: 157).

It is a matter of fact that the family is central to the whole scheme of social life envisaged by Islam (McDermott and Ahsan 1980: 13). During the first phase of immigration, migrants were mostly single men who came for a limited period. The fact that they were men on their own often meant that requirements of religious practice were minimal. There was a strong sense that the family at home remained the focus of cultural and religious identity. During that phase, migration had, if anything, strengthened familial obligations rather than weakened them (Ballard 1982: 188). When the British immigration restrictions began to curtail free movement within the Commonwealth, Muslim men started to reunite their families in the diaspora. Consequently, immigrants have tended to retain their traditional, regional cultures, languages, religions and kinship ties. The settlement patterns of the Muslim population have served the recreation and reproduction of Islamic identity in Britain. Each settlement became a home and within each home honour (*izzat*) has tried to be sustained (Ballard 1994a: 15). As ethnic 'colonies' grew in size and sophistication, migrants' confidence grew as well so that they could reconstitute their families despite the alien surroundings (Ballard 1982: 189). Importantly, this new migration affected religious practice. First, the sense of temporariness began to weaken and was replaced by a sense of permanence. Second, the presence of wives and children critically widened the scope for interaction with the surrounding society (Nielsen 1991a: 43). Most migrants made great efforts to reunite their families.

Many Muslims privately confess to being more devout in this corrosive alien atmosphere than in their previous homeland (Wahhab 1989: 5). Presence of wives and children undoubtedly served this phenomenon. Recent research showed that 'many wives saw themselves as joining their husbands to 'save' them from being estranged from their culture and religion' (Nielsen 1991a: 47).[13] According to many Muslims, Western society is meaningless, aimless, rootless, characterized by vandalism, crime, juvenile delinquency, the collapse of marriages, a growing number of illegitimate children, and psychiatric disorders. Only Islam could provide an alternative lifestyle. The arrival of women and children led to a gradual increase of awareness of the need to preserve the community's Islamic identity vis-à-vis the host society (Shaw 1994: 49-52). While the religious observance had previously slid into abeyance, family reunion has brought a change. Shared religious and sectarian commitments have proved to be the catalyst around which most communities have coalesced. As numbers grew, a network of mosques began to spread across the country (Ballard 1994a: 18).

Muslims enjoy a relatively high degree of religious and cultural autonomy in

[13] Indeed, 'Western influences' on the men when they were alone were widespread. Many had girlfriends. Although their activities were not openly approved, spending time with a woman or even drinking was tolerated in the early years; see in detail Shaw (1988: 43-44).

Britain now. Living in relatively self-contained communities in Britain, they are committed to stay and determined to pass on to their children their religious and cultural values. Thus, they want to reproduce their traditional social and cultural world, and have made vigorous efforts to reconstruct almost every aspect of their traditional and original socio-cultural life. As a result of this reconstruction of religion and the competition of *izzat* (honour), individuals felt themselves under constant pressure to be committed Muslims (Ballard 1994a: 18).

## Muslim Responses and Interaction of Laws

Muslims did not come to England expecting to 'do as the Romans do'. Most of them have desired to maintain their own distinct culture and traditions, including their laws. This desire has been coupled with ignorance of many requirements of English law. Muslims were then confronted with a number of problems and tried to find solutions to their problems by themselves in the absence of official response and recognition.

As a result of the continuing existence of the unofficial Muslim laws and customs, there are a number of possibilities. Muslims have developed some responses and offered some solutions to the above-mentioned predicaments.[14] First, it is a possibility that the Muslim unofficial law could be incorporated into the official English law. Second, by recognizing the lack of sensitivity of the legal system, Muslims have employed informal methods of conciliation. Thirdly, they have continued to seek for official recognition and formal methods of conciliation compatible with Muslim law. As a fourth option, they have developed a hybrid rule system to satisfy the requirements of both official English law and the unofficial Muslim law. Now, these possibilities will be discussed one by one.

### *Incorporation of the Unofficial Law into Official Law*

Muslims will not only wish to be regulated by the principles of Islamic law when they are living in a non-Muslim state, they will also seek to formalize such an arrangement within the state's own legal system (Poulter 1990b: 147). Although, even in the Islamic world, the principles of Muslim law are not always applied in total, Muslim family law usually prevails, in one form or another. In most Muslim countries, the states have regulated the public or general law, but family law has remained almost untouched. During colonial periods, colonial western powers more or less followed the same strategy. Thus, it is 'natural that Muslims expect the application of Muslim family law, even from a non-Muslim government' (Jansen 1994: 42). Muslims view and argue the issue principally in terms of religious freedom and they expect Islam's past respect for Jewish and Christian minorities in Muslim lands to be reciprocated in the West (Poulter 1990b: 148).

During the 1970s, the Union of Muslim Organizations of UK and Eire

[14] It must be underlined that some non-Muslims scholars of the field also have been offering solutions that will be discussed below as well.

(hereinafter UMO) held a number of meetings for this purpose and in 1976 proposed a separate system of Islamic family law (Muslim personal law) which would be applicable to all British Muslims (UMO 1983).[15] This attempt proved unsuccessful. Although, since then, such demands have been made intermittently, they have been rejected. These demands, 'perceived as threatening an established order and a well-functioning system of legal regulation, have led to an essentially defensive, reactionary response' (Menski 1993a: 256). The official legal system proposes some justification in rejecting incorporation of Muslim family law into the official legal system. First of all, as is stressed above, it is against the very notion of a uniform legal system (Poulter 1990b: 158). It is widely believed that it 'would be impossible in Britain because the law covers everyone, even nationals of another state, in all areas' (Joly 1995: 15; Poulter 1990b: 158). However, as Poulter (1990b: 158) rightly points out, 'it is not wholly accurate'. This is not an accurate justification since one can possibly call attention to the situation of Jews and Quakers. A second reason might be the practical difficulty of applying Muslim family law because there are so many versions of Muslim family law. Thirdly, would cases be decided by the existing civil courts or by a specially established religious court staffed exclusively by Muslims? Poulter (1990b: 158) asserts that civil courts will hardly be legitimate in the eyes of Muslims, and plurality of Muslim views and their non-uniform structure will prevent the latter option. According to Poulter (1990b: 159), the fourth difficulty stems from the human rights dimension: Muslim family law is seen as contradictory to fundamental human rights (see in detail Poulter 1990b: 159-166). According to Poulter (1993: 184-185) 'on human rights grounds, Muslims should not be allowed to operate a system of Islamic personal law in England because of the risk that the rights of women will be violated in a discriminatory fashion thorough such practices as polygamy, *talaq* divorces and forced marriages'.

At that point, the issue of incompatibility between 'universal' human rights and Muslim law could be debated further. Obviously at this point, this has to be extremely brief.

The universality of human rights concepts has always been debated. Many scholars, especially in the west, have depicted Muslim law 'as incompatible with modernity and more particularly with what is seen as one of its greatest achievements: the Universal Declaration of Human Rights' (Mitri 1995b: vii; for instance see Poulter 1986; 1990a; 1990b; 1990c; 1997: 52-53).

However, this reading of human rights has some technical flaws. It is not an easy task to refer to European or Western-made conceptions, since the universality of such concepts has always been debated (see for example Cassese 1990b: esp. chapter 3; Schmale 1993; Kazmi 1987; Pollis and Schwab 1979a). Even though almost all human rights documents suggest and provide for limitations, as

[15] See also Modood (1993: 515); in 1984, a Muslim charter was produced which demanded that the *Shari'a* should be given a place in personal law, see Joly (1995: 15). In Canada, Ali and Whitehouse (1992) made a proposal for Muslim personal law system, presenting Muslim law as codified whole, rather than several sometimes conflicting systems, Kelly (1998: 91).

Hamilton (1995: 29-30) argues, the issue which limits could be reasonably imposed has not been clearly elaborated. Thus, this imprecision may cause a discrimination against minority or unpopular religions (Hamilton 1995: 30).

On the other hand, Western conceptualizations of human rights have been steadily accused of being culturally and ideologically ethnocentric, a western concept with limited applicability (see for instance Pollis and Schwab 1979: 1). The definition of human rights is still subtle and highly contentious.

In addition, states' non-recognition or unawareness of dynamic Muslim pluralism perpetuates some situations to the disadvantage of those whom states are supposed to protect, a predicament confounded by failure to realize the law in praxis.

Rath et al (1991: 107) also criticize Poulter at this point: 'Poulter accepts too easily that human rights conventions are unequivocal, and represent universal norms and values... this is not necessarily the case... he bases (his assumption) on strictly formal reasoning, as if decisions by the judiciary or by the Parliament are actually based on legal considerations only'. Moreover, not all English laws are in harmony with international human rights norms as in the case of the primary purpose rule (see in detail Sachdeva 1993). Poulter should have known that forced marriages have nothing to do with neither Muslim law nor Islamic personal law. Although it is true that some South Asian families, Muslim or not, employ forced marriages, it is not legal under the Islamic personal law (see in detail Ahsan 1995: 22-23; Badawi 1995: 75).

Another scholar, Bradney (1993: 52), argues that in the area of personal law individual autonomy and complete freedom of religion are incompatible. Although in such instances the superiority of individual autonomy can justify religious discrimination, in other instances, legal rules can facilitate the wishes of individuals whose religious demands do not involve disturbing the autonomy of others. Thus, for example, a personal law system into which believers can opt if they wish to do so is entirely compatible with the demands of personal autonomy (Bradney 1993: 52). Some other legal scholars suggest that a separate law is not necessary. They emphasize that the *millet* system is not without its problems as many cases in India have shown (Hamilton 1995: 91). Instead, it is recommended that legal professionals serving in family courts should receive training in the religions and cultures of the ethnic minorities of the country and expert lay members should be included in the court hearings (Nielsen 1993a: 8). Also, they argue that Muslims 'should bear in mind just how flexible and accommodating many of the provisions of English law are and ensure that they use the existing system to the full to suit their own purposes' (Poulter 1990b: 164). Indeed, they have started to do so without an official personal law. They also became more effectively organized in their dealings with local and central governments as they gained confidence and experience (Ansari 2002: 6). The demand for an officially recognized Muslim personal law has not been fully supported by many Muslims, since they have found their own ways of reconciling Muslim law and English law (Pearl and Menski 1998: 77).[16]

---

[16] The net result of the process is the construction of *angrezi shariat*.

*Informal Methods of Conciliation*

Muslims do not expect their 'ethnic laws' to be understood, applied and tested by English lawyers and judges. The Muslim community try to keep family matters out of the hands of the courts. Thus, many cases do not come before the courts. There are many understandable reasons for this situation if the issue is seen from the Muslim perspective. First, many areas of Muslim law have traditionally and purposely been left to extra-judicial regulation. Second, in the eyes of many Muslims, 'the secular authority of western law may lack legitimacy and moral standing to deal with any intricate matter of obligations that may arise in the context of a personal law system' (Menski 1993a: 255).[17] Third, because of the *izzat* concerns, they do not want to wash their dirty linen in public. Fourth, as a result of the lack of response and recognition from the legal system, they have developed avoidance reactions.

This phenomenon coupled with the state's hesitations to recognize their Muslim identities in terms of law has led to poor communication between the community and the legal system. This not only increases the number of problems the community encounter but also engenders some negative feelings in the established legal system. Distrust of the official law and lack of respect for the lawmaker provide important feedback effects for the reconstruction of Muslim unofficial law in Britain. As Pearl (1986: 32) has already noted, Muslims have withdrawn from state institutions and developed their own methods of dispute resolution which operate both on an official and unofficial level. Pearl and Menski (1998: 77-80) draw attention to the reality that many disputes among Muslims in Britain are settled in the context of informal family or community conciliation. Senior members of the families or community leaders take their place in informal conciliation processes. Settlement patterns of the Muslims mentioned above have facilitated this process.[18]

For Muslims, there is increasing evidence of the consolidation of such bodies. Islamic *Shari'a* Councils are examples of such concerted efforts to face challenges by the official legal system (Carroll 1997: 105-110; Badawi 1995). These councils are designed to solve difficult social and legal problems which arise as a result of the application of English law to British Muslims, while Muslim law remains in the unofficial sphere (Pearl And Menski 1998: 77).

Having recognized that the official legal system has hesitated to solve their disputes in the context of Islamic family law, Muslims have established informal conciliation mechanisms (ISC 1995; Badawi 1995). They interpret Islamic law according to the needs of the Muslim community in Britain (Badawi 1995: 77).[19] Such institutions attempt to restore equilibrium between parties by enforcing an Islamic law free from cultural biases and by having no vested interest in keeping together those spouses in an empty shell of a marriage.

---

[17] Hindus and Sikhs also conceive the matter as such, Menski (1993a: 255).

[18] See also Pearl and Menski (1998: 59-61).

[19] The attempts to establish similar institutions by Canadian Muslims are interpreted as a post-modern tendency by McLellan and Richmond (1994: 673).

*Shari'a* Councils have sometimes chosen minority interpretations or views to resolve a conflict. Classical Muslim jurisprudence has provided room for this act under the heading of *takhayyur* or *takhyir* or *tarjih*: eclecticism, selection or preference from among the opinions of the different schools of law or the views of individual scholars within the schools (Coulson 1957: 135). *Takhayyur* has been the most notable basis for reforms especially in the family law field (Anderson 1976: 48ff.). Or, foraging beyond the boundaries of the general consensus, it has been possible to select doctrines from outside the four *Sunni* schools, from isolated jurists or from the Shia jurists. *Takhayyur* refers to the right of a Muslim to select the teaching of a law school other than his/her own with regard to a particular transaction (Esposito 1980b: 236). Legal provisions are reformulated by the procedure termed *talfiq* (piecing together), from a combination of the views or particular elements from the views of different schools and jurists as long as there is no departure from the spirit of Islam (Coulson 1957: 135). It is very clear that these decisions do not easily fit into traditional mainstream Muslim law but were taken as a result of living in a secular and modern country.

### *Formal Methods of Conciliation*

In 1985, the Churches' Committee on Migrant Workers in Europe (CCMWE) organized a seminar of Christians and Muslims. In the seminar, both sides reached a compromise between two extremes, separate Muslim personal law on the one hand, and the current situation of a purportedly uniform legal system of England. They offered an establishment of a tribunal which in cases involving Muslims takes full account of the parties' religious and cultural identity as a material factor if it was relevant (Nielsen 1985b: 15-18). They further commented in a later meeting that if the official legal system became more sensitized and religious experts were consulted for advice at an earlier stage, then there would be no need to undermine the 'uniformity' of the system (Nielsen 1993a: 8). After paying some attention to the processes of possible introduction of Islamic family law, they offered some form of mechanism within the family court system to take more account of Muslim needs, for example by having a quasi-judicial or arbitration hearing (Nielsen 1987b: 33).

David Pearl (1987a: 168) put forward a sort of informal family court system. He seems to suggest a body modelled on the Jewish Beth Din, which has in some cases a quasi-official capacity in that the State recognizes it as being the representative and regulatory body of most Jews in Britain (Pearl 1987a: 168). Professor van Koningsveld (1996) also espouses the idea of these informal family courts by underlining the applications of the colonial powers in the colonies. He asserts that colonial powers respected socio-legal realities in the colonies, so there is no reason to disregard this reality at home. Indeed, the Jewish Beth Din, more or less, serves this quasi-official function. As a matter of fact, the Islamic *Shari'a* Councils mentioned previously can be regarded as falling in this category (see in detail ISC 1995; Badawi 1995: 73-80). However, keeping such bodies on an unofficial level provides an important autonomy to Muslims that would be lost were control to be given to the state. This would also undermine the respect for the official legal system.

Recognizing the existence of conflicts between their own law and the official English law, the Muslim community has, in addition to bodies like *Shari'a* Councils, sought other ways to adapt their Muslim law to the non-Muslim, modern and so-called secular milieu. They have constructed new hybrid rule systems which meet demands of both official and unofficial laws. The emergence of '*angrezi shariat*' is one of the outcomes of the interaction process.

### *Code Switching and Skilled Cultural Navigators*

The literature about the interaction of South Asian laws and English law was almost non-existent till recently and with the exception of some studies such as Pearl (1972), Aurora (1967), Taylor (1976), Kannan (1978), and Watson (1977). Poulter's (1986) distinguished study is path-breaking in the field. However, most of these writings assume assimilationist trends in a one-dimensional way. Menski has shown that there is an active interaction between official English law and unofficial South Asian laws, including Muslim law.[20] This is a vivid reality, since South Asians have been following both English law and modified versions of their respective traditional laws.

As a result of living in modern societies, Muslims are faced with some new challenges. They have experienced urbanization and the spread of technology and communications. Although most Muslims are conservative in their attitudes and convinced that they have maintained traditional patterns in their entirety, it does not mean that no interaction and change have taken place.

In the British context, Wolffe (1994: 160) distinguishes four general kinds of relationships between Muslims and British society: assimilation and isolation, two extremes, and integration and redefinition, two middle courses.[21] On the other hand, although it is not easy to be British and Muslim at the same time (Modood 1992), Muslims could seek the two kind of middle way. They might remain faithful to Islam while identifying fully with Britain. In that sense, integration means the adaptation of British structures to facilitate the practice of Islam within them. To that effect, Muslim leaders have been claiming that 'Islam is flexible enough to adapt to a modern... society' (Joly 1989: 40).

The above-mentioned phenomenon of urbanization and modernization, in a long interaction process, has affected British Muslims' lives and identities. As a recent research reconfirmed, 'British Muslims have sought to adjust to and accommodate existing institutions and practices, experimenting and negotiating between the actual and perceived demands and values of British society, and the needs, beliefs and practices of Muslims (Ansari 2002: 17).

While the widely expected assimilation of English cultural patterns has not

[20] See for instance Menski (1987; 1988a; 1993a; 1993b; 1996).

[21] On the same theme, Peach and Glebe (1995: 40) underline that 'Muslims have been called upon to react in three different ways: ghettoization; political organization; liberalization'. Nielsen (1987: 389) mentions such a Muslim ghetto. They educate their own children, and organize their own family relations without reference to civil registries or English family law.

occurred and although Muslims, and many other minorities, are autonomously evolving their own distinctive lifestyles (Ballard 1982: 190; see in detail 1994; see also Joly 1995: 183), their laws and customs have undergone change and modernization. In England, as in other modern countries, the state's legal decisions and positions in a way forced Muslims to re-arrange their life-styles, which also included their laws and customs, in accordance with the respective state and its norm system.

The assumed assimilation process of Muslim ethnic minorities could be in three stages.[22] In the first stage, they might be ignorant of particular legal requirements. Customary practices would continue. At the second stage, they would learn to follow certain rules and requirements of the *lex loci*. At the third stage, it might be argued that they would completely abandon their Muslim law and, in a rational progression, would use only English law (Menski 1988a: 65). However, evidence does not suggest that this third stage has come into existence. Laws and customs of Muslims, among others, are still alive.

It will be wrong to argue that cultural norms and practices of Muslims are unchanging. They have made some modifications as well. They constructed new and varied lifestyles of their own. Migrants and their offspring readapted and continually reinterpreted their values and lifestyles in their new settings (Gardner and Shukur 1994: 164). They have launched 'a debate on the teaching of Islam within the new circumstances of living in British society' (Joly 1989: 45). Some of them have even been advocating 'modifications and adaptations capable of meeting the "onslaught of westernism"' (Joly 1989: 45).[23]

Muslim migrants followed a dual strategy for the reproduction and recreation of Islam (Joly 1989: 41). First, '(t)hey have established the necessary institutions for the essential tenets of their religious practice, addressing their efforts to the Muslim communities themselves' (Joly 1989: 41). Second, 'they have attempted to influence British institutions and individuals with a view to making a space for Muslims in their midst' (Joly 1989: 41).

As a result, Muslims in Britain, to borrow Ballard's phrase (1994a: 5), reconstructed 'a home away from home (*desh pardesh*)'. The older generation of Muslims and their British-born offspring are continuing to find substantial inspiration in the resources of their own cultural, religious and linguistic inheritance, which they have actively and creatively reinterpreted in order to rebuild their lives on their own terms (Ballard 1994a: 5).

They have become an integral part of the British society. However, 'they have done so on their own terms' (Ballard 1994a: 8). Indeed, it is remarkable that this process 'is in no way limited to the first generation' (Ballard 1994a: 34). In fact, among young people traditional beliefs and lifestyles are also very much alive (Wahhab 1989: 12).

For Muslims, this reality confirms our theoretical discussion on the place of Muslim law as higher than state law, and viewing and treating perceived Muslim

---

22 Authors use a range of terms and distinctions of meaning that are difficult to distinguish, such as assimilation, integration, and adaptation.

23 The concept *dar al-darura* could have easily served that purpose.

norms as crucially binding. Put differently, in the minds of Muslims, the 'universal' rules of Muslim law are superior to the local *lex loci*.

Especially in family issues, Muslims have found autonomy to follow Islamic and customary rules in the diaspora, too. They have not simply abandoned them. Since they are not evenly distributed across the country, the dilution of the social, religious and cultural characteristics of the community is far from possible. They have set up an internal regulatory framework to settle disputes, while tending to avoid officialdom. One of the main reasons of this is historical, for matters of family law have traditionally been dealt with outside the direct interference of the state. Settlement patterns of Muslims in Britain have helped them to continue traditional practices in their semi-autonomous communities.

In the realm of family law, ethnic minorities in England have developed new strategies to follow both the requirements of English law and their traditional religious laws. As skilled cultural navigators, Muslims, along with other ethnic minorities, have been meeting the demands of different cultures and laws. Ballard (1994a: 31) explains this phenomenon skilfully: '(j)ust as individuals can be bilingual, so they can be multicultural, with the competence to behave appropriately in a number of different arenas, and to switch codes as appropriate... they are much better perceived as skilled cultural navigators, with a sophisticated capacity to manoeuvre their way to their own advantage both inside and outside the ethnic colony'.

The assimilation thesis is no longer valid in these post-modern times and the 'immigrants' are not lost between two cultures. Constructing hybrid rule systems has allowed many Muslims to feel at ease. Redefined unofficial Muslim laws in Britain have become hybrid obligations as matter of socio-legal practice rather than official-legal fact (Pearl and Menski 1998: 74).

As a result of the development of an understanding of *dar al-ahd* and *dar al-darura* in which Muslims can live their religion peacefully, albeit with varying degrees of difficulty, they and semi-official Muslim bodies are reconstructing Muslim laws in England. In Britain today, there is 'a new form of *shari'a*, English Muslim law, or *angrezi shariat*, which remains officially unrecognized by the state but is now increasingly in evidence as a dominant legal force within the various Muslim communities in Britain' (Pearl and Menski 1998: 59).

## Reconstruction of British Muslim Laws in *Dar al-Darura*

An analysis of the position of Muslim law in England today has to take into account of the emergence of *angrezi shariat*. The reconstruction of British Muslim laws is not only a matter of continuing a traditional form of *Shari'a*. Rather, there is a variety of locally influenced sub-forms, in this case prominently South Asian British Muslim *Hanafi* law (Pearl and Menski 1998: 74-75). Today, this reconstruction is most visible in the field of family law with regards to marriage, registration of marriage, age of marriage, polygamy, divorce and much more. There is now significant evidence that British Muslims marry twice, divorce twice, and do many things twice in order to meet the demands of Muslim legal pluralism.

*Arranged Marriages*

Marriage practices of Muslims in Britain generally reflect the fact that family and kinship groups are seen as the basic units of social organization. Marriage is therefore a matter which is of concern to the group generally, and the interests of individuals in this matter are conceived as being subsumed within the wider group. Thus marriage in this understanding has above all involved the formation or maintenance of family alliances, even though nominally the event is organized between individual members of such groupings (Oakley 1995: 11; see also Werbner 1995: 139). Anwar (1998: 106) underlines that '(w)hen a marriage is arranged, it is seen as a contract between the two families and not two individuals'.

Arranged marriages among South Asians have been the object of several studies; they are an important mechanism to reconstruct family lives in the new country (Kannan 1978: 130-132; Ballard 1979: 124-125). The power of tradition over religion has been enormous among Muslims as well as among other South Asians. Although Islam stipulated that a girl's permission must be obtained before marriage, until recent times very few parents asked or discussed marriage prospects with them (Mirza 1989: 18). Since *izzat* and *purdah* are considered very crucial in the lives of South Asian Muslims, the practice of arranged marriages is a matter of great importance. *Izzat* is advanced by arranging prestigious matches for the family's daughters. Any misbehaviour according to *izzat* could ruin the marriage prospects not only of the girl concerned, but also those of her sisters (Wolffe 1994: 158).

Yet generational conflict among Muslims, and among other Asians, too, is often misinterpreted by 'whites' in quite ethnocentric terms, as involving excessively authoritarian parents (Ballard and Ballard 1977). One should not assume that all young Muslims are hostile to arranged marriages (Oakley 1995: 13). Indeed, according to a recent research, out-of the twenty-two people interviewed, only two people strongly objected to it in principle (Joly 1995: 170).

The practice of arranged marriage continues in Britain, as the table below shows:

**Table 4.3 Parents' decision over marriage partner by age and gender**

| Age group | Men | Women |
|---|---|---|
| 50+ years | 62 | 87 |
| 35-49 years old | 59 | 78 |
| 16-34 years old | 49 | 67 |

*Source*: Modood et al (1997: 318).

Such marriages are treated as perfectly valid in themselves (Poulter 1990b: 151). Although the consent of both prospective spouses is essential in Muslim law, there are instances where a young person may be validly married simply on the basis of his or her guardian's consent. This marriage is unlikely to prove acceptable in England (Poulter 1990b: 152). In some cases, parents faced with disgrace might resort to coercive measures, including violence, transport to the country of origin, or threats. To describe this, the term 'forced marriage' is sometimes used (Poulter 1986: 22). Oakley (1995: 13) emphasizes that although in some specific instances this term may be clearly appropriate, this term is not an accurate description of the traditional cultural practice, but rather of its abuse.

If the marriage is a forced marriage, such a marriage is treated as voidable under the English law.[24] The ground for annulment is that the party concerned did not validly consent to the marriage as a result of duress (Poulter 1990b: 151).[25] In that situation, courts try to determine what constitutes duress.

In Singh v Singh, the court advocated the view that it must be proved that the person's will was overborne by a genuine and reasonably held fear caused by threat of immediate danger to life, limb or liberty.[26] As is seen, this was a narrow interpretation of duress. However, in a later case, Singh v Kaur, it was held that fear of social and financial ruin and exposure was sufficient to constitute duress.[27] Two years later, the courts took a more liberal approach and held that the test was simply whether the petitioner's will had been so coerced as to vitiate consent.[28] Thus, the requirement that a threat to life, limb or liberty appears to have been dropped.

Beside these developments in the legal field, during the last decades in Britain, second-generation Muslims have started to challenge conventions. They are looking for a greater autonomy for Muslim women within an Islamic context (Mirza 1989: 9, 14, 24; Wolffe 1994: 158-159; Sharif 1985; Joly 1995). Moreover, some 'Muslim parents are now letting their children make the final marriage decision' (Mirza 1989: 28; Ballard 1979: 125). Also, an increasing number of matches can be made in Britain. This stems from both demographic self-sufficiency of the population and shifting aspirations and attitudes (Gardner and Shukur 1994: 156). Recent changes in the immigration laws have also contributed to the process (Ahsan 1995: 24).

Consequently, liberal versions of the arranged marriage have evolved in Britain. When a boy or girl has reached marriageable age, parents start looking for a suitable prospective spouse for their child through a network of relatives and friends. When a family is satisfied with the boy's background, education and financial situation, or the girl's character, family background and ability to manage a home, the stage is set for the next step and photographs of the prospective spouses are exchanged. If a mutual tendency appears between the boy and girl, then a meeting under parental guidance may be arranged. The candidates meet and may talk to each other, then the marriage may be agreed. In this way, the final decision is up to the prospective spouses, and not to the parents. By the late 1980s,

---

[24] Matrimonial Causes Act 1973, ss 12, 13. See Singh v Singh (1971) P 226; (1971) 2 All ER 828; (1971) 2 WLR 963; Singh v Kaur (1981) 11 Fam Law 152; Hirani v Hirani (1982) 4 FLR 232.

[25] Matrimonial Causes Act 1973, s 12.

[26] Singh v Singh ((1971) 2 All ER 828; (1971) P 226; (1971) 2 WLR 963.

[27] Singh v Kaur (1981) 11 Fam Law 152.

[28] Hirani v Hirani (1983) 4 FLR 232.

this well-defined 'assisted arranged marriage' has emerged within the Muslim community and other South Asian communities (Hiro 1991: 159). A new trend in assisted arranged marriage has started to come into operation recently. In that, parents advertise for their offspring in matrimonial sections of community newspapers or young people do this themselves. Recently, there has been a tremendous increase in the number of Muslim matrimonial companies and internet websites.[29]

In another increasingly prominent scenario, the children take the initiative to make the first introduction, the parents are brought in through the process of negations at a later stage. Thus the final arrangement still looks like the product of a family consensus (Nielsen 1995a: 115). In conclusion '(i)t seems that arranged marriage will endure, but it will increasingly be adapted and accommodated to children's opinions' (Joly 1995: 172).

*Solemnization of Marriage: Nikah*

Like every society, Muslims also have some rules regulating entry into marriage. These rules concentrate generally on such matters as who may marry, who can marry who, who has to agree to the marriage, what ceremonies and what formalities must be accomplished etc.

Although marriage is a divinely ordained institution in Islam, each marriage as such is in the nature of a contract. The word *nikah* used for marriage in the *Qur'an* and the *Sunna*, means *aqd*, or contract. 'Thus, as with any contract, several elements are considered essential to its existence' (Büyükçelebi 2003: 280).

This contract is a strong covenant. The marriage contract in Islam is not a sacrament. It is revocable. Both parties mutually agree and enter into this contract. Offer and acceptance is the essential part of this contract and both sides should do this with their own free will. Both bride and groom have the liberty to define various terms and conditions of their liking and make them a part of this contract. Büyükçelebi (2003: 280-281) lists the conditions for a sound marriage contract as follows:

- The offer and acceptance is permanent and certain. If anything in the contract includes something of a temporary and uncertain nature, the marriage is invalid. This is why the words of acceptance must be in present tense to emphasize certainty.
- Two credible witnesses must be present, and the marriage should be announced and publicized.
- Both parties have willingly accepted the marriage.
- The bride and groom are identified and known.
- The parties and witnesses are not bound to keep it quiet.
- The man and woman must be legally competent (adult and sane).

---

29 See *Muslim Guide* (2004).

- The woman cannot be one of those forbidden to the man by relation, nursing, or any other preventing factors.
- The offer and acceptance of the contract must be done in one sitting.
- The bride must receive a dowry (*mahr*). The groom gives *mahr* to honour the bride, to show his respect and his sense of responsibility.

Marriage ultimately leads to a number of relationships and engenders a set of mutual rights and obligations. Each contract, however, is not a sacrament; it is not irrevocable.

According to Muslim law, the state has nothing to do with marriage, but in modern legal systems states, for several reasons, claim authority to interfere and supervise marriages.[30] At this point, a number of problems arise between the official law and unofficial Muslim law. As (Hamilton 1995: 39-40) summarizes, where a religious marriage takes place, but the parties have failed to fulfil the preliminary civil requirements, the question arises whether the state will recognize this ceremony as conferring the status of marriage on parties. The law favours the validity of marriage, particularly where the parties have not knowingly and wilfully contracted a marriage in defiance of the legal requirement to obtain a licence. The English courts do not overlook a flagrant disregard of the appropriate civil formalities to marriage. They do not treat a religious marriage, even one valid according to the particular religious law, celebrated in the absence of these, as creating a marriage at all.[31] This means that the possibility of nullity proceedings, even to declare a marriage void, is not open nor, therefore, is there a possibility of claiming some form of matrimonial relief.

The cases of R v Bham and R v Ali Muhammed clearly illustrate this. In both cases, the court accepted that 'neither the parties nor the celebrants intended to effect a valid English marriage, only an Islamic one' (Hamilton 1995: 41). It is obvious that the law is in a rather uncertain position. Thus, 'parties who have gone through a religious ceremony without first fulfilling the civil preliminaries, will be treated as never having contracted a marriage, if the parties knew that the marriage would not be valid under English law' (Hamilton 1995: 41).

Until 1753 when Lord Hardwicke's Marriage Act enacted, there were various ways of solemnizing a valid marriage. The Church of England sought to exert more controls over marriage solemnization in the seventeenth century. The Lord Hardwicke's Act regularized the performance and registration of marriages. To effect a marriage the Act required that the marriage be solemnized, according to rites and rules of the Church of England, in the parish church where one of the parties resided, in the presence of two witnesses and clergyman. Marriages were to

---

[30] Justifications for this vary: From the need for protection of the vulnerable, to the need for certainty and equality between men and women, and the need to ensure public morality, Hamilton (1995: 38). Moreover, rights of property and inheritance, the role of determination of validity, the welfare state's demands for the knowledge of the status of individuals to calculate entitlements are some other reasons.

[31] See R v Bham (1965) 3 All ER 124.

be entered into the parish register and signed by two parties. The Quakers and Jews, but not other religious groups such as Catholics and Protestants, were exempt from these requirements. They were allowed to marry according to their own customs and usages. All others had had to marry according to Anglican rites, in an Anglican church to contract a valid marriage, a restriction that remained in force until the Marriage Act of 1836 (Hamilton 1995: 43). With the Marriage Act of 1836, parties, after obtaining a licence, were able to marry through a completely civil ceremony in the presence of a registrar and two witnesses. The Act also recognized the other churches where parties could contract a valid marriage according to their rites as long as there was, at some stage, *per verba de preasenti*, that the parties took each other as husband and wife (Hamilton 1995: 44).

Minority religious groups have complained of discrimination with regards to the formalities and requirements placed on them, and those of the adherents of the Church of England, the Quakers and the Jews. In 1973, the law Commission took the view that it would be impossible to reform the system unless uniform civil preliminaries were made compulsory for all marriages (Hamilton 1995: 51). However, this recommendation has never been the subject of legislation (Hamilton 1995: 51).

Until 1990, Muslims and other ethnic minorities could only marry in a register office or a registered building.[32] A registered building needed to be a separate building certified under the Places of Worship Registration Act, 1855 as a place only for worship. Thus, although Christians could use churches according to this rule, most Muslims could not have solemnized their marriages officially in a mosque or community centre and public places, since most mosques are not separate buildings but are cultural centres used for different purposes, such as community events and public meetings; they are more like community centres and these places are not separate places for worship. As a result, Hamilton (1995: 48) notes that in 1991 only 74 mosques were registered buildings out of a total 452 registered as places of worship according to the 1855 Act. However, an adjustment was made in easing the requirement that there must be a separate building in order for a place of worship to be qualified as a registered building. The Marriage (Registration of Buildings) Act, 1990 and the Marriage Act, 1994 are two recent amendments in the Marriage Act, 1949 that allow buildings to become registered as 'approved premises' where a valid registration can take place.

Some mosques, rather than having present an official of the local registry office at the ceremony, have sought recognition for one of their own officials to act on behalf of the registry. In such cases, a fully legalized marriage can be performed by a Muslim official according to both Muslim law and the English law, an interesting feature of plural legal reality.

Islamic law does not distinguish between civil and religious marriages. However, the state in England wishes to supervise the actual process of civil marriage in order to prevent fraud and abuse (Poulter 1986: 33; 1998: 205). Should a religious ceremony take place in England without fulfilling the preliminary civil requirements, the official law will not recognize this marriage as legally valid. If a

---

[32] Marriage Act, 1949, ss 12, 45(1).

civil ceremony in an English register office is followed by a religious ceremony in an unregistered building, the religious ceremony does not supersede or invalidate the civil ceremony and is not registered as a marriage in any marriage register book.[33] In other words, the civil ceremony is the only marriage which English law recognizes. An unregistered Muslim marriage will be void even if the parties knowingly and wilfully contracted the marriage (Hamilton 1995: 41).[34] However, it is not clear what the law's approach will be when the parties marry in this form believing that they are contracting a valid marriage according to both their religious tradition and English law (Hamilton 1995: 42).

Another problem regarding Muslim marriage is the attendance of the couple. According to Muslim law, a marriage is capable of being effected by an exchange of declarations between representatives (*wakil*) of the couple acting on their behalf. In Muslim ceremonies, one often finds the couple in separate rooms, making the declaration separately. Such marriages would not be valid under the English law, the bride and bridegroom have to attend in person and exchange their vows using a standard form of words.[35] Otherwise, this would amount to an invalid marriage ceremony (Hamilton 1995: 50; Poulter 1990b: 150).

Muslims have reconciled these conflicting points by reconstructing newly adapted Muslim law rules. As a result, it appears that not many Muslim cases have come before the courts regarding these matters in the last few years. Analyzing why a low rate of marriage registration was reflected in the census, Hamilton (1995: 50) concludes that: 'Another possible reason for the low rate of Muslim marriages is that Muslims are deliberately circumventing marriage laws and marrying according to Muslim customs with no registration of marriage.' This concurs with the findings of Menski (1987, 1988, 1993) that Muslims 'have, for some time, been engaged in law-making processes of their own, while admitting the importance of formal obedience to English law' (Jones and Gnanapala 2000: 104). Thus, today there is 'an intricate combination of Muslim *nikah* and English registered marriage' (Pearl and Menski 1998: 168).

Solemnization of marriages according to Muslim law was so evident that social scientists have started to observe this phenomenon among Muslims in Britain since the 1950s (see Collins 1957). Many Muslims, along with other ethnic minorities, have sought to preserve customary patterns of marriage solemnization. While they consider this area of law central to their traditions, the courts in England are reluctant to recognize the validity of ethnic minority marriages solemnized in England that fail to comply with the requirements of the marriage acts (Jones and Gnanapala 2000: 132).[36]

Earlier research in the late 1950s showed that Muslims in Britain have three types of marriages: the first is a legalized British marriage, the second is a Muslim form of marriage and the third is the relationship known as common-law marriage (Collins 1957: 160). In these years, couples started to observe both English and

---

[33] Marriage Act, 1949, s 46(2); Qureshi v Qureshi (1972) Fam 173.

[34] R v Bham (1965) 3 All ER 124.

[35] Marriage Act, 1949, ss 44(3), 45(1).

[36] R v Bham (1965) 3 All ER 124; Rahman (1949) 2 All ER 165.

Muslim laws, for mainly two reasons. First, some Muslim couples formerly married by a registrar later, for religious reasons submitted to a *nikah* as well. Secondly, wives who only had a *nikah* asked that the union be ratified by an official marriage as well, so as to safeguard their own and their prospective children's status and rights (Collins 1957: 160). After an initial period of insecurity, when some unregistered Asian marriages in Britain had been abused, communities quickly learned the *lex loci* and constructed their new rules in these matters. Virtually all Asians now register their marriages in accordance with English law. It is now observable that 'a trend to build the registered ceremony, which remains prior to the religious wedding in most cases, into the Asian wedding rituals' has developed (Menski 1993a: 262). Recent research has confirmed that 'the registration ceremony of English law has been built into the customary "Asian" patterns of marriage solemnization in such a way that it constitutes something like an engagement in the eyes of the "Asian" spouses and their families' (Menski 1988b: 15; see also Hamilton 1995: 50; Pearl and Menski 1998: 169).

With the official registration of the marriage, the prospective husband is legally tied down to the obligations of the marriage, but curiously it does not, in the eyes of the bride, groom and community, amount to the couple being considered truly married but only that they have committed to being truly married (Menski and Shah 1996: 7). As a result, the couple are expected to abstain from all kind of intimate interactions and by all means should most definitely not consummate the marriage, as they are yet to be married. Only after the religious marriage will they be able to consummate their marriages. Otherwise, their marriage would be regarded as sinful and illegitimate from a religious and cultural point of view. This indicates that it is the religious marriage that determines the nature of the relationship and is perceived as the one that really matters; the official one is only seen as a mere formality which is imposed by the state with certain beneficial implications.[37]

Superiority of the *nikah* in the eyes of the Muslim community can be detected from the statements of an 'insider researcher'.[38] She notes that 'in recent years Muslim weddings in Britain have become very elaborate affairs... Even the registry office wedding is now deemed an integral part of the Muslim marriage ceremony and is seen as binding' (Mirza 1989: 22).

Now, most Muslims in England register their marriage first because of concerns of izzat, knowing that the couple are not actually fully married till the completion of the *nikah*. In that way, they prevent the groom's possible abuse of the socio-legal situation of the Muslim minority by just walking away after the first night. It is obvious that there are some potential dangers of abuse at the expense of women in that type of marriage, since there is no recognition by the official

[37] See also Hiro (1991: 159); Hamilton (1995: 74); Menski (1993b: 8).

[38] Mirza (1989: 5) defines herself as an 'insider researcher'.

authority.[39] If the man simply leaves his wife-in-religion, the woman would have no recourse and rights whatsoever before the courts under the official law. After losing her virginity, which is so very important in the Muslim culture, she would have to face difficulties in getting religiously divorced and then remarried. Even worse, if she has a baby from the previous relationship, the remarriage option would be even more complicated and difficult.

Sometimes, before solemnization couples want to end their 'engagement', in other words nullify their official marriage. It must be emphasized that English law's 'approach fails to recognise the religious values of a number of religious minorities, and the importance that is attached by these groups to the religious ceremony of marriage' (Hamilton 1995: 78). In a number of Sikh cases, courts refused to grant nullity and forced couples to use the divorce law. Communities, as a result of this, now try to keep official and unofficial marriages as close together as possible (Menski and Shah 1996: 7).

On the other hand, a very recent research found that unregistered *nikah* is still common among British Muslims. (Shah-Kazemi 2001: 31) reports that out of the total 287 case files she examined a significant 57 per cent of women did not register their marriages in the UK according to civil law at all, but did have an Islamic *nikah* ceremony. In 27 per cent of those cases where the *nikah* ceremonies did take place in the UK, the women did not go on to register their marriages; hence these women did not acquire valid marriage status according to UK civil law. Out of the minority of women who did register marriages according to civil law, only 37 per cent had their civil marriages before the *nikah* ceremony. The others had their civil registration ceremonies on the same day as their *nikah* ceremonies, or thereafter (Shah-Kazemi 2001: 31).

In conclusion, the total picture is that under this British Muslim law if a Muslim couple want to marry, they will actually marry twice. Thus, they meet the requirements of both Muslim law and the English law. In addition, they fortify the strength of the *nikah* by incorporating official legal rules into their unofficial laws.

### *Age of Marriage and Marriages within Prohibited Degrees*

The official law on age of marriages is obviously in conflict with traditional Muslim law. In the eyes of the people and Muslim law, when a girl or boy reaches puberty, he or she can marry whatever his or her age is. However, the official legal system never allows this.

Muslim men cannot marry women who belong to one of the following categories: The mother, sister (including half and stepsisters), daughter, niece, paternal aunt, maternal aunt, father's wife (whether divorced or widowed), foster mother, foster sister, mother-in-law, stepdaughter, daughter-in-law, sisters and aunts as co-wives, married women, idol worshippers, atheists and men. In addition, Muslim women cannot marry non-Muslim men (Büyükçelebi 2003: 276-277).

---

[39] In the Turkish context, this is seen as a widespread problem and both the public and the scholars are very much concerned with this issue. To some of them, this type of marriage is not Islamic, since it is hidden. See in detail below.

A marriage in which either party is within the prohibited degrees of relationship as defined in the Marriage Acts 1949-1996 will automatically be null and void.[40] The English legal system completely disregards the Islamic prohibition on marriages between Muslim women and non-Muslim men and between Muslim men and polytheist or atheist women. Any such marriage entered into in England will be fully valid (Poulter 1990b: 151). Although there has been no decided case about such issues, it is definite that English law would disregard these prohibitions falling outside its rules (Poulter 1993: 177). However, since the Muslim community will not recognize such marriages, the occurrence of such marriages is very rare. Societal pressure reduces the possibility of these marriages. If they occur, it may well be that the 'offending' party is excommunicated.[41] However, most of the time, the non-Muslim party converts to Islam to please the Muslim parents and the Muslim milieu.

A marriage in which either party is under the age of 16 years will automatically be null and void in England, regardless of circumstances.[42] The minimum marriage age was raised in 1929 from the old common law ages of 14 for boys and 12 for girls, to 16 for both.[43] Where either party is between the age of 16 and 18, the under-age party needs parental consent. If a parental responsibility holder refuses to consent, the child may seek the consent of the court. Failure to obtain such consent renders the marriage voidable (Hamilton 1995: 57). While it is an offence under English law to have sexual intercourse with a girl under 16, in one case it was held that this was not applicable where the parties were married (Hamilton 1995: 61; Poulter 1986: 19-20).[44]

On the other hand, in Muslim law there is no age limitation; focus is on puberty. Some parents, although rare, tend to marry their offspring just after puberty which may well be before the age of 16. In these cases, families employ only Muslim law rules and solemnize marriages according to these rules. Getting married by *nikah* only, spouses can cohabit, which is absolutely legitimate in the eyes of the community. If, after reaching the age of 16 years, they register their marriages, there may not appear to be any problem. One should perhaps add that the issue of age of marriage is more theoretical than practical in Britain; in practice, it appears that conflicts between Muslim law and the official English law rarely occur.

### *Polygamy*

Pertaining to polygamy, there is an obvious conflict between Muslim law and

---

[40] Matrimonial Causes Act, 1973, s 11.

[41] It is possible to see some news about such incidences in British 'Asian' newspapers.

[42] Matrimonial Causes Act, 1973, s 11.

[43] Age of Marriage Act, 1929 s. 1, re-enacted in the Marriage Act 1949 s. 2.

[44] Sexual Offences Act, 1956, s. 6(1); Alhaji Mohamed v Knott (1969) 1 QB 1 (1968) 2 All ER 563. Although the criminal law is designed to prohibit the exploitation of young girls and sets up the minimum age for consent to sexual intercourse as 16, it is usually only enforced strictly where an older man is involved, Poulter (1986: 22).

English law.[45] In England, marriage is defined as a monogamous union between one man and one woman. Matrimonial Causes Act 1973, s 11(b) provides that a marriage will be void if, at the time of the marriage, either party was already lawfully married. The state des not allow polygamous marriages to be contracted within the jurisdiction. Under classical Muslim law, a man is permitted to marry up to four wives at any one time.

If the marriage takes place in a country in which polygamy is illegal, then the second or subsequent marriage cannot be regarded as polygamous in nature. Such a marriage would be deemed as being bigamous according to English law and as a result would be considered void. A marriage celebrated in England polygamously and without any civil ceremony is invalid, whatever the domicile of the parties.[46] Moreover, a polygamous marriage contracted abroad by a person domiciled in England is void.[47]

English law allows for no flexibility among English domiciliaries regarding polygamous marriages. That means a person domiciled in England cannot marry polygamously under English law. As mentioned above, if a person is a party to a subsisting marriage, he or she cannot validly contract a second or subsequent marriage.[48] This marriage will be *void ab initio* and the offending party might be charged with the offence of bigamy.[49]

British Muslims employ Muslim law rules to continue the practice of polygamy, although it must be said that occurrences of such marriages are now very rare due to reasons such as economic conditions and improving levels of education of women.

A Muslim man would marry the first wife under *angrezi shariat* fulfilling all legal requirements under the English law as well as in Muslim law. He then may choose to marry a second wife under *Shari'a* only, contracting *nikah* with her, but not any form of official registration. The official legal position of the second woman in English law would rather be a concubine or a cohabitant in the technical language of the modern English law (Pearl and Menski 1998: 277).

According to Aina Khan, a Muslim solicitor who is a specialist in Islamic family law, usually the courts just regard the second wife as a cohabitee while the first wife retains all normal rights.[50] She then goes on to say that '(t)he average man seems to want to exercise his religious right to marry more than once although in my experience they want to do so without taking on any of the attendant responsibilities (sic)'.[51] As a result, it is not surprising to see advertisements in newspapers where a man is seeking a second spouse, or a woman is advertising to

[45] Actually there are two kinds of polygamy. The first is where the husband is allowed to take more than one wife (polygyny) and the second is where the wife is allowed to have more than one husband (polyandry). Since polyandry is most uncommon and prohibited by Muslim law, in this study I use the term polygamy to mean polygyny.

[46] R v Bham (1961) QB 159 (CCA), overruling R v Rahman (1949) 2 All ER 165.

[47] But see Radwan v Radwan (No. 2) (1972) 3 All ER 1026.

[48] Matrimonial Causes Act, 1973, s 11(b).

[49] Offences Against the Person Act, 1861, s 57.

[50] In an interview by *Q-News*, N. 270-271, June 1997, p. 8.

[51] *Q-News*, N. 270-271, June 1997, p. 8.

become a second wife of a married man.[52]

Among the Muslim community, there are also some cases in which the man is already married and his existing wife and child(ren) are in Pakistan or elsewhere abroad. He then marries a second time with *nikah* only, without divorcing his first wife.[53] Under such conditions, he can still bring his first wife and child(ren) from abroad, if he so wants (see also Shaw 1988: 173).

There is also another variant of polygamous arrangement in *angrezi shariat*. The husband divorces the first wife under the English law but not under Islamic law; he does not pronounce *talaq*. Thus, she is still his wife in Muslim law. Then he takes a second wife under *angrezi shariat*, with *nikah* and official registration (Pearl and Menski 1998: 277).

In a nutshell, Muslim law in relation to its most criticized field, is in full operation, whether the state recognizes it or not. A Muslim man can effectively have more than one wife if he wants, enjoy the community recognition of all his marriages and therefore suffer no real detriment from not having his polygamous marriage recognized in law. If anything, with the exception of the possible conviction, non-recognition of polygamous marriages works in favour of the husband as he avoids the implications involved.

On the other hand, non-recognition may cause some problems for the wife in custom, since one cannot argue that polygamous marriages do not occur among English domiciliaries. A polygamist wife can hardly claim her rights of maintenance other than by confronting the problem of a limping marriage.[54]

*Divorce*

In Muslim law divorce can be obtained in a number of extra-judicial ways like *talaq*. In its primitive sense, the word *talaq* means dismission, but in law it signifies a release from the marriage tie. The Islamic law of divorce is founded upon express injunctions contained in the *Qur'an*, as well as in the *hadith* literature, and its rules occupy a very large section in all *fiqh* works. Divorce is an abominable transaction in the sight of God, therefore such an act should only take place from necessity, and it is best to only make the one sentence of divorce (i.e. *talaq al-ahsan*). Divorce may be given either in the present time or may be referred to some future period. It may be pronounced by the husband either before or after the consummation of the marriage. It may be either given in writing or verbally.

The words by which divorce can be given are of two kinds: *sarih*, or 'express,' as when the husband says, 'Thou art divorced'; and *kinayah*, or 'metaphorical', as

---

52 See such a matrimonial advertisement by a woman, *Eastern Eye*, May 9, 1997, p. 39. One can see such advertisements in several issues of *Q-News*. See for a recent advertisement by a wife for a co-wife for her husband *Q-News*, N. 299, January 1999, p. 59.

53 See for such a case Bibi v Ali (1997) reported in *Q-News*, N. 270-271, June 1997, p. 8.

54 Limping marriages are those marriages recognized in some jurisdictions as having been validly dissolved, but in other jurisdiction(s) as still subsisting. A husband is enabled to prevent his 'ex-wife' from remarrying in accordance with her religious belief and the dictates of her conscience. I discuss the issue of limping marriage below.

when he says, 'Thou art free; thou art cut off; veil yourself! Arise! Seek for a mate', etc.

A husband may divorce his wife without any misbehaviour on her part, or without assigning any cause. The divorce of every husband is effective if he be of a sound understanding and of mature age; but that of a boy, or a lunatic or one talking in his sleep, is not effective. If a man pronounces a divorce whilst in a state of inebriety from drinking fermented liquor, such as wine, the divorce takes place. Repudiation by any husband who is sane and adult, is effective, whether he be free or a slave, willing, or acting under compulsion; and even though it were uttered in sport or jest, or by a mere slip of the tongue, instead of some other word. A sick man may divorce his wife, even though he is on his death-bed. An agent or agents may be appointed by a husband to divorce his wife. In addition to the will and caprice of the husband, there are also certain conditions which require a divorce.

In England, while parties are free to divorce and remarry in accordance with their religious rites and rules, these divorces and marriages are unlikely to be recognized by the official law. The parties still need to have an official divorce in order to contract a second valid marriage. Recognition of religious divorces depends on where and by whom they are obtained. The courts in England have shown reluctance to cede any of their authority over domestic divorces to unofficial religious courts. The official law faces a dilemma when dealing with religious divorces: the extent to which religious traditions and laws should be accommodated in the secular system; should the official law seek to encourage and/or enforce compliance with appropriate religious laws. A failure to obtain a religious divorce may mean that the spouse, especially woman in the Muslim cases as will be seen below, is not able to remarry within her community. It is crucial to decide, as far as these women are concerned, whether religious freedom requires a positive aid by the official law to enforce religious laws and be under a duty to ensure that, in granting a civil divorce, all barriers to remarriage have been removed (Hamilton 1995: 82-83).

In England, with the Matrimonial Causes Act 1857, jurisdiction over matrimonial causes was transferred from the religious courts to the civil courts. The grounds for divorce were later extended by the Matrimonial Causes Act of 1937.

Marriage under Islam, in contrast to Hinduism, Sikhism, and Christianity, is not regarded as a sacrament but as a civil contract. Islamic law recognizes the concept of divorce and makes some provisions for it to operate. In Muslim law, there are various forms of dissolution of a marriage: at the initiative of the husband, the wife, by mutual consent, or by judicial process. *Talaq* is a unilateral repudiation by the husband; *khul* is the divorce at the instance of the wife with or without the husband's agreement and on the basis that she will forego her right to dower. *Mubaraat* is divorce by mutual consent. Divorce operates in a number of judicial and extra-judicial ways. Divorce at the instigation of the husband (*talaq*) is prominent and rather simple. However, although permitted, divorce tends to be strongly discouraged and disapproved of religiously and socially, and the families involved try to do all they can to improve the situation.

On the other hand, as indicated above, in English law there is merely one way of divorce which is through a decree granted by a court of civil jurisdiction on the ground that the marriage has irretrievably broken down.[55] It has been laid down explicitly since 1973 that no extra-judicial divorce shall be recognized in English law.[56] Section 44(1) of the Family Law Act 1986 reads as '(n)o divorce or annulment obtained in any part of the British Isles shall be regarded as effective in any part of the United Kingdom unless granted by a civil court of jurisdiction'.

The level of tolerance for religious laws is very low in England. Although the courts have been willing to lend their aid to encourage religious divorces, there is no question of recognition for any purposes (Hamilton 1995: 139). Since the introduction of the 'special procedure' or 'quickie divorce' to facilitate quicker disposal of cases, divorce is more akin to an administrative process. The Family Law Act 1996 creates a conciliatory framework in which divorcing couples are encouraged to work out their own arrangements, the role of the court being merely supervisory (Jones and Gnanapala 2000: 119).

English law recognizes foreign divorces that are valid in the law of the couple's common domicile or by the religious law of the parties.[57] If the marriage has some connection to England, the law is less generous in recognizing *talaq* divorces as the *talaq* as unilateral divorce by the husband seems to lack natural justice and the common law rule of wife's dependant domicile meant that a wife would automatically obtain her husband's domicile, so that a wife living in England might have a domicile in Pakistan (Jones and Gnanapala 2000: 121-122).

Muslims have long assumed that they could continue their customary divorce practices in England. Muslims of Pakistani origin, while domiciled in England, attempt to divorce by *talaq* or by following the requirements of the Muslim Family Laws Ordinance 1961 of Pakistan. These procedures are locally invoked in a mosque, before a solicitor or at the High Commission of Pakistan by making a proclamation of *talaq*. The English law is not prepared to recognize such a *talaq* if it is proclaimed in Britain. Recognition of overseas divorces is also not extended to cases, classed as 'transnational divorce', where only part of the proceedings takes place in Britain.[58] Thus, Muslim spouses resident in Britain can not invoke customary procedures without having to return to their country of domicile (Jones and Gnanapala 2000: 129).

It is becoming increasingly apparent that Muslims in England have not abandoned the traditional practice of divorce. Secular divorce is not regarded as

[55] Family Law Act, 1986, s. 44(1); Matrimonial Causes Act, 1973, s. 1.

[56] Domicile and Matrimonial Proceedings Act 1973, s 16; see also Family Law Act 1986, s 44(1).

[57] Pemberton v Hughes (1899) 1 Ch 881; Russ v Russ (1962) 3 All ER 193; Lee v Lau (1964) 2 All ER 248; Russ v Russ (1962) 3 All ER 193; Varanand v Varanand (1964) 108 Sol Jo 693. In Qureshi v Qureshi (1971) 1 All ER 325, this legal recognition is also extended to a *talaq* pronounced in England where both parties domiciled in Pakistan. But the Domicile and Matrimonial Proceedings Act 1973 and later the Family Law Act 1986 put that no extra-judicial divorce obtained anywhere in the UK should be recognized in England.

[58] R v Secretary of State for the Home Department, ex parte Ghulam Fatima and R v Secretary of State for the Home Department, ex parte Shafeena Bi (1985) QB 190.

sufficient to dissolve a marriage in the eyes of Muslims. A recent research showed again that the religious divorce is superior in the eyes of many Muslims: 'For the majority of the women, religious idealism also incorporates the notion that the *talaq* divorce is superior to the civil divorce... For these women the importance that the *talaq* divorce assumed was a logical concomitant of the strength of their religious identity and practice' (Shah-Kazemi 2001: 48).

Having managed to marry twice in England, Muslims have also learnt to divorce twice. This process is facilitated by the increasingly informal nature of English divorce law itself. Almost 98 per cent of all divorces in English law are undefended and effected by means of what is called the 'special procedure'. The statistics show that this procedure is the normal practice (Golden 1996: 34). Thus, divorce in English law is a kind of administrative process. Judges pronounce decree nisi without a hearing (Berkovits 1990: 136; Hamilton 1995: 98). This flexible procedure has allowed Muslims in Britain to maintain their customary procedures of divorce almost unmodified. Muslims have learnt to manipulate the official law to the effect that they use the English divorce proceedings to rubber-stamp the rather informal Muslim law procedures. After they have sorted out their affairs according to Muslim law, they follow the official divorce procedure, although by that time there is no marriage left to dissolve (Pearl and Menski 1998: 393-394).

In another scenario, they get divorced first officially then unofficially. In some of these cases, the husband refuses to pronounce *talaq*, so although officially divorced the woman can not remarry. Thus, they seek remedy by applying to unofficial *Shari'a* courts. A recent study confirms this: '55% of the women who approached the MLSC to facilitate divorces according to Islamic law, had done so after obtaining their civil divorces' (Shah-Kazemi 2001: 31).

In a nutshell, Muslim law is considered as superior and dominant over English law in the eyes and mind of the Muslim individual and community, and Muslims still follow Muslim law in England through the employment and use of a number of strategies, whatever the official law claims and whether it acknowledges this socio-legal reality or not. British Muslims operate a form of unofficial legal pluralism. In order to successfully maintain itself; Muslim law takes advantage of the English law mechanisms where it can and is of use to its continued practical existence. Muslims have been developing new techniques to satisfy the requirements of English law whilst in effect keeping true and acting in accordance with their own religious law; evidence in itself of dynamic legal pluralism and the limits of official law, which is recognized by the Muslims in England, but not by the state.

As a result of seeing that assimilationist assumptions have not turned out as expected and that there are limits to law, the English legal system has recognized some of these customs and rules as law.

English law is generally flexible enough to make concessions provided that it takes a cross-cultural and a socio-legal perspective. Thus, changing trends in society can be deduced and responded to. Law has the ability to adapt itself to changing conditions of social life. The recognition and rights given to certain ethnic minorities can and should be extended to others within the system.

The existence of this dynamic legal pluralism has crucial impacts, in particular, on the position of Muslim women in England as will be discussed in chapter 7. The book now proceeds to examine the existence of Muslim legal pluralism in another modern nation-state with a transplanted western uniform legal system and population of which 99 per cent are Muslims. In this case, the newcomer was not the Muslim individual but secular laws.

# Chapter 5

# Muslim Legal Pluralism in Turkey

Secularism or the laicist policies of the Turkish Republic did not emerge through a sudden need to convert Turkish citizens to nationalism. Turkey is one of the very first Muslim countries that encountered the modern west and its civilization and that attempted to respond to the challenges posed by the Western power and civilization. The questions surrounding these challenges, how to respond to them, preventing the collapse of the Ottoman State, modernization and transplantation of western institutions have always been on the agenda of the Turkish intellectuals.

The struggle for a secular state in Turkey neither began nor ended in 1926. The modernization attempts in Turkey had already begun in the seventeenth century when the Ottoman rulers became aware that they were far behind the European powers. Substantial discussions whether to import the European technology only or to take all its way of life, culture, laws and so on occupied the public sphere for many decades. These endless discussions were cut short by the Kemalist elite when the new republic was established: to reach the level of contemporary European civilization western way of life had to be espoused and imported with all kinds of its institutions including laws.

The tradition of secular education that began in the 1850s, and the values promoted by secular education have had a long history in Turkey. The process of disestablishment of Islamic law and the establishment of a non-religious state began in 1839 under the reformist *Tanzimat* government (Starr 1990: 78). Over five generations of families of elite reformers had experienced some of the structures and symbols of secularism, each generation moving slightly farther from immersion in Islamic symbols, rituals and practices, and closer to the symbolic patterning of secularism (Starr 1992: 15).

In the mid-1920s, Commercial Code, Penal Code and Civil Code were transplanted from different Western European countries. After almost eighty years of this revolution, when one looks at the issues from a black-letter point of view and from an armchair perspective, this has been a tremendous success in bringing a completely clean legal sheet. Yet, the socio-legal sphere needs to be analyzed before arriving at ideological conclusions. As one scholar wrote quite recently, '(h)ow much the adoption of European laws affected society remains one of the most difficult questions for sociological and historical studies of the law... One hesitates, therefore, to categorically state that the reception movement was beneficial or detrimental to Turkish society' (Bozkurt 1998: 295). Indeed, when the socio-legal reality is analyzed, it is seen that the Turkish legal transplantation experience is far from an easy-going process.

The empirical reality shows that the uniformity-focused homogenization expectations of the state and the plurality-centred survived unofficial Muslim family law conflict. This chapter shows that some Turkish Muslims have not totally abandoned their Muslim laws in favour of the transplanted 'secular' Western law, although the secular social engineers have long wished them to do so. Especially, in the issues of marriage, this chapter, based on the empirical data, suggests that some Muslim people in Turkey have not jettisoned their unofficial Muslim laws to the effect of creating 'strong' Muslim legal pluralism. They have actively assimilated to the secular law but on their own terms. They have not discarded their Muslim family laws but have adapted them to the secular milieu. By combining the rules of two different normative orderings, they have been successful in pragmatically meeting the demands of both the secular law and religious law. This phenomenon is very obvious in the realm of family issues.

To analyze this post-modern phenomenon of dynamic legal pluralism in the Turkish context, this chapter provides a historical background of the secularization of the law in Turkey, which reached its peak with the adaptation of the Swiss Civil Code and the total discarding of the Islamic laws in 1926.[1]

## Ottoman Reform Attempts and Modernization

The need for reform in the Ottoman State was first recognized in the 17th century when the state began to lose its strength. The Ottoman elite were aware that the army and other state institutions did not show their traditional vigour and that changes were needed. Early reformists' image of a properly-functioning system was the traditional Ottomans systems that had been successful in the past (McCarthy 1997: 174). Thus, reforms of the seventeenth century were generally indigenous attempts which mainly centred on strengthening the authority of the central government. They thought they were still superior to the Europeans. In the seventeenth and eighteenth centuries the Ottoman state was still a super power. Thus, there was too little to learn from Europe. Even the most reformist members of the elite believed that the Ottoman way was superior to what could be achieved in Europe. Decline or loss of territory was still attributed to a failure to apply and use the institutions, techniques and weapons (Starr 1992: 7). The Ottomans did not know of the changes in education and economy in Europe that would ultimately defeat them (McCarthy 1997: 180). As a matter of fact, the world has not waited for Ottomans to get their house in order. It was not enough to return to their strengths of the days of Suleiman. While they were at best remaining as they were, the Europeans were advancing in technology. In short, the worst aspect of traditional reform was that bringing the old Ottoman times back was seen as satisfactory, which hid the real nature of the problems (McCarthy 1997: 180). It took them a while to recognize that they were falling far behind the European powers.

[1] On 27 November 2001, the Turkish Parliament enacted a totally new civil code, replacing the former one. Many legal experts had been working on the draft of this new civil code for the last decade.

After the eighteenth century the reform efforts took on a different tone as the Ottoman state opened its doors to the West. When Sultan Ahmed III took power in 1703, his grand vizier Nevşehirli Damat İbrahim Paşa decided that the Europeans had something to be imitated. Thus, ambassadors were sent to European countries. This led to a kind of superficial westernization. Preferring show to substance, they adopted western – mainly French – dress, etiquette, lifestyle and fashion. Some matters of importance were also copied from the west as well, including the printing press that led to the publication of many scientific books (McCarthy 1997: 184). Ahmed III's successor, Mahmud I made some practical reforms of the Ottoman military.

Rather than risk changing an entire system, they naturally explained away their difficulties. The Ottoman state was only the first of many states who faced the problems of reform. Throughout the twentieth century many so-called Third World (developing or Southern) countries have endeavoured to catch up with the western economic and political power. The terms used to describe these attempts and processes indicate certain confusion. The term 'modernization' is used because all countries would like to be modern, whatever the term means to them. Yet, the word 'modernization' does not give any clue how this modernization is to be brought about. The word 'development' is not descriptive either. On the other hand, the term 'westernization' is more meaningful, precise and descriptive, that is becoming like the western (northern) countries. Yet, commitment to westernization was not an easy task. It required western way of thinking as well which leads to acculturation and adopting ways which seemed inimical to the traditional Ottoman way. Few people would want that. The problem remained how to selectively choose from Western culture, taking only technology and economy but not emulating philosophy and traditions (McCarthy 1997: 287). One can not readily say that this is an impossible endeavour but history has shown that it is one of the most challenging ones. The Ottoman State was one of the first few countries to come to grips with this and the challenges of westernization. As the reforms expanded the country became more and more western in culture. The momentous change started with European education: Students started reading not only engineering books that were necessary for a strong army but also novels, philosophy and political writings (McCarthy 1997: 287-288). Thus, the history of the nineteenth and twentieth century Ottomans became a history of the conflicts and tensions between traditionalists and reformists who defended new ways.

During the 19th century, more and more Ottoman intellectuals and statesmen had come to look at westernization as a precondition of reform in the country. Therefore, a major shift in the understanding of reform came into existence. Indigenous solutions were not taken into account any more. The dilemma of the Ottoman reformers was apparent. On the one hand, an increasing number of them came to believe that the state's salvation rested in the acceptance of Western technology and Western institutional forms. Yet, no one could come up with a formula as to how Western technology and institutions would be adapted to an Islamic society without accepting Western civilization itself. During the nineteenth century, partly under the influence of the spontaneous spread of ideas through personal contact and study, partly under direct political pressure from the Western powers, the state made periodic attempts to introduce Western political and social institutions by promulgating decrees. Rather than destroying traditional institutions, the 19th century reforms constructed new ones that were to co-exist alongside the traditional ones, which paved the way for the duality of institutions (Ortaylı 1986: 166-168; see also in detail Berkes 1978: 179-190). It was after the Ottoman state's collapse and the subsequent founding of the Turkish Republic in 1923 that this duality was finally resolved in favour of accepting Western civilization in toto (Kazancıgil 1986: 171; Tunçay 1992: 173).

The Kemalist revolution has its roots in the series of reforms and changes which are conventionally said to begin with the new model army, formed by Selim III (1789-1807), because of the serious defeats of Turks. His reform was not radical. All elements of society with the exception of the army and treasury were to be untouched; showing that he though the military reform would be enough. He established a new army called *Nizam-ı Cedid* (New Order) in modified western uniforms. He also opened western-style military schools that taught new military techniques (McCarthy 1997: 289). His successor Mahmud II totally abolished the traditional janissary army in 1826 that had been opposing reforms. Conservatists could still call upon much popular support but the opponents of reform no longer had the military power behind them. As a matter of fact, the army after 1826 became the main tool of reform (McCarthy 1997: 292).

Mahmud II published the first newspaper in the country; founded new secondary schools. He switched the linguistic orientation of the government from Arabic and Persian to French and established a translation office. Each government office was instructed to open training schools in European languages (McCarthy 1997: 295).

He changed the government infrastructure and organized along the western lines with ministers and ministries (McCarthy 1997: 293). Some changes started in the administrative and legal system. Previously the system of making laws was loose, with all laws theoretically coming from the sultan and his divan. Now legislative bodies were appointed (McCarthy 1997: 293).

These years witnessed the emergence of a circle of a protégé in the bureaucracy who shared the vision of reform, who are known as *Tanzimatçılar* (Men of *Tanzimat*, those who put things in order). They faced also certain dilemmas: '(t)he mentality of the *Tanzimat* reformers presented them with unique problems. They saw and respected the European way, but they also respected their own traditions. They had no wish to turn the Ottoman Empire into a pale reflection of Western Europe' (McCarthy 1997: 296).

On 3 November 1839, Sultan Abdulmecid declared an imperial order the '*Hatt-ı Hümayun* of *Gülhane*' by which he proclaimed his intention of reform. For the first time, a sultan had declared that reform was needed. After *Tanzimat*, parallel secular education was established as a solution to avoiding direct challenges to the *ulama*'s authority over primary education. New secular schools were opened beyond the elementary level. With the penetration of European commerce and with increasing Christian missionary activity in Istanbul, a number of foreign schools were opened (Starr 1992: 9).

The existence of the separate parallel educational systems paved the way for the division of Ottoman society and stimulated dissent (Starr 1992: 10). Reading European political writings and associating with the westerners influenced a new generation of Ottoman elite: Young Ottomans. They were trained in modern secular Ottoman bureaucratic schools, knew one or more European languages, and had lived for years in major European capitals. Thus, they developed a respect for western political institutions and affirmed that the state would never be modernized unless adopting a democratic government and a constitution. Their writings appealed to two groups: those who wanted faster liberalist reforms and those who wanted a renewed Islam to take part in the system denied by *Tanzimat* ruling elite (McCarthy 1997: 302). They had a utopian vision of an Ottoman nationalism: If all ethnic groups were given democratic freedoms, they would submerge their nationalistic feelings and come together in a new Ottoman nationality, abandoning the *millet* system. They were still far from European nationalist ideas.

Young Ottomans were also social engineers like the *Tanzimat* elite: They advocated imposing the reform from the top. Some Young Ottomans, such as Namık Kemal, also underlined that Islam was essentially democratic in nature yet could not convince the conservatists. In short, 'they were democrats in theory, but not necessarily men who understood the people for whom they avowedly spoke' (McCarthy 1997: 303).

Later, a new group of constitutionalists, Young Turks (*Jön Türkler*), like their predecessors Young Ottomans, believed that a turn to democracy was essential for the survival of the state. Unlike their predecessors they were not utopian Ottoman nationalists but Turkish nationalists. They argued that the Turks had been neglected by the Ottoman elite in favour of the non-Turkish minorities (McCarthy 1997: 315).

Nationalism – which later became in line with the *Zeitgeist* one of the major principles of the Republic – has its roots in the nineteenth century Ottoman times as well. Ottoman intellectuals had faced a dilemma: They read European political works and were imbued with western ideas such as nationalism, however, they wanted to retain the multi-ethnic state at the same time. In other words, they were eager to strengthen their 'Turkishness' but also were afraid of alienating non-Turks of the country (McCarthy 1997: 209). Two main factors that paved the way for Turkish nationalism were the emergence of nationalisms of non-Turks who declared Turks to be 'the enemy' and the simmering western interventions of Ottoman internal affairs vis-à-vis Ottoman ethnic minorities. Turkish nationalism is mainly a response to these. They began to think of themselves as a group that had to stand together. Then, they began to look at their own Turkish roots and history. Pre-eminent among the Turkish nationalists was Ziya Gökalp (1876-1924) who translated Emil Durkheim's works into English and wrote extensively on Turkish nationalism. Gökalp and his friends underlined the importance of Turkish folk culture, pre-Islam Turkish history, a pure Turkish uncorrupted by Arabic and Persian, political traditions of the Central Asian Turks, secularism, diminishing the role of Islam in the public sphere and replacing its dominance with nationalistic fervour (McCarthy 1997: 209).

These Young Turks organized the *Ittihad ve Terakki Cemiyeti* (the Committee of Union and Progress, CUP) and soon spread to all advanced schools, including the military school. In 1908 they, including many who were officers in the army, revolted against the Sultan with a demand for restoring the constitution and calling for elections. Sultan Abdulhamid gave in on 23 July 1908 when after a pause for three decades Ottoman 'democratic' political life began again. Turkish nationalists had triumphed and immediately set upon reform (McCarthy 1997: 316-319). 'The Young Turk revolution was extremely nationalistic, and secret organizations, such as Freemason Lodges in Italy and the Bektashi dervish orders in Anatolia, had played some part in it' (Starr 1992: 12). As these Young Turks were influenced by the nationalistic ideas, they supported nationalist initiatives. Some talked about relinquishing the Ottoman state and creating a Turkish nation, and some among these envisioned that it would be a secular state (Starr 1992: 13). They even attempted to introduce a new Turkish alphabet to replace Arabic characters. They introduced the teaching of Turkish into the school curriculum which was to be applied in even non-Turkish regions of the country (McCarthy 1997: 209). Little consideration was given to how the non-Turk ethnic minorities would fit into their scheme (Starr 1992: 12).

During the period of 1908-1917 when the CUP was in power, religion and nationality, Islam and secularism, freedom and loyalty were debated (Starr 1992: 12). The CUP government took a major step against the duality of Islamic/secular institutions which started with *Tanzimat* by asserting the dominance of state over religion. Islamic judges were made paid officials of the state and their decisions subject to appeal to secular courts. The state started overseeing the training of the members of the religious courts (McCarthy 1997: 324). Turkish nationalism intensified during World War I but it triumphed and took its radical form only after the establishment of the new Republic in 1923.

## Secularization of the Ottoman Law and Legal Transplantation

Western law had been in the process of being received into Turkey for a period of about one hundred years before the establishment of the Republic. In fact, although the pace of legal reforms quickened after the formation of the republic in Turkey, the law actually started to be taken up during the times of the Ottoman State, and then commenced being put into written form.

Turkish legal history presents three different aspects. The first, which started in the beginning of the 14th century and ended in 1839, was the period of Islamic law based upon the principles of the *Qur'an* and administered by religious courts throughout the Ottoman State. The second period began in 1839 with the Charter of *Gülhane* and the *Ferman* of Reforms. For the first time, new secular courts were established and compilation of secular laws and transplantation of European laws and regulations began to appear, including the Charter of *Gülhane* and the *Ferman* of Reforms, Ottoman Penal Codes of 1840 and 1858, the Ottoman Commercial Code of 1850 and some other laws and regulations of European origin, especially in the French pattern.

The third phase starts with the declaration of the Republic in 1923 when new ideas of a complete westernization and establishment of a secular state led Turkey to the enactment of a civil Code adopted from Switzerland with minor modifications; which went into force on October 4, 1926. In the same manner, the Turkish Criminal Code was adopted from the Penal Code of Italy of 1899 and the Turkish Criminal Procedure Code was adopted from the German Criminal Procedure Code. Switzerland became the source of most Turkish laws, including the Turkish Code of Obligations, the Turkish Code of Civil Procedure, and the Turkish Code of Execution and Bankruptcy. With the enactment of these laws, especially the Civil Code, Turkey became and still remains under civil law jurisdiction.

The precedents for the introduction of Western-based systems of law into Ottoman State were in addition to and not a replacement of the Muslim law. There was a dualist legal structure. The development of western-style laws and courts in the nineteenth century reflected a struggle between conservatives and reformers (Starr 1992: 21). The Ottoman reformers dealt with the quasi-legal institutions by creating parallel legal institutions. As trade and commerce increased with the Europeans and ethnic minorities were rebelled, new secular laws and courts were devised. With the exception of family law, secular laws took precedence (Starr 1992: 24).

The legal system of Ottoman law was based on *Shari'a*. In the Ottoman legal system, non-Muslims were subject to their own ethno-religious groups in the field of private law and in public law they were subject to Islamic law as it was applied to *dhimmis* (protected persons, non-Muslim minorities). Islamic law was not applied to non-Muslims except in cases where non-Muslims came into litigation with Muslims or where both parties agreed to be judged by Islamic law when their own religious laws were insufficient. It was left to the non-Muslims to use their own laws and institutions to regulate behaviour and conflicts under the leaders of their religion. Divisions of society into communities along religious lines formed the *millet* (nation) system. Different denominations dealt with the ruling power through their *millet* leaders.

Constitutional movements during the Ottoman period commenced towards the end of the 18th century. In the hope of gaining the loyalty of all the subjects, Ottomans reformists endeavoured to save the state by granting equal rights to Muslim and non-Muslim subjects alike (Bozkurt 1998: 284).

During the period 1789-1808, Sultan Selim III envisaged the formation of an advisory assembly, called the *Meclis-i Meşveret*, within the context of the New System (*Nizam-ı Cedid*) that he wanted to have set up, which is seen as a major step towards a constitutional government system.

The '*Sened-i İttifak*' (Charter of Alliance) is seen as the first important document from the point of view of a constitutional order. Whilst the 1808 charter restricted the Sultan's exercise of power, it also delegated some authorities to a senate body, the *Ayan*. The charter is a significant document as it was also recognized by the Sultan. The *Tanzimat* era commenced with the issue of the decree entitled '*Gülhane Hatt-ı Hümayunu*' in 1839. The subjects of the Ottoman Sultan were assured that their basic rights would be respected. The document is especially significant for its recognition of equal rights in education and in government administration for those of Christian persuasion, exemplifying egalitarian principles. The Edict of *Islahat* (*Islahat Fermanı*) of 1856 was supplement to the Edict of *Tanzimat*. The Edict of *Islahat* re-declared equality between Muslim and non-Muslims and at the same time reaffirmed the privileges given to non-Muslims (Bozkurt 1998: 284).

Ottomans had already during their reign developed secular law called *qanun* (imperial law) that was 'an independent category of law derived directly from the sovereign will of the ruler' (İnalcık 1964: 57). These directives issued by the ruler were justified as they were not in contradiction with *Shari'a*, they were regarding the new developments in life and they were in most cases secondary rules. From the study of the *fatawa* and the Ottoman law it becomes apparent that many points of law were interpreted by the Turkish jurisconsults (*muftis*) in accordance with secular necessities rather than with the doctrinal principles of the *fiqh* (Ülken 1957: 53).

Early forms of secular law could also be found in the special licences given to European traders and later to non-Muslim Ottomans. A person holding such a licence was exempt from the jurisdiction of religious courts. When disputes occurred, these disputes would be settled by special councils set up by the Ministry of Commerce. These councils later extended their jurisdiction to Muslim/non-Muslim disputes. The concept of secular legal forums to hear commercial disputes was expanded again in 1847 when civil and criminal courts were set up in Istanbul with a regularized system of selecting judges. Rules of evidence were taken from the European Law Merchant rather than the Ottoman law (Starr 1992: 29). The Ottoman Penal Code of 1840 was made under the influence of the French criminal law but was largely still within the framework of the Islamic penal laws. For the first time in history, an Ottoman *qanun* was in the form a secular European code. The Ottoman Penal Code of 1858 was based on the Napoleonic Code of 1810, putting aside Islamic punishments. It established a French-type system of courts, with tribunals of first instance, courts of appeals and a high court of appeals. These were the first distinct hierarchy of a secular court system in the country (Starr 1992: 31). This secular criminal Code and court system remained in operation till 1923.

The government sanctioned traders' courts already established, to the effect of circumventing traditional Islamic law and creating new secular commercial courts. The first Ottoman secular criminal courts were established in the 1840s in police headquarters. They were operating under a new secular penal code. A mixed court of maritime commerce was established in 1850. In these mixed courts, half of the judges were European. Ottoman commercial courts were also established. A new chain of jurisdiction was established that extended upward through the secular provincial governor to the capital, bypassing links with *Shari'a* courts. In 1850, the Ottoman Commercial Code was promulgated, which was an adopted version of the French Commercial Code. This is the first clear example of legal transplantation in Turkey (Starr 1992: 29). The Ottoman Land Code of 1858 was inspired by the French freehold farming system.

The 1839 decree gave the *Meclis-i- Vala-yı Ahkamı Adliyye* (the Supreme Council of Judicial Ordinances) impetus to become a serious legislative council. The 1839 decree declared that this council should be increased in size and made more representative. The Sultan promised to accept its recommendations if a majority vote of its members concurred (Starr 1992: 25). *Meclis-i Vala* was given the responsibility of discussing legislative matters. The new legislation was to be recommended to the Sultan. In most cases, with his power decreased, the sultan had to rubberstamp these decisions. This council successfully operated for 15 years. Later, a new generation of Ottoman reformers wanted to weaken the power of the older generation so they divided the *Meclis-i Vala*'s functions in to two, making *Meclis-i Vala* only a judicial organ under the name then *Encümen-i Ali* (High Council) and creating a council of ministers (*Meclis-i Vukela*). The High Council's main task was to complete and extend the reforms of *Tanzimat*. It was also mandated to study all existing regulations for all state organs and was empowered to change these regulations in order to meet new conditions (Starr 1992: 27).

Even though secular commercial and criminal courts were established earlier, the true beginning of the secular legal system can be said to start in 1868 at the division of *Meclis-i Vala* into two organs: the Council of State (*Şuray-ı Devlet*, today's *Danıştay*), a legislative body and a court of appeal (the *Divan-ı Ahkam-ı Adliyye*) which was divided into civil and criminal sections. The *Divan-ı Ahkam-ı Adliyye*'s name was later changed to *Adliyye Nezareti* (Ministry of Justice).

During the entire *Tanzimat* period, the *Majalla* (the Ottoman Civil Code) was one of the most characteristic achievements. It was felt that a Civil Code was greatly needed and its preparation appeared on the agenda. Ali Pasha proposed the adoption of the French Civil Code but was opposed by Ahmet Cevdet Pasha who supported a Civil Code compatible with Islamic law; his view was accepted and he prepared the *Majalla* (Bozkurt 1998: 292).

The new secular courts often had to resolve by recourse to commercial law, but the judges were rarely knowledgeable about the *fiqh*. Initially, this problem was tried to be solved by the president of the religious court becoming the president of the secular court as well but this proved unsatisfactory, and a decision was made to codify the Islamic law of obligations (Starr 1992: 34). Thus, for the first time in the Muslim history, Islamic law was codified, which was developed between 1867 and 1876. It codified the *Hanafi fiqh* on transactions, contracts, and obligations, leaving the family law out. The *Majalla* was applied in both religious (*Shari'a*) and secular (*nizamiye*) courts. The Penal Code and Commercial Code were the predecessors of the Ottoman Civil Code but they were largely based upon or inspired by European codes. The *Majalla* was purely Islamic in content but European in form, it is a joint venture between conservatists and reformers, exemplifying the negotiation and compromise between these groups (Ostrorog 1927: 79).

Reformers in 1876 took advantage of the chaos in the country and pressed for a constitutional government. Young Ottomans endeavoured to put their ideas into practice and the first Ottoman constitution (*Kanun-i Esasi*) was promulgated on 23 December 1876, which also started the period known as the First *Meşrutiyet*, or First Constitutional Period, a period of a liberal constitutional monarchy. The 1876 Constitution was a document that resembled written western constitutions. It was modelled on the Belgian Constitution of 1931 and the Prussian Constitution of 1851 (Bozkurt 1998: 285). It is the first constitution of an Islamic state in history.

Islam remained the official religion of the state. For the first time in history, all subjects were declared to be Ottomans regardless of their religion. All subjects were equal; all were to enjoy liberty; a person's home was declared inviolable.

In addition to defining the main organizational structure of the state, it also set forth basic rights and liberties of Ottoman subjects and stipulated that the courts and the judges be secure from all external interventions; such a written principle thus took place in this Constitution for the first time. The basic concept in the 1876 constitution is that, although somewhat restrictive in the exercise of powers, it nevertheless, for the first time, recognized a legislative assembly partially elected by the people. This parliament was divided into two chambers, an elected *Meclis-i Mebusan* (Chamber of Deputies) and *Meclis-i Ayan* (Chamber of Notables), appointed directly by the Sultan. A grand vizier would perform the duties of a prime minister with his ministers. The *Şuray-i Devlet* (Council of State) was retained as the supreme court of appeal for administrative law cases and was to continue its legislative function. A new high court (*Divan-ı Ali*) was also established to hear cases against members of the government. *Meclis-i Mebusan* 'was granted certain powers to enact certain laws and to exercise control over the executive' (Özbudun 1978: 24). The entire secular court system evolved during the *Tanzimat* period was incorporated into the constitution. This constitution has provisions covering basic rights and privileges, the independence of courts and the safety of judges, among other aspects. Concepts such as equality, personal immunity, commercial freedom, freedom of press, freedom of education, right of petition, right to work in public services, sanctity of property, prohibition of angaria and torture and collection of taxes by means of codes are introduced (Güven 1996: 143). The judges were to be appointed for life, courts to be organized by law, and no outside interference was allowed. Religious courts were retained in matters of religion.

The first secular law school, the Istanbul Law Faculty, was established in 1875 to train judges, advocates and public prosecutors for the non-Islamic courts (Bozkurt 1998: 290). After the promulgation of the 1876 constitution, a system of public prosecutors and of judicial inspectors was established. The Constitution regulated the 'security for judges' and introduced the institutions of attorney and notary public. The ministries of Justice and Religious Affairs were united under the one ministry: the Ministry of Justice and Religious Affairs (*Adliyye and Mezahib Nezareti*) that had the mandate of jurisdiction of the secular *nizamiye* courts, regulated by written laws. In 1879, the French Criminal Procedure Code was transplanted that was the basis for the establishment of modern criminal courts and for the public prosecutors. In the same year, the Civil Procedure Code was enacted which was also modelled on the French law. In 1911, nearly 70 articles from the Italian Zanardelli Criminal Code were transplanted into the Ottoman Criminal Code (Bozkurt 1998: 288).

However, Sultan Abdulhamid dissolved the parliament in 1878 and ended this period. But, the influence of liberalism continued and eventually the Sultan was forced to restore the Constitution in 1908 and the Second *Meşrutiyet* period started (Özbudun 1978: 24). In 1909, the 1876 Constitution was substantially amended to the effect of increasing the power of the legislature and restricting those of the

Sultan. As a result, a truly constitutional system was established. But this system did not last long as the ruling *İttihad ve Terakki Party* quickly transformed the system into a dictatorship of the dominant party. With the defeat of the Ottomans in WWI, the government collapsed and maintained only a shaky existence under the control of the occupying Allied forces whilst the nationalist resistance movement to the occupation established a new governmental structure in Ankara under the leadership of Mustafa Kemal (Atatürk) (Özbudun 1978: 24-25).

Ottoman law was developing not only through reception of Western Codes, but also through doctrine, following the prevailing mode of western jurisprudence. But his reform process was not without problems. It was not only conservatists who opposed the law reform but also European powers who worried that they could not interfere in the internal affairs of the Ottomans. 'One of the interesting problems that emerged from this development was the objection of foreigners to the application of this procedural law to Muslims and non-Muslims alike' (Bozkurt 1998: 288). These European powers demanded a return to the previous system arguing that new reforms 'undermined the Capitulations and privileges of non-Muslims. Ironically, the Ottoman State was compelled to defend its reception of Western laws against Western critics who preferred to see the old system (which they criticized) maintained' (Bozkurt 1998: 290).

Despite secularization in several fields of law after the *Tanzimat*, the laws of marriage, divorce, inheritance, and custody of children for Muslims continued as before. The *Majalla* was meant to express law common to all Ottoman subjects, whatever their religion. Thus, it left out the family law and laws of inheritance and wills, and laws of foundations (*waqf*s) as the separate non-Muslim minorities had different and autonomous laws in the *millet* system (Ostrorog 1927: 79). Some reformists objected to this situation arguing for a total reform. A number of Western civil codes were translated into Turkish. Some scholars even published articles comparing the French Civil Code and *Majalla* article by article (Bozkurt 1998: 292-293). Without knowing that it would become the Civil Code of Turkey 14 years later, another scholar translated the Swiss Civil Code into Turkish in 1912. The German Civil Code was translated in 1916 (Bozkurt 1998: 293).

In 1916, the state established a committee to draft a civil code. This committee studied Roman, British, French, German, Swiss, American, Austrian and Hungarian laws (Bozkurt 1998: 293). On 25 October 1917, the Ottoman Family Laws Ordinance (OFLO) (*Hukuk-u Aile Kararnamesi*) was enacted. It was the first codification of Muslim family law in history.

This was a revolutionary law in the sense that it eclectically reflected and amalgamated the views of different juristic schools of Islam. The law tried to give marriage a more official character by stating that the unilateral *talaq* in the presence of two witnesses did not suffice to terminate a marriage. The presence of a judge or a deputy was required by the law. Moreover, every marriage and divorce had to be legally organized according to state procedures. The law also granted a wife two new grounds of divorce. For the first time, age limits for marriage were set. The new law also allowed women, at the time of betrothal, to incorporate into the marriage contract a condition that a second marriage by the husband whilst still married to the first wife would automatically make the second marriage null and void (see in detail Tucker 1999: 6-10). With this law, for the first time, religious courts were placed under the authority of the Ministry of Justice (Starr 1992: 40). This law 'grouped separately the rules related to marriage and divorce for Muslims, Jews, and Christians, but authorized the *qadi* courts to handle cases related to the marriage and divorce, and dowry and trousseau claims for non-Muslims. This drew sharp criticism from the diplomats of great powers' (Bozkurt 1998: 293). After WWI, the British occupied Istanbul and forced the government to repeal this law in 1919.

## Republican Era: Continuity and Change

Turkish nationalism became the driving principle of the Republican elite. During World War I and especially the War of Independence (1919-1922), the popular will changed and they started identifying themselves as Turks as they were forced to stand together against invaders. Turkish nationalism was directed at raising the prestige of Turkey by efficient Westernization rather than by an attempt to recover the Empire (Stirling 1965: 5).

Mustafa Kemal Atatürk emerged from the war as a great war hero who saved the nation. With this great prestige and popularity he drew on the new national identity and feeling to create a new government, radically changing the Ottoman way and creating the Turkish Republic on 29 October 1923. In creating new symbols and institutions for the republic, Atatürk drew on the ideas, programmes, and leaders of the Young Turks, paving the way for a remarkable degree of continuity in both the core members of bureaucracies and in the political elites (Starr 1992: 13).

The Republican elite's passion for modernization, seen as an escape from backwardness, translated itself into a total dislike and distrust of all things associated with the ancient regime and the old way of life. Topping the long list of suspect establishments were religion and the religious institutions. The culture associated with religion and religiosity, such as dress code, was also deemed antithetical to contemporary civilization (Barkey 2000: 88). Thus, to the Kemalist élite, the question was no longer that of finding some means to integrate Islamic institutions with the Western ones. They categorically decided to destroy the former (Yazıcıoğlu 1993: 180; Toprak 1981: 33).

The Turkish state under the reins of the Kemalist elite assumed that cultural change and modernization could be imposed from above through the force of law. One of the major expected changes was the secularization of the society.

From the ruins of the Ottoman era the Turks, under the leadership of Mustafa Kemal Atatürk, managed to found a new modern nation-state. The territory encompassed and concentrated on ancient Turkish land, with Anatolia at its centre. This state was proclaimed to be a Republic in 1923 with a president and a parliament and thereby abolished the Sultanate. The urgent aim of the founders of the state was to transform the 'backward', traditional, and religious society into a modern, secular and 'civilized' one. They already had their model for this transformation in the form of European civilization and wanted Turkey to be as much of an exact copy of this civilization as was humanly and physically possible.

For the Kemalist elite, to reach the level of contemporary civilization, i.e. the European civilization, the modern, Western way of life had to be espoused and imported with all that it included and entailed; the package was non-negotiable and if you wanted a part you had to get the lot. However, it is no real myth that the Kemalist elite not only wanted to import everything European for the sake of modernizing Turkey, but that equally and maybe even more so they wanted to transplant the whole European lifestyle to get rid off all the remaining and existing remnants of the Ottoman history, time and values. They asserted that '(t)raditions are to be respected as long as they do not jeopardize the interests of a society and prevent the community from reaching a certain level of civilization' (Timur 1957: 36).

In other words, whether the European lifestyle was transplanted to Turkey for the sake of modernizing it, or for the sake of what the Kemalist elite saw as ugly and repugnant is a question that has yet to be conclusively settled. A quick scan in Turkish dailies will show that the simmering tensions between the officials who enthusiastically aim to secularize the society from above and some people who stick to the neo-traditional Muslim culture still continue, showing that the two sides have not yet given up. The head scarf issue at the Turkish universities is only one of such tensions.

Secularism was implemented through a series of decisive steps taken to disestablish Islam from a role in law and education, and as the official religion of the state (Weiker 1981: 105). Founders of the Republic believed that there was not enough time to wait for 'the slow process of evolution; people must use their energy and will to force every material element of life through modern moulds and modern patterns' (Saeed 1994: 162; see also Göle 1994: 66-70).

Toprak (1981: 40) distinguishes four phases of secularization in Republican Turkey: Symbolic secularization, institutional secularization, functional secularization and legal secularization. Secularization of the first phase enforced changes in aspects of national culture or social life which had a symbolic identification with Islam. This includes a transformation in the connotations of a set of symbols from the sacred to the profane. Concepts of dress, time, the uses of public spaces, the calendar, the written language, its script, and the numerical system were changed from what they were in Ottoman times (Starr 1992: 503; Toprak 1981: 40). The reformers imagined a new community of loyal citizens inhabiting a new world – that of secularism where the Islamic cognitive framework was replaced by a secular one that would change individuals' very notions of themselves. Their concept of time and calendar, their conception of self and other, the work world, family relationships, dress, names, language, script, alphabet, numerical system, neighbourhoods, education, public behaviour, and especially 'mentalities' would be changed (Starr 1992: 89).

The easiest cultural symbol to identify people by is through their language (Toprak 1981: 40). Thus, the Kemalist government launched some radical reforms with the language of the Turks. The first phase was the change of the alphabet from the Arabic to the Latin script in 1928. This was followed by a concerted effort to change the vocabulary by substituting new words derived from Turkish roots in place of the Arabic and Persian derivatives that had been integrated and evolved into the language over the centuries through cultural contacts. The second phase of cultural reform was the attempt to substitute the pre-Islamic history of the Central Asian Turks with the Ottoman past so that a common basis for national identity other than religion could be established. In this reading of the new Turkish history, the Turks, who until then had been identified with Islam, are presented as a nation of people who have great innate cultural characteristics that shines through them throughout their history regardless of the religion they adopted subsequently, whether that be Shamanism or Islam. In search of a unifying myth to replace Islam, which was the language of society, long forgotten roots of the pre-Islamic era were introduced. Yet this process of re-writing history to build a nation was construed not as scientific endeavour but as ideological glue for national cohesion (Ergil 2000: 50). Disregarding the Islamic view of Turkish history, the new historiography declared the Islamic period to be only one of the episodes in the national and civilization aspects of Turkish history. All subjects of the state became equal citizens regardless of their religion. The abrogation of the Caliphate in 1924 was another radical and crucial act of symbolic secularization (Starr 1992: 14).

Second, institutional secularization covered the changes in organizational arrangements designed to destroy the institutional strength of Islam. It was claimed that Turkey must be freed from the backward-looking institutions of Islam. In the eyes of the Kemalist elite, Islam was 'responsible for Turkey's backwardness' (Allen 1968: 173).

The source of all evil was the unity of state and religion. The Kemalist élite proceeded to disestablish the *ulama* and tried to destroy the sources of power of the Islamic hierarchy (Starr 1989: 502). The abolition of the Caliphate in 1924, in addition to its symbolic significance, was the first step in the deinstitutionalization of religious involvement in politics. This was followed by the abolition of the Office of the *Şeyhü-l-İslam* (the highest Islamic authority in the state) and the Ministry of Religious Affairs and Pious Foundations (*Şeriye ve Evkaf Vekaleti*) on the same date. These steps together with the recognition, in both the 1921 and the 1924 Constitutions, of the principle that political authority derived its legitimacy from the concept of national sovereignty, rather than divine will, constituted major stages in the direction of releasing the religious hold and influence from the state mechanics. This movement reached its high water mark in 1928: The second article of the 1924 Constitution which recognized Islam as the state religion was abrogated. After the abolition of institutions of the past, new but official institutions were established with a view of controlling religious activity, and concerted efforts were made to destroy the institutional strength of local Islam (see in detail Toprak 1981: 40; Heper 1986a: 373).

The third type of secularization is one which includes changes in the functional specificity of religious and governmental institutions (Toprak 1981: 40). In the *Tanzimat* era, an effort was made to codify the law for the first time in Turkish history. Although such codification was based on the Muslim law, it was nevertheless an important step towards the secularization of law in that it was the first recognition of the necessity to establish legal codes that were written and distinguishable from religious provisions. During the *Tanzimat* and the following periods, a number of secular codes were enacted in the fields of commercial, penal, and civil law that supplemented the religious ones. At the same time, a parallel effort was made to establish secular courts, in which the new codes would be applied. The abolition of the *Shari'a* courts as the final secularization of the court system was accomplished in 1924, with the subsequent unification of the court system under the jurisdiction of the Ministry of Justice and the enactment of distinctly secular codes. As a result, the religious institutions officially lost their former judicial functions (Toprak 1981: 48).

Symbolic, institutional and functional secularization in the Republican era paved the way for the legal secularization that needs more detailed elaboration.

## Speeding up the Legal Reforms and Total Secularization

Symbolic, institutional, and functional secularization were reinforced by a legal framework which attempted to eliminate the religiously-sanctioned provisions of law. According to Hooker (1975: 306), Turkey's experience 'is an excellent example of a state undertaking the process of legal importation as a result of fundamental revolution, and under the impetus of that upheaval, attempting to establish a completely clean legal sheet' (Hooker 1975: 306). The Kemalist élite espoused a legal modernist discourse that – they believed – has conferred legitimacy on them as this modernist and revolutionist legal discourse 'sketch pictures of widely shared, wistful, inchoate visions of an ideal' (Gordon 1986: 16). Thus, the minister of Justice of the time, Mahmut Esat Bozkurt, 'declared that what he desired was not reform but a revolution of Law' (Bozkurt 1944: 7 cited in Bozkurt 1998: 294).

Transformation of society would start with the very smallest unit, the family. Thus, after the proclamation of the Republic in 1923, radical reforms were introduced in family law matters as well. In the field of family law, all earlier reforms, however extensive they seemed, had not affected the traditional Muslim law which governed family life. Family law had been one of the last bastions of Islamic law and the most resistant area of the legal system to secularization. The attempt to change the Muslim family laws is one of the most daring experiments for the modernizing élite in Muslim societies. However, such an attempt was perceived as necessary by the Kemalists since the family plays an important role in transmitting dominant cultural values to younger generations, and the aim of the Kemalist nationalists was the cultural transformation of society (Toprak 1981: 54). They thought that starting with individual males and females, new selfhoods would flourish within ancient shrouded bodies. To enhance the status of all women law was selected as one of the instruments of change (Starr 1992: 89-90). The purposeful action by the Kemalist elite in supplanting Muslim family law with secular laws was meant to create a more egalitarian relationship within the domestic household (Starr 1992: 112).

Atatürk expressed his revolutionist tendency in his speech during the inauguration of the National Assembly in 1924: '(t)he direction to be followed in civil law and family law should be nothing but that of Western civilization. Following the road of half measures and attachment to age-old superstitions is the gravest nightmare that impedes the awakening of nations. The Turkish nation cannot tolerate this nightmare' (cited in Berkes 1964: 469-70).

To Bozkurt, the European model was essential; he told Leon Ostrorog in 1925 when they met in Ankara that '(w)e are badly in want of a good scientific code. Why waste our time trying to produce something new when quite good codes are to be found ready made? ...The only thing to do is to take a good ready-made Code to which good commentaries exist, and to translate them wholesale. The Swiss Code is a good Code; I am going to have it adopted' (Ostrorog 1927: 87-88).

The Kemalists made their first attempt to change the legal system by the appointment of special committees of the Ministry of Justice to prepare the framework for a new set of secular codes in 1924 (see in detail Aydın 1995: 167-172; see also Berkes 1978: 519). However, the results of the reports showed the heavy influence of the traditional Muslim law in the proposed changes.[2] The project was thus dropped and the government decided to adopt the Swiss Civil Code, the Italian Criminal Code, and the German Commercial Code (Güriz 1996: 9-10).

By 1926 an entirely secular legal system was put in place. Law was precisely aimed at behaviour, in the hope that attitudes would follow (Boulding 1986: 4). As a result, in attempting to build a new national identity for Turkey, the secular legal system became the very foundation of the modern Turkish state (Starr 1992: 169).

The legal culture has become an amalgam of predominantly Swiss, German, Italian and French legal cultures, and the legal system is based totally on large-scale eclectic receptions from Western models. As a part of the secularization of the legal system 'a new law school was opened in Ankara in 1925 to train judges and lawyers in the new secular law' (Starr 1992: 16).

With regards to the transplantation of the Swiss Civil Code, in addition to the above elaborated ideological reasons, there is also a political dimension. Turkey having secured the need of the Capitulations concessions with the Lausanne Treaty praised her sovereignty very highly (Postacıoğlu 1957: 54). The rights of ethnic minorities were debated during the Lausanne treaty. This treaty imposed heavy restrictions and obligations upon Turkey 'to provide for non-Turkish minorities an adequate modern legal system. A general reform fulfilled this obligation without appearing as a slavish compliance with the Treaty' (Lipstein 1957: 73). Aydın (1995: 171-172) concurs: the heavy pressures regarding this matter led the Kemalist elite to adopt a Western law to accommodate the demands of Western powers to prevent lingering interference. The western powers renounced their privileges under the Capitulations regime conditionally on minorities in Turkey being exempted as regards to personal law from the provisions of Turkish law which was based on Islamic law. Under article 42 of the treaty, it was conceded that each minority should be governed by its own customary/religious law in matters of personal status, the rules of which were to be established by *ad hoc*

[2] See for details and comments in the press about the mentioned proposal, Abadan-Unat (1986: 130-131). See also Aydin (1995: 168-169).

commissions. Turkey perceived this as a breach of its sovereignty and its intended uniform legal system. Thus, to render the privileges of minorities pointless, the Swiss Civil Code was transplanted (Postacıoğlu 1957: 54).

Secular law was alien for both Muslim citizens and non-Muslim minorities. Under Ottoman rule, the denominational groups called *millet* had the right to choose their own leader, practise their own religion, and follow their own family laws. After the acceptance of the Civil Code, the non-Muslim minorities, to whom article 42 of the Treaty of Lausanne had recognized legal autonomy in family and personal matters, decided to give up that prerogative. All the members of the *millet*s lost their separate status and became individual citizens of the Turkish Republic. Their religious courts were also replaced by secular ones.

The Civil Code differs fundamentally from the provisions of the Muslim law (Aydın 1995: 172). The new secular law was meant to change the core structure of Turkish domestic life to bring it closer to Western models (Starr 1992: 91). As Berkes (1978: 522) points out, the Civil Code was perceived by the élite as an instrument of achieving what ought to be rather than regulating what in reality exists.

When the new secular Turkish Civil Code became effective on October 4th 1926, it caused an anomaly. Family law in Turkey was now governed by non-Islamic secular laws for the first time in its history, whilst the citizens of this new Republic remained and continued to be Muslims. Those parts of the new legal 'system which conflicted most with the former order of things, in particular with established institutions and practices in family relations, land-holding and the law of succession, exposed both the new legal order and society to strains and stresses which raised the problem whether the Civil Code or society was to prevail in the end' (Lipstein 1957: 73).

## Expected Legal Secularization, State Islam versus Muslim Local Law

In the Republican epistemology, religion is imprisoned into the conscience of the individual and places of worship in the society and is not allowed to mix with and interfere in public life (Mardin 1982: 180). On the other hand, the application of laicism in Turkey has taken on a slightly different form, in that religious affairs in Turkey have been placed under the auspices of the state and justification for doing so have been explained in reference to Turkey's 'special and unique' circumstances (Sarıbay 1986: 200). As Laicism as a concept espouses the idea that religion and state are kept distinct and separate, the Turkish version of laicism would appear to be self-contradictory. The Kemalist élite however, thought that if religion and state are non-separable components in Islam, then the best way of keeping Islam out of the public and political life would be to place it under the control and supervision of the state. As a result, religious institutions were linked to state bureaucracy. Then, the state started to interfere in religious affairs during the Republican era. A Directorate of Religious Affairs was established in 1923 at the instigation of the members of the Grand National Assembly as a replacement for the Ottoman Ministry of Religion. Later constitutions that were prepared after the coup d'etats of 1960 and 1980 re-confirmed its place in the system. Now, article 136 of the 1982 constitution provides that the Directorate is directly responsible to the Prime Minister and has no direct contact with daily politics (Shankland 1999: 29).

Soon after the establishment of the Republic, the Directorate of Religious Affairs was established, and all Islamic activities were tried to be placed under the auspices of this organ of the state, with the Prime Minister of Turkey in 'firm control' (Starr 1992: 15). As a result, religious institutions are linked to the state bureaucracy, without any autonomy. As Shankland (1999: 9) portrays it, the Republican elite and especially the army regard their 'ultimate task to preserve the Republic and its borders. This means that, if necessary, it is fully prepared to use orthodox Islam as a bulwark against communism or as a means of achieving harmony in the community'. As was earlier observed 'it is plain that one cannot categorically assert either that the government is favorable or that it is hostile to Islam. The truth of the matter seems to be that it is distinctly opportunist in its attitude' (Allan 1968: 175; see also Kadıoğlu 1998: 11).

Establishment of the Directorate of Religious Affairs with a substantial budget and over 80 thousand employees is a result of this understanding of 'Turkish type of laicite'. It has an extensive organization. The Directorate controls all 86 thousand mosques and employs the *imam*s, *mufti*s and *muezzin*s who 'are the salaried employees of the state who have to follow instructions which are derived from state policy' (Mardin 1983: 149). The *mufti* acts as a local link between the believer and the state; he also administers the *imam*s attached to every mosque and distributes sermons and other materials sent to them from above. The *imam*s are not just part of an administrative structure; they are also subject ideologically to the decisions made by their superiors in the announcements that they make and the sermons that they preach. This tight supervisory structure leaves '*imam*s with little leeway to create their own interpretation of religion' (Shankland 1999: 29). The teachers, textbooks, and curricula of all religious schooling are under the direct supervision of the Director-General of Religious Education, a separate office of the Ministry of Education.

The Republican elite have 'claimed that true expression of religion could be found through the use of Turkish prayer, a language that all could understand, through translating the Koran into Turkish, rather than Arabic. They also drew historical parallels, asserting that their revolution mirrors the Protestant battles against Papism in its dislike of intermediaries and direct access to the faith for all. Thus, it was cleansed religion, without mysticism, without saints, and without independent religious institutions that was aimed at. It was also one closely controlled' (Shankland 1999: 23). As Shankland (1999: 31) concludes, 'the Directorate's role has primarily been to oversee, ratify and steer the massive expansion of Islamic activity within the population as a whole rather than actually provide it'.

The Turkish version of secularism is unique, although the Turkish State defined its attitude toward religion as 'laicism', an intellectual inheritance from the French Third Republic (Başgil 1962; 1991; Yazıcıoğlu 1993: 180; Toprak 1995: 91); there are certainly some elements that make the Turkish application unique. One of the most conspicuous of these elements is that the Turkish state has assumed a role of a 'secular *mujtahid*' and has been interpreting Islam in the lines of its ideological vision. I will term the outcome of this secular official *ijtihad* '*Lozan Islamı* (Lausannian Islam)' which has been the state Islam or official version of Islam of Turkey. In the state version of Islam, there is no conflict between the religion and Turkish modernity that covers the modern nation-state, secularism, democracy and no public role for religion. To subordinate religion to the political establishment, the state has long tried to create its own version of Islam. The reason d'etre of the Directorate of Religious Affairs has been to create a tailor-made national modern Turkish-Islam, definitely suppressing the transnational links and role, cut off from all international and transnational ties, specific and limited to the nation-state's official borders that were drawn with the Lausanne Treaty of 1924 between Turkey and the European powers. The main task of the Directorate has been to control Islam in accordance with the needs of the secular nation-state to the effect of creating a secular, modern, official, 'Lausannian-Islam'.

Although, it has been claimed that the state in Turkey has tried to make religion a private belief not affecting the public sphere with its adamant secularization ideology, this is not entirely true. The state has tried to made use of religion as a 'helping hand' (King 1995c: 105). This idea of religion has formulated religion in terms of its responsibility for the moral health of the nation (King 1995c: 106). Theoretical foundations of this mentality could be traced back to Durkheim who influenced Atatürk's 'intellectual father' Ziya Gökalp who also translated Durkheim's works into Turkish.

Durkheim's main thesis was that religion plays a significant role in uniting a society together. In his view, any coherent society must be at base a religious collectivity. He conceived the integral nature of religion as the ceremonial and expressive glue that binds any social organization together, or, more boldly put, religion as society's worship of itself, was Durkheim's essential insight. He pointed out that the collective act of worship integrates social institutions. It does this in a special way with 'collective effervescence', which is a dynamic social force produced when people get together. It is the life of the group over and above the lives of the individuals who make up the group.

Gökalp had systematically advocated domination of Turkish culture with forms of western civilization rather than importing institutions as they had developed in the west. His sociological orientation, taking a nation as a political and cultural unity, helped him in his advocacy of Turkism. Atatürk's movement and Gökalp's ideas had a close interaction in that Kemalism was affected by Ziya Gökalp in the formulation of nationalism as a principle, and Gökalp was affected by Kemalism which rejected any ambition beyond the borders of the new Turkey (Kongar 1986).

So, in this Durkheimian mentality, an approved version of Islam, *Lozan Islamı*, could and should play a public role. That is why when a financial crisis erupted in 2001, the Directorate prepared a Friday sermon to discourage the faithful from using US Dollars and this sermon was delivered – as it is obligatory – by *imams* in 86 thousand or so mosques of Turkey.

Prior to the establishment of the Turkish Republic, the Ottoman State had always been focused on Islam. Islam existed as an all-embracing life system, providing Muslim citizens with a framework of meaning to interpret their lives. However, as seen above, after the establishment of the Republic, Islam was completely disregarded. It was relegated to a matter of conscience, which was left solely to the private sphere. Citizens could be Muslims in their private lives, yet they could not claim any room for Islam in the public arena. The Civil Code is applied in all parts of Turkey and all Turkish citizens and residents are subject to it.

The Republic focused most of its political energies on creating a truly unitary nation-state in place of the pluralistic Ottoman State. The *millet* system was no longer considered as an appropriate system in the eyes of the Republican élite. Personal laws were unified under the title of a modern civil code. Indeed, uniformity attempts in the family law of Muslims had started in Ottoman times. The Ottoman State intervened in marriages and divorces of the people and employed local governments in the process. These units were responsible for the registration of the family law affairs. With this development, the secularization of family law can be said to have started in Ottoman times (Alkan 1990: 89). However, radical changes were introduced after the construction of the new state. The élite hoped that, through the secular legal system, it would gain complete monopoly of legitimate power and not have to share this with religion or custom. Thus, as a dominant element of the state, the élite for whom law-making was the primary tool of social change rather than the product of large-scale demands 'attempted to present one consistent image of justice and one unified legal system. Islam fell under the control of the modern state through laicism, which intended that no Islamic competition could again challenge the secular state's monopoly over law' (Starr 1992: 170). One system of nation-state law framed by the Constitution of the state, entirely secular, and one system of state courts administered by the Ministry of Justice, also secular, constitutes the official legal system in the country. The modern Turkish Constitution takes it for granted that Islam in today's Turkey does not offer a competing legal sensibility to secular law (Starr 1992: xix). Religion as a source of law has been abolished; the Western idiom of state law has triumphed.

Even though Islam has been officially removed from public life, which was firmly based on the theory and practice of the Ottoman State, it is still deeply rooted in the minds and hearts of the people. Although the state has kept an eye on the former religious leaders, their successors and the religious functionaries, they have regained something of their influence in public life by attracting masses into their religious atmosphere (Rosenthal 1965: 61). It is reiterated frequently that 'revolutionary efforts through law have only resulted in partial changes' (Abadan-Unat 1986: 125). The Kemalist ideology, which had national, secular and modern elements, could not fill the gap which Islam was supposed to have forcefully vacated (Mardin 1982: 180-181; Saeed 1994: 164). The state, through its secular policies and programs of westernization, threatened the value system of the Muslim people in the country without providing, at the same time, a satisfactory and all-encompassing ideological framework which could have mass appeal and was capable of replacing Islam (Saeed 1994: 165). Bifurcation between the élite and the masses made it difficult for the Kemalists to carry out their reforms from above (Saeed 1994: 172). Mardin (1982: 181) underlines this: 'neither Kemalism nor its associated doctrines could replace Islam in the lives of the peasantry, and the provincial and lower-class populations'. Local Islam survived despite all attempts of the state (Öktem 1995: 49). Islam is pervasive in a modern sense in Turkish society, and this exemplifies the failure of the Republican elite's attempts at encapsulating, restricting and imprisoning religion to the individual's consciousness and private realm 'Atatürk wanted to make religion a private concern, but unanticipated social consequences soon caught up with him. As the boundaries of the private have become enlarged in Turkey an unforeseen development has occurred. As private every-day life has increasingly been given new richness and variety, religion has become a central focus of life and acquired a new power' (Mardin 1989: 229).

As a recent study on Turkey reconfirmed '(t)he vibrancy of Islam is remarkable in almost all areas of Turkish life... This Islam is neither a replacement for, nor an alternative to, the modern world: it is an integral part of life' (Shankland 1999: 15, see for detailed data Shankland 1999: 54-61). Shankland (1999: 17) further states that even though the Kemalist system has survived, 'the situation today differs in this, and other ways, from that future envisaged by many of the Republic's founders' (Shankland 1999: 17). It was the introduction of Democracy in the late 1940s that provided the key link between rulers and ruled. As elections campaigning began, despite the repeated emphasis on ensuring that politics and religion were henceforth to be separate, politicians were hardly able to resist the offer to support Islamic mores to attract votes (Shankland 1999: 35).

In the legal field, too, Islam continues to affect people's lives. For instance, as early as in 1955 a group of Turkish and foreign scholars examined the question whether legislation has succeeded in displacing Turco-Islamic traditions with reference to the adoption of Swiss family law and answered the enquiry with a qualified 'no' (Magnarella 1974: 108). Communities, especially in rural areas, regard official law as 'government' law and it has little effect on the life of the village mechanism (Hooker 1975: 366-371). With the passage of time, the expectation that people would learn and follow only the official *lex loci* by entirely abandoning the Muslim law turned out to be untrue. In the mid-1990s, there were still conflicts between the official legal system and the local law (Ansay 1996: 110).

The Civil Code differs from the provisions of the Muslim law (Aydın 1995: 172). Although, it was claimed that the potentialities and possibilities inherent in and derivable from the Muslim canonical law had been taken into consideration before enforcing the new code, the enactment of the Civil Code aimed to achieve a complete separation between religion and law. As Berkes (1978: 522) points out, the Civil Code was perceived by the élite as an instrument of achieving what ought to be rather than regulating what in reality exists.

There exist a number of differences between the secular civil law of Turkey and the Muslim local law. These differences include the secularization of the marriage ceremony. A legal marriage has to be registered with the civil authorities and must be concluded in their presence. Religious ceremony was made optional and carried no legal weight. A religious marriage without official registration was made a criminal offence. The adoption of the principle of monogamy meant that polygamy was under no circumstances allowed and became a criminal offence. The secularization of divorce proceedings was another key reform. The new law gave both parties an equal right to sue for divorce. *Talaq* was no longer recognized. Divorce could only be granted by an official court.

As a natural result, these differences led to confusion in the lives of the people. They have been faced with a certain dilemma between the unrecognized Muslim law and the official but secular state law. Stirling (1965: 209) had earlier observed that many provisions of the new codes were not being followed. Some segments of the society have been passively resisting abandonment of their traditional practices for the sake of the civil Code (Kruger 1991: 203). Many men and women were marrying without going through a state-recognized civil marriage ceremony and they were remarrying without a 'legal' divorce (Kruger 1991: 203-204, 206). Thus, in the eyes of the official law, some couples were living in adulterous or bigamous relationships. However, according to the local law, only the celebration of religious wedding (*nikah*) can legitimatize the marriage (Stirling 1965: 209).[3]

Muslim Turks have sought other ways to adapt their Muslim law to the modern and so-called secular milieu. Again, as in the more recent British case, they have reconstructed their Muslim laws to meet the demands of both official and unofficial laws, as the subsequent chapters further analyze.[4]

## Reconstruction of the Turkish Muslim Law

People in Turkey, after the reception and transplantation of the Swiss Civil Code have had three alternative routes from which they could choose in conducting themselves that relate to the secular law: Avoidance of the official law, following the Turkish state law or following a combination of the requirements of the Muslim law and Turkish law. Evidence has shown that the Turkish populace has preferred the third choice. They have developed a new Muslim law which amalgamates the rules of Muslim law as well as those of the secular Turkish law, as in the British case.

As marriage is such a basic institution of society, it is not a coincidence that

---

[3] Actually, the term '*nikah*' is used in Turkish both to refer to the official marriage ceremony and the religious one. To be more precise, Turkish people call the official ceremony '*resmi* (official) *nikah*', and the religious ceremony '*ımam nikahı*'. In Islamic law, there is no institution like '*ımam nikahı*', since almost every individual adult Muslim male is capable of solemnizing the marriage in the presence of two witnesses. Even the bride-groom or one of the witnesses can perform this function. There is no special formula or required status to do this job, see for example Günenç (1990b: 117). However, in Ottoman times, the state tried to register the marriages and gave this registration duty to *imams* in local units, see in detail Alkan (1990: 89); see also Cin (1974: 287); Abadan-Unat (1986: 183). As a result, Turkish people started to call religious marriage '*imam nikahı*'. In short, this term although not necessarily Islamic, is a product of Turkish culture. In this study, I use the terms '*nikah*' and '*imam nikahı*' to refer only to a religious marriage.

[4] Yet in the Turkish case, the issue is not a minority case. In contrast, it pertains to the majority. Also, in this case, the new-comer is not the immigrant group or ethnic minority, but the transplanted Western law.

family formation would be the first target of legal penetration. The Turkish Constitution refers to the family as the basic institution of the society. It is considered that if the institution of family is healthy, then the society and the state will be healthy as well. Thus, by protecting and regulating the family, the state protects and empowers itself (Toroslu 1984: 154). To that effect, the legal system imposes upon the state certain 'duties' towards the family. As a result, it is stated in Article 41: '(t)he state shall take... measures and establish the necessary organisation to safeguard the peace and well-being of the family'.

The protection of mothers and children and family planning are especially stated as the duties of the state under the Turkish Constitution. At this point, 'for a considerable part of the population, there has been some contradiction between their traditional social practice and the law' (Ansay 1996: 110). In the case of marriage, the attitude to the Code turns to one of outright conflict between the official law and Islamic rules or, more accurately, what the people regard as rules of Islamic law (Hooker 1975: 367).[5] Thus, a number of problems have arisen between the official law and unofficial Muslim local law. Turkish Muslims have reconciled these conflicting points by employing certain strategies and methods in matters such as solemnization of the marriages, age of marriage, polygamy and divorce. As a result, only a few cases have appeared before the courts.

### *Solemnization of Marriage: Nikah*

Under the official law, only civil marriages performed by authorized marriage officers are allowed and recognized and this is safeguarded by the constitution.[6] Article 134 of the new Civil Code states that the formalities of celebration commence with the submission of the necessary documents by the parties to the marriage office at the place where they are residing at the time. The authorities start inquiries to check whether impediments to the marriage exist. Article 143 of the new Civil Code provides that a marriage may be solemnized in accordance with any religious rites if the parties desire, but registration of marriage preceding such a solemnization is necessary. Only after the celebration of the civil marriage is a *nikah* permitted and the parties should present their marriage document to *imam* before the religious marriage.[7] If a civil ceremony in a register office is followed by a religious one, the religious ceremony does not supersede or invalidate the civil ceremony and is not registered with any authority.[8] The civil ceremony is clearly the only marriage which the official law recognizes. The men and women who perform a religious marriage ceremony without having made the legal marriage contract are considered to be punishable. Article 237 of the Criminal Code states that:

---

[5] In order to emphasize that point I use the term 'local Muslim law' which covers the rules that the people consider Islamic, whether they are genuinely Islamic or not.

[6] Article 174/4 of the Turkish Constitution.

[7] Article 143 of the new Civil Code and Article 237/3 of the Criminal Code.

[8] Article 143 of the new Civil Code.

> A marriage officer who knowingly solemnizes the marriage of persons who are not legally entitled to marry, parties to such a marriage, and appointed or natural guardians who consent or lead the parties to such a marriage, shall be imprisoned for three months to two years.[9]
>
> A public officer issuing marriage certificates without abiding by legal requirements shall be punished by imprisonment for not more than three months.
>
> Whoever performs a religious ceremony for a marriage without seeing the certificate indicating that the parties are lawfully married shall be punished by the punishment prescribed in the foregoing paragraph.[10]
>
> Men and women who cause a religious ceremony to be performed prior to being married lawfully shall be punished by imprisonment for two to six months.[11]

Despite all the legal measurements such as this article, the authorities will not know of the incident unless a dispute arises. The majority of the perpetrators of these alleged 'crimes' remain unpunished. There is almost no punishment for *imams* who celebrate such marriages unofficially (Kruger 1991: 209). Or, as in many cases, judges would be tolerant with the convicted and would change the punishment from imprisonment to a pecuniary punishment, which shows the perpetuating impact of the legal postulates.[12]

It is a well-known reality that 'many Turkish citizens still prefer the informal or consensual marriage, or *imam nikahı*' (Abadan-Unat 1986: 172; Zevkliler 1995: 705; Kümbetoğlu 1997: 121). Sometimes they marry with *imam nikahı* without registration, which is not recognized under the Civil Code. Marriages are performed by *imams* without prior celebration (Ansay 1996: 113; Kümbetoğlu 1997: 121).

Some 70 years after the transplantation of the Civil Code, the norms which consider a child born only of non-religious (civil) wedlock a 'bastard' are quite dominant (Balaman 1985: 211; Talay 1994: 34), since 'legitimacy for the villagers still rests solely on the *nikah*' (Stirling 1965: 209).[13] In the 1990s, it is an undeniable fact that 'many unmarried couples, and the society they live in, believe that the religious ceremony provides enough evidence for the validity of their marriage' (Talay 1994: 34).[14]

An earlier study (Timur 1972: 92) found that 35.4 per cent of all marriages in

---

[9] Y2HD 04. 06. 1985 E 985. 5223 K 985. 5310; Y4CD 09. 12. 1986 E 986. 9510 K 986. 9813.

[10] Turkish Criminal Code, Article 237/3. Y4CD 09. 12. 1986 E 986. 9510 K. 986. 9813; Y4CD 28. 04. 1992 E. 992. 2504 K. 992. 3125; Y4CD 14. 03. 1990 E. 990. 916 K. 990. 1435. Y4CD 09. 12. 1986 E 986. 9510 K 986. 9813; Y4CD 28. 04. 1992 E. 992. 2504 K. 992. 3125; Y4CD 14. 03. 1990 E. 990. 916 K. 990. 1435.

[11] Ansay et al (1965: 85). For some cases which appeared before the Court of Cassation, see Y4CD 06. 06. 1983 E 983. 2664 K 983. 3310; Y4CD 09. 12. 1986 E 986. 9510 K 986. 9813; Y4CD 28. 04. 1992 E. 992. 2504 K. 992. 3125. Y4CD 14. 03. 1990 E. 990. 916 K. 990. 1435; Y2HD 04. 06. 1985 E. 985. 5223 K. 985. 5310.

[12] Y2HD 06. 06. 1983 E 983. 2664 K 983. 3310; Y2HD 04. 06. 1985 E. 985. 5223 K. 985. 5310; Y 4CD 28. 04. 1992 E. 992. 2504 K. 992. 3125.

[13] Y2HD 28. 03. 1968 1366 E. 1984.

[14] A woman journalist in eastern Turkey states that everybody in the region marries by *nikah*, and official marriage is also common, see *Sabah Melodi*, 25 March 1998, p. 2.

Turkey were civil, 49.2 per cent were mixed civil-religious (concluded in the presence of civil authorities and later, an *imam*), and 15.0 per cent were only religious and hence carried no official legal weight. Whereas the percentage of civil marriages was only 54.1 in the three largest cities – Istanbul, Ankara, and Izmir – this figure dropped to 29.8 in the villages. In both urban and rural areas, approximately half of the marriages were mixed civil-religious. Finally, whereas the percentage of religious marriages unregistered by civil authorities was 5.6 in the cities, it went up to 21.3 in the villages. According to another researcher, 15.4 per cent of all marriages in Turkey are celebrated without a civil ceremony at all (Alkan 1981: 80). Balaman (1985: 211) proves that there are a number of people who were married only by religious ceremony. Moreover, according to this author, in the researched population 'no marriages take place without a religious ceremony' (Balaman 1985: 211). Data from the 1990s show that the importance of the religious marriage in the eyes of the people still continues (see table 5.1).

**Table 5.1 Percentage of married population by type of marriage**

| | Total | % | Rural | Urban |
|---|---|---|---|---|
| Total | 25,678,892 | 100. 00 | 100. 00 | 100. 00 |
| Civil | 2,455,418 | 9. 56 | 5. 11 | 13. 59 |
| Religious | 1,256,980 | 4. 89 | 6. 89 | 3. 09 |
| Both | 21,806,832 | 84. 92 | 87. 38 | 82. 70 |
| None | 38,525 | 0. 15 | 0. 18 | 0. 13 |
| Unknown | 121,137 | 0. 47 | 0. 44 | 0. 50 |

*Source*: Adapted from SPO (1992: 42, table 31).

It is also clear from table 5.1 that Turkish people have learnt to combine the official and unofficial marriage. Even in the villages, the ratio of performing both marriages is 87.38 per cent. On the other hand, religious only marriages still occur in substantial numbers, in opposition to the directives of the official law.

Other evidence that proves that people have learnt to combine the rules of the secular and religious laws is the decreasing time interval between the religious and secular marriages (Yıldırak 1992: 22; see table 5.2 below). Again this mirrors the British experience.

**Table 5.2 Interval between religious and official marriages by age groups**

| | Age group | | |
|---|---|---|---|
| Time of official marriage | 15-29 | 30-44 | 45+ |
| At the same time as *nikah* | 73 | 75 | 62 |
| After *nikah* | 10 | 12 | 24 |
| After the first child | 8 | 8 | 5 |
| After two or more children | 2 | 4 | 2 |
| Ones without official marriage | 7 | 1 | 5 |
| No answer | - | - | 2 |
| Total | 100 | 100 | 100 |

*Source*: Adapted from Yıldırak (1992: 23, table 7).

The table shows that people have realized to a great extent that marrying religiously only has disadvantages, whilst having married secularly in addition to the religious marriage has substantial benefits, especially for the women concerned. Research conducted by Hacettepe University in 1988 and 1993 (HUNEE 1993) also confirms the above-mentioned official research:

**Table 5.3 Type of marriage by region (1988)**

| Region | Civil only | Religious only | Both |
|---|---|---|---|
| Western Anatolia | 13. 9 | 3.2 | 82.9 |
| South Anatolia | 6.8 | 11.4 | 81.5 |
| Central Anatolia | 9. 9 | 5.3 | 84.4 |
| Northern Anatolia | 6.3 | 8.5 | 85.2 |
| Eastern Anatolia | 11.3 | 20.8 | 65.7 |

*Source*: HUNEE (1993), cited in Kümbetoğlu (1997: 122).

It is worth noting that after five years, the ratio of performing both marriages has remarkably increased. In addition, the ratio of civil only marriages decreased which could be interpreted as a result of the Islamic revivalism in the country:

**Table 5.4 Type of marriage by region (1993)**

| Region | Civil only | Religious only | Both |
|---|---|---|---|
| Western Anatolia | 5.4 | 2.2 | 92.4 |
| South Anatolia | 2.0 | 7.6 | 90.0 |
| Central Anatolia | 1.9 | 6.4 | 91.7 |
| Northern Anatolia | 2.7 | 5.0 | 92.3 |
| Eastern Anatolia | 1.7 | 22.4 | 75.9 |

*Source*: HUNEE (1993), cited in Kümbetoğlu (1997: 122).

According to recent research conducted by the Directorate of Religious Affairs, 54.8 per cent of the university youth in Turkey want *nikah* in addition to official registration.[15]

People prefer *nikah*, according to Yıldırak (1992: 22), mainly for two reasons: First they need to sanctify their marriages to be happy and secondly, the formalities of official marriage seem difficult to handle. Compulsory medical inspection and a number of documents required make people hesitant about official marriage (see also Kruger 1991: 209; Abadan-Unat 1986: 172).[16] Early marriage is another reason for marriage by *nikah*. It is even argued that the difficulty of divorcing is the main reason for the popularity and widespread practice of *imam nikahı* (Fişek

[15] See *Hürriyet*, 23 February 1998, p. 12.

[16] Compulsory medical inspection prior to marriage has been imposed by the Public Health Act of 1930, number 1593, see Fişek (1985: 293).

1985: 295).

The state's desire for uniform legal standards is opposed to the religious and cultural diversities of the people. As a matter of fact, as the empirical research shows, social reality is not responding fully to the desires of the secular law. Even the state accepts this phenomenon. In a publication of the State Institute of Statistics, it is stated that in spite of the legal prohibition:

> ...it is assumed that religious marriages (not accompanied by official marriages) often take place, especially in the Eastern and Southeast parts of Anatolia. Therefore the number of marriages appears to be lower than they actually are, since religious marriages are not included in these statistics (SIS 1997a: ix).

In another scenario which exemplifies another kind of *nikah* arrangement, people marry religiously with a *nikah* and count this as an engagement (diametrically opposite of the British Muslim practice of the solemnization of the marriage), and if they agree in all aspects during engagement, they register their marriages and become a 'real' married couple.[17] The reason for this practice can be explained by reference to the modernization of Turkey. As indicated above, most marriages are still of an arranged marriage nature in the country. Generally speaking, there are two types of arranged marriages. The first is the more strict practice, usually more widespread in rural regions with however a receding trend, and is where all arrangements of choosing the bride and groom are handled and determined by the parents with their children given no vote of disagreement. In this case, the bride and the groom often see each other very briefly if they see each other at all and always in the presence of a third party. The second, more popular method is where the parents often select an appropriate candidate for their son, as it is still norm that the man proposes, and the prospective groom then meets with the prospective bride. In this case the first meeting is usually in another room from where all the parents are sitting, in again the presence of a third person. Upon some consideration and as an initial step the couple are often engaged, if they feel comfortable in doing so, in order to be able to have more contact and legitimize this in the eyes of the community. In this case however, the prospective couple are expected and allowed to find out more about each other to ascertain the likelihood of compatibility. However, doing so intrinsically means committing sin. In order therefore to legitimize this meeting in religion and solidify its place in the community, the parents more often insist that the two be religiously married. When the couple are religiously married then they can, in theory, engage in sexual intercourse without this strictly speaking counting as fornication in religion. However, in custom the couple are married for the purposes of being engaged, can only see and meet each other now more comfortably – often with the guardian younger brother lagging behind and checking the moves of his future-brother-in-law – and are expected to use this limited freedom to get to know each other more. This way, the couple are saved from committing sin by the legitimization of the *nikah*, the bride's often unblemished record is kept clean in the eyes of the

[17] *Kadın ve Aile*, July 1987, pp. 40-45; *Yeni Bizim Aile*, February 1994, p. 20.

community and the parents saved from the scruples of the 'what if' every time their children meet.[18]

In the course of the last decades, changes in marriage patterns and realization of the legal security of civil marriage have led to an increase in the number of civil marriages (Abadan-Unat 1982b: 17). This trend still steadily continues in the 1990s. Even in rural areas, people have started to register their marriages whilst still giving essential importance to the *nikah* (Kongar 1992: 432). According to Turkish Muslim law, Muslims will marry twice with several permutations to satisfy the competing demands of secular law and religious belief (Williams 1982: 163).

In summary, therefore, it can be concluded that there are five different patterns of solemnization of marriage in the Turkish context: Civil marriage, religious marriage, both civil and religious marriages at the same time, civil first without solemnization for a period and then the religious marriage, and finally religious first and after a while the civil marriage.

### *Age of Marriage*

In Ottoman times, there was no minimum age prescribed for marriage; it was up to the parents to decide until the child reached puberty. Later, the Ottoman Family Laws Ordinance (OFLO) of 1917 prescribed a minimum age of 9 for women and 10 for men. Then, in the Republican period, the age of marriage was taken over from Swiss law as being 18 years for males and 17 years for females. However, it proved to be unsuitable for Turkish conditions, which are based upon different biological and geographical facts and was reduced to 17 (15 with the permission of the judge) and 15 (14 with the permission of the judge) respectively in 1938 (Lipstein 1956: 17).[19] Now, with the Article 124 of the new Civil Code of 2001, marriage age for both parties is 17.

Permission is granted as a result of one of the following: Elopement and deflowerment, pregnancy, or living together as husband and wife. For such a permission to be granted, males should have completed their 16$^{th}$ year of age and females their 14$^{th}$. They should have physical and mental maturity and parental consent is required.[20] With the new civil Code the new limit is the completion of the 16$^{th}$ year of age for both parties.[21] The Court of Cassations has cancelled some decisions of judges if it did not see an exceptional point to allow marriage in the case[22]

This rule is obviously in conflict with traditional Muslim law. In the eyes of the people and Muslim law, when a girl or boy reaches puberty, he or she can marry

[18] *Kadın ve Aile*, July 1987, pp. 40-45; *Yeni Bizim Aile*, February 1994, p. 20; Kerimoğlu (1989b: 23-26); Vefa (1990: 197-208).

[19] Act No. 3453. 1938.

[20] Act No. 3453, 1938.

[21] Article 124 of Civil Code 2001.

[22] Y2HD 28. 04. 1986, E. 4269- K. 4463.

whatever his or her age is.[23] However, the official legal system never allows this.[24] A number of cases have come before the courts whilst many have not. Especially parents in rural areas or illiterate ones, although rare, tend to marry their offspring just after puberty which may be reached well before the age of 15. In these cases, families at first employ only Muslim law and solemnize marriages according to Muslim law rules. Married only by *nikah*, the spouses' cohabitation is absolutely legitimate for the community. After reaching the age of 15, they can register their marriages with the state.

In a reported case, the judge had allowed a girl who was 11 years old to marry but the Court of Cassation had cancelled that decision.[25] In another case, a boy under the age of 15 took permission from a judge to marry but the Court of Cassation held that the judgement was void.[26] Şahinkaya (1983: 26) mentions a girl married at 12. Another woman married at the age of 13, but the parents officially increased her age and she was married in both civil and religious ceremonies (Şahinkaya 1983: 30). In another case, the court gave permission to a girl aged 11 to marry and it was not appealed. However, the Courts of Cassation overruled that decision.[27]

Statistical data shows that people in many cases do not take into account the provisions of the Civil Code. According to earlier research conducted in 1972, the rate of under-age marriages for women was almost the same in urban and rural areas, 13 per cent and 14.5 per cent respectively. As far as males were concerned, the rate in three big cities was 8.1 per cent and in rural areas 23.3 per cent. About 10 years later, another research conducted in Diyarbakir's central villages showed that 10.87 per cent of the married women were married at the age of 13 (Şahinkaya 1983: 25).

In the late 1980 and earlier 1990s, the State Planning Organization conducted some research which is considered to be representative of the whole of Turkey (SPO 1992). This comprehensive research was done with 18,210 households from urban and rural communities.[28] The sampling data were then generalized to apply to all Turkey. According to this research, the percentage of under-age marriages (under age 16 years) in Turkey is about 9 per cent (SPO 1992: 39).

---

[23] According to a recent research, the parents may marry off their daughters when they are 11 and their sons when they are 14, Elmacı (1996: 105).

[24] Y2HD 07. 05. 1985, E. 4496- K. 4385.

[25] Y2HD 28. 12. 1987, E. 11288- K. 10889.

[26] Y2HD 24. 09. 1985, E. 8499- K. 7437. For other such cases see Y2HD 07. 05. 1985, E. 4496- K. 4385; Y2HD 28. 12. 1987 E. 11289- K. 10888.

[27] Y2HD 28. 12. 1987, E. 11288- K. 10889.

[28] Cities and regions included are: Istanbul, Izmir, Bursa, Sakarya, Denizli from Western Anatolia, Gaziantep, Adana, Antalya, Hatay from South Anatolia, Ankara, Eskişehir, Konya, Kütahya from Central Anatolia, Samsun, Zonguldak, Trabzon, Kastamonu from Blacksea, Malatya, Erzurum, Diyarbakır, Sivas, Van, Kars, Şanlıurfa, Adıyaman, Siirt, Ağrı from East and South East Anatolia, SPO (1992: 9).

**Table 5.5 Under-age marriages (of all subsisting marriages, 1992)**

| Marriage age | Total | % | Rural | Urban |
|---|---|---|---|---|
| -12 | 93,878 | 0. 37 | 0. 46 | 0. 28 |
| 13 | 231,733 | 0. 90 | 1. 07 | 0. 75 |
| 14 | 562,685 | 2. 19 | 2. 33 | 2. 07 |
| 15 | 1,382,296 | 5. 38 | 6. 26 | 4. 59 |
| Total | 2,270,592 | 8. 84 | 10. 12 | 7. 69 |

*Source*: Adapted from SPO (1992: 39, table 27).

In another recent research which is also representative of Turkey, Yıldırak (1992: 21) has found that the median marriage age of women is lower than the official figure.[29] Religious/illegal marriages are regarded as one of the causes of under-age marriages (is it conclusive that religious marriages cause under-age marriages or under-age marriages cause religious marriages. Which one comes first? People want to marry under-age and use religion to do so. Or religion allows for under-age marriage and this causes people to take advantage of this), since the couples below the age limit determined by the state law, 15 for a man and 14 for a woman, cannot marry legally (Fişek 1985: 293). Secondly, it is argued that in rural areas people firstly marry with *nikah* and then after two or three years of cohabitation and matrimonial life, they feel a need to register their marriages (Yıldırak 1992: 21). Sometimes, when their child reaches school age, they have to pay a certain amount of fine and register their marriages in order to get the compulsory identity card for their child (Yıldırak 1992: 21).

Even official statistics show the reality of under-age marriages. In a recent publication of the State Institute of Statistics (SIS), it is very clear that even in 1990, some 60 years after the transplantation of the Swiss Civil Code the ratio of marriages in the age group of 12-14 was 0.54 per cent for females and 0.88 per cent for males. Moreover, it must be emphasized that these figures are not reflective of the true proportion of experience since most of the time people are not eager to report such 'illegal' marriages to civil servants.

**Table 5.6 Ratio of ever-married population by age group (12-14) and census years**

| Gender | 1965 | 1970 | 1975 | 1980 | 1985 | 1990 |
|---|---|---|---|---|---|---|
| Female | 0. 98 | 1. 89 | 2. 02 | 1. 11 | 0. 96 | 0. 54 |
| Male | 0. 47 | 0. 80 | 2. 22 | 1. 02 | 0. 94 | 0. 88 |

*Source*: Adapted from SIS (1996: 20, table 9).

In his research, Yıldırak (1992: 21) found that when a girl and a boy inform the

[29] This research was conducted in 14 different cities of Turkey, which are from various geographical regions, Yıldırak (1992: 8).

*imam* about their consent to marry, it is sufficient for the *imam* to solemnize their marriage. Women marry despite being at the age of 10-11. In these cases, *imam* neglects or forgets to ask the bride her age (Yıldırak 1992: 22). Even in some western Anatolian villages and towns, there are many under-age brides. As reported in Daily Milliyet in 12 February 2001, in Acarlar Town of Aydın City, there were 100 girls between the ages 10-13 who were married by their parents in return for 5-6 thousand US dollars. As a precaution, Governor of the town, Kamil Köten, declared that all village weddings celebrated without prior permission from him would be illegal (Ata 2001).

Fieldwork has also shown that in some regions of Turkey, despite what the law asserts or prohibits, people marry off their daughters after the age of 11 and sons after the age of 14 (Elmacı 1994: 105). Turkish culture does not condone marriage before puberty. Thus, it is virtually non-existent. In some statistics, minimum marriage age in practice is taken as 10 years, since marriage below that age is only rarely possible in Turkey's conditions.

These data plainly show that in spite of all the efforts by the state, under-age marriages, although rare, are a part of socio-legal reality in Turkey. In some cases, people have even succeeded to register under-age marriages illegally.[30]

*Polygamy*

As concerns polygamy, there is an obvious conflict between traditional Muslim law where a man is widely assumed to be permitted to marry up to four wives at any one time and the official law of Turkey. When polygamy was abolished by the Civil Code in 1926, the religious custom justifying polygamy became officially null and void (Güriz 1996: 4). Thus, a marriage in which either party is already married to someone else will automatically be null and void according to the official law. The official law has no flexibility regarding polygamous marriages; that means a person cannot marry polygamously in Turkish law. If a person is a party to a subsisting marriage, he or she cannot validly contract a second or subsequent marriage. Articles 92, 113, 114, 115 of the Civil Code 1926 and Article 130 of the Civil Code 2001 provide that no person shall marry again unless he proves that the earlier marriage has been dissolved by death or by divorce or by a decree of nullity, and that a second marriage shall be declared invalid by the court on the ground that a person had a spouse living at the time of the subsequent marriage. In other words, the second marriage is absolutely void, or *void ab initio*.[31] Parties that knowingly contract such a marriage are seen to have committed a criminal offence under Article 237/5 of the Criminal Code, which states that 'if the man is already married he shall be punished by imprisonment for six months to three years. If the woman knowingly marries such a man she shall be given the same punishment'.[32] However, where a person marries in good faith with

[30] Y4CD 14. 03. 1990 E. 990. 916- K. 990. 1435.

[31] YHGK 26. 03. 1986, E. 2. 751- K. 287; Y2HD 27. 02. 1986, E. 1729- K. 2054; Y2HD 03. 06. 1990 194. 2546.

[32] Ansay et al (1965: 86).

another person who is already married and the former marriage is subsequently dissolved, the second marriage shall not be declared invalid.[33]

Having noted the above, polygamous marriages have not been totally eradicated in Turkey (Abadan-Unat 1986: 173; Kümbetoğlu 1997: 121). Turkish society is generally a monogamous society. Polygamous marriages are only exceptional. Although it varies from region to region, the ratio of polygamous marriages has been minimal in the history of Turkey. According to recent research, in contrast to legendary stories about the harems in the Ottoman state, in 1885, the proportion of polygamous marriages in Istanbul was only 2.51 per cent (Duben and Behar 1996: 161). In 1907, the figure was 2.16 (Duben and Behar 1996: 162). Moreover, most of the polygamous marriages have been bigamous (Duben and Behar 1996: 162). Now, although the Civil Code abolished polygamy, the polygamous local tradition, in the same proportion in which it existed in the past, is still rife (Coşar 1978: 127; Güriz 1996: 4; Kümbetoğlu 1997: 121).

Social acceptance of succeeding wives is gained by performing *imam nikahı* (Coşar 1978: 127). Numerous first marriages are also only religious but not registered (Coşar 1978: 127). Estimates of the proportion of polygamous marriage in rural areas during the present century ranges between 2 and 10 per cent. According to a study sponsored by the Turkish Ministry of Justice in 1942, almost all polygamous marriages involved two wives (Magnarella 1974: 126). A study based on a survey research found that approximately 2.0 per cent of all marriages in Turkey were polygamous in the early 1970s (Timur 1972: 93). Whereas the percentage of men with more than one wife was 1.6 per cent in the cities, the figure increased to 2.7 per cent in the villages (Timur 1972: 94). In the early 1980s, Şahinkaya (1983: 50), in Eastern Anatolia, found the rate of polygamy to be about 4.4 per cent. According to another research (Gökce 1991: 113 cited in Elmacı 1994: 84), the polygamy rate for the whole of Turkey is approximately 2 per cent.

A religious wedding utilizes polygamy in a particular way. Some polygamists reported that if they had to divorce their wives to remarry, they could not have married, since the issue of divorce is not conceived positively in the community (Elmacı 1994: 109). The two most common reasons given for these bigamous unions were the need for another female helper and the suspected sterility of the first wife. In Turkish society, the most important ground for legitimising divorce was the infertility of the wife. 97.3 per cent of women and 80.4 per cent of men agree that it is appropriate for a husband to have a second wife if he has no male offspring (Başaran 1990: 187). In cases of infertility the perceived problem is thus solved by the polygamous marriage of the husband to a widow or an unmarried woman (Elmacı 1994: 101-104). A third reason for polygamy, according to some research, was the institution of the levirate or widow inheritance by married kin of the deceased (Magnarella 1974: 126). In these cases, polygamy is regarded as a social duty or a pious obligation. However it must be emphasized that there are many polygamists who had neither such excuses nor reasons prior to their second marriages other than those of satisfying their whims and desires.

[33] Y2HD 25. 05. 1981 E. 2573- K. 4025; Y2HD 29. 12. 1981, E. 7888- K. 8649; Y2HD 25. 03. 1985 E. 2463- K. 2779; Y2HD 02. 06. 1981 E. 2838- K. 4288.

In the Turkish context, it can be contended that the practice of polygamy is customary more than religious.[34] The role of religion in this case is to legitimize the polygamous unions (see Elmacı 1994: 89-90). In that respect, in most cases, Islam is just manipulated and abused by the people (see Tosun 2001; Karlığa 2001). Kandiyoti (1997: 106) goes further to assert that the patriarchal system that transcends the borders of Islam paves the way for most practices in Muslim communities. Most of the time it is not the practising religious people who perform polygamy. Rather, people wish to live with another woman for several other reasons and they try to satisfy social pressures and their minds by employing Turkish Muslim law rules (see for a detailed research confirming this Elmacı 1994, Tosun 2001).

Several studies have shown that polygamy remains socially acceptable in certain situations (see for example Elmacı 1994). In public, the number of males who marry polygamously and defend that state of affairs has been steadily increasing (Kümbetoğlu 1997: 121, 127; Altuntek 1993; Elmacı 1994). However a crucial point should be stressed here: Polygamy, or more generally, survival of the local law is not a rural phenomenon although most writers tend to see it as such. Even in big cities and metropolitan areas, despite the smaller figures, dynamic Muslim legal pluralism is a reality. Sometimes it is easier to continue a polygamous life free from pressure of a *Gemeinschaft* in a crowded metropolitan city (see Elmacı 1994: 105; 108, Tosun 2001). A quick scan in Turkish newspapers would show that polygamous marriages are not only confined to the rural and eastern parts of Turkey (Kümbetoğlu 1997: 123). In that context, one can see in urban areas people who have polygamously married, too. For instance, there are some politicians, businessmen, singers, actors, members of parliament and even ministers of the cabinet who are known to be polygamists, despite the legal systems stance on the issue.[35] A former cabinet minister who was also chairman of a very popular football club, was noted to be freely talking about his second wife in an interview.[36] Earlier research found that polygamous marriages established after 1926 exist under the following two types: The first marriage was with a civil wedding and the *nikah*, while the second was with the religious wedding only due to the impossibility of a civil wedding since polygamy is illegal. In the second type, both marriages were solemnized only by a traditional and religious wedding. However, in contemporary Turkey, one observes more than two patterns of polygamy which is more complex and sophisticated than the findings of earlier

[34] Local law may or may not contain Islamic elements, Hooker (1975: 366); Stirling (1957: 26-27).

[35] For a recent case concerning a minister of the cabinet, as he then was, a member of the then ruling Welfare Party, which became a controversial issue between European and Turkish politicians with regard to human rights issues in Turkey, see *The Independent*, 17 April 1997, p. 14. For another case regarding another former minister of the cabinet who is also former chairman of a very popular football club, see *Hürriyet*, 7 November 1997, p. 27. In another recent case, the second wife of a polygamist businessman who had a *nikah* only claimed in court that after her husband's death she was given only 3 companies, while the first wife received 23. She claimed that that was injustice and she deserved much more applying for the annulment of the contract left by the husband regarding inheritance. Reported in *Hürriyet*, 20 March 1998, p. 43.

[36] *Hürriyet*, 7 November 1997, 27.

researchers. According to Turkish Muslim law rules, there are at least four patterns of polygamy. However that figure can easily increase depending on the number of the wives concerned. In the first pattern, the man marries two or more wives with only a *nikah* and no registration. In the second pattern, only one of the women is a wife by civil ceremony. If, for instance, the first marriage was civil, the second will be religious as polygamy is illegal according to the code (Elmacı 1994: 108).

Significantly, the first wife then becomes the legal mother of the children born to the second wife. Birth certificates and identification documents are arranged accordingly (Balaman 1985: 211; Elmacı 1994: 109). Yet it is quite possible that a second, third or fourth wife could be the official wife if the husband did not prefer to register the earlier marriage. In this third pattern, the husband takes his first wife without official marriage, then he marries the second one both officially and unofficially. In the fourth pattern, the husband divorces his wife officially but does not pronounce *talaq* so that she is still his wife in religion. He marries another woman both officially and unofficially (with '*imam nikahı*') (Beşer 1993: 162). Thus, it is made sure that the children of the first wife and the second wife are legitimate in the eyes of both Muslim law and the official legal system. These scenarios can be adapted to the cases of the possible third or fourth wives with different permutations.

Whilst one can argue by looking at the empirical reality that legal reform from above has not had an absolute impact on the institution of polygamous marriages, it is also worth emphasising that although the official prohibition of polygamy has not worked effectively, it has created a social sense to a certain extent that polygamy is no longer acceptable, but this is a change in social psychology, a field in which legislation is at best of dubious value (see already earlier Hooker 1975: 366).

Prohibition of polygamy was a radical step in Turkish history. Yet, this was not a great revolution or a big change, since the society was anyway more or less monogamous. Polygamous marriages were already minimal. This minimal ratio has continued to exist in spite of all legal actions against it. One can say that the state did not wish to be tough, probably espousing the saying that 'as you make your bed, so you lie on it', at the expense of women, as is always the case. Thus, many Muslim scholars have been advocating the view that when there is not a state recognition, Muslims should stay away from polygamy (see for instance Tosun 2001).

### *Divorce*

The divorce rate in Turkey has been relatively low.[37] Thus, the case of *talaq* is not a big issue in terms of numbers. People in Turkey generally react negatively to the idea of divorce. It is conceived as an unpleasant experience and it may be

[37] The most detailed research on divorce in Turkey is Zwahlen's (1981) study which surveys the issue from ancient Turks to modern Turkish society. Another detailed study on Turkish law is Williams (1982).

condemned by families and friends (Levine 1983: 339).[38]

Even though in Muslim law divorce can be obtained in a number of extra-judicial ways like *talaq*, in secular Turkish law there is solely one way of divorce, which is through a decree granted by a court of civil jurisdiction on the ground that the marriage has irretrievably broken down. In an earlier case, the Court of Cassation did not recognize the *talaq*, stating that there is only one type of dissolution of the marriage under the Civil Code.[39] Muslim law's prohibition on the marriage after three *talaq*s between the couple was refused on the ground that there is no such rule in the Civil Code.[40]

Marriage may be terminated by the death of one of the spouses or by the declaration of a judge (Ansay 1996: 116). In other words, the Civil Code restricts the incidence of divorce, for, although the right to divorce is accorded to both men and women, divorces can be obtained only through a court decision based on specific and proven circumstances. The judge can either declare the marriage void, if the conditions for a valid marriage do not exist; or grant an annulment; or decide to grant a divorce or separation. The Civil Code 1926 had made divorce by collusion or mutual consent difficult for many years.[41] Now, Article 166 of the new Civil Code 2001 makes a divorce by mutual consent possible.

On the other hand, since marriages are religious, divorces are also made by *talaq* to terminate the religious marriage, the *nikah* (Altuntek 1993: 77). Although statistical records 'do not include the number of dissolved informal marriages' (Abadan-Unat 1986: 177), husbands still divorce their wives with *talaq* and devout Muslim wives have to agree to the official divorce. However, this type of easy divorce is not an easy option in Turkish society where most marriages are still arranged and therefore what in theory appears to be an easy divorce mechanism is in fact more difficult than effectuating an official divorce (Balaman 1985: 214). Effectivity and intensity of the relationships between families make it almost impossible for an individual to reach a decision to divorce so that individual whims and desires cannot easily be put into effect (Balaman 1985: 215). Yet it is evident that with the waning of the institution of the arranged marriages, *talaq*s could become easier in practice as they are in theory. In the cases of 'hidden marriage', for example, *talaq* is always used. Also in urban areas, due to the declining intensity of social pressures and rising individualism, divorce would inevitably become an easier option.

In the final analysis, empirical data and the case law prove that Turkish people have reconstructed their religious law in spite of all the claims of the secular legal system, particularly in the cases of marriage and divorce, manifestly showing that law has its limits. By developing a new Turkish Muslim law, today's Turks, as skilful legal navigators, have met the demands of both the secular Turkish legal system and the Muslim law in a dynamic legal pluralist context.

---

[38] As will be analysed below. limping marriages are a matter of concern in Turkey as in the British case, Beşer (1997: 302); Kerimoğlu (1989b: 23-26).

[39] Now, Articles 161-173 of Civil Code 2001.

[40] YHGK 08. 06. 1968 E. 1966. 2-1487- K. 425 T.

[41] Article 150 of the Civil Code 1926.

## Unofficial Muslim Legal Postulates in Turkey

The socio-legal reality in Turkey has been noted not only by the general public and scholarship but also by the state officials as well. Yet this does not mean that the state has recognized this reality. On the other hand, it has not been very harsh on the so-called law-breakers, thanks to the Muslim legal postulates.

One can detect Muslim legal postulates regarding marriage issues from the survey research on public opinion regarding relevant phenomena, acts of officials, and responses of legislation to the socio-legal reality and decisions of the judges in the lower courts.

### *Public Opinion*

It is common to come across news in the media about a celebrity who has recently got married by only having a *nikah* with no accompanying negative comment despite the fact that the marriage is religious, unofficial and illegal.[42] As seen above, although many children are perceived as illegitimate by the legal system if they are the offspring of a couple unofficially married, they are not illegitimate in the eyes of the community as the religious ceremony is still regarded as valid in itself. The legalization of the sole *nikah* as a valid form of marriage was an election promise of the Welfare Party.[43] In the columns of the scholars who answer questions of people regarding religion and society, these issues are discussed freely as if these are not 'illegal' in law.[44]

Regarding polygamy, several studies have shown that it remains socially acceptable in certain situations (see for example Elmacı 1996). Social acceptance of succeeding wives is gained by performing only '*imam nikahı*' (Coşar 1978: 127). Successful polygamy can even be a source of prestige (Stirling 1965: 197; see also on this, Altuntek 1993; Elmacı 1996).[45] As noted above, it is possible to come across people in urban areas who have also married polygamously.

### *Officials*

State officials, most of the time, being aware of the socio-legal reality that Muslim legal pluralism is operating in the country, organize special ceremonies where many unofficially married couples get married with the help of the state. They try to encourage the unofficially married people to get married officially. To that effect, in some parts of Turkey, the state organizes big official marriage ceremonies where many unofficially married couples get married with the help of

[42] See for an example, *Milliyet*, 6 March 1998, p.3.

[43] *Yeni Yuzyil*, 7 December 1996, 8.

[44] It is so common that one can find many examples for this, see for instance, *Zaman*, 11 April 1998, 11.

[45] See for an example, *Milliyet*, 6 March 1998, p.3.

the state.[46] No mention is made at these ceremonies of the Criminal Code or any kind of punishment. In such a recent case, the Secretary of State Responsible for Women and Family started a new campaign: '*Resmi nikahsız aile kalmasın*' (Let there be no family remaining without an official marriage). In the first event of that legal literacy campaign, the Minister and the Director of Religious Affairs bore witness in a state-sponsored official marriage ceremony of 12,000 couples who were married with *imam nikahı* but not with official marriage.[47] A quick scan at the press shows that this practice still continues. For instance, daily *Milliyet* of 19 November 2001 reports that governor, military officers and some students bore witness to the official marriage of 130 already married (unofficially) couples.[48]

*Amnesty Laws*

The state law needed to come to terms with the socio-legal reality and provided for ad hoc legislation (see Lipstein 1956: 19). As early as 1957, socio-legal scholars noted that 'for even at the present time, when the Civil Code has been in existence only 30 years, it has changed its form and content owing to certain extraneous conditions' (Fındıkoğlu 1957: 13).

As seen, although illegal, there are still some marriages performed by the *imams* without the prior celebration. This state of marital affairs has given rise to the long-standing problems of couples who are not legally married, but regard themselves, and are regarded in their social sphere, as married, and their children who are illegitimate under the Civil Code (Fişek 1985: 289). These officially 'illegitimate' children face many problems during their lives (Kümbetoğlu 1997: 121).

The response to the great increase in illegitimacy as defined in the law has been the passing of a series of enactments to make legitimization an extremely simple procedure (Hooker 1975: 367; Fişek 1985: 290; Ansay 1996: 119).[49] Thus, 'amnesty laws are almost periodically enacted which allow the registration of "consensual marriages", if a child has been born out of such a relation and if no marriage impediment between the parties exists' (Ansay 1996: 113). The most recent of these laws is dated 8 May 1991 and was valid for five years (Ansay 1996: 113).[50] New draft law legislation on this matter is at the legislative stage at the Grand National Assembly.[51]

Whilst the primary concern in Western societies has been to improve the legal status of the illegitimate child, in Turkey, the legislator has provided for the legitimization not only of the child, but of the extra-marital union from which the

[46] See for a recent case, *Hürriyet*, 9 March 1997.

[47] *Hürriyet*, 14 November 1997, p. 11.

[48] *Milliyet*, 19 November 2000, p. 21.

[49] Between 1933 and 1965, benefiting from five such bills, 2,739,379 unions were registered as marriages and 10,006,452 illegitimate children were legitimized, Fişek 1985: 292.

[50] Law no. 3716, promulgated on 16 May 1991. Previous laws nos. 2330, 4727, 5524, 6652, 1826, and 2526.

[51] *Hürrıyet*, 04 February 2003.

child has been born (Fişek 1985: 291).[52]

According to the Turkish Amnesty laws, the children could be registered as legitimate if they were born to parents who had been living together continuously as husband and wife. The Constitutional Court also espoused the same view.[53] Based on this decision of the Constitutional Court, the Court of Cassation has also followed this reasoning.[54]

Children who were born out of an occasional relation may, however, not be registered as legitimate under such laws (Ansay 1996: 120). This is an extraordinary development since the official law, although covertly, accepts the reality of *imam nikahı* which on its own terms has no official standing.

*Decisions of the Judges*

As seen above, the public medium does not generally see the existence of unofficial law as a breach of law. Many people in society in one way or another are related to people who are unofficially married. It would be naive to expect that many cases will come before the courts on this matter alone. Only in conflict situations, one of the parties discloses such a thing to the courts. Despite all the legal measurements, the authorities will not know of the standing of the marriage unless a dispute arises. Thus, the majority of the perpetrators of these alleged 'crimes' remain unpunished (Özgen 1985: 315). Kruger (1991: 209) confirms Özgen on this point by stating that there is almost no punishment for *imams* who celebrate such marriages unofficially (Kruger 1991: 209). Or, as in many cases, as will be seen below, judges would be tolerant with the convicted and would change the punishment from imprisonment to a pecuniary punishment which shows the perpetuating impact of the legal postulates.[55]

Thus, a number of cases have come before the courts whilst many have not. In some cases, one can easily detect that judges have taken into account the public opinion and local legal postulates on the matter and have as a result been tolerant.

The judges in the lower courts have tolerated a number of under-age marriages yet the Court of Cassation has cancelled these decisions if it did not see an exceptional reason to justify such an approach in the case.[56] In one case, the court gave permission to a girl aged 11 to marry and it was not appealed. However, the Courts of Cassation overruled that decision.[57]

In another case, a boy under the age of 15 took permission from a judge to marry but the Court of Cassations held that the judgement was void.[58] Only a few

---

[52] This does not apply to polygamous marriages. It is only for unmarried persons.
[53] 21.5.1981, No. 29.22.
[54] Y2HD 1.3.1983, S 1627.18-25.
[55] Y2HD 06.06.1983 E. 983.2664- K. 983.3310; Y2HD 04.06.1985 E. 985.5223- K. 985.5310; Y4CD 28.04.1992 E. 992.2504- K. 992.3125.
[56] See for such an example, Y2HD 28.4.1986, E. 4269- K.4463.
[57] Y2HD 28.12.1987, E.11288- K.10889.
[58] Y2HD 24.9.1985, E. 8499- K.7437. For a similar case, see Y2HD 7.5.1985, E.4496- K. 4385.

examples of such cases have been noted here that were overruled by the Court of Cassations as these are the only reported cases. The highest court, the Court of Cassations, strictly applies the letter of the law. Presumably, there are a number of unreported similar cases that have never come to the Court of Cassations and have therefore not been overruled.

The tolerant approach of the judges is also the case with *nikah*- only marriages and polygamy. The judges in Turkey have, thus, been accused by some extreme-leftist writers as being tolerant to 'fundamentalist' tendencies and attitudes (see for example Öztemiz 1997: 125).

In some cases, courts treat the second wife with some recognition despite the fact that she was only married unofficially. In one recent case, the judge held that second wife should be paid some compensation from the insurance company because of the death of her unofficial husband at work.[59]

Here again, the legal postulates are in operation. Although unofficial (and illegal), the *nikah* and polygamy were taken into consideration by the judges, since the legal postulates of the society include these practices. These decisions in the lower courts prove that the legal postulates of the society influence the decision and thinking of the judges, making them sympathetic to the demands of local unofficial laws. Since the legal postulates, in this case interwoven classical and local Muslim laws and morality, permit and condone an unofficial marriage, a judge may not consider it as a serious criminal offence or intrusion of the rights of the minor, although a western judge would treat the case differently.

Thus, it might be said that, in the Turkish context, due to the legal postulates, judges are tolerant, understanding, patient and sympathetic toward the local people in the matter of unofficial and under-age marriages and polygamy (Starr 1992: 169). This phenomenon has paramount importance since, '(t)he success of any reform is dependant upon two main factors: the attitude of the public toward it; and the interpretation given to it by judges' (Shaham 1995: 259).

The attempt to change the legal rules concerning family matters is one of the most daring experiments for the modernizing elite in Muslim societies. However, such an attempt was perceived as necessary in the Republic of Turkey in the 1920s after the collapse of the Ottoman State as the family plays an important role in transmitting dominant cultural values to younger generations and the aim of the new modern Turkish nation-state was the cultural modernization of the society.

Although the Turkish state tried to abolish Muslim law by transplanting new secular and uniform laws, the result has been that Turkish Muslims have not abandoned their local Muslim family laws. The plural socio-legal reality of Turkey stems from the tensions between secular, Islamic and customary rules that cohabit in the practical daily lives of the Muslim citizens. This is nothing but a '*sujet de droits*' situation. Yet not surprisingly in the issues of marriage and divorce, evidence suggests that some Muslim people in Turkey have found ways to reconcile the demands of both the secular official law and unofficial Muslim law, and it manifestly indicates the creative capacity of Muslim individuals as skilful legal navigators in daily affairs. This experience provides instructive lessons

[59] Y21HD 21.03.1996, E. 1604- K. 1661.

showing the possibilities and limitations of attempting to reconstruct society by restructuring its law.

The socio-legal reality of Muslim legal pluralism stemming from resistance of local Muslim law has, for many years, been seen as a rural phenomenon in Turkey. However, it is becoming clear that Muslim legal pluralism, especially in family matters, is a reality of urban areas too. The state and the élite expected that by means of education, members of society would learn the rules of the official legal system, and they believed that with the increase of urbanization, which is considered to be the same as modernization and 'development', people would give up their local customs and religious laws and would follow only the official law. However, the Turkish empirical data have not confirmed this expectation. Rather, Turkish people have reconstructed their unofficial religious laws in spite of all the claims of the secular legal system, particularly in the issues of marriage, manifestly showing that state law has limits to shape the society. By developing this new Turkish Muslim law, as skilful legal navigators and law-inventing citizens, which is a result of the interaction of official and unofficial laws, these Turks have met the demands of both the secular Turkish legal system and the unofficial Muslim law in a dynamic legal pluralist context. This is an excellent, culture-specific illustration not only of Ehrlich's 'living law', but of Chiba's intricate theory of the continuous interaction of official and unofficial laws (Menski 2000: 308). It also proves our formulation of dynamic legal pluralism in which hybrid laws are continuously created as a result of the interaction.

Since Turkish Muslims have reconciled these conflicting points by employing Turkish Muslim law rules, only a few cases have appeared before the courts. Even though this book only deals with family law issues, it is also observable in the Turkish society that in other fields such as finance, banking, economy, insurance, and in all sorts of spheres of life, Muslim law is referred to and obeyed by many people despite the non-recognition of the state.[60]

A post-modern legality is visible in Turkey where the traditional Muslim law was totally but only officially abolished and replaced by transplanted secular laws. Local and unofficial Turkish Muslim laws have resisted the unification and assimilation purposes of the modern nation-state. People have not abandoned their

---

[60] Contemporary and frequently asked issues in Turkey: working in Europe, *madhhabs*, using amplifier when reading *azan*, Friday prayer and work, *dar al-Islam*, fasting and travelling by train, stock exchange, tax, *halal* meat, marrying non-Muslim woman, *talaq*, court divorce, polygamy, nationalism, unemployment benefit, inflation, interest, customs tax, bribery, depositing money at a bank in non-Muslim countries, selling alcohol in a non-Muslim country, gambling in *dar al-harb*, sterilization, plastic surgery, using perfumes, abortion, *ijtihad*, military service, and so on, see TDV (1999). Beşer (1991), organ transplantation, prayers (*salat*) on bus, VAT, mortgage, European union, gold tooth, alcohol in medication, eau de cologne, life insurance, Kurucan (1998), interest, inflation, insurance, life insurance, feminism, *nikah*, and fertility clinics. *Fatwa* books are bestsellers in Turkey. Moreover, many newspapers have *fatwa* columns. Recently, the number of Turkish *fatwa*s sites on the internet has increased. Also, through various popular newsgroups and e-mail discussion lists, Turkish Muslims solicit information about what 'Islam' says about any particular problem.

local and religious laws and customs whether legal modernity recognizes them or not. There have been limits to official laws to shape society from above and resistance to official laws stemming from the challenge of heterogeneity of society and post-modern legal pluralism. Now, secular official and Muslim unofficial laws co-exist in the Turkish socio-legal sphere.

Turkish Muslims not only have challenged the presumptions of legal modernity but have also shown that 'they can become citizens while at the same time retaining their Muslim identity' (King 1995: 112). They retain their Muslim law in even secular and modern contexts in a post-modern way without violating the democratic order although a purportedly uniform legal system wishes to transform society through law, aiming for homogenization with a mentality of the nineteenth century militant positivism. Yet it is now post-modern times and legal pluralism is here to stay where cultural plurality exists. In the final analysis, Turkey continues to be a Muslim country, no matter what changes may have taken place in Turkey's Islam. Islam is pervasive in Turkish public sphere and this shows the partial failure of the Kemalist elite's attempts of making religion a private belief.

As prominent Turkish sociologist Nilufer Göle aptly puts it, Muslim identity is in a process of normalization, transforming from being Islamist to Muslim,[61] showing that 'buzzwords such as "fundamentalism", and catchy phrases such as Samuel Huntington's rhyming "West versus Rest" and Daniel Lerner's alliterative "Mecca or mechanization" are of little use in understanding this reformation' (Eickelman 1998:, 82). Factors such as a desire to join the EU, civil society's growth, independent media, telecommunications technology, globalization, foreign encouragement and support, and the role of religious leaders, are all dynamically interlinked and intertwined in transforming the Turkish society.

[61] Nilufer Göle, *Zaman*, 4 June 2000.

# Chapter 6

# Muslim Legal Pluralism in Pakistan

Pakistan provides many examples of interaction of religious and local customary traditions and extremely instructive debates about the role of the modern state vis-à-vis the scope and problems of Islamic legal reform. Islam is the foundation of state legitimacy in Pakistan and the state law is used as an instrument by the state to serve the purposes of Islamic modern nation-state ideology. Modern Pakistani law, despite its constitutional commitment to observe the injunctions of Islam, operates on the basis that the state law is the only legal authority. In other words, it follows the Western model of political ideology which is characterized by the paradigm of legal modernity in the normative realm but tries to match this model with Islamic concepts.

This chapter analyzes the results of the attempts of the Pakistani state's reform of elements of Muslim family law, and the failure of those attempts because of stiff opposition. That opposition is reinforced by local understandings and practices. I argue that this is a clear example of the limitations of the state's power to shape society through legislation from above. The state's effort to 'engineer' a modernization of Muslim family law has met with intense opposition not only from some of the *ulama* but also from the Muslim public.[1] Some segments of society simply refused to adhere to the law as reformed by the state. Case law and research suggest that, 'civil disobedience' is particularly marked in relation to issues of marriage, polygamy and divorce.

Following a brief account of Pakistani law, attempts at reform, the background of the 'civil disobedience' and the failure in particular of the reforms related to marriage, polygamy and divorce, I will examine and try to show that the socio-legal sphere in Pakistan is fragmented resulting from clashes between the official law and civil disobedience.

---

[1] The role of the *ulama* and *madrasah*s in shaping and mobilizing public opinion in Pakistan is a factor that must be taken into account, given that the influence of the state bureaucracy and schools is particularly limited because of a lack of resources and poverty. *Ulama* have a monopoly over *madrasah*s without sharing it with the state. The proliferation of *madrasah*s paves the way for the increasing role of *ulama* and traditional understandings. While in 1947 there were only 147 *madrasah*s in the country, today the figure is around 8000. On the role of *ulama* and *madrasah*s, see in detail Nasr (2000). It goes without saying that when the degree of *ulama*'s influence increases, the state's influence would decrease.

## The Personal Law System, Reform and Expected Uniformity in Muslim Laws

During the Raj, the British approached the Muslim law from their own frame of reference and evolved a somewhat hybrid Anglo-Muhammadan law, which nevertheless left the Muslims' family law virtually untouched. In this respect, the British rulers were following earlier practice. The situation changed in the South Asian context only with the emergence of the modern nation-state of Pakistan, which sought greater control over societal processes through codified statute law. Early 20th century reforms of family law in the Ottoman State opened the gates of legislative activity and had a significant impact elsewhere in the Islamic world, including Pakistan.

As in the Ottoman reform of 1917, in Pakistan, the local forms of Islamic family law were reformed through modern legislative process, either by adopting provisions of different schools of Muslim law itself or by subjecting some of the institutions of Islamic law to certain regulatory measures (see in detail Pearl 1979: 197). The locally prevalent forms of Islamic family law have been reformed through the modern legislative process, either by adopting provisions of the various other schools of Islamic law itself, or by subjecting some of its institutions to certain regulatory measures. Early reforms of family law in the Ottoman state opened the gates of legislative activity, which has had crucial impacts in Pakistan as well as in the world.

However, simmering tensions regarding many legal issues between supporters of tradition and supporters of modernity continue (Donohue and Esposito 1982: 200). As Pearl (1987: 244) observes: 'there are those who believe that the reforms in the family laws... have undermined the basic values of the Muslim way of life'. In their view, the reforms militate against the basic tenets of Islam (see Tanzilur-Rahman 1997). The tension has emerged in a conflict between official and unofficial laws in the daily lives of Muslims.

Modern Pakistani law, despite the constitutional commitment to observe the injunctions of Islam, operates 'on the basis that the modern state law is the dominant legal authority' (Menski 1997: 20). In other words, it follows the legal modernity paradigm except that it seeks to adapt this paradigm to Islamic concepts. Perhaps unsurprisingly, the attempts of the Pakistani state to introduce a number of important reforms have been perceived as anti-Islamic by some Muslim scholars and some people.

The Muslim Family Laws Ordinance (MFLO) 1961, is a particular focus in this controversy. The official law is widely perceived as being different from immutable religious law and not accepted as the just law. Muslims have felt themselves 'repelled by the state legal system which co-opted but did not truly include them' (Kozlowski 1998: 87). This led to 'civil disobedience' that rendered the official law ineffective: there is an observable gap between state law and popular practice.

After the emergence of modern nation-states, Muslims have tried to define 'Islam' as the ideology of the state. In the Pakistani context, the religious Islamic ideology forms an important part of the general social, political and legal superstructure (Haque 1983: 368). The rulers of Pakistan have desperately wanted to develop a dominant ideology to provide legitimacy and justification for the creation and existence of Pakistan and to hold together the various ethnic groups. Thus, Islam has become the foundation of state legitimacy in the country. Still in that context, law is used as an instrument by the state to serve the purposes of an Islamic modern nation-state ideology (Mehdi 1994: 16).

For centuries, the family law of Muslims had been the only legal topic left untouched by rulers (Coulson 1964: 161). In the history of South Asia, villages have maintained a degree of autonomy. Justice was nominally administered by the kings, but judicial administration was not centralized, and was in practice conducted by village tribunals known as panchayats, which applied local laws. Later, while the Muslim administration of justice was centralized, the local structures persisted and remained autonomous. Even though political centralization has been established under British rule and later in independent India and Pakistan, the local legal structures remained strong (Mehdi 1994: 4).

Under colonial domination, the *Shari'a* was reformulated according to European terms. It remained a 'Muslim' personal law, restricted in scope and confined to matters of family law. Interference by the British with the Muslim law of the subcontinent started in 1772. They approached South Asian laws from their own framework of reference and drew a distinction between the public and private spheres, and between the religious and the secular. The Warren Hastings Scheme of 1772 differentiated the general law and the personal laws of Muslims and Hindus, who continued to be governed by their respective personal laws. Although no neat distinction can really be made, this basic division is still applied in South Asian countries, including Pakistan. The British then embarked on a programme to codify major areas of the general law. This was realized from 1860 onwards, once British sovereignty had been firmly established in 1858. Despite their guarantee of 1772, that the Muslim and Hindu laws would be in accordance with their own indigenous rules, the British soon began to create laws in order to overcome certain social problems among the people.[2] Muslim law in the Indian subcontinent was restricted to the domain of family law, and those laws have remained almost completely uncodified (Esposito 1982b: 77; Amin 1996: 135; Kozlowski 1998: 72).

By following British practice, the courts started to operate on a case-law system which was a direct departure from Islamic jurisprudential theory and practice. As a result of these changes and the adoption of English juristic methods, 'Anglo-Muhammadan law' emerged, which was a legal practice very much influenced by the British (Esposito 1982b: 76).

In 1929, the Child Marriage Restraint Act was promulgated (Balchin 1994: 32). The Act set up minimum marital ages for both males and females which were different from the traditional interpretations of Muslim law, where puberty is taken as the main criterion. After a decade, the Dissolution of Muslim Marriages Act, 1939 came into existence, which aimed to grant women some judicial relief through establishing additional grounds for divorce, most of which were not recognized by the Muslim law of the country (Balchin 1994: 32; Esposito 1982b:

[2] Mainly this happened in Hindu law, see Sati Regulation, 1829.

76).[3]

These very mixed systems of law were inherited by all three major South Asian countries. Many of these laws are still in force today. Following the independence of Pakistan, Anglo-Muhammadan law became the official state law of Pakistan. However, the simmering tensions between the forces of tradition and modernity continue to contribute to lingering debates on many legal issues (see Mehdi 1994: 9).

In matters relating to marriage, divorce, dower, inheritance, succession, and family relationships, the system of personal law is applied in Pakistan. Thus, Muslim, Christian, Hindu, Sikh, Buddhist and Parsi family laws can be applied in the country (see in detail Anwari 1988).[4] Muslim personal law is applied by courts, in accordance with the sect to which an individual Muslim belongs. The Muslims of Pakistan are divided mainly into two sects, namely the *Sunni*s and the *Shia*s (Mahmood 1993: 13). Majority of Pakistani Muslims are *Hanafi Sunni*s. The *Shia*s are divided into many groups; *Ithna Ashari*, and *Ismaili* are the two main schools of *Shia* Muslim law in the country. There is an initial presumption that a Muslim is governed by *Hanafi* Muslim law, unless the contrary is proven by good evidence (Mahmood 1993: 13). As for non-Muslims who profess to be bound by the same law as Muslims, the option of following *Hanafi* law is also possible provided it is *bona fide* (Mahmood 1993: 13).

Legal reforms to the personal laws in South Asia have always focused on the laws of the majority, while minority laws have been almost totally ignored, although for different reasons.[5] For instance, unlimited polygamy under Hindu law in Pakistan is still allowed, although it is forbidden in India.[6] Conversely, Indian Muslims may marry up to four wives in accordance with Muslim law, while the Pakistani law, in section 6 of MFLO 1961, made attempts to provide some legal controls. Although in the case of Pakistan the state has been trying to reform the Muslim family law of the majority, it will be seen below that this has not been successful. The modern nation state of Pakistan has tried to achieve greater state control over societal processes by using statute law, prominently the Muslim Family Laws Ordinance, 1961. These attempts to Islamize the law threw up the problem of the internal diversity of conceptualizations about Islam, showing that 'Pakistan could not claim to be uniform in its understanding of *Shari'a*' (Menski 1997c: 22). The religious groupings themselves are divided by sectarian differences (Pearl 1990: 328). Regarding this issue, a crucial debate between traditionalists and modernists has been continuing in the country (Donohue and

---

[3] *Hanafi* law is followed by most Muslims in the Indian subcontinent. Moreover, it is more or less the official version of Muslim law in Pakistan. In *Hanafi* law, the right of women to seek divorce was restricted by juristic interpretation.

[4] The personal law system in the country is a natural continuation of South Asian personal laws. akin to the *millet* system which has been applied in Muslim countries for centuries.

[5] Approximately 97 per cent of the population of Pakistan are Muslims. Most of them (over 80 per cent) are *Sunni*, Ahmed (1982: 274).

[6] In the same vein, Muslim polygamy is not restricted in India by statute, whereas the state has tried to restrict and control it in Pakistan.

Esposito 1982: 200). As Pearl (1987b: 244) underlines, 'there are those who believe that the reforms in the family laws... have undermined the basic values of the Muslim way of life'. According to them, these reforms militate against the basic tenets of Islam. Consequently, this has led to a conflict between official and unofficial laws in the daily lives of Muslims.

In the first fourteen years of Pakistan's history, no reforms had been made regarding Muslim family law. In May 1954, the Punjab Legislative Assembly presented a Marriage Reform Bill. In August 1955, the government set up a Marriage and Family Law Commission (Esposito 1982b: 83; see also Balchin 1994: 33-34). In June 1956, the Commission submitted its report. Maulana Ihteshamul Haq, one of the members of the commission, submitted a long dissenting note which represents a traditional viewpoint on family law issues. In the main report of the commission, it was accepted that family laws as presently applied were the result of misinterpretations of Islam, that the resultant laws were un-Islamic, and that the existing judicial machinery was slow and dilatory (Patel 1979: 90). As the reports have shown, there are two main perspectives regarding family law: that of traditionalists and modernists (see in detail Tanzilur-Rahman 1997: 3-7).[7] Indeed, the publication of the report brought in its wake serious political controversies between these two spectrums. As a result, the report was shelved. After five years, the MFLO 1961 was promulgated. In 1962 the West Pakistan Muslim Personal Law (*Shariat*) Application Act was enacted, inter alia, to extend the MFLO 1961 to the whole of West Pakistan except the tribal areas. The Act of 1962 was significant in its attempt to bring greater uniformity in the application of the Muslim personal law.

These acts reflect a desire to change from extra-judicial patterns to more state control. However, they were half-hearted attempts and did not constitute full legal reforms (Patel 1979: 11; 1991: 99). Though the MFLO purported to be based on the recommendations of the Commission on Marriage and Family Laws, 'the force of the traditionalists' opposition is reflected in certain omissions and also in the relatively mild punishments for offenders' (Esposito 1980b: 224-225; see also Carroll 1982: 60).

The MFLO did not abolish the statute law concerning family affairs in force before 1961, which had been made as early as 1929 and 1939. The Ordinance had the effect that the old case law system of legally binding precedents continued even after the Islamization of the law in the seventies (Mehdi 1994: 158).

However, the official law is sometimes perceived as being different from religious immutable law and is not accepted as the just law. Some traditionalist Muslims felt that the state legal system co-opted but did not truly include them (Kozlowski 1998: 87). This in turn led to an ineffectiveness of the official law and a gap between state law and popular practices. Patterns of diversified and plural practices persisted and remained active (Mehdi 1994: 8). In the course of the past few decades, there has been a trend towards the 'Islamization' of law and increasing the Islamic content of substantive law in Pakistan. However, in the final analysis, one can say that Islamization of law in Pakistan has neither destroyed

[7] Also see in detail Firdous (1990).

Anglo-Muhammadan law nor local folk laws. It has only increased the inconsistency and instability of the system, leading to fragmentation of the legal sphere.

## Major Differences between Unofficial Muslim Laws and the Official Law

Although Islam is the religion of adherence for the majority of the population and is the state religion of Pakistan, Muslim law alone does not determine the public or private obligations of Muslims. In Pakistan, with the quest for modernity, by embodying Islamic precepts in Code form, and providing for their administration in courts, the authority of law has been transferred from the religious ethic to the state. Although Islamic private law is a part of the state system of law, its implementation and some substantive provisions bearing directly on Islamic jurisprudence are secular in origin. Even Islamization is a 'positivist, state-driven phenomenon, another method of social engineering through law' (Menski 2000: 310).

The new laws of the state that pertain to Muslim personal law are crucially different from the traditional normative understanding of Muslim law and local practices. As Coulson (1964: 214) noted '(t)he *ijtihad* on which the reforms are allegedly based is of a very different nature from the conscientious reinterpretation of the original sources as practised by the Middle Eastern reformers'.

Moreover, jurists and judges generally are from Western educational backgrounds and in most cases they interpret the law not from a traditional Islamic perspective but from a point of view of legal modernity. Kozlowski (1998: 74) claims that this is the case even with the judges of the *Shari'a* benches.[8] Moreover, the Islamic law created and enforced by the government bears 'only a faint resemblance to *Sharia/Fiqh*' (Kozlowski 1998: 76). Yet, there is another form of law, Muslim law, which is not superseded by any form of state law.

However, although these reforms were made, the so-called un-Islamic practices could not be controlled and have continued to exist. These reforms only resulted in causing a conflict between the reformed modern Islamic laws, which are imposed by the state and the traditional Muslim laws and local customs. As the traditionalists had serious reservations about the proposed state of Pakistan and distrusted the leadership of the 'Westernized Muslims', who often seemed to lack a real understanding of Islam (Ahmed 1982: 263), the reforms could not gain a ground of legitimacy in the eyes of the traditionalists or at the grassroot level.[9] Muslim law, distinct from state-sponsored Islamic law, has historically anchored itself in local communities. Regional identities combined with multigenerational

[8] Kozlowski (1998: 74) notes that the *Shari'a* courts consisting of these judges lack profound learning in *Shari'a*, as taught in traditional religious academies, have disappointed many religious scholars. For such an example see Tanzilur-Rahman (1997: 221).

[9] Kozlowski (1998: 83) states that the *Barelvi* scholars have issued a number of *fatwa*s claiming that they are the only true Muslims living in the country. As government is in the hands of 'false' Muslims, they have argued that they cannot be bound by the state's regulations.

attachments to particular lineages of *ulama* and *mullah*s lead people to give their primary loyalty to one of several distinct interpretations of *Shari'a*, since the ordinary people know their practitioners best. As a result, the state has been unable to 'obliterate the thousands of local societies in which the day-to-day practice of Islam takes place' (Kozlowski 1998: 84).

Thus, as the case law and research that shall be referred to below have repeatedly shown, the wide gap between the laws of the state and the plurality of legal practices still exists in Pakistan. While some of these differences have their roots in the conflicts between the modern state law and Muslim law, some of them stem from the local 'un-Islamic practices' of people that have mainly been fostered by ignorance and low literacy levels.[10]

The main conflicting points between *Hanafi* law in Pakistan and the official law are as follows:

- The age limit set by the official law contradicts the Muslim law, which puts emphasis on puberty rather than prescribing a certain age;[11]
- In traditional law there is no mandatory marriage registration, while the official law appears to require this;[12]
- In traditional law there is no need to get permission from an existing wife or wives to marry another wife, however, section 6(1)the MFLO 1961 appears to make such a written permission compulsory;
- By *talaq-al-bida*, commonly practised in the country, divorce is irrevocable as soon as it is pronounced. There is no room for reconciliation, while the official law provides for reconciliation;
- Traditional law does not require notice of divorce to any person or entity, not even the wife, whereas the official law with section 7 of MFLO 1961 requires notice to be given to the chairman of the Union Council and a copy of the notice sent to the wife;
- In traditional law, if after a third divorce a man wants to marry the same woman, an intervening marriage is required. The official law has abrogated this restriction in section 7(5).

In addition to these cleavages between the official law and traditional Muslim

---

[10] Only about 15 per cent of the Pakistani population can read and write. Only 1 per cent of the population have a college or university education. This low degree of education is primarily responsible for the lack of adequate reform in Islamic thought, Ahmed (1982: 282). Recent research gives similar figures: Only 16 per cent of the total female population qualify as literate and 75 per cent of the people live in rural areas, Jalal (1991: 77); Weiss (1994b: 413). The literacy level of the country has recently been estimated as 35 per cent by the government, however, this figure is highly optimistic, MPDGP (1998: 4). According to a recent publication of the Ministry of Education, the female literacy for rural areas is not more than 8 per cent, GPME (1998: 26). Approximately 75 per cent of the population live in rural areas, Rashid (1987: 314); Jalal (1991).

[11] Section 12 of the MFLO. See Tanzilur-Rahman (1997: 290-293) on this.

[12] Section 5(1) of the MFLO.

law, there are also many differences between the official law and local laws of the people, which involve many un-Islamic customs. The main reason often given for this is that the majority of Pakistanis are descendants of Hindu converts to Islam, who even today firmly adhere, if unknowingly, to certain customs, beliefs, and practices of their Hindu ancestors (Ahmed 1982: 270; see also Saifi 1980; Kozlowski 1998: 83). Islam spread in the subcontinent through a slow process of evolution rather than a thoroughly homogeneous diffusion. The result was a spontaneous and haphazard process of acculturation in which the people became nominally Muslim while remaining culturally Hindu at least in some aspects. Hence, especially in villages 'the traditional Hindu outlook and social forms were retained' (Ahmed 1982: 271; see also Saifi 1980).

Differences of opinions in textbooks and between religious scholars within the same *madhhab* stood side by side with a liberal acceptance of local as well as caste custom. Individual lineages likewise tended to identify as 'Islamic' any forms of behaviour enforced by a group's elders (Kozlowski 1998: 79). There exists a great confusion about what is repugnant to religion and what is not. Some practises are so common that, for an average person, it seems impossible to doubt the validity of these practices (Saifi 1980: 188). More dramatically, the majority of women are unaware of the genuine marriage system of Islam. Thus, any attempt to eliminate some of the Hindu-oriented marriage customs has been viewed as a departure from the Islamic marriage system (Saifi 1980: 190).

This fact coupled with the above-mentioned deep cleavages between the official law and traditional Muslim law, has led to the state's attempts to reform the personal laws of Muslims being faced with intense confrontations by the grassroots, to the extent that it could be termed as civil disobedience.[13] That civil disobedience has paved the way for the current dynamically legal pluralist situation of the Pakistani legal system. In addition, some groups mount active protest in favour of the traditional Muslim law against the kind of state sponsored Islamic law (Kozlowski 1998: 82). Now the hyper-fragmented Pakistani socio-legal sphere will be analyzed in some detail.

## Persistence of Muslim Legal Pluralism and Hyper-Fragmented Socio-Legal Sphere

As discussed previously, the main area of reform regarding the personal law of Muslims was the marriage sphere. The official law tried to regulate the age of marriage, registration of marriages, polygamy and divorce issues; an attempt that has brought the official law into conflict with the local law.

[13] Civil disobedience is a public, non-violent, conscientious yet political act contrary to law usually done with the aim of bringing about a change in the law or policies of the government, Rawls (1977: 90). See also Bedau (1961), King (1969), Zinn (1968) and Cohen (1969).

*Solemnization of Marriage: Nikah*

The need for compulsory marriage registration is felt because in both civil and criminal cases questions often arise concerning the existence of a marriage contract and the marital status of the parties involved. In the absence of such registration, uncertainty and confusion are usually inevitable. In certain cases, the factum of marriage is often alleged, and its proof is merely based on oral evidence, which by nature is uncertain (Patel 1991: 139).[14]

The MFLO 1961 provided under section 5 for the compulsory registration of marriages. The section reads as follows:

> 5. Registration of marriages. (1) Every marriage solemnized under Muslim Law shall be registered in accordance with the provisions of this Ordinance.
> (2) For the purpose of registration of marriages under this Ordinance the Union Council shall grant licences to one or more persons, to be called *Nikah* Registrars. but in no case shall more than one *Nikah* Registrar be licensed for any one Ward.
> (3) Every marriage not solemnized by the *Nikah* Registrar shall for the purpose of registration under this Ordinance, be reported to him by the person who has solemnized such marriage.
> (4) Whoever contravenes the provisions of subsection (3) shall be punishable with simple imprisonment for a term which may extend to three months or with fine which may extend to one thousand rupees, or with both.
> (5) The form of *Nikahnama*, the registers to be maintained by *Nikah* Registrars, the records to be preserved by Union Councils, the manner in which marriage shall be registered and copies of *Nikahnama*, shall be supplied to the parties and the fees to be charged therefore, shall be such as may prescribed.
> (6) Any person may, on payment of the prescribed fee, if any, inspect at the office of the Union Council the record preserved under subsection (5), obtain a copy of any entry therein.

However, under the Ordinance, the non-registration of marriage does not make the marriage invalid or unlawful, although registration is obviously of important in proving the existence of a marriage. This 'loophole left in the law of registration to satisfy the orthodox is that non-registration does not make a marriage invalid or unlawful' (Mehdi 1994: 159; see also Carroll 1979: 119-121). Thus, '(j)udicial relief is not denied to unregistered marriages in Pakistan, if they can be proved by other means' (Mehdi 1994: 159; see also Esposito 1980b: 225).

For registration of marriage the MFLO 1961, and rules thereunder authorize the Union Council to appoint *nikah* registrars, and to supply to every such registrar a bound register of the *nikahnama* in the prescribed form and a seal. However most of the records and functions of the Union Councils have been transferred to the municipal offices and to the offices of the commissioners or deputy commissioners (Patel 1979: 55). In many instances, it was found difficult to locate the relevant records of *nikah* registers and to obtain the necessary copies. There is always the

[14] For example, when a person was sued for abduction of a female, his defence often was that he had married the woman with her own free will and as there was no machinery for the compulsory registration of marriage, the factum of marriage was difficult to decide, Patel (1991: 139).

danger of interpolations, where proper records are not maintained carefully (Patel 1991: 143).

Traditionalists conceive compulsory registration as interference by the state in the sacred law (see in detail Tanzilur-Rahman 1997). They agree on the importance of registration, but are opposed to criminal sanctions to enforce its implementation. Thus, though this law remains in force, many marriages in Pakistan are still not registered. Moreover, the courts have held that an oral and unregistered marriage is valid (Balchin 1994: 51; Mehdi 1994: 159).[15] Further, lawyers point to the fact that 'there is a lot of corruption in the registration of marriages... *nikah* registrars will, for a very small sum, enter a forged *nikah* or any previous date in the records to oblige a customer' (Mehdi 1994: 160). Earlier research has also shown that marriages are not generally registered or, even if they are registered, 'the registers and files are not properly kept and no supervision is maintained of the staff charged with that function' (Mehdi 1994: 160; Tanzilur-Rahman 1997: 115). A recent social survey indicates that '(e)verything as to the registration of marriages, especially in the villages, is in a hotch potch' (Tanzilur-Rahman 1997: 115). As a result of insufficient measures and safeguards to protect the people, especially the women, 'their rights are in great jeopardy' (Tanzilur-Rahman 1997: 115).

Mehdi (1994: 160) highlights that there are several reasons for the shortcomings of the official law. Firstly, failure to register a marriage does not effect the validity of the marriage; secondly, the maximum custodial sentence for non-registration is only three months; thirdly, judicial relief is not denied in the cases of unregistered but proven marriages; lastly, because of the temporary abolition of the Union Councils, the functioning of the system of registration has suffered. Their role is usually performed by a civil judge. Illiteracy and ignorance of the law on the one hand and deliberate non-compliance on the other are further reasons for the ineffectiveness of the official law. Put in a nutshell, marriages are still simply solemnized in 'people's own customary ways' (Mehdi 1994: 160), whatever the official law says or expects.

### *Age of Marriage*

Under-age marriages in the country have been encouraged due to the fear of increasing sexual immorality of not having married at an early age and the concept of *izzat*. Arranged and infant marriages can be counted as other reasons for leniency and encouragement of under-age marriages (Choudry 1993b: 3).

Under-age marriages are theoretically restricted by the Child-Marriage Restraint Act, 1929, which prescribed penal sanctions where the bridegroom had not reached the age of eighteen and the bride fourteen (Carroll 1982: 60; Patel 1991: 149; Tanzilur-Rahman 1997: 290). With the promulgation of section 12 MFLO 1961, the age of fourteen was substituted by the age of sixteen.[16] A female

[15] Habib PLD (1980) Lah 791; Abdul Kalam (1987) MLD 1637.

[16] Sections 12 and 13 were omitted by the Federal Laws (Revision and Declaration) Ordinance (XXVII of 1981), Second Schedule, Pat II, Item 18.

under 16 years of age is defined as a 'child' and it is an offence to marry her off.[17] However, traditionalists vehemently oppose the age restriction. The '209 *ulama* of Pakistan' categorically declared that '(i)t is repugnant to the clear injunctions of the Holy *Qur'an*' (see in Tanzilur-Rahman 1997: 291).

According to section 13 of the MFLO 1961, should an under-age marriage take place, the woman may repudiate the marriage when she reaches the age of eighteen.

However, a marriage contracted after the attainment of puberty and before the age of 16 years for females and 18 years for males is valid under Pakistani Muslim law. The Child Marriage Restraint Act does not make such marriages invalid or void. The Act prescribes punishments for the groom who marries a child considered to be under-age for the purposes at hand, the person who performs, conducts or directs any under-age marriage, and where a minor contracts such a marriage, the person with charge of the minor. The female who enters into an under-age marriage is not liable to any punishment under the Act. Having stated the above it is important to note that under-age marriages are still deemed valid.[18] On the other hand, in practice, it is almost impossible for a child to repudiate the marriage without her family's support. Indeed, it is abundantly plain that almost all under-age marriages are, by nature, arranged marriages. Thus, it would be naive to expect families who arrange the marriages themselves, in which they marry off their under-age daughter usually without much of her input and say, to then a few years later support their now grown child to repudiate the marriage contract.

Research shows that a great number of parents have been marrying off their daughters at an extremely early age, despite the rising trend in the age of marriage due to economic and educational factors (Mehdi 1994: 195; Alam and Karim 1986: 91).[19] This practice is especially prevalent in rural parts of the country and in some segments of society it is a matter of custom (Choudry 1993b: 3; Mehdi 1994: 194). However, it is difficult to know the precise figures of under-age marriages in Pakistan. One of the basic reasons for this is the element of corruption. It is not uncommon for a *nikah* registrar to be bribed into registering a marriage of a girl and boy who are under the legal marriage age (Mehdi 1994: 196).

Mehdi (1994: 196) notes that during her field research she met a boy of ten married to a girl of twelve, who has four other married male classmates of the same age. In addition, Mehdi (1994: 196) points out that people in villages often do not know their age, another factor contributing to the difficulty in finding out the precise number of under-age marriages in Pakistan.

In short, even though the age of marriage is continuously rising, it cannot be said that the official law has had its intended effects and is closely adhered to by

[17] However, under the Offence of *Zina* (Enforcement of *Hodood*) Ordinance, 1979, the term 'adult' is defined as a person who has attained, being a male, the age of eighteen years or, being a female, the age of sixteen years, or has attained puberty whichever is earlier.

[18] See for instance Bakshi PLD (1970) Lah 386; Sughran Mai PLD (1980) Lah 386.

[19] A research which is helpful in understanding South Asian Muslim patterns of marriage conducted in India among Indian Muslims has found that 19 per cent of married women were married under the age of 15, Ashrafi (1992: 74).

one and all. It is especially common in rural regions of the country to marry off young girls before they reach the age of puberty and consequently before the prescribed age of sixteen years. Researchers have pointed out that the Act did not have the effect of an immediate deterrent to under-age marriage and the practice of under-age marriage still exists (Wakil 1991: 44; Patel 1979: 61).

*Polygamy*

All Muslim law schools agree that a Muslim man does not require permission to contract a second or subsequent marriage up to a maximum of four marriages at any one time. And, he does not have 'to submit himself to examination by any person or institution in advance of the final decision to contract a second or subsequent marriage' (Pearl 1987b: 77). However, section 6 of the MFLO tried to restrict the male's right of polygamy. Under section 6 of the MFLO, polygamy is restricted to the extent that a man who is planning to marry a second or subsequent wife must submit an application for permission to the chairman of the Union Council stating the justifying reasons for the proposed marriage and also whether the consent of the existing wife or wives has been obtained. The council may then grant permission if it is satisfied that the proposed marriage is necessary and just. The relevant section reads as follows:

> 6. Polygamy. (1) No man, during the subsistence of an existing marriage shall, except with the previous permission in writing of the Arbitration Council, contract another marriage, nor shall any such marriage contracted without such permission be registered under this Ordinance.
>
> (2) An application for permission under subsection (1) shall be submitted to the Chairman in the prescribed manner, together with the prescribed fee, and shall state the reasons for the proposed marriage and whether the consent of the existing wife or wives has been obtained thereto.
>
> (3) On receipt of the application under subsection (2), the Chairman shall ask the applicant and his existing wife or wives each to nominate a representative. and the Arbitration Council so constituted may, if satisfied that the proposed marriage is necessary and just, grant, subject to such conditions, if any, as may be deemed fit, the permission applied for.
>
> (4) In deciding the application the Arbitration Council shall record its reasons for the decision, and any party may, in the prescribed manner, within the prescribed period and on payment of the prescribed fee, prefer an application for revision (to the Collector) concerned, and his decision shall be final and shall not be called in question in any Court.
>
> (5) Any man who contracts another marriage without the permission of the Arbitration Council shall-
>
> (a) pay immediately the entire amount of the dower, whether prompt or deferred, due to the existing wife or wives, which amount if not so paid, shall be recoverable as arrears of land revenue; and
>
> (b) on conviction upon complaint be punishable with simple imprisonment which may extend to one year, or with fine which may extend to five thousand rupees. or with both.

The Council has general powers to decide what is just and necessary for granting polygamous marriage permission, and has to consider circumstances such as sterility, physical unfitness for conjugal relations, wilful avoidance of a decree for restitution of conjugal rights, or insanity on the part of an existing wife. Section 6 of MFLO categorically lays down that no man shall contract another marriage without the permission of the Arbitration Council. However, the MFLO does not specifically state that a polygamous marriage entered into without the permission of the Council is illegal, void or voidable (Mehdi 1994: 164). In that regard, Balchin (1994: 77) points out that subsequent marriages contracted in contravention of section 6 of MFLO remain valid, and that it makes the official law less effective against arbitrary and unjustified polygamy (see also Mehdi 1994: 160).

Despite the expectations of the legal system, these regulations faced stiff opposition on account of the conditions they place on polygamy (Balchin 1994: 40).[20] It has been argued that section 6 'must be deleted in toto, for, in its present form, it is totally repugnant and foreign to the words and spirit of the Holy *Qur'an* and *Sunna* and the fundamental principles of Islamic jurisprudence' (Tanzilur-Rahman 1997: 131). The arguments for and against polygamy's legality and morality continue unabated (Hodkinson 1984: 107).[21]

Although it appears at first sight that Pakistan has outlawed Muslim polygamy through section 6 of the MFLO 1961, close scrutiny shows that this is a misrepresentation of the facts and the effects of the provision. As numerous court decisions confirm, almost all Muslim polygamists in the country 'remain unpunished and husbands are not put to rigorous tests over the issue of permission of an existing wife or wives' (Menski 1997c: 29). In addition, if a man marries another woman without the permission of the existing wife or wives, although he is liable to punishment, the second or subsequent marriage is still considered valid.[22] Thus, such a law cannot guarantee a woman that her husband will not bring a co-wife into the house. Saifi (1980: 203) mentions the possibility of cases 'when a wealthy and amorous man would happily pay the fine and undergo six months sentence, but in return have his 'sweetheart' as his second wife'. Indeed, many men risk the penalties in section 6(5) (a) and (b) of the MFLO 1961, and contract polygamous marriages without bothering to apply to the Arbitration Council for

[20] Firdous (1990) analyzes in depth the discussions of polygamy by Muslim modernists in South Asia.

[21] For justifications of polygamy, see in detail Hodkinson 1984: 107-108.

[22] Cases where the husband contracts a subsequent marriage without the permission of existing wife/wives include: Sana PLD (1967) Pesh 324; Mohd. Zaman PLD (1967) Lah 1109; Abdul Basit (1970) SCMR 753; Zulai Khan PLD (1986) Quetta 290; Sher Muhammed (1986) PCrLJ 1510; M. Ashraf PLD (1987) Lah 27; Faheemuddin PLD (1991) SC 1074; Nazar Hussain (1991) CLC Note 238; Tofazal Hussain Shah (1991) PCrLJ 1063.

approval (Mehdi 1994: 165).[23]

Arranged marriages have a crucial impact on the institution of polygamy. It is customary to marry off the boy of the family at a fairly young age to a cousin in order to keep the property within the family. Often, such marriages prove unsuitable when the boy attains manhood. He, then, takes a second wife (Patel 1979: 85). When men attain wealth or position they may seek younger wives (Patel 1979: 85). These rich men 'do resort to polygamy, justifying it either by the first wife's failure to produce a male child or in order to have a love-match' (Saifi 1980: 202). This also becomes a device through which the men claim to avoid *zina*.

Even though 'polygamy is resorted to by a very small minority in Pakistan, as men realize that domestic harmony is almost impossible when two or more wives share one husband' (Saifi 1980: 203), there is significant evidence that some women 'prefer the shelter of a polygamous arrangement over a stigmatised post-divorce life' (Menski 1997c: 29). Indeed, 'a woman will often prefer to be a co-wife rather than a divorcee, particularly if she is of an age where remarriage is a remote possibility' (Carroll 1982: 61). The socio-economic pressures upon a woman are so intense and her future so insecure that the majority of husbands manage to get written permission from the wife under immense pressure and duress. The result of non-compliance with the 'command' of the husband would be divorce. Therefore, many wives give the required written permission (Ali et al 1990: 17).

In a recent case, which was decided by the Federal *Shari'a* Court of Pakistan, it was held that the several provisions of the MFLO were violative of the injunctions of Islam (see in detail Menski 2000: 321).[24] The judges in this case 'found that the section should be read as seeking to ensure that the polygamous man treats his wives equally' (Menski 2000: 321).[25]

In short, though Pakistan has put impressive restrictions on the traditional right of man to polygamy, in practice these regulations appear to be mere formalities rather than effective deterrents. Whatever the official law commands, the practice of polygamy is accepted and practiced.

### *Divorce*

In *Hanafi* law, neither the wife nor any witnesses are required to be present at the time and place when a husband is divorcing his wife.[26] The *talaq* is effective orally

[23] For relevant cases see: Fauzia Hussain PLD (1985) Lah 165; Iftikhar Nazir PLD (1968) Lah 587 (fifth wife). Sana PLD (1967) Pesh 324; Muhammed Zaman PLD (1967) Lah 1104; Ahmad ullah and another PLD (1968) Lah 703; Abdul Basit (1970) SCMR 753; Sardar Begum (1982) PCrLJ 1298; Zulai Khan PLD (1986) Quetta 290; Sher Muhammad (1986) PCrLJ 1510; Jamila Begum NLR (1986) CrLJ 212(1); Khadim Hussain (1986) SCMR 1821; Inayat Khan (1980) PCrLJ 2023; M. Ashraf PLD (1987) Lah 27; Faheemuddin PLD (1991) SC 1074; Nazar Hussain (1991) CLC. Note 238; Tofazal Hussain Shah (1991) PCrLJ 1063; Ghulam Fatima (1981) CLC 1651; Nadir Khan (1990) CLC 293. See however Faheemuddin PLD (1991) SC 1074.

[24] Allah Rakha v Federation of Pakistan, 2000 CLR 349.

[25] Allah Rakha v Federation of Pakistan, 2000 CLR 395.

[26] See succinctly Balchin (1994: 43-46), see in detail Pearl (1987: 100-106).

and in writing. Any order or form of words can be used to the express the meaning. However, Section 7 of the MFLO 1961 has attempted to convert the *talaq al-bid'a*, which is an irrevocable divorce, into a revocable divorce.[27] The objective of section 7 is to prevent hasty dissolution of marriage by *talaq* pronounced unilaterally by the husband. The section reads as follows:

> 7. *Talaq*. (1) Any man who wishes to divorce his wife shall, as soon as may be after the pronouncement of *Talaq* in any form whatsoever, give the Chairman notice in writing of his having done so, and shall supply a copy thereof to the wife.
>
> (2) Whoever contravenes the provisions of subsection (1) shall be punishable with simple imprisonment for a term which may extend to one year or with fine which may extend to five thousand rupees or with both.
>
> (3) Save as provided in subsection (5), a *Talaq* unless revoked earlier, expressly or otherwise, shall not be effective until the expiration of ninety days from the day on which notice under subsection (1) is delivered to the Chairman.
>
> (4) Within thirty days of the receipt of notice under subsection (1), the Chairman shall constitute an Arbitration Council for the bringing about of a reconciliation between the parties, and the Arbitration Council shall take all steps necessary to bring about such reconciliation.
>
> (5) If the wife be pregnant as the *Talaq* is pronounced, *Talaq* shall not be effective until the period mentioned subsection (3) or the pregnancy, whichever be later, ends.
>
> (6) Nothing shall debar a wife whose marriage has been terminated by *Talaq* effective under this section from remarrying the same husband, without an intervening marriage with a third person, unless such termination is for the third time so effective.

Although the official law appears to deviate drastically from the traditional Muslim law, it fails in practice to restrict the man's right of divorce.[28] As in the case of polygamy, the divorce procedure provided in the official law has become a mere formality instead of deterring and regulating the unilateral use of divorce by the husband. (Carroll 1979: 125; see also Pearl 1971b: 565; Mehdi 1994: 171). In a recent case, even the Supreme Court observed that sending notice to the Chairman Union Council is a mere formality.[29] The MFLO 1961 endeavours to incorporate a procedure for reconciliation before a divorce is effectuated. It provides for an Arbitration Council, with a chairman and two arbitrators, one on behalf of the husband and one on behalf of the wife, for purposes of seeking to reconcile the two parties. The husband's unilateral right to divorce his wife remains intact, except

---

[27] *Talaq-al-bid'a* is not much approved but is widely practised among the Muslims of Pakistan. It consists of three declarations of divorce occurring at one time and the marriage is then irrevocably dissolved, Mehdi (1994: 167). In addition 'if divorce has become irrevocable... he is not permitted to marry her again until she has taken another husband and lived with him as a wife; after she has parted from her new husband, the first husband then may remarry her', Mehdi (1994: 167); see also Maududi (1981: 180.

[28] For a detailed study regarding the discussions of divorce by Muslim modernists in South Asia, see Firdous (1990).

[29] Kaneez Fatima PLD (1993) SC 905.

that the procedure of notice of divorce and reconciliation has to be adhered to (Patel 1979: 103). As mentioned above, section 7 of the Ordinance requires that any man who wishes to divorce his wife shall, as soon as may be, after the pronouncement of *talaq* in any form whatsoever, give the chairman notice in writing of his having done so, and shall supply a copy thereof to his wife.[30] The mere pronouncement of *talaq* without notice to the chairman theoretically means that the divorce is not effective as far as the official law of the land is concerned[31] (repetition).[32] However, in Mirza Qamar Raza, the Federal *Shari'a* Court even questioned whether that was the case, stating 'the effectiveness of the *talaq* cannot be subjected to the service of notice on the Chairman'.[33] Quite frequently divorce is pronounced on a wife, but the husband deliberately or owing to lack of awareness, does not get the divorce deed registered. Although the responsibility of registration is on the husband, the onus of proof is on the former wife. This puts women in jeopardy, owing to the loopholes in the legal system. In such cases the 'divorced' wife can be charged with *zina* on remarriage.[34] An obviously anguishing prospect not knowing what your marital status in law is, especially when so much is made to made to depend on it (Patel 1979: 111; Mehdi 1994: 201).

Section 7 of the MFLO 1961 has been opposed by the traditionalists. To them, this section 'is against the injunctions of Islam' (Tanzilur-Rahman 1997: 195). They feel that this law 'has made an absolute right of divorce, granted to a husband by God, subject of and dependent on the actions of a third agency, i.e. an Arbitration Council' (Mehdi 1994: 170-171). Thus, according to them, the official law creates a conflict between the law and the conscience of the people.

The official law is not clear on many points on the matter of divorce. For instance, whether giving notice to the wife is a necessary condition does not seem to be clear.[35] In some cases, it was held that the non-supply of a copy of divorce notice to the wife does not prevent the divorce from becoming effective after ninety days.[36] On the other hand, in some cases, the courts espouse the view that the service of the copy on the wife is as important as service of the notice on the chairman.[37] If authorities fail to form an arbitration council, it is deemed that this

---

[30] Ali Nawaz Gardezi PLD (1963) SC.51; Abdul Mannan (1970) SCMR 845.

[31] Ali Nawaz Gardezi PLD (1963) SC 51; Tauquir Fatima PLD (1964) Kar 306; Abdul Mannan (1970) SCMR 845; Inamul Islam PLD (1982) FSC 156; Shera PLD (1982) FSC 229; Muhammed Salahuddin Khan (1984) SCMR 53; Malik Javed Ali (1987) SCMR 518; Abdul Mannan (1970) SCMR 845; Kaneez Fatima PLD (1989) Lah 490; Aijaz Haroon PLD (1989) Kar 304; Ayyaz Aslam (1990) ALD 702. However, in Parveen Chaudry (1976) Kar 416, the court held the view that absence of the communication does not invalidate the divorce.

[32] Mirza Qamar Raza PLD (1988) Karachi 169.

[33] Muhammad Sarwar PLD (1988) FSC 42.

[34] Noor Khan PLD (1982) FSC 265.

[35] Naziran PLD (1990) SCMR 803; Ashique Hussain PLD (1991) Kar 174; Kaneez Fatima PLD (1993) SC 901 at 916-917.

[36] See for instance Zikria Khan PLD (1985) Lah 319.

[37] See for example Inamul Islam PLD (1976) Lah 1466.

has no effect upon the validity of the divorce.[38]

Another major loophole in the restriction on divorce is that failure to comply with the procedure prescribed by the official law, though it incurs penalties, does not affect the validity of the divorce (Esposito 1982b: 85; Carroll 1979: 124; Mehdi 1994: 170).

After Islamization in 1977, courts have taken a more traditionalist approach towards section 7.[39] While in some cases the courts held that the MFLO was not repugnant to Islam,[40] in some others, it was held that the ineffectiveness of *talaq* in the absence of the notice was against the injunctions of Islam.[41] In such a case, the *Shari'a* Appellate Bench of the Supreme Court declared that section 7 of the MFLO 1961 is repugnant to the injunctions of Islam and held that divorce would become effective even in the absence of a notice to the chairman of the Union Council since notice to a Chairman is not mandatory under the injunctions of Islam.[42] Moreover, it was held in the same case that if there is a clash between an existing law and the injunctions of Islam, then the latter shall prevail whether it is recognized by the official law or not.

As a consequence, it has become evident that the traditional form of divorce, *talaq*, is still predominant in Pakistan. In legal advice given by lawyers in reply to readers' questions in newspapers and magazines, they suggest that people should follow the official law, but only as a procedural formality (Mehdi 1994: 172). It was further reported that villagers are not prepared to condone any person who remarries his divorced wife without an intervening marriage of the woman with someone else (Mehdi 1994: 172).

Some experts, like Tanzilur-Rahman, have been arguing that the protections extended to the MFLO had (that the provisions in the MFLO had) become 'nugatory' because it was in contradiction to the Objective Resolution 1949 which manifests that sovereignty belongs to Allah (see now Tanzilur-Rahman 1997: 46-50).[43] In June 1993, the position of the MFLO 1961 vis-à-vis the Federal *Shari'a*

---

[38] Fahmida Bibi Muhtar Ahmad PLD (1972) Lah 694; Maqbool Jan (1975) PLD Lah 147; Akhtar Hussain PLD (1977) Lah 1173; M. Zikria Khan PLD (1985) Lah 319.

[39] Noor Khan PLD (1982) FSC 265.

[40] Kaneez Fatima PLD (1989) Lah 490; Ayyaz Aslam (1990) ALD 702.

[41] An important case in this respect is Mirza Qamar Raza PLD (1988) Kar 169; Allahdad (1992) SCMR 1273.

[42] Allahdad (1992) SCMR 1273. On the issue of deciding the repugnancy to the injunctions of Islam, see Kennedy (1992). He shows that there is no consensus in regard to either the content or the desired pace of Islamic reform in the country and the superior courts are in a position of being activist in the Islamization process (Kennedy 1992: 787).

[43] Mirza Qamar Raza PLD (1988) Kar 169. Tanzil-ur-Rahman's view was upheld in Muhammad Sarwar PLD (1988) FSC 42. See however Kaneez Fatima PLD (1989) Lah 990; (1993) SC 905. For the Objectives Resolution, see in detail Shah (1992b); Tanzilur-Rahman (1997: 47-48). The first paragraph reads as follows: Whereas sovereignty over the entire universe belongs to Allah Almighty alone and the authority which he has delegated to the State of Pakistan, through its people for being exercised within the limits prescribed by Him is a sacred trust (now Article 2-A of the Constitution of Pakistan). It became a part of the Constitution in 1985 with the Revival of Presidential Order, Presidential Order 14 of 1985.

Court changed. The Supreme Court reviewing its earlier decision in a case ruled that the Federal *Shari'a* Court was competent enough to examine the MFLO of 1961.[44] As a result, it is quite fair to conclude that the MFLO, 1961 is no longer sustainable as the governing law although it has not been repealed or abrogated (Pearl 1990: 335). This proves once again that the Pakistani official law has accepted defeat, albeit covertly, vis-à-vis the unofficial local Muslim law and legal pluralism in the field of divorce, too.

[44] Mahmood-ur-Rahman Faisal PLD (1994) SC 507.

# Chapter 7

# Post-Modern Muslim Legality and its Consequences

The three case studies analyzed here suggest that state law has limits and dynamic Muslim legal pluralism is a perpetual, and most probably ubiquitous, fact. In other words, our three cases are different manifestations of the same reality.

## Dynamic Muslim Legal Pluralism and Post-Modern Muslim Legality

Legal modernity and legal centralism are being challenged in the post-modern condition. It is becoming increasingly recognized that social space is not a normative vacuum. Local laws, along with local cultures and identities, are preserved (McLellan and Richmond 1994: 666). Thus, totality in the legal arena is questioned. Post-modern analyzes of law and social movements have challenged the claims of universal theories. Legal pluralism has become a key concept in a post-modern view of law (Santos 1987: 297). This broader conception of law indicates a more complex relation between law and society (Santos 1987: 281). Law is regarded as more plural and not only located within the state (Merry 1995: 12). This plural notion of law, in which state law is only one of many, does not give any privilege to centrality (Merry 1995: 23). While legal officials and scholars assume state monopoly of legal production, research on legal pluralism maintains the existence and circulation of different legal systems in society, of which the state law forms one (Santos 1987: 280). Thus, the whole structure of law of a people is not limited to the monistic system of state law. The whole structure of law as an aspect of culture should include all regulations which the people concerned observe as law in their cultural tradition, including value systems (Chiba 1986a: 4). Law is inseparably rooted in society so as to be approachable by sociological methods. In this reading, law is understood as an aspect of the total culture of a people. Law is a socio-cultural construct.

In the socio-legal realm, 'the different forms of law create different legal objects upon eventually the same social objects' (Santos 1987: 287). Various legal scales do not exist in isolation but rather interact in many ways (Santos 1987: 288). Indeed interlegality, which is the phenomenological counterpart of legal pluralism, is a highly dynamic process (Santos 1987: 298). The result of this intersection and interaction among legal spaces is that one cannot speak of law and legality but of interlaw and interlegality, which are the conceptions of different legal spaces that are superimposed, interpenetrated, and mixed in people's minds as much as in their actions (Santos 1987: 298).

Global and societal changes in the post-modern condition are producing radical transformations in construction of identity. No identity is grounded in ontological truth. There is a visible and growing rejection of fixed identities, while new emerging identities are fluid and hybrid.[1] The idea of an integrated personality within a bounded or self-contained community is replaced by interplay of synchronic and diachronic perspectives that continually construct and reconstruct identity. Individuals are increasingly subject to competing ethnic, national, cultural, religious and legal reference points (McLellan and Richmond 1994: 669). In the legal realm, this type of individual is called a '*sujet de droits*' (see in detail Vanderlinden 1989).

The whole structure of law of a people is not limited to the monistic system of state law, but is plural, consisting of different systems of law interacting with one another harmoniously or conflictingly. Three dimensions (society-state-religion) of the socio-legal sphere always interact with each other. Moreover, there is a three-level structure of law consisting of official law, unofficial law and legal postulates and there is a dynamic interaction between all these. As our analyzes of three cases have shown, these interactions pave the way for the continuous construction of new hybrid laws.

The self is a normative construct. Yet it is normatively constructive as well. Law's true authority is located in the constructive capacity of the subject. Internormative dialogue also exists at the level of the individual who is a *sujet de droits*. The self is being continuously constructed and constructs as a skilful legal navigator in the socio-legal climate of the post-modern condition. In the dynamic legal pluralist spheres, skilful legal navigators invent, combine, mix, construct and reconstruct laws as an aesthetic creation process.

On the other hand, it is contended that there is no sharp line between individuals and collective actions. There are cross-cutting ties that are maintained by skilful cultural and legal navigators on various levels in the post-modern condition (Richmond 1988: 2). These ties do not replace territorially-based communities or bureaucratically organized formal organizations, but are superimposed on them. The self-identified and reflexive post-modern navigator is in continual dialogue with formal organizations and with ethno-religious communities whose boundaries are not necessarily defined by geography. The boundaries of a society or of a community no longer correspond to the political borders of the modern nation-state (McLellan and Richmond 1994: 665). In that condition, '"the local" does not remain local' (Hunt 1992b: 58) since '(i)n the multicultural context of a country... ethnic or religious groups may appear as relatively isolated minorities, but when expanded into the global framework, their relationships must be understood as part of an international network' (McLellan

[1] Santos (1987: 297) draws attention to this fluidity and hybridity in the socio-legal sphere: '…our century has been too much overridden by the opposition between the formal and the informal... Now, it is time to see the formal in the informal and the informal in the formal'.

and Richmond 1994: 665).[2] In the post-modern condition, various local insertions into the global system are represented and reproduced (McLellan and Richmond 1994: 667).

As the present study substantiates, the post-modern challenge of multiculturalism exists in the legal sphere as well. The metanarrative discourse of uniform national legal systems, and of modernity, is challenged by local folk, ethnic and small cultures, their 'unofficial' obligation systems, and other normative orders. There is always a resistance from the periphery. In other words, there are limits to the role of state law in shaping societies. People do not simply obey the rules which are enforced by the state from above, and they do maintain their own self-perceptions of legal affairs. Unofficial laws co-exist with official ones, so that legal pluralism arises as a factual situation where different modes of legal regulation overlap in their application to and within society. All three cases studies explored show clearly that the reality of dynamic legal pluralism might be a matter of concern everywhere. The failure of legal modernity is obvious. The powers of tradition, local customs, and resistance to change from the top and cultural diversity are inevitable realities of everyday life. Since law is a socio-cultural construct, legal diversity is a fact and not a fiction like legal modernity.

As regards Muslims in particular, the inescapable conclusion is that despite the uniformity claims of the modern nation-states in the socio-legal sphere, expulsion or non-recognition of unofficial Muslim laws has not proved a total success, as Muslims have developed their own ways of reconstructing the legal arena, paving the way for dynamic Muslim legal pluralism.

In all three cases it was found, especially regarding family law issues where change occurs but tradition governs, that state law has no monopoly over the socio-legal sphere, that law has limits, that the growth of unofficial laws is a reality, and that dynamic Muslim legal pluralism is a recalcitrant fact. In these dynamic contexts, new laws are being continuously constructed by skilful post-modern legal navigators. These developments have crucial impacts on the ideas of how law, women, the state and religions interrelate.

This study has argued that legal pluralism could exist for Muslims at four different levels: Individual, communal, national and global. The present study mainly analyzed the reality of legal pluralism at individual and national levels. At the individual level, many laws interact with each other in the very same individual's mind and conscience. *Shari'a*, could be seen as a bundle of legal postulates and Muslim individuals are bound by rules of Islam and legal postulates as a total way of life wherever they go. Thus, most of the time, they are subject to more than a single legal order meeting at the level of a 'sujet de droits'.

Secondly, dynamic legal pluralism exists at the community level, stemming from the differences between local cultures, customs, ethnicity, traditions, and

[2] So far as the Muslim minorities and their laws and customs are concerned, this phenomenon is of paramount importance, since Muslims and Muslim law issues have started to frequently occupy the global public sphere, see Vertovec (1996). Although they might be minorities in some non-Muslim States, they are, at the same time, a part of an *ummah* with 'universal' laws that, at times, clash, and interact with modern nation-state laws, see in detail King (1995b; 1995c).

local laws of different communities.

Thirdly, dynamic legal pluralism could exist at a national level in which there are interactions between state law, local variations, ethnic differences, recognized Muslim laws, and unofficial local Muslim laws.

A fourth case is the trans-national and global legal pluralism. *Ummah* as the universal Muslim interpretative community, a community consisting of individuals bound together by shared knowledge, terminology, discourse, and a basic corpus of ideas, beliefs and attitudes, poses two different manifestations of dynamic legal pluralism. One is internal. There are many variations among different schools of law, jurists, applications, understandings and practices of Muslim law. The second is external. There are a number of clashes and differences between Muslim law (with all its variations) and modern state laws. A third type could be among Muslim laws and other unofficial laws as a different manifestation of cross-national legal pluralism.

This book has endeavoured to show that a new dimension to legal pluralism studies ought to be inserted: That being religion. This study has also indicated that dynamic legal pluralism will also arise in Muslim majority situations, as the examples of Turkey and Pakistan have shown. Thus, legal pluralism is not only relevant in relation to ethnic minorities or indigenous peoples. It persists everywhere where different socio-cultural contexts exist, be it due to political, ethnic or religious reasons. The present study has also indicated the importance and effects of judicial legal postulates, based especially on the evidence in Turkey. Another crucial result of this study is that it has demonstrated once again that legal pluralism is not only a matter for the Southern countries or those countries with personal law systems; it is a universal post-modern phenomenon.

In this post-modern condition, individuals are subject to more than one legal order such as legal orders of states, localities, religions, ethnicity, supra-national entities, international and transnational institutions, and so on. Different laws interact at the levels of the individual, community, nation-state and globe, either harmoniously or conflictingly. In other words, legal pluralism is a phenomenon of different legal spaces first superimposed, interpenetrated and intermingled in the individual mind and behaviour, then at the communal, national and global level. However, *sujets de droits* can handle with dexterity the conflicting situations arising from dynamic legal pluralism and as skilful legal navigators; they invent, manipulate and construct new laws.

This is most patently the case with Muslim law, a strong example of this phenomenon. Although post-modernity and Muslim law diametrically oppose each other in certain aspects (because Islam is another metanarrative), Muslim legal pluralism stemming from the existence of unofficial Muslim laws and their interaction with state law proves post-modernity's existence, while post-modern formulations accommodate and tolerate, at least theoretically, the existence of this special kind of Muslim legal pluralism. In other words, there is a mutual, if not symbiotic, relationship between Muslim legal pluralism and the post-modern condition, and this phenomenon is global. In all cases, Muslim law takes different forms as the supreme law according to the mind and conscience of Muslim individuals who are *sujets de droits*. However, as skilful legal navigators, they would combine the provisions of different rule systems and would try to meet the demands of these legal frameworks. I would call this entity the 'post-modern legal identity'. Thus, in the socio-legal sphere being a *sujet de droits* is not a totally contradictory situation.

One can expect post-modern legal identities to become the main actors of socio-legal spheres at all levels from communal to global in the next few decades. Among Muslims, this trend of reconstructing unofficial laws will steadily continue, so that Muslims will not lose their distinctive identities but will find ways to adapt their religious life-styles to modern and even secular milieus. In that sense, they can even be called 'law-manipulating citizens', where they utilize the official laws in favour of their unofficial Muslim laws.

As seen throughout this study, legal non-recognition of this social reality is not a viable option for scholarship. As will be seen below, non-recognition causes a number of difficulties that present a problematic situation regarding religion, ethnicity, culture, differential legal treatment, vulnerable members of society and respect for the law and authority. As a result, both state law and '*ulama*' could possibly lose their control over the socio-legal domain as a result of the growth of unofficial legal alternatives and hyper-fragmentation of the socio-legal sphere.

## Consequences of Post-Modern Muslim Legality

### *Differential Legal Treatment*

In the British context, as seen above in chapter 4, Muslims have not been able to convince the English law and courts that religious discrimination amounts to unlawful indirect discrimination against a particular religious group (Jones and Gnanapala 2000: 55).[3]

At present the picture is unclear. A number of important cases have been settled out of court to avoid that the law become clarified. It is evident that the current situation is perceived by Muslims as discriminatory.

The state is willing to accept social, but not legal, pluralism. Thus, the state's desire for uniform legal standards is diametrically opposed to the cultural diversities of the people. Obviously, this has put the burden of assimilation on Muslims and other minorities.

Indeed, there exists a long-standing dissatisfaction among members of the Muslim community. They feel 'that the structures of white British society are, at best, blind to the existence of a Muslim community in the country' (Nielsen 1987: 384). A recent poll showed that 69 per cent of Muslims felt that 'the rest of society does not regard them as an integral part of life in Britain' (Ansari 2002: 17). Ansari (2002: 22) further puts that '(m)any Muslims feel a mixture of resentment, anger and despair, and it is not surprising that substantial numbers of them remain alienated from Mainstream British society'. Muslims argue that they 'are among

[3] Farhat Malik v British Home Stores (1980); Yasin v Northwest Home (1993), Azam, Bhayat and others v J H Walker (1994).

the very worst-off group, and yet, unlike religious groups like Sikhs and Jews, they are not deemed to be an ethnic group and so are outside the terms of existing anti-discrimination legislation' (Modood 1994: 14; see also UKACIA 1993, Rath 1991: 106, Q-News, June 1997).

Muslim writers frequently make such referrals to the legal positions of Jews and Sikhs.[4] As a result of such unequal application of legal principles, there has been widespread alienation from the state among members of ethnic minorities in Britain. They feel that the human rights of non-white Britons are less valued than those of whites. Muslim writers frequently stress that 'Islam is explicitly a dimension of racial abuse and incitement to hatred... cultural-racism' (Modood 1994: 7). Muslims have a feeling of persecution, oppression and hostility towards the authorities (Modood 1993: 517). It is ordinary to see similar themes in Muslim newspapers, magazines and conferences.

Muslim writers have continuously pointed out that Muslims 'may be driven into a deeper more antagonistic isolation from wider society' (see McLoughlin 1996: 221). A quick scan of 'the Muslim press certainly creates an impression of victim mentality' (Jones and Gnanapala 2000: 55).

It appears that the official legal system is unable to command the respect and attention of a large segment of the Muslim minority population. There exists distrust towards the English system of justice. As a consequence of the predicaments of the legal system, the state has failed to comprehend the problems of the ethnic minorities.

### *'Illegitimate' Children*

As seen above, the existence of Muslim legal pluralism in Turkey has given rise to the long-standing problems of couples who are not legally married, but regard themselves, and are regarded in their social sphere, as married, and their children as legitimate who are actually, under the Civil Code, deemed illegitimate.

Although amnesty laws are almost periodically enacted which allow the registration of 'consensual marriages'. This is only possible if no marriage impediment between the parties exists. Moreover, children who were born out of an occasional relation may, however, not be registered as legitimate under such laws.

These 'illegitimate' children face many problems during their lives (Kümbetoğlu 1997: 121). For instance when they reach the correct age to start their education, they face difficulties since most of the time they are not officially recognized or not 'known' by the state.

### *Abuse of Nikah*

As explained above, people in Turkey marry religiously with *nikah* and count this as an 'engagement', and if they find themselves compatible and would like to

[4] See for example Modood (1993: 516), for a comparison between Asian Muslims and Hindus and Sikhs, see also Ellis (1991).

proceed then they register their marriages and thereby become a 'real' married couple.[5]

The reason for this practice can be explained by reference to the modernization of Turkey. Most marriages are still arranged in the country. However, the parents and the children agree that it is they who must make up their minds as to whether they want to marry each other. The meetings in the presence of their parents is simply not enough and having to have a third person wherever they go can be annoying; so the have the religious marriage to legitimize their rendezvous in the eye of the public, save themselves from guilt and sin in the eyes of religion for meeting so regularly[6] and alleviate the scruples factor of the parents. Obvious in this practice, the official marriage is regarded as the 'decisive marriage'.

However, this application causes many problems in certain circumstances. Young couples sometimes consider the *nikah* to be sufficient in permitting them to engage in sexual behaviour, including intercourse, since they are married under Muslim law.[7] Yet, if a problem arises and the, in theory, unofficial marriage but, in practice, engagement ends, then the woman faces problems.[8] Since they are not officially married, she cannot claim any legal rights from the former husband, in the absence of the Muslim law's legal weight (Beşer 1997: 302; Beşer 1993: 161).[9] Therefore, the former husband is not legally tied down to the obligations of the unofficial marriage, whether it is dissolved or not. The woman loses her virginity, which is considered very important and sacred in the eyes of the Turkish people.[10] A second marriage for her will be very difficult and she will be categorized as 'second class value'. More dramatically, in some cases, the woman becomes pregnant. Since they are not officially married and entered into sexual intercourse secretly, they may employ abortion, which is not a positive experience for young couples.[11] Consequently, depressions, psychological problems and even suicides, although rare, may occur.[12] Also, with the dissolution of the engagement, the woman may face additional problems to those discussed above; very similar in nature to the matters of limping marriages and difficulties arising from hidden *nikah*'s which will be discussed below.

---

[5] *Kadın ve Aile*, July 1987: 40-45; *Yeni Bizim Aile*, February 1994: 20.

[6] *Kadın ve Aile*, July 1987: 40-45; *Yeni Bizim Aile*, February 1994: 20; Kerimoğlu (1989b: 23-26); Vefa (1990: 197-208).

[7] *Kadın ve Aile*, July 1987, p. 41.

[8] Such a case is elaborated by Kerimoğlu (1989a: 23-26) according to Muslim law. In this case, after the engagement ended, the then prospective couple decided not to marry. However, they got married by *nikah*, and the man has not given her *talaq* for five years to the effect of creating a limping marriage. He demands some money to give the poor girl her *talaq* and is already married to another woman. See also Vefa (1990: 197-208); Beşer (1997: 302). I discuss limping marriages in the Turkish context below.

[9] See in detail *Kadın ve Aile*, July 1987, p. 41; *Yeni Bizim Aile*, February 1994, p. 20.

[10] *Yörünge*, 28 July- 3 August 1996, p. 10; even the state is very careful about virginity, see *Sabah*, 17 October, 1997, p. 4.

[11] *Kadın ve Aile*, July 1987, p. 42.

[12] *Yörünge*, 28 July- 3 August 1996, pp. 5, 9; *Kadın ve Aile*, July 1987, p. 42.

*Limping Marriages*

The legal systems in England and Turkey pay insufficient attention to the role which religious beliefs play in divorce (Conway 1995: 1618). It has been consistently argued that 'the failure of the legal system to allow a religious law influence in the dissolution of marriages has the potential to cause injustice to members of religious minorities' (Conway 1995: 1618). In that context, the main problem is the occurrence of limping marriages which are those marriages recognized in some jurisdictions as having been validly dissolved, but in other jurisdiction(s) as still subsisting.

As Menski and Shah (1996: 10) state 'the purportedly egalitarian law further disadvantages Muslim women in Britain'. A husband is enabled to prevent his 'ex-wife' from remarrying in accordance with her religious belief (Berkovits 1990: 138-139; Hamilton 1995: 83; 116).

In both Islam and Judaism, in order to remarry, a woman must obtain a religious decree of divorce. Under Jewish law, the wife must obtain a *get*, in Islamic law, a religious divorce must be accomplished in one of the ways of *talaq*, *khul* or *mubaraat*. If the woman is not religiously divorced from her husband, it does not matter that she is divorced under the civil law, in the eyes of the community her remarriage will be regarded as adulterous and any possible offspring will be illegitimate since it is not allowed under the religious law. So, in reality, until the religious divorce is obtained, the civil divorce remains ineffective because one party is unable to remarry (Schuz 1996: 135).

Sometimes, capricious husbands divorce their wives officially but do not want to pronounce *talaq* or deliver the *get* to prevent the women from remarrying (see Berkovits 1990; Reed 1996; Hamilton 1995). Knowing the value placed on a religious divorce by their wives, such men have used their power to grant or withhold divorce to negotiate favourable settlements on the issue of finance, property and/or contact and custody relating to any children (Hamilton 1995: 118-120; Schuz 1996: 150; Carroll 1997: 100). In some other cases, a Muslim woman could obtain a civil divorce, valid under the state law, but subsequently find out that her husband, at the time of the divorce, did not use the required Islamic formula for divorcing her (Chryssides 1994: 66; Badawi 1995: 77).

There are many cases also in Turkey where a woman obtains a civil divorce, yet is not divorced by her husband in religion with a *talaq* and therefore is made to suffer (Beşer 1993: 161; Kerimoğlu 1989b: 23-26).[13] Thus, parents, family members, relatives and religious community leaders who are usually well-respected in the community, try to resolve family conflicts.[14]

It is obvious that limping marriages causes hardship to the female in the former relationship , and there is 'the potential for great bitterness between the spouses' (Hamilton 1995: 121). The ultimate outcome is 'acute misery and frustration' (Reed 1996: 103). In this context, Hamilton (1995: 117) argues that the official law creates injustice (Hamilton 1995: 117). Indeed, '(w)hilst preventing

13 See also in detail *Kadın ve Aile*, July 1987, pp. 41-44.

14 *Kadın ve Aile*, July 1987, pp. 41-44.

discrimination against women may be a laudable aim, it is unclear whether it is either an appropriate or realizable objective in this context' (Schuz 1996: 141). It is abundantly clear that 'non-recognition will not prevent the discriminatory practice' (Schuz 1996: 141).

Limping marriages are the metaphorical offsprings of the union of legal systems and their denial of the existence of the reality of legal pluralism. The irony of course is that enactment of state law in the issues of marriage and divorce and family matters are usually based on the rationale that women will benefit as a result. However, the very same law's non-recognition approach of legal pluralism is what disadvantages the women so greatly in this situation.

*Hidden (Gizli) Nikah*

Shadid and van Koningsveld (1991: 112) observed another phenomenon regarding unofficial *nikah* marriages and its abuse among some Muslims in the Netherlands. In this scenario, youngsters have a *nikah* only marriage in the ignorance of their parents and try to legitimize their relationship although at first instance their intentions might not be to really and truly get married: '(t)he main motive for this practice is to avoid pre-marital intercourse which is strongly condemned by Islam. This type of marriage creates the possibility for Muslim youngsters of opposite sexes to live together as is the case with Dutch youngsters' (Shadid and van Koningsveld 1991: 112).

It is obvious that there are some potential dangers of this abuse at the expense of women, since there is no recognition by the official authority of their *nikah* only marriage. If the man wants to leave and walks away, the woman would have no rights whatsoever before the courts under the official law nor will there be any community pressure on the husband as continues to be the case in traditional Muslim societies. After losing her virginity, which is very important in the Muslim culture, the woman will face difficulties in getting remarried. Even worse, if she has a baby from the previous relationship, the remarriage option of the woman on her own terms and preferences would be even more unlikely and problematic.

In the Turkish context, this type of marriage is getting more common. It is called hidden (*gizli*) *nikah*. Young people, generally university students, have a '*nikah*' only marriage, without informing their parents.[15] In the absence of an official registration, these marriages are not legitimate in the eyes of the state law.[16] More interestingly, these marriages are also not seen as an actual marriage by many parents because of the absence of the legal framework.[17] This practice of hidden *nikah* is followed by those other than young people: From time to time, the

[15] See for a recent comment and a response to a letter by a popular *fiqh* columnist about hidden marriage. He declares that he receives a number of letters from young people regarding hidden *nikah*. He also emphasizes that most of the time, women are affected very negatively, Sohbetler, Ahmet Şahin, *Zaman* 2, 26 February 1998, p. 3.

[16] At this point, it is superfluous to emphasize that with polygamous marriages an absence of legal framework is of course the case.

[17] *Kadın ve Aile*, July 1987: 45; *Yörünge* 28 July- 3 August 1996: 5-10.

country is shaken by some news about hidden and/or polygamous marriages of popular and celebrity personalities as well.[18]

'Hidden *nikah*' is a kind of Islamically legitimized flirt, according to some Islamic scholars (see in detail Eren 1995).[19] For instance, according to the theology professor Bekir Topaloğlu, this kind of *nikah* is a type of covert flirt.[20] Hamza Aktan, a professor of Islamic jurisprudence, emphasizes by a reference to a *hadith* that the distinction between *halal* and *haram* lies in the announcement of the marriage to the public. Thus, he concludes that 'hidden *nikah*' is un-Islamic and one cannot show a similar application in the time of the prophet.[21] According to another prominent scholar, Ali Rıza Demircan, this kind of *nikah* is a social catastrophe and most probably is illegitimate according to Muslim law since it is hidden and this situation is in conflict with the idea and purpose of the marriage institution in Islam.[22]

This practice, not surprisingly, has caused social problems for women. As a result of the practice of the hidden *nikah*, columns of Islamic scholars who reply to the questions of individuals in the newspapers and in some Islamic periodicals are frequently occupied by questions or complaints from girls taken advantage of, after they have been deserted by their unofficial young 'husbands' with or without any excuse (see Beşer 1997: 302). Since they are not officially married, the former-unofficial-wife cannot claim any legal rights where Muslim law is not applied as official state law and as a result the former-unofficial-husband will not be made to comply with his religious but unofficial Islamic duties (Beşer 1997: 302; Beşer 1993: 161).[23]

Having stated all these, one should again draw attention to the socio-legal reality that, as a result of the interaction between the official and unofficial laws, official marriage has become a part of the 'real' marriage. Most parents and couples want to register their marriages. The statistical data suggest that most people marry by employing a religious ceremony but at the same time they officially register their marriages, too. This has become a new custom of marriage among the people which is evolving. They marry twice, officially and religiously. Then, if something goes wrong and they decide to get divorced, they get divorced twice, officially and religiously, again. Only in some rural areas and in polygamous or under-age marriage cases do the couple not register their marriages since it is not possible to do so in the context of modern Turkish law.

---

[18] See for instance all nation-wide Turkish daily newspapers of the 1-15 January 1997. See for a more recent case about *imam nikahı*, *Milliyet*, 6 March 1998, p.3. See also about the popularity of *imam nikahı* among Muslim Turks, *Sabah*, 29 March 1998.

[19] *Kadın ve Aile*, July 1987: 41, 45; *Yörünge* 28 July- 3 August 1996: 5-10.

[20] *Yörünge* 28 July- 3 August 1996: 9.

[21] Zaman, 12 January 1997, 2. See for the same view Ahmet Şahin, *Zaman* 2, 26 February 1998: 3.

[22] *Yörünge* 28 July- 3 August 1996: 9.

[23] See in detail *Kadın ve Aile*, July 1987: 41; *Yeni Bizim Aile*, February 1994: 20.

*Super-hybrid Laws*

Among the Muslims in England, 250,000 to 300,000 are people of Turkish origin. 90 per cent of these Turks live in London, concentrating in certain parts, to the effect of creating 'Turkish towns'. Preliminary observations and anecdotal evidence suggest that there is an emergence of a hybrid Anglo-Turkish Muslim law that is a combination of Turkish Muslim law and *angrezi shariat*. Preliminary observations and anecdotal evidence suggest that there is a process of super-hybridization of Turkish-English-Islamic law to the effect of the construction of an Anglo-Turkish-Muslim law that is in some ways also a combination of Turkish Muslim law and *angrezi shariat*.

I will now shortly explain the development of a hybrid form of marriage solemnization among Anglo-Turkish Muslims in London. In doing so I first trace the background of most Turks who have lived under, or are aware of, a legal system in Turkey which has already been transformed by attempts at secularization within a Muslim social context. Thus, Turkish Muslims have already had some historical experiences of combining an officially secular legal system with the demands of their unofficial laws. Therefore at least five patterns of marriage making can be discerned among Muslims in Turkey. In Britain, these patterns have altered again to lead to the creation of further hybrid forms of marriage solemnization.

*Turks in Britain* Most of the research on British Muslims has focused on South Asians while the Turkish community in Britain is under-researched. Due to the nature of data sources available in Britain, it is not possible to verify the estimates precisely because the census data seem to have failed to measure the Turkish population in Britain accurately. Thus, there are a number of estimates ranging between 65,000 and 300,000 people of Turkish origin in Britain.[24]

Britain was one of the first countries to accommodate a large number of immigrant workers. Stemming from the colonial history, these immigrants were coming largely from the Commonwealth. Turkey was not a main source in this regard. Even though a number of Western European countries such as Germany made bi-lateral arrangements regarding Turkish immigrant workers, there was no such arrangement undertaken between Turkey and Britain.

In the late 1950s and 1960s a large-scale labour migration had taken place from Turkey to Western Europe. Although many of the immigrant Turks went to Germany, other receiving countries included France, the Netherlands, Belgium, Sweden and Britain.

Yet Turkish migration to Britain could be traced back a little further. The British Empire annexed Cyprus in 1914 and the residents of Cyprus became subjects of the Crown and a migration from Cyprus to Britain started in the early

---

[24] Definition of a Turk in this study includes: All Turkish nationals including the ones who are ethnically Kurdish, Turkish-Cypriots, and British citizens who are ethnically Turkish or originally from Turkey.

1920s. By the 1930s, there were almost 1,000 Cypriots in the country, even though most of them were Greek-Cypriots; a few of them were Turks (Oakley 1979: 13).

During the 1950s, Turkish-Cypriots began to immigrate to Britain for economic reasons (Sonyel 1988: 12). By 1958, the number of Turkish-Cypriots in the country was 8,500 (Bhatti 1981: 2). Their numbers increased each year as rumours about immigration restrictions appeared in the media (Bhatti 1981: 2).

After the independence of Cyprus, the country joined the Commonwealth and until the Immigration Act of 1962, significant numbers of Cypriots migrated to Britain. This Act affected the migration of Turkish Cypriots as when there were problems and unrest on the island, they were allowed to come to Britain. By 1964, the estimated number of Cypriots in the country was 78,846. Economic underdevelopment, communal hostilities and political uncertainties resulted in emigration from the island in substantial numbers (Bhatti 1981: 17). The political unrest in Cyprus after 1964, with violence, curfews and psychological frustration caused a sharp increase in the number of immigrants to Britain.

After the 1962 Act, smaller numbers of migrants continued to come to Britain. Following the war in 1974, several thousand Cypriots entered Britain (Oakley 1979: 13). The number of Cypriots in early 1980s was estimated at 160,000 and 20-25 per cent were estimated to be Turkish (King 1982: 93).

The existence of Turkish Cypriots was instrumental in establishing links with the Turks living on the mainland. Some of the early Turkish immigrants to Britain in the 1960s and 1970s were recruited as workers and chefs in restaurant businesses of already established Turkish Cypriots.

As Turks were not required to have visas till 1989, many of them came to Britain freely (Küçükcan 1999: 62). The majority of Turks initially subscribed to the idea of return but only a handful of them could actually do so. The migration of Turks to Britain took place mostly on an individual basis, not as families. Almost all of the early generation came to London as single men, either unmarried or leaving their wives and children behind. The intention of returning and the feeling of insecurity prevented immigrants from bringing their wives and children with them. Intentions to return back were strengthened by sending money home and investing there. Yet at later stages as the myth of return began vanishing, family re-unification started. Several developments such as changes in the country of origin, changes in the host society and internal changes either to the individual or to the immigrant community acted as forces for migrants to reconsider their position abroad. Eventually the idea of return lost its salience by the increasing number of family unions that led to permanent settlement abroad (Küçükcan 1999: 7). Now what happens is that other than having properties in Britain they also own properties in Turkey and every year spend their summer holidays there. This suggests that they are here to stay without jettisoning, if adapting, their cultural background.

The 1991 census seems to have failed to measure the Turkish population in Britain accurately, as is the case with the Cypriot population (Küçükcan 1999: 63). The growing number of new Turkish-owned businesses in various fields, the increasing number of social, welfare and religious organizations addressing a larger clientele and the growth in the population of school-age children and asylum-seekers in recent years suggest that the number of Turks is now somewhere between 250,000 and 300,000.

Turkish community is not evenly distributed across the country. As a result of the process of 'chain migration', a reconstruction of their traditional milieus in Britain became possible. Ladbury (1979: 309) earlier found that there was a willingness to stay here among the Turks. The use of social networks, kinship relations and patronage has perpetuated the concentration of the Turks in the same quarters of the city (Küçükcan 1999: 65). Now almost all Turks live in Greater London and in surrounding districts of London, and there are many Turks from the same village or district of a particular city. A kind of village transplantation has taken place. An earlier research on Turks found out that 54 percent of the Turkish respondents preferred living with Turkish neighbours (Dokur-Gryskiewicz 1979: 187). Turks in London live mostly in northeast London. Today, the Turkish community is visible in certain areas of North and North-East London such as Barnet, Enfield, Edmonton, Wood Green, Palmers Green, Islington, Stoke Newington, Haringey, Hackney and Tottenham. In South London, they live in Elephant and Castle, Lewisham and Peckham. Some others have settled in Lewisham, Southwark, the city of Westminster, Barnet, Kensington and Chelsea.

Whilst Turks are not evenly distributed across the country but concentrated in certain areas to the effect of reconstructing Turkish *mahalla*s or neighbourhoods, on the other hand, diversity among these Turks along the lines of ethnicity, ideology, culture, identity and religion is another obvious characteristic. As a direct result, the traditional homeland Turkish culture, identity and diversity are, to a great extent, reproduced and reconstructed in the British context as well, which paved the way for the emergence of the Anglo-Turkish Muslim law in Turkish London.

*Emergence of super-hybrid Anglo-Turkish Muslim law* As we have seen above, there are five different patterns of solemnization of marriage in Turkey: (a) Civil marriage, (b) religious marriage, (c) both civil and religious marriages at the same time, (d) civil first without solemnization for a period and then the religious marriage, and (e) religious first and after a while, civil marriage.

On the other hand, in *angrezi shariat*, most British Muslims register their marriage first because of concerns of *izzat*. If a Muslim couple want to marry, they will actually marry twice. By doing so, they meet the requirements of both Muslim and English law. In addition, they fortify the strength of *nikah* by incorporating official legal rules into their unofficial laws.

Küçükcan summarizes the types of marriages between Turkish indivudials in London as follows: (a) Marriages between individuals living in England and living in Turkey; (b) Marriages between individuals living in England and living in Cyprus; (c) Marriages in London (i) between mainland Turks; (ii) between Turkish-Cypriots; (iii) between mainland Turks and Turkish-Cypriots; (iv) outside the Turkish community (Küçükcan 1999: 85, 99).

Among the Turkish community in London, it is observable that 'the migration experience and diaspora situation has changed some facets of wedding rituals and marriage presentations' (Küçükcan 1999: 98). Küçükcan notes, '(T)here was a new type of network developing, in addition to that of kin and friendship networks. I would like to refer to it as a 'religious network' originating not in blood relations, neighbourhood or in village origin but belonging to particular religious movement' (Küçükcan 1999: 108). He goes on to explain that:

> ...religious families and Islamically educated young people within the Turkish community would like to marry someone who has similar tendencies. In many cases this is seen as the precondition of mutual understanding and compatibility... an ideal marriage is based on Islamic rules whereby religious rituals are observed and children are brought up according to Islamic principles (Küçükcan 1999: 109).

Our participant observation on the Turks in London confirms the above-mentioned phenomenon. Over the last nine years I have been observing Turkish marriages in London. In May 2001, I have interviewed six newly married couples. For our research purposes, this sample was selected on the basis that the bridegroom was originally from Turkey who did not have an indefinite residence permit but had only a visa for a limited period of stay. In all these six cases, the bridegroom is from Turkey and came here to study with the intention of going back to Turkey. Then they met suitable candidates and decided to marry and stay. Four of the brides are from the London Turkish community, one is of Pakistani origin and the other of Kenyan origin who were all born and raised in the UK.

In all these six cases, they married religiously with a *nikah* at the engagement ceremony and counted this as only an engagement (diametrically opposite of the *angrezi shariat* practice of the solemnization of the marriage), even though they were rightfully and legitimately married in Islamic law. The underlying reason was as follows: These marriages were all arranged. In these arranged matching attempts, the girl and boy might meet and talk in the presence of a third person. If they like each other, they can get engaged, and during this period they need to get to know each other more closely. To legitimize their meetings without attendance of the third person, parents wanted them to marry religiously in order not to commit a sin.[25]

When they agreed on all aspects during engagement they registered their marriages with the English law. Yet still at this stage they were not seen as married in the eyes of the community, although even according to *angrezi shariat* there is nothing more left to do. The reason that they wanted to register their marriages has immigration or visa purposes. Although they sincerely intended to get married, it was not time yet. They may not be ready for *düğün* (the real wedding ceremony) for different reasons. But, the bridegroom's visa vas limited and in order to have him stay in Britain they officially married but did not solemnize the marriage till

---

[25] Küçükcan's findings concur with our observations. He observed that 'As soon as the engagement was announced, a religious wedding contract (*dini nikah*) took place in order to enable the couple to see each other in accordance with the Islamic rules. Generally after six months engagement the couple married in Germany and the wedding ceremony was repeated in London'. He also notes a similar wedding that took place between a Turkish man and a French convert woman, Küçükcan (1999: 111).

*düğün*. Although, as we underlined above, both in Muslim law and English law they were legitimately married. These two marriages were not enough for the solemnization of marriage in the eyes of Anglo-Turkish community. The prospective couples had to wait for *düğün*, which is the traditional wedding ceremony that takes place in banqueting suites, hotels, restaurants, or a mosque's meeting and wedding hall (a separate function room which is not a prayer area) to get the parents' and community's recognition that they were husbands and wives.

They also needed to register their marriage with the Turkish consulate as in all these cases the bridegrooms were Turkish citizens and in four of the six cases the brides were Turkish nationals who had to inform authorities of their marriage under the Turkish law.

In the Kenyan and Pakistani brides' cases this was much more important for if they did not register the marriage with the Turkish consulate within four weeks of the official English marriage, they would have lost their right to become a Turkish citizen automatically on the grounds of marrying a Turk. After the four week period elapses, the automatic right to citizenship expires and they need to learn Turkish and stay in Turkey for a period of minimum five years to become a Turkish citizen.

In sum, in the area of marriage, many Muslim Turks in London marry three times in accordance with this new hybrid law. First, they employ *nikah*, during their 'engagement' period without consummating their marriage, even though they are rightfully and legitimately married in Islamic law following their *nikah*. Then, they register their marriage with the English state for immigration and civil purposes, so that the bride or bridegroom can stay in the country if his/her visa is expiring. In some cases, the civil registration takes place before *nikah*. Yet these two marriages are still not enough for the solemnization of marriage in the eyes of Anglo-Turkish community. The prospective couple has to wait for *düğün*. Moreover, they will need to register their marriage with the Turkish consulate as well if they have a Turkish nationality. In sum, whilst an ordinary English couple marries once, for some Muslim Anglo-Turks, at least three marriage procedures are needed before it is solemnized and consummated.

### *Post-Modern Hyper-Fragmentation*

In these *darura* times, some young people have developed adaptive strategies to cope with the challenges of modern life. These young Muslims navigate at the *madhhab* level across unofficial Muslim law. The legal pluralism inherent in Islamic jurisprudence helps them to find answers to their everyday life dilemmas. They select, eclectically and also pragmatically, a convenient answer from one of the *Sunni* mainstream *madhhabs*. By employing this kind of modern individual *takhayyur*, a Muslim 'becomes his/her own mufti',[26] or a micro-*mujtahid*, making sometimes swift decisions in face of a minor but instant problem. In the British context, a recent research has found that: '(e)ven on… points where Muslims

[26] Murad (1999).

believe that English law is incompatible with Islamic law, they have found little difficulty in living within its strictures, partly because there is no consensus on these issues among Muslims themselves and partly because they are not considered obligatory from a religious point of view' (Ansari 2002: 23).

One can observe many Muslims surfing on the inter-*madhhab*-net. A *Hanafi* follows the *Shafii madhhab* and combines the noon prayer with the afternoon one or the evening prayer with the night one.[27] Normally *Hanafi* law does not permit this. Or, surfing in the area of ablution is also possible:[28] according to *Shafii madhhab*, if a man touches a woman, he will need to renew his ablution before praying, but if he bleeds, he will not. In the *Hanafi madhhab*, the two instances are diametrically opposite. Also, in the *Hanafi madhhab*, when performing ablutions, one has to wash one's feet completely. Then, if the person wears a tight leather sock during the next 24 hours and wants to renew his ablution during the day, then it is enough that he/she simply touches this leather sock with a wet hand symbolically instead of washing the whole foot. In the *Hanbali madhhab*, one can do this with a normal sock as well. It is thus not surprising to see some *Hanafi*s taking advantage of this *Hanbali* view when they perform ablutions in non-Muslim environments where it is not convenient to wash the feet. A golden tooth or filling is not permitted under *Hanafi* law, so Muslims follow the *Shafii* views when wanting to do so (Beşer 1991: 180). Regarding alcohol, although there is a consensus that drinking is prohibited, the external usage is permitted by some *Hanafi* scholars (Beşer 1991: 183-187). Thus, surfers from other *madhhab*s usually benefit from this. Regarding interest, Abu Hanifa and Muhammad al-Shaybani are of the view that in *dar al-harb*, it is permissible between a Muslim and a non-Muslim. Others oppose this opinion, so if an individual wants to accept interest, he follows the former view (Beşer 1991: 192-193). This is not an exhaustive list of examples.

While some of these micro-*mujtahid*s confine their rulings to the boundaries of the four *madhhab*s, many others claim that they can deduce their own interpretations directly from the *Qur'an* and *Sunna* (see Murad 1999). It is even suggested that 'in the absence of sanctioned information from recognized institutions, Muslims are increasingly taking religion into their own hands' (Mandaville 1999). Thus, one frequently hears young Muslims say that one can now find all the necessary information on *Qur'an* and *Hadith* DVD-ROMs. A kind of access which the *madhhab imam*s did not have (Islahi 1999).

Muslims in the post-modern age, have not abandoned their religious laws in favour of the *lex loci* but have found ways to reconstruct it under the conditions of *asr al-darura*, paving the way for a new Muslim legal pluralism and that new *ijtihad*s take place, showing the dynamic character of Muslims and their unofficial laws. Although nobody would flag it as such, these decisions exemplify modern *takhayyur* and new *ijtihad*, slowly paving the way for a new *fiqh*. Thus, forgetting about the simmering and heated discussions on the opening of the gate of *ijtihad*, in practical life under the conditions of *asr al-darura*, Muslims have been

---

[27] See for such a permission, TDV (1999, 43).

[28] See for examples, http://www.Sunna.org/msaec/articles/madhhab_issues.htm.

exercising *ijtihad*, maybe showing the irrelevancy of theoretical discussions.

It is obvious that at the end of the day this state of affairs may lead to millions of *madhhabs* and there will be a post-modern fragmentation in the Muslim socio-legal sphere(s).[29] In *asr al-darura*, there is a danger of post-modern fragmentation as individuals claim to be and act as *mujtahids*. In traditional Islamic jurisprudence, consensus (*ijma*) contributed to the creation of a relatively fixed body of laws (Esposito 1998: 83). As a leading British Muslim scholar, Dr. Abdal-Hakim Murad of the University of Cambridge, strongly asserts 'with every Muslim now a proud *Mujtahid*, and with *taqlid* dismissed as a sin rather than a humble and necessary virtue, the divergent views which caused such pain in our early history will surely break surface again. Instead of four *madhhabs* in harmony, we will have a billion *madhhabs* in bitter and self-righteous conflict' (Murad 1999).

In the English (and possibly Turkish) context, lack of responsiveness of the official system to the expectations of Muslims 'may to a very large extent have been responsible for the now commonly observed phenomenon of "avoidance reaction"' (Menski 1993a: 241). Muslims, thus, try to avoid getting involved with the official legal system. It appears that the official legal system is unable to command the respect and attention of a large segment of the Muslim minority population. There exists a distrust of the official system of justice.

One of the leading *fiqh* experts of Turkey, Professor Hayrettin Karaman, points out another danger in that if there are no clear answers to contemporary questions, then Muslims might be confused and follow un-Islamic ways (Karaman 1996: 536).

To prevent all these, a new activity is required that will respect the tradition but will also satisfy the demands of Muslims in the post-modern age.

---

[29] For a strong but informed critique of micro-*mujtahids*, see Murad (1999). On this, see for another critique by Sa'id al-Buti, http://www.Sunna.org/fiqh/buti_vs_salafi.htm.

# Chapter 8

# Looking to the Future

## Legal Uniformity

In practice the claims of legal modernity do not fully work and official state law has limits, a situation which feeds legal pluralism. Thus, social engineering through law is not a simple but rather a highly contentious matter. Despite the claims of legal modernity, socio-legal studies have repeatedly discovered that there are alternative normative orderings in society and that resistance to official law is always an issue at stake. As one writer comments, 'the "reach" of state power and state law is subject to specific conditions and always falls short of its ideological pretensions' (Hunt 1992b: 59).

Some problems emerge during modernization: The lack of power behind modernization programmes can cause failure, there may be a difference between reality and over-ambitious aims, insufficient knowledge of reality or ignorance of it, the lack of exploration of the possible consequences, and the neglect of social phenomena, cultural conditions, religious and customary traditions (Kulcsar 1987: 81). At times state law can be seen as unnecessary, avoidable, and remediable by the people or society. Laws do not work effectively if they are not congruent with their social context. It is evident that no law can ultimately compel action. All the law can do is 'try to induce someone, by order or by persuasion or by suggestion, to a certain course of action' (Allott 1980: 45-46).

This might easily cause differential treatment to the different ethnic minorities that can possibly undermine the respect for the lawmaker. The view from within the ethnic minorities is that therefore the law and its personnel are biased.

As the present study substantiates, the post-modern challenge of multiculturalism exists in the legal sphere as well. The metanarrative discourse of uniform national legal systems, and of modernity, is challenged by local folk, ethnic and small cultures, their 'unofficial' obligation systems, and other normative orders. There is always a resistance from the periphery. In other words, there are limits to the role of state law in shaping societies. People do not simply obey the rules which are enforced by the state from above, and they do maintain their own self-perceptions of legal affairs. Unofficial laws co-exist with official ones, so that legal pluralism arises as a factual situation where different modes of legal regulation overlap in their application to and within society. All three case studies explored clearly show that the reality of dynamic legal pluralism might be a matter of concern everywhere. The failure of legal modernity is obvious. The powers of tradition, local customs, and resistance to change from the top and cultural diversity are inevitable realities of everyday life. Since law is a socio-cultural construct, legal diversity is a fact and not a fiction like legal modernity.

As regards Muslims in particular, the inescapable conclusion is that despite the uniformity claims of the modern nation-states in the socio-legal sphere, expulsion or non-recognition of unofficial Muslim laws has not proved a total success, as Muslims have developed their own ways of reconstructing the legal arena, paving the way for dynamic Muslim legal pluralism.

Uniform official laws are not always absolutely effective. Official law alone cannot deal with social problems and it has a limited capacity to enforce social change. States should acknowledge that there are limits and resistance to official laws in the community where their sovereignty is not absolute and that legal pluralism is a fact. However, this does not mean that unofficial laws always exist in direct opposition to the official law. The process is more complex and dynamic.

## Official Legal Pluralism

It should also be discussed here whether the application of a Muslim personal law is practical, viable and possible in England and/or Turkey. As seen above, the Union of Muslim Organizations of UK and Eire (UMO) has been campaigning for a separate system of Islamic family law (Muslim personal law) which would be applicable to all British Muslims. This attempt proved unsuccessful. Although, since then, such demands have been made intermittently, they have been strongly rejected.

Another scholar, Bulaç, also proposes that marriage affairs and solemnization should be left to communities and the state's role must be reduced to registering what happened.[1] In 1996, one of the deputies in the Grand National Assembly made a proposal of a similar nature. He proposed that *mufti*s should be given rights to solemnize and register marriages and *nikah* should be made legal and permissible before registration, which is a punishable offence under the Criminal Code, 237/4.[2] Already earlier Fındıkoğlu (1957: 16) made such a suggestion: 'it is expected that Turkish legal experts and sociologists will collaborate to combine civil and religious elements in one form of marriage which can be celebrated by men of religion, as is the practice in northern countries, or one which is celebrated with full ceremony after a civil marriage, as is the practice in some Western countries'.

In Turkey, some Muslim activists are very keen on the enactment of new laws regarding the Civil Code. They do not only wish to be regulated by the principles of Muslim law when they are living in a modern and secular nation-state, but also when they seek to formalize such an arrangement within the state's own legal system. They have come up with their alternative solutions, trying to legalize '*imam nikahı*' to prevent abuses and misuses. They propose some changes to the Civil Code.[3]

---

[1] *Yeni Şafak*, 11 April 1996, p. 12.

[2] *Milliyet*, 1 April 1996, p. 23.

[3] See for instance *Bizim Aile*, July 1993, pp. 18-19.

Demands to return to Islamic law in Turkey have constituted a vivid part of the political and academic agenda, although the majority of people do not seem to be interested in these issues.[4] In the legal realm, the élite carried out a power struggle for control of the state. Turkish law became an arena in which rival visions of the social and political world could be located. The legal discourses espoused by Islamic and secular law practitioners and users project two different visions of the world and the place of Islam in people's lives (Starr 1992: xxii).

In that context, some scholars and politicians espouse the very idea of an Islamic social, political and legal system called '*adil düzen* (just system)'. Since it is legally forbidden to include Islam in political life, they use metaphors, never tacitly referring to any kind of Islamic system. Supporters of this view envisage a kind of *millet* system in the country. The main concern in this proposal is not the non-Muslims living in the country, since they have virtually no problems with the Civil Code, but the Muslim majority's own official local law. Thus, some Muslim reformers want to eliminate this conflicting situation, and favour only (at least for now) application of the Muslim family law which would be applicable to all Muslims.

From time to time, these Muslim activists voice their demands in the public medium. For example, Prime Minister Necmeddin Erbakan, as he then was, the leader of the Welfare Party, called for the *millet* system or personal law system.[5] In the academic field, Ali Bulaç is the most prominent example of a writer who advocates such a system.[6] He refers to the Medina society of the time of the Prophet and the 'Medina Constitutional Charter',[7] the first application of a *millet* system in Muslim history.[8] In this multi-religious and legally pluralist project (Bulaç 1995a: 161-167; 1995b: 84; 1997: 113), each block would have their religious, cultural and legal autonomy (Bulaç 1995b: 85; 1995a; 163; 1997: 89). They would be independent in their internal affairs (see in detail Bulaç 1995a: 161-167; 1995b: 82-87; 1997). There are also some other projects offered by Muslim scholars which claim to directly refer to the *Qur'an* rather than to the historical experience of Muslims (see Gürpınar and Malkoç 1994: 169-172).[9]

---

[4] The main reason for this is the construction of Turkish Muslim law. Since they have found ways of coping with the conflicts between the official legal system, the Muslim family law and the contemporary social realities by employing Turkish Muslim law rules, they do not feel any necessity to change the system as a whole, which would anyway be very difficult to do under existing circumstances.

[5] *Yeni Yüzyıl*, 7 December 1996, p. 12.

[6] Bulaç (1992a; 1992b; 1992c; 1993a; 1993b; 1995).

[7] For a detailed study on the Medina Constitutional Charter and the English translation of the full text see Ahmad (1993), see also Ishaq (1968: 231-232).

[8] For a detailed discussion about the original Medina Constitutional Charter of the time of the Prophet and its main articles see Karaman (1993: 166-171).

[9] Moreover, it is well known that a huge body of literature exists regarding human rights in Islam. In that context, the *millet* system, the Medina Constitutional Charter and the situation of non-Muslim minorities in Muslim countries have been continuously referred to and discussed. This issue at times constitutes an important section in contemporary books about Islamic law and society in Turkey. For such an example see Aydın (1995; 1996: 229-236).

Some minor changes are proposed as well. For instance, the Welfare Party, the party in power during the first half of 1997, proposed a more limited legal reform in the form of a change for the recognition of *nikah*.[10] Some members of the party even ventured to declare that law should not be produced by the state but by individuals and communities. The state must assume the role of a co-ordinator.[11] However, Akyol (1996: 12) harshly criticizes this view and asks what will be the law of this co-ordinatorship, and who would produce the law. In the end he seems to conclude that an apparatus, whether the state or not, will have to be in the role of ultimate authority of producing or enacting laws and of being a co-ordinator in Zengin's terms (see in detail Akyol 1996).

On the other side of the fence, the official law still expects to assimilate the unofficial law and to acquire a monopoly over the socio-legal sphere. As seen in chapter 5, official marriage campaigns for already married couples with *nikah*, and amnesty laws for officially 'illegitimate' children are clear evidence of the hope of state law to assimilate 'the other' on its own terms. Thus, it would be reasonably fair to say that there is no reconstruction on the official side with regard to family law, despite sharp awareness of the perpetual survival of the unofficial Muslim law.

As far as the application of Muslim personal law in England is concerned, although Muslims would argue that the application of Muslim family law is based on the right of the freedom of religion, the counterargument would be that freedom of religion is subject to limitations if these are necessary to protect public welfare, order, morals, or the fundamental rights of others. At that point, it is also argued that the priority of individual autonomy justifies religious discrimination (Bradney 1993: 52).[12]

It was offered that there could be an establishment of a tribunal which decides cases relating to Muslim family issues, taking into account their religious and cultural values and norms. It was further commented that if the official legal system became more sensitized and religious experts were consulted for advice at some early stage in the trial, then there would be no need to undermine the 'uniformity' of the system (Nielsen 1993a: 8). Some form of mechanism within the family court system could take more account of Muslim needs, for example by having a quasi-judicial or arbitration hearing (Nielsen 1987b: 33). David Pearl (1987a: 168) also put forward a type of informal family court system. He seems to suggest a body modelled on the Jewish *Beth Din*, which has in some cases a quasi-official capacity in that the state recognizes it as being the representative and regulatory body of most Jews in Britain (Pearl 1987a: 168). Professor van Koningsveld (1996) also espouses the idea of these informal family courts by

---

[10] *Yeni Yüzyıl*, 7 December 1996, p. 12.

[11] Bahri Zengin of the Welfare Party is the champion of these ideas. See for example, *Milli Gazete*, 14 November 1995, p. 12.

[12] At the same time, however, he points out that in other instances legal rules can facilitate the wishes of individuals whose religious demands do not involve disturbing autonomy of others. Thus, for example, a personal law system into which believers can opt if they wish to do so is entirely compatible with the demands of personal autonomy.

underlining the applications of the colonial powers in the colonies. He asserts that colonial powers respected socio-legal realities in the colonies, so there is no reason to disregard this reality at home. Indeed, the Jewish *Beth Din*, more or less, serves this quasi-official function. Islamic *Shari'a* Councils can be considered to be the Muslim counterpart of the Jewish *Beth Din* (see in detail ISC 1995; Badawi 1995: 73-80). Significantly, however, this is evidence of Muslim self-organization, rather than a state-sponsored institution. Badawi (1995: 78-80) emphasizes the dangers in state sponsorship, contending that the Muslim community is not homogeneous and these councils may be seen as lackeys of the state.

However, keeping such bodies on an unofficial level provides an important autonomy to Muslims which would be lost were control to be given to the state. This would also undermine the respect for the official legal system.

Poulter (1995: 86) suggests, on the same lines as van Koningsveld (1996 and earlier), that the state should encourage institutions like *Shari'a* Councils in the settlement of family disputes between Muslims by mediation in England. In this situation, the 'remedies' of the English legal system will still be available. Dissatisfied individuals can always go to the English courts if not happy with *Shari'a* Councils (Poulter 1995: 86) or they can chose not to go to the council in first place. Yet if someone is unhappy with the English law, there is usually no other option for them. Muslim wives whose husbands do not wish to give them *talaq* would find that recourse to English law does not solve their problems, as long as their minds are under the influence of Muslim law concepts (Pearl and Menski 1998: 76).

Poulter (1995: 87) also suggests that Muslims should be involved in all questions of law reform so that a Muslim perspective contributes to legal change in England. Fourthly, judges could be trained to be more sensitive to the religious and cultural needs of Muslims and other minorities (Poulter 1995: 87). As Nielsen (1985: 17) suggests, the courts could be made aware of the parties' religious identity and this could be a material factor in deciding a case. Or, Muslim lawyers well versed with Muslim law could be attached to British family courts as adjudicators (Speelman 1991: 10).

In view of Poulter, the wisest strategy would be to retain the present policy of adapting an essentially monistic structure on an ad hoc basis so that the reasonable religious and cultural needs of the ethnic minority communities are satisfied. He argues that the English legal provision is adequate for Muslims and their families (Poulter 1998: 204). Poulter also suggests that Muslims should hope that as English law goes through the regular procedures of being updated the underlying spirit of the fundamentals of the *Shari'a* is increasingly embodied in its provisions (Poulter 1998: 233). In this regard, Muslim organizations must be encouraged to become fully involved in the general law reform process. Attention should be turned away from such a grandiose scheme to more mundane local initiatives with greater potential for achieving practical results (Poulter 1998: 233-234). It is also recommended that legal professionals serving in family courts should receive training in the religions and cultures of the ethnic minorities of the country and expert lay members should be included in the court hearings (Nielsen 1993: 8).

On the issue of incorporation of Muslim family law into the English law, Pearl and Menski (1998: 77) state that the demand for an officially recognized Muslim personal law has not been fully supported by enough Muslims, concurring the earlier observation that 'soundings among ordinary Muslims seem to suggest little active support for the idea' (Nielsen 1992: 53).

It seems clear that for the above-mentioned reasons and many others not explicitly stated that a separate Muslim personal law cannot and will not be introduced in England. In short, it does not seem plausible in the foreseeable future that demanding an application of Muslim personal law in England would prove successful. Moreover, the Pakistani experience shows clearly that having a personal system will not ultimately solve the problem of concern.

As for Turkey, it is immediately striking that the Welfare Party, which was the main political force advocating a personal law system in the country, was abolished on 14 January 1998 (see for details, Gülalp 1999; Boztimur 2001). One of the grounds for its abolition according to the published report of the Supreme Court, was the party's stand vis-à-vis a personal law system in Turkey.[13] The Supreme Court held that:

> ...application of a legal pluralist system based on belief prevents social development and destroys national unity. However, one of the conditions of being a nation is to reach legal and judicial unity. Law must be organised in accordance with the modern values not religious, sectarian or ethnic differences. It is clear that legal pluralism which would pave the way for individuals to be subject to different laws based on belief differences would cause religious discrimination and shake the secular system based on reason and modern science. It is not possible that such an idea would enjoy protection under the Constitution and human rights conventions that reflect universal values.[14]

That shows again that the Turkish state is very sensitive about uniformity of the legal system, while the Turkish society, as far as the man in the street is concerned, sees less of a problem, as people have already reconstructed their own Muslim laws to govern family affairs as skilful legal navigators.

As in the case of Pakistan, although there is a personal law system in the country, the state has felt a need to reform the personal law of the Muslim majority. This shows that the modern nation state will always want to interfere and regulate the family law issues of the people, at least of the majority, which will lead to dynamic legal pluralism whether or not the state has a purportedly uniform legal system or a personal law system.

As a matter of fact, it seems that modern nation-states under the heavy influence of legal modernity will always need to harmonize, regulate, unite, control and supervise the society, which in all cases shows a tendency to be legally plural. For a number of concerns such as human rights, protection of women and children, prevention of crimes and demands of the welfare state, the modern state has felt a need to interfere.

The official legal system proposes some justification in rejecting incorporation

[13] *Zaman*, 23 February 1998, p. 10.

[14] *Official Gazette of Turkish Republic*, 22 February 1998, p. 12.

of Muslim family law into the official legal system. First of all, as is stressed above, incorporation of a personal law into the law is against the very notion of a uniform legal system. A second is given as the practical difficulty of applying Muslim family law. Third is the question of interpretation. Who will interpret the Muslim law? It is also asserted that civil courts will hardly be legitimate in the eyes of Muslims, and plurality of Muslim views and their non-uniform structure will prevent the latter option. The fourth difficulty stems from the human rights dimension: Muslim family law is seen as contradictory to fundamental human rights. In short, there seems no justification for acceding to the claim of establishing a separate system of Muslim personal law.

Some other legal scholars also suggest that a separate law is not necessary. They emphasize that the *millet* system is not without its problems as many cases in India have shown (Hamilton 1995: 91). It was also argued that a unified system of law has in the past helped to create a more cohesive society (Poulter 1990b: 158; Speelman 1991: 7). In this context the socio-legal reality in Pakistan regarding the application of the *millet* or personal law system and its problems will be briefly analyzed.

Pakistan provides many examples of interaction of religious and local customary traditions and instructive debates about the role of the modern state vis-à-vis the scope and problems of Islamic legal reform. Islam is the foundation of state legitimacy in Pakistan. The official law is used as an instrument by the state (regime) to serve the purposes of Islamic modern nation-state ideology.

Legal reforms to the personal laws in South Asia have always focused on the laws of the majority, while minority laws have been almost totally ignored, although for different reasons. For instance, unlimited polygamy under Hindu law in Pakistan is still allowed, although it is forbidden in India.[15] Conversely, Indian Muslims may marry up to four wives in accordance with Muslim law, while the Pakistani law, in section 6 of MFLO 1961, made attempts to provide some legal constraints to this practice.

In the Pakistani case, although there is a quest for modernity, traditional Muslim law has not been completely abandoned. Rather, there has been an attempt by the state to reform, limit, regulate and restrict it. Regarding this issue, a crucial debate between traditionalists and modernists has been continuing in the country. According to traditionalists, these reforms militate against the basic tenets of Islam. Consequently, this has led to a conflict between official and unofficial laws in the daily lives of Muslims. Recent research confirms that these reform attempts of the state have led to intense clashes between two types of Muslim personal law, the local Muslim law rules and the state-sponsored codified Muslim personal law.

Thus, the reforms of the MFLO have failed to a certain extent in producing the expected and desired outcomes. There are several reasons for this. Some scholars, firstly list the failure of democracy in the country (Patel 1979: 92; Mehdi 1994: 198). Secondly, although some acts are conceived by the MFLO as illegal they are neither void nor invalid. Thirdly, the ad hoc nature of the reforms and lack of

[15] In the same vein, Muslim polygamy is not restricted in India by statute, whereas the state has tried to restrict and control it in Pakistan.

systematic Islamic rationale creates serious problems. Fourthly, the apparent discontinuity of the reforms within traditional Muslim law subjects them to heavy fire from the traditionalists. Thus, ordinary people tend to be very sceptical about 'Islamization' although they are not sceptical about Islam itself, which continues to be the source of legitimization. They view themselves as Islamic, but in different terms. In that sense, non-observance also stems from the unawareness of ignorant and illiterate people who unfortunately constitute the overwhelming majority of the Pakistani populace. Especially the people in rural areas and women are the most disadvantaged.[16] The fifth problem in the system is the diversity of opinions concerning family law issues, which causes the legal system to have a fragmented structure. Sixthly, it is widely believed that the introduction of the official law is for the poor and that the rich always escape from its application (Rashid 1987: 314). Seventhly, because of the above mentioned ignorance and low literacy level, women by and large are not aware of their rights, and even where they are, they do not have the courage nor are in the socio-economic position to fight legal battles with close relatives in a highly patriarchal society (Ali et al 1990: 28).

The role of the *ulama* and *madrasah*s in shaping and mobilizing public opinion in Pakistan is a factor that must be taken into account, given that the influence of the state bureaucracy and schools is limited especially because of a lack of resources and poverty.[17] *Ulama* have a monopoly over *madrasah*s without sharing it with the state. The proliferation of *madrasah*s paves the way for the increasing role of the *ulama* and traditional understandings. While in 1947 there were only 147 *madrasah*s in the country, today the figure is around 8000. It goes without saying that the *ulama*'s and the state's influence advance in indirect proportion to each other.

In conclusion, reform attempts of the state in Muslim family law have been challenged by the local, unofficial Muslim law. Now, despite the state's attempts, there is still more than one type of legal norm governing Muslim family law issues in Pakistan, as has always been the case. The Pakistani case is instructive in the sense that it is irrelevant whether the state has a personal law system or not; legal diversity and legal pluralism will not be overcome.

## Civil Neo-*Ijtihad*

As a result of the non-recognition of the dynamic Muslim legal pluralism, Muslim scholars and academics have been producing new *ijtihad*s to face the above-mentioned challenges. Thus, in the Turkish context, although some religious scholars are of the opinion that *nikah*, although unofficial, is sufficient for a couple

[16] The literature on the ignorance and illiteracy is vast, for some examples, see Samar Fatima Saifi (1980); Kozlowski (1998: 83); Jalal (1991: 77); Patel (1991); Wakil (1991: 42-77); Ali et al (1990: 9-31); Alam and Karim (1986: 87-106). For government publications admitting the reality, see MPDGP (1998).

[17] On the role of *ulama* and *madrasah*s see in detail Nasr (2000: 139-180).

to be married in Islam[18] there are now other Islamic scholars, religious academics and Islamic community leaders who strongly advise the official registration of the marriage. They are of the view that in the absence of recognition of Muslim law, official registration of the marriage is absolutely necessary to avoid the kind of problems and complications mentioned above (see for example Beşer 1993: 161; 1997: 302).[19]

In the conditions of Turkey in which Muslim law carries no legal weight, it will be beneficial for couples, especially for women, to register their *nikah* (Beşer 1997: 302; 1993: 161).[20] Otherwise, husbands can easily walk away without any legal remedies and financial responsibilities (Beşer 1997: 302; 1993: 161).[21] As a result, they conclude, it would be wrong to marry without official registration. They indirectly, by emphasizing the drawbacks, reject unofficial marriages without registration.[22]

Moreover, Aktan (1997) underlines that the official marriage ceremony is also adequate for the purposes of Islam.[23] He says, unofficial '*nikah*' stems from just a psychological necessity.[24] To him, official marriage is sufficient and meets all demands of Muslim law in effectuating a *nikah*.[25] In addition, the Directorate of Religious Affairs espouses the very same idea (see Balcı 1994: 100). Some academics in Islamic Theology Faculties and the Directorate of Religious Affairs also support this view (Kerimoğlu 1989b: 17). A recent publication on Islamic marriage by a respected scholar also confirms that a civil marriage provided that it

18 *Kadın ve Aile*, July 1987, p. 43; *Yörünge*, 28 July- 3 August 1996, pp. 5-10.

19 See in detail *Kadın ve Aile*, July 1987, pp. 40-45.

20 *Kadın ve Aile*, July 1987, pp. 40-45.

21 Islamic periodicals in the country from time to time devote their issues to these matters. See for instance *Kadın ve Aile*, N. 28, July 1987; *Yeni Bizim Aile*, N. 49, February 1994; *Yörünge* 28 July- 3 August 1996, pp. 5-10. In a more recent comment on this, a popular religious columnist and authority in Islamic jurisprudence, Ahmet Şahin, in his column disapproves this practice not on the basis of the classical Muslim law but on the basis of social experience *Zaman*, 11 April 1998.

22 See for ideas of some religious scholars (Dr. Faruk Beşer, A. Rıza Demircan, Lütfi Doğan (ex-Director of the Directorate of Religious Affairs), Halil Günenç, Prof. Dr. Mehmet Hatipoğlu, Prof. Dr. Hayrettin Karaman, Selahattin Kaya (*Mufti* of Istanbul)) *Kadın ve Aıle*, N. 28, July 1987, pp. 40-45; and for the views of Kazım Güleçyüz, Ali Eren, Dr. Semra Yenigün, Ali Rıza Demircan, Ali Rıza Temel, Dr. Abdulaziz Bayındır, Halil Günenç, Prof. Dr. Bekir Topaloğlu, Nuriye Çeleğen, *Yörünge* 28 July- 3 August 1996, pp. 5-10. See also *Yeni Bizım Aile*, February 1994, p. 20. See also Günenç (1990b: 117).

23 *Zaman*, 12 January 1997, p. 2.

24 Since a civil marriage is a completely secular act. people do not feel comfortable when they are entering a new stage in their lives. Regardless of whether they are an observant (or practising) Muslim or not, they usually make sure that they get married by *nikah* as well. This phenomenon is very remarkable in the sense that it shows us how sometimes tradition might be confused with the religious law. As is known, in Islamic jurisprudence, marriage is not a sacrament but a civil contract and the only conditions attached to it are the existence of offer and acceptance and the presence of two witnesses.

25 Also Aktan (1997) espouses the same idea, although to him it is not necessary according to Muslim law. See *Zaman*, 12 January 1997, p. 2.

is in line with the Islamic law is also *sahih*[26] (Özcan 2001: 281).

In order to satisfy the psychological needs of people, some scholars propose that, a combination of the religious and official marriages would be ideal (see for instance Balcı 1994: 100-102). The suggested solution is to use a 'religious official' (in the majority of cases an *imam*) to conduct an official marriage ceremony in which both religious and civil elements are combined (Hooker 1975: 365). Balcı (1994: 102) argues that as funerals are administered by *imams* who are employed by the municipal governments, in the same way municipal governments can employ *imams* to register and solemnize marriages to meet the demands of both Muslim law and the official legal system and thereby satisfy and put to rest the doubts and scruples of the people. Marriage formalities can also be checked by the Directorate of Religious Affairs, which has an excellent network throughout the country via mosques and employees. They could solemnize and register marriages in tune with the provisions of the Civil Code and Muslim law. Aktan (1997) also supports the idea, yet he is not so optimistic on the ground that some groups would consider this proposal to be against the principle of *laicité*.[27] One of the prominent religious scholars, Günenç (1990b: 117) supports the idea that there is no difference between a civil servant and an *imam* under the Islamic jurisprudence regarding solemnization of marriage. Neither of them has a special role in conditioning a *nikah* (Günenç 1990b: 117). Thus, although he does not put it explicitly, Günenç (1990b: 117) seems to suggest that if official law modifies itself to meet some requirements of the local Muslim law, which are mostly psychological such as reciting a part of *Qur'an* or some prayers, then the civil servants could also solemnize the *nikah*.

As another solution, an Islamic jurisprudence professor, Hayrettin Karaman, proposes the idea of giving the right to divorce to women.[28] To him, this purely Islamic application will absolutely prevent limping marriages.[29] All that those who are getting married need to do, is before the religious marriage takes place the prospective husband accepts the prospective wife's right of divorce in the presence of two witnesses.[30] Indeed, if the point which is drawn by Aktan that the fundamental principle in marriage according to Islam is to protect the woman's rights is taken into account, then Karaman's proposal becomes even more important.[31]

On the other hand, some scholars argue that there are some essential differences between *nikah* and the official marriage ceremony (see for example Kerimoğlu

[26] Islamically valid.

[27] *Zaman*, 12 January 1997, p. 2.

[28] *Kadın ve Aile*, July 1987, p. 44. As a matter of fact, the Islamic *Shari'a* Council of the United Kingdom which is an unofficial Islamic court deals with the religious law issues of the Muslim minority in the country has been employing such a contract, ISC (1995); on these Muslim *Shari'a* Councils, see Badawi (1995); Surty (1991); Pearl and Menski (1998). Term 2 of this contract stipulates that the wife is entitled to obtain a *talaq* if her husband enters into a polygamous marriage without her written consent.

[29] This is the position also taken by the Islamic *Shari'a* Council of Britain.

[30] *Kadın ve Aile*, July 1987, p. 44.

[31] *Zaman*, 12 January 1997, p. 2.

1989b: 17; Beşer 1997: 300-302). Under Muslim law, a Muslim woman cannot get married to a non-Muslim as official law allows (Kerimoğlu 1989b: 18). There is nothing about *mahr* in official marriage, which is obligatory under Muslim law (Kerimoğlu 1989b: 17; Beşer 1997: 301). Third, the official ceremony allows for two females to count as the necessary number of witnesses for the marriage. This, however, is not acceptable in Muslim law.[32] Fourth, although non-Muslim witnesses are acceptable in the official law, this is not acceptable under Muslim law (Beşer 1997: 301-302). Fifth, the bar of fosterage is not recognized under the Civil Code (Beşer 1997: 301). Finally, official law prohibited an Islamic right, namely that of polygamy (Kerimoğlu 1989b: 17-18).[33]

It is clear that there are also some flaws in these arguments against the idea of considering the official ceremony to suffice as the *nikah*, since people can themselves adjust their official marriage ceremonies to meet the demands of Muslim law. They can have two male witnesses, they can decide the *mahr* which official law does not prevent and they can avoid marrying Muslim women to non-Muslims. Moreover, juristic discourse does not support the idea that if a law does not recognize some rights or restricts them, and then it is totally objectionable and illegitimate in Islam to conduct by or through them. Thus, if an intended marriage is monogamous and the above mentioned matters concerning the ceremony are observed, then people can easily use the official law to satisfy the demands of Muslim law as well.

Regarding polygamy, many religious scholars discourage it by reference to fundamental sources of Islam (see for example Ateş 1997: 12-16). Some others discourage it because of the unofficial position of Muslim law and its lack of official legal weight. Beşer (1993: 161), for example, underlines that without official registration, it is not Islamically right to get married polygamously since Muslim law has no legal weight, which causes many problems for women regarding limping marriages, maintenance rights, inheritance and so on. Aktan (1997) asserts that it is quite possible to suspend the right to get married polygamously by reference to some of the applications of Caliph Omar.[34]

## Muslim Alternative Dispute Resolution

In England, Muslims enjoy a relatively high degree of religious and cultural autonomy. They have adapted and continually reinterpreted their values and lifestyles for their new settings. Muslims in Britain have tried to construct a home away from home (*desh pardesh*) to be part of British society and to keep their

---

[32] In Muslim law, witnesses must be two males or one male and two females in civil law cases.

[33] Another religious scholar, Günenç (1990b: 117), puts that under the *Shafii* law, the consent of the parents of the bride is necessary and essential. However, the official does not seek such consent if she is over 18, thus the official marriage is invalid in the eyes of the *Shafii* Muslims, Günenç (1990b: 117).

[34] The second Caliph after the Prophet. He had suspended the right of Muslim men's marriage to the women from the people of the book. See *Zaman*, 12 January 1997, p. 2.

culture. Research has shown that that many important disputes among them never come before the official courts. Many disputes among Muslims in Britain are settled in the context of informal family or community conciliation (Pearl and Menski 1998: 77-80). Senior members of the families or community leaders take their place in informal conciliation processes. Though customary arbitration procedures may not fit in with the western legal system, their decisions are generally honoured and implemented through a mix of sanctions and ostracism (Jones and Gnanapala 2000: 103-104).

As mentioned above, having recognized that the official legal system has been hesitant to solve their disputes in the context of Islamic family law, Muslims have established informal conciliation mechanisms.

One of the objectives of the ISC is 'establishing a bench to operate as court of Islamic *Shari'a* and to make decisions on matters of Muslim family law referred to it' (ISC 1995: 3-4). The ISC is a quasi-Islamic court that applies Islamic rules to deal with 'the problems facing Muslim families as a result of obtaining judgments in their favor from non-Islamic courts in the country, but not having the sanction of the Islamic *Shari'a*' (ISC 1995: 7).

A characteristic feature of the work of the ISC is its eclectic approach to Muslim law. It is not bound by or tied to any particular *madhhab* and is prepared to offer the parties the benefits of any *madhhab* which suits their particular need regardless of whether this conforms to the school prevailing in their country of origin, domicile, or nationality. These Councils' verdicts are 'based upon rulings derived from the main four schools of thought together with other sources within the *Sunni* Tradition, as well as the Literalist School' (ISC 1995: 7). Scholars are from 'all major schools of thought among the *Sunni*s' (ISC 1995: 5, 7). These councils have called upon the wider heritage of Muslim law to avoid the difficulties faced by Muslims. Sometimes, they have chosen minority interpretations or views to resolve a conflict by employing *takhayyur*.

If a woman seeks divorce, she must have a valid reason. Women who want divorce apply to the Council in writing. Then the Council tries to contact the husband at least three times at monthly intervals and advertises in a local newspaper. If they contact him they try to reconcile the situation. If they fail to reconcile, then they apply *khul* (Shah-Kazemi 2001: 12-13, 17-18). This divorce nullifies the Islamic marriage only. Obviously, *khul* right is not within the *Hanafi madhhab*.[35] The Council grant *khul* in the following circumstances: the husband is missing; the husband suffers certain physical defects; when the wife embraces Islam but the husband refuses to do so after the waiting period being notified of the change; when the husband ill treats the wife or fails to perform his marital

[35] The reason I highlight that these rulings are not based on the *Hanafi* School but were eclectically selected from other schools is that the majority of Muslims in Britain are from the Indian subcontinent and an overwhelming majority of them are *Hanafi*s. Even though classical Muslim jurisprudence allowed individuals under necessity to follow another school for a specific issue, which is called *takhayyur*, for centuries, this has not been applied for a number of reasons. Now, what the Islamic *Shari'a* Council is doing is institutionalising this classical right of the individual.

obligations or does not maintain her, in spite of having the means to do so; when the husband does not or refuses to comply with the judge's order to divorce his wife for one of the mentioned reasons (ISC 1995: 5, 7, 12-13). Most of these circumstances are not in the *Hanafi madhhab* either. This is nothing but a neo-*ijtihad*, exercised in the face of the necessities and demands of dynamic Muslim life in England.

The unofficial *Shari'a* courts in England are now the places where neo-*ijtihad*s take place, showing the dynamic character of Muslims and their unofficial laws. Although nobody would flag it as such, the decisions taken by these *Shari'a* courts exemplify modern *takhayyur* and new *ijtihad*, slowly paving the way for a new *fiqh* for the Muslim minority.

## Official *Ijtihad* Committees

The Turkish state expected that through education, legal literacy campaigns, and urbanization, the populace would give up its local customs and religious laws and would only follow the official law. However, it is becoming clear that Muslim legal pluralism is a metropolitan reality, too.

In addition to family law, many refer to Muslim law in their dealings in business, finance, and insurance matters, despite the non-recognition of this law by the state. An indication of this phenomenon is the fact of that *fatwa* books are now bestsellers in Turkey. Moreover, many newspapers have *fatwa* columns, and recently, the number of Turkish *fatwa* sites in cyberspace has increased. Scholars have been asked about such contemporary topics as working in Europe, *madhhab*s, using amplifiers when reading the call to prayer, Friday prayer and work, *dar al-Islam*, fasting and travelling by train, the stock exchange, tax, halal meat, marrying non-Muslim women, *talaq*, court divorce, polygamy, nationalism, unemployment benefits, inflation, interest, customs tax, bribery, depositing money at a bank in non-Muslim countries, selling alcohol in a non-Muslim country, gambling in *dar al-harb*, sterilization, plastic surgery, using perfumes, abortion, *ijtihad*, military service, organ transplantation, prayers (*salat*) on the bus, VAT, mortgages, the European Union, alcohol in medication, eau de cologne, life insurance, feminism, fertility clinics, etc.[36] In this regard, it is also worth mentioning that a recent survey has found that 14.1 per cent of the Turkish people have accounts with interest-free Islamic finance institutions despite the fact that such finance institutions carry no state guarantee for any losses, as opposed to mainstream banks.[37]

Albeit secular, the state has set up an *ijtihad* committee, *Diyanet İşleri Başkanlığı Din Işleri Yüksek Kurulu* (The Directorate of Religious Affairs Higher Committee of Religious Affairs). The pervasiveness of Islam and Muslim law in Turkish society is so evident that the state has needed to respond to this socio-legal reality by establishing this committee. In Turkey, religious institutions are linked to state bureaucracy, without any autonomy. Soon after the establishment of the

[36] See Beşer (1991); Kurucan (1998); TDV (1999).

[37] See 'Anar Anketi March 2001', http://www.anararastirma.com.tr.

Republic, the Directorate of Religious Affairs was established and all Islamic activities were placed under its auspices. The state has also tried for a long time to create its own version of Islam. The HCRA is a result of this scheme.

This organ of the state has a somewhat awkward status. While the state does not recognize Muslim law, and arguing for its application is a criminal offence, the HCRA bases its arguments on officially non-recognized Islamic legal and jurisprudential sources. This committee endeavours to produce *fatwa*s to the questions put to it.[38] The HCRA responds to the socio-legal reality by exercising *ijtihad* and by also employing *takhayyur*.

There is a problem of doctrinal authority and legitimacy in this Turkish case, similar to the Pakistani one. Some people do not see the rulings and *ijtihad*s of the HCRA as legitimate for it is an organ of a modern secular state with the scholars of the HCRA being paid civil servants of the state. These scholars must act within the limits of the secular law and try to adapt the Muslim law to state law; scholars at the HCRA are not free to operate within the realm of *Shari'a*. If there is a clash between *fiqh* and secular state law then the *lex loci* must prevail. Indeed, on controversial issues such as head-scarves, these scholars have had to either keep silent or to advocate the state's position.

## Faith-Based Movement Leaders to Implement Neo-*Ijtihad*

The examples of *Shari'a* Councils in Britain, the Higher Committee of Religious Affairs in Turkey, and micro-*mujtahid*s show that the question is no longer whether the gate of *ijtihad* is open or not but which *ijtihad*s are necessary and which ones are to be followed. Many people and institutions claim a right to exercise *ijtihad* and indeed do practice *ijtihad*. Whether these are legitimate in the eyes of the people or not is another question. The problems of doctrinal authority, legitimacy, and post-modern fragmentation will still need to be dealt with.

To prevent post-modern fragmentation but at the same time implement new changes and *ijtihad*s without confronting problems of civil disobedience or lack of legitimacy, it seems that faith-based movement leaders with effective organizations to implement their ideas have a role to play. In this respect, Fethullah Gülen has found a wide audience for the implementation of his ideas, which are described as reformative by some scholars (Eickelman 1999: 89).

### *Ideas Implemented in the Public Sphere: Gülen and His Movement*

Fethullah Gülen is an Islamic scholar, thinker, writer, and poet. He was born in Erzurum, in the east of Turkey, in 1938. He was trained in the religious sciences informally by several Muslim scholars and spiritual Sufi leaders. In 1958 he was awarded a state preacher's license and in the following years expanded his

[38] These *fatwa*s can be found in book form published in 1999, see TDV (1999); a *fatwa* website of the committee is in service, too: the Directorate of Religious Affairs *Fatwa* Site, http://www.Diyanet.gov.tr/dinibilgiler/dinibil.html.

audience base. In his sermons and speeches he emphasized the pressing social issues of the times. He has inspired many people in Turkey to establish educational institutions that combine modern sciences with ethics and spirituality. His efforts have resulted in the emergence of the faith-based Gülen movement, whose boundaries are loose and difficult to specify.

By exercising *ijtihad* without flagging it as such, Gülen reinterprets Islamic understanding in tune with the *Zeitgeist* and develops a new Muslim discourse that is based on 'the synthesis of Islam and science; an acceptance of democracy as the best form of governance within the rule of law; raising the level of Islamic consciousness by indicating the connection between reason and revelation; and, achieving this-worldly and other-worldly salvation within a free market and through quality education' (Yavuz 2000, see also Altınoğlu 1999, 102). Stated summarily, Gülen's interpretation of Islam seeks a compromise with the modern living world. He claims that an understanding of secularism existed among the Seljuks and Ottomans: they employed *ijtihad* in worldly matters, and enacted laws and decrees to respond to the challenges of their times.

Some of the elements, if not all, in Gülen's discourse may not be unique to him; there have been a number of Muslim intellectuals and *mujtahid*s who developed new ideas and understandings in the face of the challenges of modernity, without making concessions from the Islam of the past. Yet what makes Gülen unique is that as a leader he has successfully persuaded and mobilized many people – numbering a few million at the present time – to establish institutions and to put into practice his discourse in over 60 different countries.

Given his strong influence in particular on his followers and in general on the Turkish society, Gülen's ideas regarding legal pluralism, renewal, *takhayyur*, and *ijtihad* are likely to find an appeal and to have a chance of being implemented in the future. What follows is an outline of some of his ideas on some issues relevant to this study.

Gülen sees diversity and pluralism as a natural fact.[39] By making reference to the Turkish Islam of the Seljuks and Ottomans and to their practice of religious pluralism, he underlines that a legally pluralist system existed during those times as well.[40] Gülen believes that there is a need for *ijtihad* in our age. He says that he respects the scholars of the past but also believes that *ijtihad* is a necessity: to freeze *ijtihad* means to freeze Islam and to imprison it in a given time and space. He argues that Islam is a dynamic and universal religion that covers all time and space, and renews itself in real life situations; it changes from one context to another, and *ijtihad* is a major tool in enabling this. But he affirms that sometimes the ideas about *ijtihad* are luxurious, as there are many more serious problems challenging Muslims, and that everybody could claim to be a *mujtahid* in today's circumstances. He puts a strong emphasis on raising and educating strong believers, and is of the opinion that it is important to raise individuals who would meet the criteria of a *mujtahid*.[41]

---

[39] http://www.fethullahGülen.org/articles/interfaith.html.

[40] http://www.m-fGülen.org/eserleri/kk/laiklik.htm.

[41] Author's interview with Gülen (Yilmaz 2000b).

Regarding *takhayyur*, Gülen believes that under *darura* an individual can follow another *madhhab* by judging the situation with his conscience, ensuring that he is truly under *darura*. While opposing *talfiq*, Gülen argues that keeping *madhhab*s separate will always give people a chance to navigate across these *madhhab*s if any problems arise.[42]

With regard to the definition of *darura*, Gülen underlines that an individual can define whether a particular situation is one of *darura* or not. Yet he goes on to say that if everything is left to the individual to define what *darura* is, then there is a danger of arbitrariness, and this could possibly be against the spirit of *Shari'a*, which states that believers should sometimes endure difficulty as life is essentially a test. Gülen emphasizes that in the name of *maslaha* and *darura*, people, by nature, are inclined to follow the easiest option at all times;[43] if everything is permitted in the name of *darura*, then the essence of religion will not remain. He argues that if the earlier generations had given permission to everything and relaxed the requirements, then today there would not be anything remaining as far as religion is concerned.[44] Gülen suggests that a consultative body or a group of scholars can define specific *darura* conditions in detail, which individuals can use as guidelines.[45]

Gülen strongly advocates such *ijtihad* committees (Gülen 1995: 288). He is of the opinion that it is no longer possible for individuals to be *mujtahid*s on all matters (*mujtahid-i mutlaq*); *ijtihad* committees should perform this task instead. In Gülen's view, it is quite possible that in the future people from all sorts of disciplines will come together in research centres and constitute *ijtihad* committees. He argues that these committees should consist of scholars from different subject areas who advise on particular issues. They should also use the latest technological advances of the age, including computers, cyberspace, DVD-ROMs, and so on.[46]

To Gülen, even today scholars can come together and try to answer some contemporary questions put to them. In the future, he says, if more suitable *mujtahid*s emerge, they can come up with their own better solutions and *ijtihad*s. For *ijtihad* committees, theology faculties could be suitable bases or the Directorate of Religious Affairs could set up such a committee or could evolve its already existing *fatwa* committee (HCRA) into an *ijtihad* committee. The state can choose to enact any of these *ijtihad*s. Then Muslims would be following such enacted official law, since they are ordered to obey their rulers (*ulul amr*), as long as the latter act within the realm of *Shari'a* and are not against its spirit. In Gülen's view, states should establish these committees as a service to society, and he gives as an example the Directorate of Religious Affairs Higher Committee of Religious

42 Ibid.

43 Ibid; see also Gülen (1995, 285-286).

44 Author's interview with Gülen, Yilmaz (2000b); see also Gülen (1995, 285-286).

45 Author's interview with Gülen, Yilmaz (2000b). On psychology and warning of caution, see also Karaman (1999, 327-332); Beşer (1991, 7, 8, 265); Sa'ban (1996, 450, 451); Gülen (1995, 295-286, 288, and 309).

46 Author's interview with Gülen, Yilmaz (2000b).

Affairs (HCRA). Yet if a state fails to do this, Muslims should employ civil *ijtihad.*

*Implementation of the New Discourse and Ijtihad in the Public Sphere*

Gülen's discourse is not only meant on a rhetorical level; he encourages all his followers and sympathizers to realize his ideals and to put into practice his discourse. He is now 'one of the latest and most popular modern Muslims which Republican Turkey has produced' (Kadıoğlu 1998: 18). His biography, published in 1995, has entered into its fiftieth edition. Every year in the print media roughly 1,000 news items are reported on Gülen.[47] The actual number of Gülen's millions of followers and sympathizers is not known, but it is agreed that it is the largest civil movement in the country (Sadowski 1999). He is now described as an opinion leader in Turkey.[48] In newspapers he is at times referred to as the unofficial civil religious leader of Turkey.[49]

His movement is deemed to be moderate; it 'can be considered "modern" in the sense that it espouses a world view centered around the self-reflexive and politically participant individual's ability to realize personal goals while adhering to a collective identity, and it seeks to shape local networks and institutions in relation to global discourses of democracy, human rights, and the market economy' (Yavuz 1999a: 195). The movement has a television network (Samanyolu TV) and two radio channels (Burç FM, Dünya FM), broadcasting in Europe, the Near East, Central Asia, and the Indian sub-continent; a daily newspaper, *Zaman*, with a circulation of 300,000 in Turkey, and is also published in 16 countries including Europe and the USA; a number of periodicals specializing in various fields; and a news agency (Cihan News Agency).

Gülen has also been successful in transforming and even revolutionizing the Muslim educational discourse by taking it from its traditional form as practised in the *madrasah* and *Qur'an*ic literacy courses to the modern high school and university format. He has encouraged people to establish modern schools rather than traditional ones. Businessmen who follow Gülen's message are very active in education and have 'built up a vast educational empire in over 50 countries' (Pope 1998). People inspired by Gülen have established more than 500 elementary and secondary schools, of which almost 250 are outside Turkey, in Europe, the USA, the Central Asian republics,[50] Tanzania, Senegal, Nigeria, Russia, Japan, South Africa, Australia, and Cambodia; a number of language and computer courses; hospitals and health clinics; tutoring chains, six universities in Turkey and Central Asia; and almost 600 student hostels only in Turkey. The movement has also an Islamic bank (Asya Finans), and an insurance company. The movement has also a share in the music industry of Turkey.

Modern sciences are taught in the schools operated by Gülen's followers. Another progressive aspect of the Gülen movement in the field of education

---

47 See http://www.m-fGülen.org.

48 Enis Berberoğlu, *Hürriyet*, 10 August 2000.

49 Avni Özgürel, *Radikal*, 2 March 2001.

50 See for a list of some of these schools, Yavuz (1999b: 599).

pertains to the raising of the educational standards of women. In the words of Yavuz, 'A decade ago, this religious community was not even willing to allow their daughters to go to secondary or high schools. They preferred to send female students to the *Qur'an*ic courses or the strictly female *Imam Hatip* schools. For years, Gülen publicly and privately encouraged the community to educate all their children regardless of gender. Today, there are many all-female schools and many of their graduates go on to universities' (Yavuz 1999c: 125).

Gülen has changed the traditional tutoring practice of teaching by making available printed texts and audio-visual material. Recently, cyberspace has also come into play. Moreover, millions of copies of these materials have been sold and distributed. The daily *Zaman* alone has distributed many of Gülen's books and audiocassettes, free of charge, to all its readers in several promotional campaigns. The movement's radio channels and TV station have been broadcasting Gülen's speeches and sermons as well. Gülen's media and publishing houses have been propagating and disseminating Gülen's discourse on several issues, such as science, modernity, democracy, secularism, dialogue, modern education, etc., as well as his views amounting to '*ijtihad*s'.

Daily *Zaman* also distributed an inter-*madhhab* text, Zuhayli's ten volumes *Encyclopaedia of Islamic Fiqh* (1997). 300,000 copies of this set were distributed to *Zaman*'s subscribers free of charge. In this work, the author cites views of the four *Sunni madhhab*s. In some cases even, he cites the fifth *madhhab*.

Interfaith dialogue is also on the movement's agenda, all over the world. In the countries where it operates, it either establishes interfaith organizations, associations, and societies or is in close contact with men of faith. In the schools Gülen encouraged to establish, Muslims, Christians, Jews, Buddhists, Shamans, and others study together.[51] Daily *Zaman* employs Jewish and Christian columnists, who contribute regularly.

The movement brings together scholars and intellectuals regardless of their ethnic, ideological, religious, and cultural backgrounds. The Journalists' and Writers' Foundation functions as a think-tank on related issues. The Abant Platform is a result of the attempt to find solutions to Turkey's problems regarding sensitive issues such as laicism, secularism, and religion.[52] A new theology, as it were, has been created by this movement in the Abant Platform. For the first time on 19-20 April 2004, Washington DC hosted the 7th annual meeting of the Abant Platform. The April 19-20 meeting was organized with the help of the Journalists and Writers Foundation as well as Johns Hopkins University Paul H. Nitze School of Advanced International Studies (SAIS).[53]

---

[51] Author's interview with Cemal Uşşak, Yilmaz (2000d).

[52] http://www.turkishdailynews.com/old_editions/07_14_01/dom.htm#d5.

[53]http://www.sais-jhu.edu/pubaffairs/media_events/PDF_Events/Conference%20Program.pdf. The Daily *Zaman* reports that this year's topic was 'Islam, Democracy and Secularism: The Turkish Experience'. According to SAIS Vice Dean John Harrington the School hosted Abant Platform because of Turkey's experiences with Islam and secularism, particularly after September 11th. The first day of the meeting was a scientific conference in which many Turkish and American intellectuals participated. On

Gülen has also encouraged his sympathizers to work on contemporary issues such as genetic engineering, organ transplantation, music, art, modern theology, tafsir, Muslim-Christian dialogue, secularism, and possible Islamic responses to these issues.[54] The movement's publishing houses – Nil, Kaynak, Töv, Truestar, Fountain – have supported and published these works. Many of Gülen's followers publish papers and books and write Ph.D. theses on these very topics. New *fatwa* books are published by these publishing companies, too. The theology journal Yeni Ümit has been disseminating these ideas for the last decade. A new intelligentsia in the lines of Gülen's discourse has also been evolving.

In short, 'Gülen is the engine behind the construction of a "new" Islam in Turkey' (Yavuz 1999c: 121). Even though there has not been any discussion of *ijtihad*, neo-*ijtihad* or *tajdid* within the movement, it is obvious that all these developments and activities are results of Gülen's *ijtihad*s, even though he would neither claim nor admit that they were so. Put differently, what he does can be labelled as, '*ijtihad* (and *tajdid*) by conduct'. People in his movement, believing that he is capable of reinterpreting Islam to respond to the necessities of the time, follow in his footsteps, put into practice his discourse, and realize his ideals.

*Neo-Ijtihad and Faith-Based Movement Leaders*

Muslim legal pluralism is an everyday reality in both Muslim and non-Muslim environments. By surfing on the inter-*madhhab*-net, Muslims have successfully responded to the changing social and cultural contexts and have found solutions within Islam without abandoning their Muslim identity and law. Even though such surfers are not always psychologically comfortable with what they do, at least it helps them to feel that they are still operating within the boundaries of the *Shari'a*.

Muslim legal pluralism, skilful legal navigators, surfers on the inter-*madhhab*-net, and post-modern micro-*mujtahid*s paving the way for possible socio-legal fragmentation will be part of Muslim community life for years to come, and the challenge of the future will be to accommodate this reality within traditional Islamic jurisprudence. It is clear that at this point a new understanding and application of *ijtihad*, responding to and reflecting the *Zeitgeist*, will take place.[55]

To prevent post-modern fragmentation but at the same time to implement new changes and *ijtihad*s without inciting civil disobedience, it seems, as the Gülen case exemplifies, that civil faith-based movements have a role to play. Having almost replaced the *ulama*'s doctrinal authority, faith-based movement leaders

April 20, participants in round table meetings discussed Turkey's experiences with Islam and secularism and the applicability of those experiences to the Middle East, Central Asia as well as the Caucasus. Turkish State Ministers Mehmet Aydın and Ali Babacan as well as Republican People's Party (CHP) member and Istanbul Deputy Kemal Derviş attended the Platform. Well-known academic Francis Fukuyama from SAIS and Bilgi University's Prof. Mete Tunçay, representing Abant Platform, made the opening remarks, http://www.zaman.com/?bl=national&alt=&trh=20040419&hn=7537 on 19 April 2004.

[54] Author's interview with Gülen, Yilmaz (2000b).

[55] See for a succinct summary of new *ijtihad* and *mujtahid*s in the contemporary Muslim world, Karaman (1985a); Karaman (1985b).

exercise or advocate *ijtihad* and, most importantly, have the means to implement their ideas in the civil realm, even though in most cases they do not label or flag this as *ijtihad* or *tajdid*. Individuals are not coerced into following a faith-based leader and tend to judge the leader with different criteria: the level of piety, appearance, honesty, knowledge, sincerity, and so on. Whether these criteria are relevant, scientific, or correct is beside the point; they are enough to legitimize a faith-based leader, his discourse and practice for the followers in one way or another.[56]

The function of a faith-based movement leader in relation to *tajdid* could present itself in three ways. First, the leader maybe a *mujtahid* himself and practice *ijtihad*. Second, he may follow the *ijtihad*s of certain other individuals or institutions, and by doing so, legitimize their *ijtihad*. Third, the leader may set up an *ijtihad* committee, the *ijtihad*s of which will (may) be followed first by the leader and then by his followers. In this way fragmentation of the Muslim socio-legal sphere as a result of activities of post-modern Muslim surfers and micro-*mujtahid*s can be avoided while Muslim legal plurality and diversity are maintained.

At this point, it must be emphasized that it is the duty of Muslim scholars to research Muslim legal pluralism and its consequences in real life other than in marriage issues and to develop a sociology of *fiqh*. It is also important that this socio-legal reality be closely monitored both by scholars and the legal system to secure a healthy future. This requires a supra-modern standpoint as will be elaborated below.

## Supra-Modern State Laws

The post-modern legality's challenge comprises of resurgence of local laws, dynamic legal pluralism, and the continuous construction of hybrid unofficial laws, all of which show the limits of modern state law. An escape from this socio-legal cul-de-sac requires a transcendence of the status quo and the challenges posed by post-modern legality. The new conceptualization of a legal system needs to be elastic, not rigid, in order to come to grips with reality, which is innovative and not anachronistic. It also needs to transcend internal fragmentation and the loss of autonomy. Otherwise, where the official law does not deal with reality, it would be unable to claim the loyalty of at least some Muslims.

History has shown that the very existence of states is a must. Human beings have not found any another viable framework within which to preserve communal life. Thus, the problems of legal organization have to be discussed within the context of the state paradigm. However, that condition does not mean that one has to accept the presumptions of legal modernity. Dynamic legal pluralism as a post-modern phenomenon is here to stay. On the other hand, if the state is an apparatus of society, and the raison d'être of the state is to serve society; the state law has to

---

[56] A writer reports that 'some *Hanafi* Nurcus follow the *Shafii* rites during their daily prayers due to their loyalty to Said Nursi', (Yavuz 1999b: 586).

be realistic, taking cognisance of the fact of post-modern legal conditions and religion, multiculturalism, transnationalism, globalization, internationalization, supranational entities, multiple modernities and resurgence of the local. Only in this way would state law be able to sustain its credibility.

The state's move should be a supra-modern multi-cultural response. I offer the term 'supra-modern legality' to mean a legality of the supra-contemporary situation. Supra-modernity does not have to be directly linked to modernity, which is an accidental result of the unique developments in the Western world. That perspective could be sustained in all eras, pre-modern, modern and post-modern. It is not a result of historical developments. From a higher point of view, which is supra-modern, the socio-legal sphere could still be seen as unified. But the perspective to be taken is very important. Differences could be seen as embroideries of a carpet or different colourful stones of a mosaic.

Law is a very complicated process. Speculation of the future in the socio-legal realm is not an easy task. State law must behave like a chameleon, adapting itself to its changing surroundings (Santos 1987). Thus, the state should constantly check the socio-legal sphere with a multiculturalist and post-modern mentality which does not presume a culture's superiority to the others and adapt its law to the demands of reality. It must be noted, as this study has tried to indicate, that law is a socio-cultural construct and not only specific conditions of the socio-legal situation of a locality or a country. Law is a local knowledge. Perhaps, a supra-modern law should take into account that, in today's global village where transnational movements and diasporas are important actors, it is also relevant to speak of law in terms of 'glocal' knowledge. Multi-culturalism is here to stay. As post-modern theory has constantly reminded us no culture is superior to others. Thus, a supra-modern law should treat all cultures equally in theory and equitably in practice with a view of positive discrimination vis-à-vis vulnerable members of the society in terms of gender, age, religion, culture and ethnicity. This of course implies constant bargaining processes where communities, civil society institutions and public bodies constantly engage with each other.

Supra-modern legality admits post-modern legality and constantly adjusts itself to the living reality. Otherwise, legal pluralism, like legal modernity, could be repressive to women and children if the state purports to be unaware of factual situations in the socio-legal sphere. The most viable option is not to disregard dynamic legal pluralism but rather to recognize it and to act in accordance with this perpetual fact. Otherwise, the vulnerable members of society will continue to be vulnerable. The problem is not whether to have a personal law system, but to have a sensitive legal system that constantly monitors the socio-legal sphere and develops itself accordingly to protect the members of society.

In this mentality, an umbrella law to prevent post-modern hyper-fragmentation of the socio-legal sphere would be needed. It does not matter whether the legal system is personal or not. It could be a uniform legal system but not homogeneous, in that it provides exceptions for local laws but still constantly monitors the living reality of dynamic legal pluralism, and makes proper adjustments. A supra-modern legal system is still formally a uniform legal system within the boundaries of a state. Thus, it does not lead to anarchy or nihilism as in the post-modern theory, but recognizes diversity as part of the mosaic. 'Unity within diversity' is flagged in this understanding with themes of tolerance, multi-culturalism and post-modernity.

A supra-modern mentality and mechanism takes into account the demands and necessities of people from all backgrounds, especially with regard to culture, religion and ethnicity. This method should not be enforced in an ad hoc character in the hope of the demise of all unofficial laws, but should try to strike the delicate balance between the demands of the socio-cultural legal sphere and the political stand of the state.

Supra-modern mentality reflects the specifications of legal pluralism as there is an umbrella state law to prevent post-modern anarchy yet it is still different from weak legal pluralism. In a supra-modern legal system, instead of different personal laws within a specific code, adjustments are made in accordance with different local laws, reflecting the awareness of post-modern legality.

As a matter of fact, the English legal system is a likely candidate to this kind of supra-modern legality with its tradition of flexibility, adjustment to changing conditions and tolerance to other cultures. Yet as I noted above, it is still not an example to a supra-modern model as there is no mechanism to monitor the socio-legal sphere and certain objective criteria to take into account different local laws. Moreover, the English law makes its adjustments in an *ad hoc* fashion with the hope of the demise of local laws and the success of homogeneity. It is also relatively slow to respond to the challenges of socio-legal reality, as is seen in the case of Muslims' legal discrimination and limping marriages.

In conclusion, within the reality of post-modern legality, dynamic legal pluralism, unofficial laws and legal postulates are here to stay. The challenge of the future is to make their ever-present co-existence as conflict-free as possible. However, in the near future, the onus of the survival of the reality of Muslim legal pluralism will still be mainly on the shoulders of skilful Muslim legal navigators and their leaders.

# Bibliography


Abadan-Unat, Nermin (1978) 'The modernization of Turkish women'. In: V. 32 N. 3 *Middle East Journal*. 291-306.

Abadan-Unat, Nermin (1981) (ed) *Women in Turkish society*. Leiden: E. J. Brill.

Abadan-Unat, Nermin (1986) (ed) *Women in the developing world: The evidence from Turkey*. Denver: University of Denver.

Abdulhalim, Shaikh (1993) *Muslim family laws*. 4th ed. Lahore: PLD Publishers.

Abdullah, Ahmed (1973) *The historical background of Pakistan and its people*. Karachi: Tanzeem Publishers.

Abdur Rahim, M. A. (1988) *Principles of Muhammadan jurisprudence according to the Hanafi, Maliki, Shafi'i and Hanbali schools*. Reprint. Lahore: Mansoor.

Abdur Rahim, M. A. (1994) *Principles of Muhammadan jurisprudence*. Reprint. Lahore: Mansoor.

Abedin, Syed Z. and Ziauddin Sardar (1995) (eds) *Muslim minorities in the West*. London: Grey Seal.

Abel, Richard L. (1974) 'A comparative theory of dispute institutions in society'. In: V. 8 *Law and Society Review*. 217-347.

Abel, Richard L. (1979) 'The rise of capitalism and the transformation of disputing: From confrontation over honor to competition for property'. In: N. 27 *UCLA Law Review*. 223-255.

Abel, Richard L. (1981) 'Conservative conflict and the reproduction of capitalism: The role of informal justice'. In: V. 9 *International Journal of the Sociology of Law*. 245-267.

Abel, Richard L. (1982) (ed) *The politics of informal justice*. V. I-II. New York: Academic Press.

Abu-Rabi, Ibrahim M. (1995) (ed) *Islamic resurgence. Challenges, directions and future perspectives. A roundtable with Prof. Khurshid Ahmad*. Islamabad: Institute of Policy Studies.

Acar, Feride (1990) 'Türkiye'de Islamcı hareket ve Kadın. Kadın dergileri ve bir grup üniversite öğrencisi üzerinde bir inceleme'. In: Şirin Tekeli (ed) *Kadın bakıs açısından 1980'ler Türkiyesinde Kadınlar*. Istanbul: İletişim. 69-101.

Acar, Feride (1994) 'Women in the ideology of Islamic revivalism in Turkey: Three Islamic women's journals'. In: Richard Tapper (ed) *Islam in modern Turkey: Religion, politics and literature in a secular state*. London. New York: I. B. Tauris. 280-303.

Adal, Erhan (1991) *Fundamentals of Turkish private law*. Rev. 3rd ed. Istanbul: Beta.

Afshar, Haleh (1989) 'Gender roles and the 'moral economy of kin' among Pakistani women in West Yorkshire'. In: V. 15 N. 2 *New Community*. 211-223.

Afshar, Haleh (1995) 'Islam empowering or repressive to women?' In: Michael King (ed) *God's law versus state law: The construction of Islamic identity in Western Europe*. London: Grey Seal. 54-61.

Afzal, Mohammad (1974) *The population of Pakistan*. Islamabad: Pakistan Institute of Development Economics.

Afzal, Mohammad et al (1973a) 'Muslim marriages: Age, mehr and social status'. In: V. 12 *The Pakistan Development Review*. 48-61.

Afzal, Mohammad et al (1973b) 'Marriage patterns in a rural agglomeration'. In: V. 12 *The*

*Pakistan Development Review*. 272-282.

Agnihotri, R. K. (1990) 'Conflicting pressures. The case of Sikh children in Leeds (UK)'. In: N. 6 *South Asia Newsletter* (of University of Amsterdam). 18-22.

Ahmad, Feroz (1969) 'Age at marriage in Pakistan'. In: N. 31 *Journal of Marriage and the Family*. 799-807.

Ahmad, Feroz (1977) *The Turkish experience in democracy, 1950-1975*. Boulder, Co: Westview Press.

Ahmad, Furqan (1994) *Triple talaq: An analytical study with emphasis on socio-legal aspects*. New Delhi: Regency.

Ahmad, Gulzar (1993) *Muhammad and his constitutional charter*. Rawalpindi: Institute of Islamic Culture.

Ahmad, M. B. (1951) *The administration of justice in medieval India*. Karachi: The Manager Publications.

Ahmed, Akbar S. (1992) *Postmodernism and Islam: Predicament and promise*. London.New York: Routledge.

Ahmed, Akbar S. (1993) *Living Islam: From Samarkand to Stornoway*. London: Penguin.

Ahmed, Akbar S. (1995) 'Islam and the district paradigm: Emergent trends in contemporary Muslim society'. In: T. N. Madan (ed) *Muslim communities of South Asia: Culture, society, and power*. New Delhi: Manohar Book Review Literary Trust. 63-102.

Ahmed, Akbar S. and David M. Hart (1984) (eds) *Islam in tribal societies. From Atlas to the Indus*. London et al: Routledge & Kegan Paul.

Ahmed, Akbar S. and Hastings Donnan (1994a) (eds) *Islam, globalization and postmodernity*. London: Routledge.

Ahmed, Akbar S. and Hastings Donnan (1994b) 'Islam in the age of postmodernity'. In: Akbar S. Ahmed and Hastings Donnan (eds) *Islam, globalization and postmodernity*. London: Routledge. 1-20.

Ahmed, Ishtiaq (1987) *The concept of an Islamic state: An analysis of the ideological controversy in Pakistan*. London: Frances Pinter.

Ahmed, K. N. (1972) *The Muslim law of divorce*. Islamabad: Islamic Research Institute.

Ahmed, Khursheed (1961) *Studies in family laws of Islam*. Karachi: Chirach-e-Rah Publications.

Ahmed, Munir D. (1982) 'Pakistan: The dream of Islamic state'. In: Carlo Caldorola (ed) *Religions and societies: Asia and the Middle East*. Berlin et al: Mouton Publishers. 261-288.

Ahmed, Shama (1981) 'Asian girls and culture conflict'. In: Juliet Cheetham et al (ed) *Social and community work in a multiracial society*. London: Harper and Row. 133-138.

Ahsan, Menazir (1994) 'Islam and Muslims in Britain'. In: Hussin Muttalib and Taj ul-Islam Hashmi (eds) *Islam, Muslims and the modern state: Case-studies of Muslims in thirteen countries*. London: St. Martin's Press. 339-361.

Ahsan, Menazir (1995) 'The Muslim family in Britain'. In: Michael King (ed) *God's law versus state law: The construction of Islamic identity in Western Europe*. London: Grey Seal. 21-30.

Akgündüz, Ahmet (1991) *Eski anayasa hukukumuz ve İslam anayasası*. 3rd impression. Istanbul: Timaş.

Akhtar, Shabir (1995) 'Relationships between Muslim parents and children in a non-Muslim country'. In: Michael King (ed) *God's law versus state law: The construction of Islamic identity in Western Europe*. London: Grey Seal. 31-43.

Akınturk, Turgut (1975) *Aile hukuku*. 2nd ed. Ankara: Sevinç.

Akınturk, Turgut (1991) *Medeni hukuk*. Ankara: Savaş.

Akipek, Jale S. (1961) *Türk medeni hukuku*. Ankara: İstiklal.

Akram, M. (1974-5) 'Pakistani migrants in Britain'. In: V. 4 N. 1 *New Community*. 116-118.

Akşit, Bahattin (1986) '*Imam*-hatip and other secondary schools in the context of political and cultural modernization of Turkey'. In: V. 5 N. 1 *Journal of Human Sciences*. 25-41.

Aktan, Hamza (1992) 'İslam aile hukuku'. In: BAAK *Sosyo-kültürel değisme sürecinde Türk ailesi*. Ankara: B Aile Araştırma Kurumu. 396-433.

Aktan, Hamza (1997) 'Interview with Hamza Aktan on Islamic family law'. In: *Zaman* (12 January 1997). 2.

Akyol, Taha (1996) *Medine'den Lozan'a*. Istanbul: Milliyet Yayınları.

Al-Abdin, Tayyib Z. (1995) 'The implications of *Shari'ah, fiqh* and *qanun* in an Islamic state'. In: Tarek Mitri (ed) *Religion, law and society: A Christian-Muslim discussion*. Geneva. Kampen: WCC Publications. Kok Pharos. 20-26.

Al-Ahsan, Abdullah (1992) *Ummah or nation. Identity crisis in contemporary Muslim society*. Leicester: The Islamic Foundation.

Alam, Iqbal and Mehtab S. Karim (1986) 'Marriage patterns, marital dissolution, and remarriage'. In: Nasra M. Shah (ed) *Pakistani women. A socio-economic and demographic profile*. Islamabad. Honolulu: Pakistan Institute of Development Economics and East-West Institute. 87-106.

Alavi, Hamza (1986) 'Ethnicity, Muslim society, and the Pakistan ideology'. In: Anita M. Weiss (ed) *Islamic reassertion in Pakistan*. Syracuse: Syracuse UP. 21-47.

Al-Azmeh, Aziz (1996) *Islams and modernities*. 2nd ed. London. New York: Verso.

Albrow, Martin et al (1994) (eds) *Local/global relations in London. Shifting boundaries and localities*. London: Roehampton Institute.

Alem, Syed Iqbal (1968) 'Age at marriage in Pakistan'. In: V. 8 *The Pakistan Development Review*. 489-498.

Ali, Ahmed et al (1990) 'Sociological difficulties in the implementation of legislation pertaining to women in Pakistan'. In: V. 9 N. 14 *Journal of Law and Society*. 9-31.

Ali, Muhammad Mumtaz (1992) *The concepts of Islamic ummah and Shariah*. Selangor: Pelanduke.

Ali, Parveen Shaukat (1986) *Status of women in the Muslim world*. Lahore: Aziz Publications.

Ali, Syed Mumtaz and Enab Whitehouse (1992) 'The reconstruction of the constitution and the case for Muslim personal law in Canada'. In: V. 13 N. 1 *Journal of Muslim Minority Affairs*. 156-172.

Ali, Yasmin (1992) 'Muslim women and the politics of ethnicity and culture in Northern England'. In: Gita Sahgal and Nira Yuval-Davis (eds) *Refusing holy orders: Women and fundamentalism in Britain*. London: Virago. 101-123.

Alkan, Mehmet O. (1990) 'Tanzimattan sonra 'Kadın'ın hukuksal statüsü ve devletin evlilik sürecine müdahalesi üzerine'. In: N. 3 *Toplum ve Bilim*. 85-95.

Alkan, Türker (1981) *Kadın-erkek eşitsizliği sorunu*. Ankara: Faculty of Political Sciences.

Allen, Elisha Henry (1968) *The Turkish transformation: A study in social and religious development*. New York: Greenwood Press.

Allott, Antony (1980) *The limits of law*. London: Butterworths.

Allott, Antony (1983) 'The limits of law: A reply'. In: V. 21 *Journal of Legal Pluralism*. 147-153.

Allott, Antony (1985) 'Popular law-making in Western society'. In: Gordon R. Woodman and A. Allott (eds) *People's law and state law. The Bellagio papers*. Dordrecht: Foris Publications. 21-34.

Allott, Antony and Gordon R. Woodman (1985) 'Introduction'. In: Gordon R. Woodman and A. Allott (eds) *People's law and state law. The Bellagio papers.* Dordrecht: Foris Publications. 1-9.

Ally, M. M. (1979) *The growth and organisation of the Muslim community in Britain.* Muslims in Europe Research Papers 1. Birmingham: CSIC-MR.

Altınoğlu, Ebru (1999) *Fethullah Gülen's Perception of State and Society.* Istanbul: Bosphorus University.

Altschull, J. Herbert (1984) *Agents of power.* New York: Longman.

Altuntek, N. Serpil (1993) *Van yöresinde akraba evliliği.* Ankara: Kültür Bakanlığı Yayınları.

Alum, Rolando A. Jr. (1985) 'Cultural ideology and empirical reality: Case studies in contemporary law management'. In: Gordon R. Woodman and A. Allott (eds) *People's law and state law. The Bellagio papers.* Dordrecht: Foris Publications. 35-54.

Amin, Mohammad (1989) *Islamization of laws in Pakistan.* Lahore: Sang-e-Meel Publications.

Amin, Syed Hasan (1985a) *Middle East legal systems.* Glasgow: Royston.

Amin, Syed Hasan (1985b) *Islamic law in the contemporary world.* Glasgow: Royston.

Amin, Syed Hasan (1989) *Islamic law and its implication for modern world.* Glasgow: Royston.

Amin, Syed Hasan (1996) 'Classification of legal systems in the Muslim countries'. In: H. S. Bhatia (ed) *Studies in Islamic law, religion and society.* New Delhi: Deep & Deep. 133-144.

Anderson, Benedict (1983) *Imagined communities: Reflections on the origin and spread of nationalism.* London: Verso.

Anderson, Benedict (1991) *Imagined communities: Reflections on the origin and spread of nationalism.* 2nd ed. London: Verso.

Anderson, J. Norman D. (1960) 'The significance of Islamic law in the world today'. In: V. 9 *American Journal of Comparative Law.* 187-198.

Anderson, J. Norman D. (1970) 'Reforms in the law of divorce in the Muslim world'. In: V. 31 *Studia Islamica.* 41-52.

Anderson, J. Norman D. (1971) 'Modern trends in Islam: Legal reforms and modernisation in the Middle East'. In: V. 20 *Islamic and Comparative Law Quarterly.* 1-21.

Anderson, J. Norman D. (1975) *Islamic law in the modern world.* Westport: Greenwood Press.

Anderson, J. Norman D. (1976) *Law reform in the Muslim world.* London: Athlone Press.

Anderson, Walter Truett (1995a) 'Four different ways to be absolutely right'. In: W. T. Anderson (ed) *The truth about the truth: De-confusing and re-constructing the postmodern world.* New York: G. Putnam's Sons. 110-116.

Anderson, Walter Truett (1995b) (ed) *The truth about the truth: De-confusing and re-constructing the post-modern world.* New York: G. P. Putnam's Sons.

Andrews, Ahmed (1996) 'Muslim attitudes towards political activity in the UK: A case study of Leicester'. In: W. A. R. Shadid and P. S. van Koningsveld (eds) *Political participation and identities of Muslims in non-Muslim states.* Kampen: Kok Pharos Publishing. 115-128.

Anis, Ahmad (1996) *Women and social justice. Some legal and social issues in contemporary Muslim society.* Islamabad: Institute of Policy Studies.

Ansari, Humayun (2002) *Muslims in Britain. Report.* Richmond: Minority Rights Group International.

Ansay, S. Şakir (1952) *Medeni kanunumuzun 25. yılı münasebetiyle eski aile hukukumuza bir nazar. Hukuk inkılabımızı aydınlatan tarihi teşri vesikalar.* Ankara: AUHFY.

Ansay, Tuğrul (1983) 'Review of Mary Zwahlen's *le divorce en Turquie*'. In: N. 31 *The*

*American Journal of Comparative Law*. 751-753.
Ansay, Tuğrul (1996) 'Family law'. In: Tuğrul Ansay and Don Wallace, Jr. (eds) *Introduction to Turkish law*. The Hague et al: Kluwer Law International. 109-123.
Ansay, Tuğrul and Don Wallace Jr. (1966) (eds) *Introduction to Turkish law*. Ankara: Güzel Istanbul Matbaası and The Hague et al: Kluwer Law International.
Ansay, Tuğrul et al (1965) (eds) *The Turkish criminal code*. London: Sweet & Maxwell.
Anthias, Floya and Nira Yuval Davis (1993) *Racialised boundaries*. London: Routledge.
Anwar, Muhammad (1979) *The myth of return: Pakistanis in Britain*. London: Heinemann.
Anwar, Muhammad (1992) 'Muslims in Western Europe'. In: Nielsen, Jorgen S. (ed) *Religion and citizenship in Europe and the Arab world*. London: Grey Seal. 71-93.
Anwar, Muhammad (1994) 'Muslims in Britain. Demographic and social characteristics'. In: V. 14 N. 12 *Journal of Muslim Minority Affairs*. 347-361.
Anwar, Muhammad (1998) *Young Muslims in Britain: Attitudes, educational needs and policy implications*. Leicester: The Islamic Foundation.
Anwari, A. M. (1988) *The manual of family laws*. Lahore: Khyber Law Publishers.
Apter, David E. (1965) *The politics of modernization*. Chicago: The University of Chicago Press.
Arai, Masami (1994) *Jön Türk dönemi Türk milliyetçiliği*. Istanbul: İletişim Yayınları.
Aral, Vecdi (1992) *Hukuk felsefesinin temel sorunları*. Istanbul: Filiz.
Arat, Necla (1986) (ed) *Kadın sorunu*. 2nd ed. Istanbul: Say.
Arat, Necla (1994) (ed) *Türkiye'de kadın olmak*. Istanbul: Say.
Arat, Necla (1996) (ed) *Türkiye'de kadın olmak*. 2nd ed. Istanbul: Say.
Arthurs, H. W. (1985) *Without the law: Administrative justice and legal pluralism in mid 19th-century England*. Toronto: University of Toronto Press.
Ashraf, Ali (1981) 'The challenge of modernisation and the response in Turkey and India'. In: V. 12 N. 3 *Islam and the Modern Age*. 169-181.
Ashrafi, Talat Ara (1992) *Muslim women in changing perspective*. New Delhi: Commonwealth Publishers.
Ata, Yalçın (2001) 'Ortaçağ gelinleri', *Daily Milliyet*. 12 February 2001.
Ataay, Aytekin (1957) 'Neden İsviçre medeni kanunu?'. In: V. 9 N. 1 *International Social Science Bulletin*. 65-69.
Ataay, Aytekin (1970) 'Neden İsviçre medeni kanunu?' In: *Medeni Kanunun 50. yılı sempozyumu. Tebliğler*. Istanbul: Fakülteler Matbaası. 59-72.
Atatürk, M. Kemal (1981) *Nutuk*. V. II. Ankara: 100. Yıl Kutlama K. K.
Ateş, Süleyman (1997) *Kur'ana göre evlenme ve boşanma*. Istanbul: Yeni Ufuklar Neşriyat.
Atiyah, P. S. (1978) *From principles to pragmatism: Changes in the function of the judicial process and the law*. Oxford: Clarendon Press.
Atiyah, P. S. (1995) *Law and modern society*. 2nd ed. Oxford. New York: Oxford UP.
Aubert, Vilhelm (1966) 'Some social functions of legislation'. In: V. 10 *Acta Sociologica*. 98-120.
Auerbach, C. A. (1966) 'Legal tasks for the sociologists'. In: V. 1 *Law and Society Review*. 91-104.
Auerbach, Jerold S. (1983) *Justice without law*. New York: Oxford UP.
AUHF (1976) *Medeni Kanunun 50. yılı: Bilimsel hafta, 15-17 Nisan 1976*. Ankara: AUHF Yayınları.
Aurora, G. S. (1967) *The new frontiersmen*. Bombay: Popular.
Austin, J. (1954) *The province of jurisprudence determined (1832)*. Ed. by H. L. A. Hart. London: Weidenfeld & Nicolson.
Austin, J. (1996) *The province of jurisprudence determined*. Ed. by W. Morrison. Dartmouth: Brookfield.

Australian Law Reform Commission (1991) *Multiculturalism: Family law*. Discussion Paper 46. Sydney: Australian Law Reform Commission.

Aydın, M. Akif (1985) *İslam-Osmanlı aile hukuku*. Istanbul: Marmara Üniversitesi İlahiyat Fakültesi Yayınları.

Aydın, Mehmet Akif (1992) 'Osmanlılarda aile hukukunun tarihi tekamülü'. In: BAAK *Sosyo-kültürel değisme sürecinde Türk ailesi*. 434-467.

Aydın, Mehmet Akif (1995) *İnsan hakları*. Istanbul: İz.

Aydın, Mehmet Akif (1996) *İslam ve Osmanlı hukuku araştırmalari*. Istanbul: İz.

Aydın, Suavi (1993) *Modernleşme ve milliyetçilik*. Ankara: Gündoğan Yayınları.

Ayhan, Riza (1991) 'Aileye yönelik hukuki düzenlemeler'. In: TCBAAK *Türkiye'de aile yıllığı*. Ankara: T. C. B. Aile Araştırma Kurumu Başkanlığı. 81-91.

Ayiter, Ferit (1956) 'The interpretation of a national system of laws received from abroad'. In: N. 5 *Annales Faculté de la droit d'Istanbul*. Istanbul: Fakülteler Matbaası. 41-43.

Ayiter, Nursin (1976) 'Medeni Kanunun nesebe ilişkin düzenlemesinin, yeni eğilim ve gereksinmeler karşısında değerlendirilmesi'. In: *Medeni Kanunun 50. yılı: Bilimsel hafta, 15-17 Nisan 1976*. Ankara: AUHF Yayınları. 43-81.

Ayiter, Nursin (1984) 'Evlilik dışı birleşmelerden doğan çocuklar'. In: Türköz Erder (ed) *Türkiye'de ailenin değişimi: Yasal açıdan incelemeler*. Ankara: Türk Sosyal Bilimler Derneği. 67-78.

Aziz, Mokhtar Ihsan (1995) 'Notes on *Shari'ah*, *fiqh* and *ijtihad*'. In: Tarek Mitri (ed) *Religion, law and society: A Christian-Muslim discussion*. Geneva. Kampen: WCC Publications. Kok Pharos. 44-47.

Badawi, Gamal A. (1996) *Polygamy in Islamic law*. Reprint. Delhi: Crescent.

Badawi, Zaki (1995) 'Muslim justice in a secular state'. In: Michael King (ed) *God's law versus state law: The construction of Islamic identity in Western Europe*. London: Grey Seal. 73-80.

Badawi, Zaki (2000) 'New *fiqh* for Minorities'. *Muslims of Europe in the New Millenium Conference*, 9-10 September, Regent's College London, AMSS (UK) and Islamic Cultural Centre, Ireland.

Badham, Paul (1989) (ed) *Religion, state, and society in modern Britain*. Lewiston et al: The Edwin Mellen Press.

Bainham, Andrew (1995) 'Family law in a pluralistic society'. In: V. 22 N. 2 *Journal of Law and Society*. 234-247.

Bainham, Andrew and Stephen Cretney (1993) *Children: The modern law*. London: Family Law.

Balaman, Ali Riza (1985) 'Family formation and dissolution in rural areas'. In: Türköz Erder (ed) *Family in Turkish society. Sociological and legal studies*. Ankara: Turkish Social Science Association. 209-219.

Balchin, Cassandra (1994) (ed) *A handbook on family law in Pakistan*. 2nd ed. Lahore: Shirkat Gah.

Balcı, Yusuf (1994) 'Türkiye'de dini nikahın gerekliliği'. In: V. 2 N. 2 *Islami Sosyal Bilimler Dergisi*. 100-102.

Balım, Ciğdem et al (1995) (eds) *Turkey: Political, social and economic challenges in the 1990s*. Leiden et al: E. J. Brill. 90-96.

Balkin, J. (1987) 'Deconstructive practice and legal theory'. In: V. 96 N. 4 *Yale Law Journal*. 743-786.

Ballard, Catherine (1978) 'Arranged marriages in the British context'. In: V. 6 N. 3 *New Community*. 181-196.

Ballard, Catherine (1979) 'Conflict, continuity and change: Second generation South Asians'. In: Verity Saifullah Khan (ed) *Minority families in Britain: Support and stress*.

London. Basingstoke: Macmillan. 109-130.

Ballard, Roger (1982) 'South Asian families'. In: R. N. Rapoport et al (eds) *Families in Britain*. London et al: Routledge & Kegan Paul. 179- 204.

Ballard, Roger (1984) 'South Asian families: Structure and process. In: The British Families Research Committee (ed) *Families in Britain*. London: Routledge & Kegan Paul.

Ballard, Roger (1990) 'Migration and kinship: the differential effect of marriage rules on the processes of Punjabi migration to Britain'. In: Colin Clarke, Ceri Peach and Steven Vertovec (eds.) *South Asians overseas. Migration and ethnicity*. Cambridge et al: Cambridge University Press, pp. 219-249.

Ballard, Roger (1992) 'New clothes for the emperor?: The conceptual nakedness of the race relations industry in Britain'. In: V. 18 N. 3 *New Community*. 481-492.

Ballard, Roger (1994a) 'Introduction: The emergence of *desh pardesh*'. In: Roger Ballard (ed) *Desh pardesh: The South Asian experience in Britain*. London: Hurst & Co. 1-34.

Ballard, Roger (1994b) (ed) *Desh pardesh: The South Asian experience in Britain*. London: Hurst & Co.

Ballard, Roger (1996) 'The Pakistanis: stability and introspection'. In: Ceri Peach (ed.) *Ethnicity in the 1991 census. Volume two. The ethnic minority populations of Great Britain*. London: HMSO. 121-149.

Ballard, Roger (1997) 'The construction of a conceptual vision: Ethnic groups and the 1991 UK Census (Review article)'. In: V. 20 N. 1 *Ethnic and Racial studies*. 181-194.

Ballard, Roger and V. Singh Kalra (1993) *The ethnic dimension of the 1991 Census: A preliminary report*. Manchester: Census Microdata Unit, University of Manchester.

Bälz, Kilian (1996) '*Shari'a* and qanun in Egyptian law: A systems theory approach to legal pluralism'. In: N. 13 *Law Department Working Papers*. London: SOAS.

Banks, Marcus (1996) *Ethnicity: Anthropological constructions*. London. New York: Routledge.

Bano, Samia (2000) 'Muslim South Asian women and customary law in Britain'. In: V. 4 *Journal of South Pacific Law*.

Banuazizi, Ali and Myron Weiner (1994) 'Introduction'. In: Myron Weiner and Ali Banuazizi (eds) *The politics of social transformation in Afghanistan, Iran, and Pakistan*. New York: Syracuse UP. 1-20.

Barkey, Henry (2000) 'The struggles of a 'strong' state'. In: V 54. N. 1 *Journal of International Affairs*. 87-105.

Barot, Rohit (1991) 'Migration, change and Indian religions in Britain'. In: W. A. Shadid and P. S. van Koningsvelt (eds) *The integration of Islam and Hinduism in Western Europe*. Kampen: Kok Pharos Publishing. 188- 200.

Barot, Rohit (1993) (ed) *Religion and ethnicity: Minorities and social change in the metropolis*. Kampen: Kok Pharos.

Barot, Rohit (1996) (ed) *The racism problematic: Contemporary sociological debates on race and ethnicity*. Lewiston et al: The Edwin Mellen Press.

Barth, F. (1989) 'The analysis of culture in complex societies'. In: V. 54 *Ethnos*. 120-142.

Barton, Stephen William (1986) *The Bengali Muslims of Bradford: A study of their observance of Islam with special reference to the functions of the mosque and the work of the imam*. Leeds: Department of Theology and Religious Studies.

Başaran, Fatma (1990) 'Birden fazla kadınla evlenmeye karşı vaziyet alışlar'. In: Behlül Dikeçligil and Ahmet Çiğdem (eds) *Aile yazilari*. Ankara: T. C. B. Aile Araştırma Kurumu Başkanlığı. 183-191.

Başgil, Ali Fuad (1962) *Din ve laiklik*. Reprint. Istanbul: Yağmur.

Başgil, Ali Fuad (1977) *Din ve laiklik*. 3rd ed. Istanbul: Yağmur.

Bassam, Tibi (1990) *Islam and the cultural accommodation of social change*. Boulder, Co:

Westview Press.

Bauböck, Rainer (1994) (ed) *From aliens to citizens. Redefining the status of immigrants in Europe*. Aldershot et al: Avebury.

Baudrillard, Jean (1993) *The transparency of evil*. London: Verso.

Bauman, Zygmunt (1992) *Intimations of postmodernity*. London: Routledge.

Bauman, Zygmunt (1993) *Postmodern ethics*. Oxford: Blackwell.

Bauman, Zygmunt (1996) *Postmodern ethics*. Reprint. Oxford/Cambridge, MA: Blackwell.

Baxi, Upendra (1986) 'Discipline, repression and legal pluralism'. In: Peter Sack and Elizabeth Minchin (eds) *Legal pluralism. Proceedings of the Canberra Law Workshop VII*. Canberra: Research School of Social Sciences, (Australian National University). 51- 62.

Baxi, Upendra (1987) 'The conflicting conceptions of legal cultures and the conflict of legal cultures'. In: Peter Sack et al (eds) *Rechtstheorie: Monistic or pluralistic legal culture*. N. 12. Berlin: Duncker & Humblot. 267-282.

Bayramoğlu, Ali (1995) *Türkiye'de toplumsal değişim*. Istanbul: Yeni Yüzyil.

Beck, Louis and Nikki Keddie (1978) (eds) *Women in the Muslim world*. Cambridge, MA and London: Harvard UP.

Beckerlegge, Gwilym (1989) *Nation formation and religious education: The concern of Muslims in Britain and Bangladesh*. Muslims in Europe: Research Papers 44. Birmingham: Centre for the Study of Islam and Christian-Muslim Relations.

Beckerlegge, Gwilym (1991) ''Strong cultures' and distinctive religions: The influence of imperialism upon British communities of South Asian origin'. In: V. 17 N. 2 *New Community*. 201-210.

Bedau, Hugo Adam (1961) 'On civil disobedience'. In: V. 58 *Journal of Philosophy*. 653-661.

Bedau, Hugo Adam (1969) (ed) *Civil disobedience*. New York: Pegasus.

Bedau, Hugo Adam (1974) 'Our knowledge of the law's limited effectiveness'. In: J. Roland Pennock and John W. Chapman (eds) *The limits of law*. New York: Lieber-Atherton. 245-255.

Beetham, David (1978) *Max Weber and the theory of modern politics*. London: George Allen & Unwin.

Behar, Cem (1985) *Nuptiality and marriage patterns in Istanbul (1885-1940)*. Istanbul: Bogaziçi University Research Papers.

Behar, Cem (1986) *Some data on polygyny in Istanbul, 1885-1926*. Istanbul: Bogaziçi University Research Papers.

Benda-Beckmann, Franz von (1988) 'Comment on Merry'. In: V. 22 N. 5 *Law and Society Review*. 897-901.

Benda-Beckmann, Franz von (1989) 'Scape-goat and magic charm: Law in development theory and practice'. In: N. 28 *Journal of Legal Pluralism*. 129-148.

Bent, Frederick (1969) 'The Turkish bureaucracy as an agent of change'. In: V. 1 N. 1 *Journal of Comparative Administration*. 47-63.

Bentham, Jeremy (1945) *The limits of jurisprudence defined*. Ed. by C. W. Everett. New York: Columbia UP.

Ben-Yunusa (1995) 'Secularism and religion'. In: Tarek Mitri (ed) *Religion, law and society: A Christian-Muslim discussion*. Geneva. Kampen: WCC Publications. Kok Pharos. 78-85.

Bergh, G. C. J. J. van den (1986) 'The concept of folk law in historical context: A brief outline'. In: Keebet von Benda-Beckmann and Fons Strijbosch (eds) *Anthropology of law in the Netherlands. Essays on legal pluralism*. Dortrecht. Cinnaminson: Foris Publications. 67-89.

Berkes, Niyazi (1956) 'Historical background of religious secularizm'. In: Richard N. Frye (ed) *Islam and the West*. The Hague: Mouton. 41-68.
Berkes, Niyazi (1964) *The development of secularizm in Turkey*. Montreal: McGill UP.
Berkes, Niyazi (1966) *Türkiye'de çağdaşlaşma*. Istanbul: Doğu-Batı.
Berki, Ali Himmet (1990) *Açıklamalı Mecelle*. Istanbul: Hikmet.
Berki, Sahir (1964) 'Türk medeni kanununda küçüklerin evlenmesi'. In: AUHF *Ernst E. Hircsh'e armağan*. Ankara: AUHFY. 387-408.
Berkovits, Bernard (1988) 'Transnational divorces: The Fatima decision'. In: V. 104 *Law Quarterly Review*. 60-93.
Berkovits, Bernard (1990) 'Get and *talaq* in English law: Reflections on law and policy'. In: Chibli Mallat and Jane Connors (eds) *Islamic family law*. London. Dordrecht. Boston: Graham & Trotman. 119-146.
Berlin, Isaiah (1995) 'The idea of pluralism'. In: W. T. Anderson (ed) *The truth about the truth: De-confusing and re-constructing the postmodern world*. New York: G. Putnam's Sons. 46-52.
Berman, Art (1994) *Preface to modernism*. Urbana: University of Illinois Press.
Berman, Harold J. (1974) *The institution of law and religion*. London: SCM Press.
Berman, Harold J. (1983) *Law and revolution: The formation of the Western legal tradition*. Cambridge, MA et al: Harvard UP.
Berrington, Ann (1994) 'Marriage and family formation among the white and ethnic minority populations in Britain'. In: V. 17 N. 3 *Ethnic and Racial Studies*. 517-546.
Beşer, Faruk (1991) *Fetvalar (fatwas)*. Izmir: Nil.
Beşer, Faruk (1993) *Fıkıh penceresinden sosyal hayatımız. V. I.* Istanbul: Nun.
Beşer, Faruk (1997) *Hanımlara ilmihal*. Istanbul: Nun.
Best, S. (1991) *Postmodern theory*. London: Macmillan.
Beteille, André (ed) (1969) *Social inequality*. Harmondsworth: Penguin.
Beyanuni, Ebu'l Feth el- (1989) *İhtilaftan Rahmete*. Istanbul: Risale.
Bhatia, H. S. (ed) (1996) *Studies in Islamic law, religion and society*. New Delhi: Deep & Deep.
Bhattacharjee, A. M. (1994) *Muslim law and the constitution*. 2nd ed. Calcutta: Eastern Law House.
Bhatti, F. M. (1981) 'Turkish Cypriots in Britain', Research Papers – Muslim in Europe, N. 11. Birmingham: Centre for the Study of Islam and Christian-Muslim Relations.
Bianchi, Robert (1984) *Interest groups and political development in Turkey*. Princeton: Princeton UP.
Binder, Leonard (1963) *Religion and politics in Pakistan*. Berkeley. Los Angeles: University of California Press.
Binder, Leonard (1994) 'Islam, ethnicity, or the state in Pakistan: An overview'. In: Myron Weiner and Ali Banuazizi (eds) *The politics of social transformation in Afghanistan, Iran, and Pakistan*. New York: Syracuse UP. 259-266.
Bistolfi, Robert and François Zabbal (eds) (1995) *Islams d'Europe. Intégration ou insertion communautaire?* Paris: Éditions de l'Aube.
Black, Donald (1976) *The behavior of law*. New York: Academic Press.
BMMT (1926) *Büyük Millet Meclisi Tutanaklari*. Ankara: TBMM.
Bodin, Jean (1576; 1995) *Les six livres de la république* (Six books of the community). Abbr. and tr. by M. J. Tooley. London: Blackwell.
Boggs, Carl (1993) *Intellectuals and the crisis of modernity*. New York: State University of New York Press.
Bohannan, Paul (1957) *Justice and judgment among the Tiv*. London: Oxford UP.
Bohannan, Paul (1963) *Social anthropology*. New York: Rinehart and Wreston.

Bohannan, Paul (1965) 'The differing realms of the law'. In: V. 67 N. 6 *American Anthropologist*. 33-42.

Bohannan, Paul (1967a) (ed) *Law and warfare: Studies in the anthropology of conflict*. Austin. London: University of Texas Press.

Bohannan, Paul (1967b) 'The differing realms of law'. In: P. Bohannan (ed) *Law and warfare: Studies in the anthropology of conflict*. Austin. London: University of Texas Press. 43-56.

Bolton, Ralph (1985) 'How the Qolla handle homicide: The demifeud in action'. In: Gordon R. Woodman and A. Allott (eds) *People's law and state law. The Bellagio papers*. Dordrecht: Foris Publications. 55-66.

Bommel, Abdulwahid van (1993) 'Old and new Europeans: Muslim resistance to 'Europanization', causes, effects and possible solutions'. In: Gé Speelman et al (ed) *Muslims and Christians in Europe: Breaking new ground*. Kampen: Kok Pharos. 112-124.

Bottomore, Tom B. (1964) *Élites and society*. Baltimore: Penguin Books.

Botwinick, Aryeh (1993) *Postmodernism and democratic theory*. Philadelphia: Temple UP.

Boulding, Elise (1986) 'Foreword'. In: Nermin Abadan-Unat (ed) *Women in the developing world: The evidence from Turkey*. Denver: University of Denver. 3-5.

Bozkurt, Gülnihal (1998) 'The reception of western European law in Turkey (From the Tanzimat to the Turkish Republic, 1839-1939)'. In V. 75 *Der Islam*. 283-295.

Bozkurt, Mahmut Esat (1944) 'Türk medeni kanunu nasıl hazırlandı?', In: *Medeni kanunumuzn XV. yıldonumu için,* Istanbul. 7-20.

Boztimur, Recep (2001) 'Political Islam in secular Turkey in 2000: Change in the rhetoric towards westernization, human rights and democracy'. In: V. 7, Ns. 1-2 *International Journal of Turkish Studies*. 125-137.

Bradford, Keith (1975) 'Marriage by proxy'. In: V. 4 N. 2 *New Community*. 254-255.

Bradley, David (1983) 'Duress and arranged marriages'. In: V. 46 *The Modern Law Review*. 499-504.

Bradney, A. (1989) 'The Dewsbury Affair and the Education Reform Act 1988'. In: V. 1 N. 2 *Education and the law*, pp. 51-57.

Bradney. A. (1993) *Religions, rights and laws*. Leicester et al: Leicester UP.

Brah, Avtah (1978) 'South-Asian teenagers in Southhall: Their perceptions of marriage, family, and ethnic identity'. In: V. 6 N. 3 *New Community*. 197-206.

Brah, Avtah (1987) 'Women of South Asian origin in Britain: Issues and concerns'. In: V. 7 N. 1 *South Asia Research*. 39-54.

Brasted, Howard (1997) 'The politics of stereotyping. Western images of Islam'. In: N. 98 *Manushi*. 6-16.

Breiner, Bert F. (1995a) '*Shari'ah* and religious pluralism'. In: Tarek Mitri (ed) *Religion, law and society: A Christian-Muslim discussion*. Geneva. Kampen: WCC Publications. Kok Pharos. 51-62.

Breiner, Bert F. (1995b) 'Secularism and religion: Alternative bases for the quest for a genuine pluralism'. In: Tarek Mitri (ed) *Religion, law and society: A Christian-Muslim discussion*. Geneva. Kampen: WCC Publications. Kok Pharos. 92-99.

Bromley, P. M. and N. V. Lowe (1987) *Bromley's family law*. 7th ed. London: Butterworths.

Bromley, P. M. and N. V. Lowe (1992) *Family law*. 8th ed. London et al: Butterworths.

Brothers, Joan (1971) *The social structure of modern Britain: Religious institutions*. London: Longman.

Brown, Colin (1984) *Black and white Britain: The third PSI survey*. London: Heinemann.

Bruce, Steve (1995) *Religion in modern Britain*. Oxford: Oxford UP.

Bulaç, Ali (1995a) *İslam ve demokrasi*. 3rd ed. Istanbul: Iz.
Bulaç, Ali (1995b) *Din ve modernizm*. Istanbul: Iz.
Bulaç, Ali (1997) *Islam ve fundamentalizm*. Istanbul: Iz.
Burke, Kenneth (1957) *The philosophy of literary form*. New York: Vintage Books.
Burman, B. K. Roy (1988) 'Persistence of folk law in India with particular reference to the tribal communities'. In: Bradford W. Morse and G. R. Woodman (eds) *Indigenous law and the state*. Dordrecht: Foris Publications. 151-165.
Burman, S. and B. Harrell-Bond (1979) (eds) *The imposition of law*. New York: Academic Press.
Buttar, P. A. (1985) 'Muslim personal law in western countries: The case of Australia'. In: V. 6 *Journal of the Institute of Muslim Minority Affairs*. 271-282.
Cain, Maureen (1995) 'Horatio's mistake: Notes on some spaces in an old text'. In: V. 22 N. 1 *Journal of Law and Society*. 68-77.
Cairncross, John (1974) *After polygamy was made a sin: The social history of Christian polygamy*. London: Routledge & Kegan Paul.
Calavita, K. and C. Seron (1992) 'Postmodernism and protest: Recovering the sociological imagination'. In: V. 26 *Law and Society Review*. 765-771.
Calder, Norman (1993) *Studies in early Muslim jurisprudence*. Oxford: Oxford UP.
Caldorola, Carlo (1982) (ed) *Religions and societies: Asia and the Middle East*. Berlin et al: Mouton Publishers.
Çalık, Etem (1994) 'Türkiye'de aile meselesi'. In: N. 30 *Türkiye Günlüğü*. 66-80.
Camaroff, Jean (1985) *Body of power: Spirit of resistance*. Chicago: University of Chicago Press.
Campbell, C. M. and Paul Wiles (1979) (eds) *Law and society*. Oxford: Martin Robertson.
Caplan, Linnel (1987) (ed) *Studies in religious fundamentalism*. Houndsmills: Macmillan Press.
Caporal, Bernard (1982) *Kemalizmde ve Kemalizm sonrasında Türk kadını, 1919-1970*. Tr. by Ercan Eyüboğlu. Ankara: İş Bankası Kültür Yayınları.
Cardozo, Benjamin N. (1921) *The nature of the judicial process*. New Haven: Yale UP.
Carmona, Ocando et al (1997) 'Postmodernism: A deconstructivist epistemology of the metanarratives'. In: V. 23 *Indian Socio-legal Studies*. 37-50.
Carroll, Lucy (1979) 'The Muslim Family Laws Ordinance, 1961: Provisions and procedures. A reference paper for current research'. In: V. 13 N. 1 *Contributions to Indian Sociology*. 117-143.
Carroll, Lucy (1981) 'Further notes on Pakistani and Indian *talaq*s in English law'. In: V. 23 N. 4 *Journal of the Indian Law Institute*. 588-595.
Carroll, Lucy (1982) 'Nizam-i-Islam: Processes and conflicts in Pakistan's programme of Islamisation with special reference to the position of women'. In: V. 20 N. 1 *Journal of Commonwealth and Comparative Politics*. 57-95.
Carroll, Lucy (1984) 'Definition of a 'potentially polygamous' marriage in English law: a dramatic decision from the Court of Appeal (*Hussain v Hussain*)'. In: V. IV, Ns. 1-2 *Islamic and Comparative Law Quarterly*. 61-71.
Carroll, Lucy (1985a) 'Muslim women and judicial divorce: An apparently misunderstood aspect of Muslim law'. V. 5 Ns. 3-4 *Islamic and Comparative Law Quarterly*. 226-245.
Carroll, Lucy (1985b) 'Wife's right to notification of *talaq* under Muslim Law Ordinance 1961'. In: *PLD*, Journal section. 272-276.
Carroll, Lucy (1986a) 'Muslim minorities and legal questions in Australia: A rejoinder'. In: V. 7 *Journal of the Institute of Muslim Minority Affairs*. 35-66.
Carroll, Lucy (1986b) 'A note on the Muslim wife's right to divorce in Pakistan and Bangladesh'. In: V. 13 N. 1 *New Community*. 94-97

Carroll, Lucy (1996a) 'Marriage-guardianship and minor's marriage at Islamic law'. In: H. S. Bhatia (ed) *Studies in Islamic law, religion and society*. New Delhi: Deep & Deep. 366-389.

Carroll, Lucy (1996b) '*Qur'an* 2: 229: 'A charter granted to the wife?' Judicial *khul'* in Pakistan'. In: V. 3 N. 1 *Islamic Law and Society*. 91-126.

Carroll, Lucy (1997) 'Muslim women and 'Islamic divorce' in England'. In: V. 17 N. 1 *Journal of Muslim Minority Affairs*. 97-115.

Carter, April (1988) *The politics of women's rights*. London. New York: Longman.

Carty, A. (1990) (ed) *Postmodern law*. Edinburgh: Edinburgh UP.

Cassese, Antonio (1990) (ed) *Human rights in changing world*. Cambridge: Polity Press.

Castles, Stephen (1994) 'Democracy and multicultural citizenship. Australian debates and their relevance for Western Europe'. In: Rainer Bauböck (ed) *From aliens to citizens. Redefining the status of immigrants in Europe*. Aldershot et al: Avebury: 3-27.

Chanock, M. L. (1985) *Law, custom and social order*. Cambridge et al: Cambridge UP.

Chattterjee, B. B. et al (1971) *Impact of social legislation on social change*. Calcutta: Minerva.

Chiba, Masaji (1985) 'The channel of official law to unofficial law in Japan'. In: Gordon R. Woodman and A. Allott (eds) *People's law and state law. The Bellagio papers*. Dordrecht: Foris Publications. 207-216.

Chiba, Masaji (1986a) (ed) *Asian indigenous law in interaction with received law*. London. New York: Kegan Paul International.

Chiba, Masaji (1986b) 'The identity postulate of indigenous law, and its function in legal transplantation'. In: Peter Sack and Elizabeth Minchin (eds) *Legal pluralism. Proceedings of the Canberra Law Workshop VII*. Canberra: Research School of Social Sciences, (Australian National University). 33-50.

Chiba, Masaji (1987) 'Legal pluralism in and across legal cultures'. In: Peter Sack et al (eds) *Rechstheorie: Monistic or pluralistic legal culture*. Berlin: Duncker & Humblot. 283-306.

Chiba, Masaji (1989) *Legal pluralism: Toward a general theory through Japanese legal culture*. Tokyo: Tokai UP.

Chiba, Masaji (1993) 'Legal pluralism in Sri Lankan society: Toward a general theory of non-Western law'. In: N. 33 *Journal of Legal Pluralism*. 197-212.

Chirane, Abdelhamit (1995) 'Conflict and division within Muslim families in France'. In: Michael King (ed) *God's law versus state law: The construction of Islamic identity in Western Europe*. London: Grey Seal. 16-20.

Choudry, Gulam W. (1993) *Islam and the modern Muslim world*. London: Scorpion.

Choudry, Salma (1993a) 'The debate on polygamy in Pakistan and India'. In: V. 12 N. 20 *Journal of Law and Society, (University of Peshawar)*. 25-32.

Choudry, Salma (1993b) 'The problem of child marriage in contemporary Pakistan'. In: V. 12 N. 21 *Journal of Law and Society, (University of Peshawar)*. 1-7.

Chowdry, A. G. (1997) *Constitutional history of Pakistan 1858-1996*. Lahore: Irfan.

Christie, Clive John (1991) 'The rope of God: Muslim minorities in the West and Britain'. V. 17 N. 3 *New Community*. 457-466.

Chryssides, George (1994) 'Britain's changing faiths: Adaptation in a new environment'. In: Gerald Parsons (ed) *The growth of religious diversity: Britain from 1945*. V. II. London: Routledge. Open UP. 55-84.

Churches' Committee for Migrants in Europe (1987) *Islamic law and its significance for the situation of Muslim minorities in Europe: Report of a study group*. Research Papers: Muslims in Europe. Birmingham: CSIC-MR.

Cin, Halil (1974) *İslam ve Osmanlı hukukunda evlenme*. Ankara: Ankara Üniversitesi

Basımevi.
Cin, Halil (1976) *Eski hukukumuzda boşanma*. Ankara: A. Ü. H. F. Yayınları.
Cin, Halil (1988a) *Eski hukukumuzda boşanma*. 2nd ed. Konya: S. Ü. H. F. Yayınları.
Cin, Halil (1988b) *Islam ve Osmanlı hukukunda evlenme*. 2nd ed. Konya: S. Ü. H. F. Yayınları.
Clarke, Colin et al (1990) (eds) *South Asians overseas. Migration and ethnicity*. Cambridge: Cambridge UP.
Clarkson, C. M. V. (1990) 'Marriage in England: Favouring the lex fori'. In: V. 10 N. 1 *Legal Studies*. 80-90.
Cohen, Julius (1974) 'Perspectives on the limits of law'. In: J. Roland Pennock and John W. Chapman (eds) *The limits of law*. New York: Lieber-Atherton. 39-45.
Cohen, Marshall (1969) 'Civil disobedience in a constitutional democracy'. In: V. 10 *The Massachusetts Review*. 218-221, 224-226.
Cohen, Marshall (1984) (ed) *Ronald Dworkin and contemporary jurisprudence*. London: Duckworth.
Cohen, Robin (1996) *Global diasporas: An introduction*. London: UCL.
Cole, J. R. (ed) (1992) *Comparing Muslim societies*. Ann Arbor: University of Michigan.
Coleman, Jules L. (1984) 'Negative and positive positivism'. In: Marshall Cohen (ed) *Ronald Dworkin and contemporary jurisprudence*. London: Duckworth. 28-48.
Collier, J. (1973) *Law and social change in Zinacantan*. Stanford: University Press.
Collier, J. (1975) Legal processes. *Annual Review of Anthropology* 4. 121-144.
Collins, Sydney (1957) *Coloured minorities in Britain: Studies in British race relations based on African, West Indian and Asiatic immigrants*. London: Lutterworth Press.
Commission for Racial Equality (1985) *Ethnic minorities in Britain: Statistical information on the pattern of settlement*. London: CRE.
Commission for Racial Equality (1990) *Britain: A plural society. Report of a seminar*. London: CRE.
Connor, Steven (1991) *Postmodernist culture: An introduction to the theories of the contemporary*. Oxford: Basil Blackwell.
Conway, Helen L. (1995) 'Divorce and religion'. In: *NLJ Practitioner* November 3. 1618-1619.
Coşar, Fatma Mansur (1978) 'Women in Turkish society'. In: Lois Beck and Nikki Keddie (eds) *Women in the Muslim world*. Cambridge, MA. London: Harvard UP. 124-140.
Cotran, E. and Chibli Mallat (1995) (eds) *Yearbook of Islamic and Middle Eastern law*. London et al: Kluwer International.
Cotterell, Roger (1984) *The sociology of law*. London: Butterworths.
Cotterell, Roger (1989) *The politics of jurisprudence*. Austin: Butterworths.
Cotterell, Roger (1992) *The politics of jurisprudence*. 2nd ed. London. Edinburgh: Butterworths.
Cotterell, Roger (1994) (ed) *Law and society*. Aldershot et al: Dartmouth.
Cotterell, Roger (1995) *Law's community: Legal theory in sociolegal perspective*. Oxford: Clarendon Press.
Coulson, Noel J. (1956) 'Doctrine and practice in Islamic law'. In: V. 18. *Bulletin of the School of Oriental and African Studies*. 211-226.
Coulson, Noel J. (1957) 'Reform of family law in Pakistan'. In: V. 7 *Studia Islamica*. 135-155.
Coulson, Noel J. (1959) *Muslim custom and case law*. V. 6 *Welt des Islam*. 13-24.
Coulson, Noel J. (1964) *A history of Islamic law*. Edinburgh: Edinburgh UP.
Coulson, Noel J. (1968) 'Islamic law'. In: J. Duncan M. Derrett (ed) *An introduction to legal systems*. London: Sweet & Maxwell. 54-79.

Coulson, Noel J. (1969) *Conflicts and tensions in Islamic jurisprudence*. Chicago: University of Chicago, Center for Middle Eastern Studies.

Coulson, Noel J. and Doreen Hinchcliffe (1978) 'Women and law reform in contemporary Islam'. In: Louis Beck and Nikkie Keddie (eds) *Women in the Muslim world*. 37-51.

Cragg, K. (1987) *Islam and the Muslim*. Milton Keynes: The Open UP.

Cragg, Kenneth (1974) 'An imperative path. Law and religion in relation. In: V. 5 N. 1 *Islam and the Modern Age*. 29-38.

Cretney, S. M. and J. M. Masson (1997) *Principles of family law*. 6th ed. London: Sweet & Maxwell.

Dahrendorf, Ralph (1969) 'On the origin of inequality among men'. In: Andre Beteille (ed) *Social inequality*. Harmondsworth: Penguin. 16-44.

Dahya, B. (1974) The nature of Pakistani ethnicity in industrial cities in Britain'. In: A. Cohen (ed) *Urban ethnicity*. London: Tavistock. 85-86.

Danelski, David J. (1974) 'The limits of law'. In: J. Roland Pennock and John W. Chapman (eds) *The limits of law*. New York: Lieber-Atherton. 8-27.

Darbyshire, Penny (1995) *English legal system*. London: Sweet & Maxwell.

Darsh, S. M. (1980) *Muslims in Europe*. London: Ta-Ha Publications.

Dassetto, F. and A. Bastenair (1984) *L'Islam transplante*. Anvers: Editions EPO.

Daura, Bello (1969) 'The limit of polygamy in Islam'. In: V. 3 *Journal of Islamic and Comparative Law*. 21-26.

Daver, Bülent (1967) 'Secularism in Turkey'. In: V. 24 *Ankara Üniversitesi Siyasal Bilgiler Fakültesi Dergisi*. 111-120.

Davies, Howard and David Holdcroft (1991) *Jurisprudence: Texts and commentary*. London et al: Butterworths.

Davies, Howard and David Holdcroft (1995) *Jurisprudence: Texts and commentary*. Reprint. London et al: Butterworths.

Davis, J. (1974) (ed) *Choice and change*. London: Athlone.

Davison, Roderic (1963) *Reform in the Ottoman empire, 1856-1876*. Princeton: Princeton UP.

Davison, Roderic (1968) *Turkey*. New York: Prentice-Hall.

Deech, Ruth (1990) 'Divorce law and empirical studies'. In: V. 106 *Law Quarterly Review*. 229-245.

Depew, Robert C. (1996) 'Popular justice and aboriginal communities: Some preliminary considerations'. In: N. 36 *Journal of Legal Pluralism*. 21-67.

Derrett, J. Duncan M. (1968a) (ed) *An introduction to legal systems*. London: Sweet & Maxwell.

Derrett, J. Duncan M. (1968b) *Religion, law and the state in India*. London: Faber.

Desai, A. R. (1963) *Indian immigrants in Britain*. London: Oxford UP.

Desai, A. R. (1971) (ed) *Essays on modernization of underdeveloped societies*. Bombay: Thacker & Co.

Desai, A. R. (1972) (ed) *Essays on modernization of underdeveloped societies*. 2nd ed. New York: Humanities Press.

Deshta, Kiran (1995) *Uniform civil code: In retrospect and prospect*. New Delhi: Deep & Deep Publications.

Diamond, S. (1971) 'The rule of law versus the order of custom'. In: N. 38 *Social Research*. 42-72.

Diamond, Stanley (1973) 'The rule of law versus order of custom'. In: Donald Black and Maureen Mileski (eds) *The social organisation of law*. New York: Seminar Press. 318-344.

Dijk, C. van and A. H. de Groot (1995) (eds) *State and Islam*. Leiden: Research School

CNWS.

Dikeçligil, Behlul and Ahmet Çiğdem (1990) (eds) *Aile yazıları*. Ankara: T. C. B. Aile Araştırma Kurumu Başkanlığı.

Dinçer, Fahriye (1993) *The Turkish women's appearance on the stage*. Istanbul: Boğaziçi University (Unpublished MA thesis).

Djait, Hichem (1978) *L'Europe et l'Islam*. Paris: du Seuil.

Dodd, Clement H. (1969) *Politics and government in Turkey*. Manchester: Manchester UP.

Dodd, Clement H. (1979) *Democracy and development in Turkey*. Hull: Ethoen.

Doe, Norman (1994) 'The legal position of religious minorities in the United Kingdom'. In: European Consortium for Church-State Research *The legal status of religious minorities in the countries of the European Union*. Thessaloniki and Milan: Sakkoulas and Giuffré Editore. 299-319.

Doğramacı, Emel (1989) *Türkiye'de kadının dünü, bugünü*. Ankara: Türkiye İş Bankası Kültür Yayınları.

Doi, Abdur Rahman (1984) *Shari'ah: The Islamic law*. London: Ta-Ha Publishers.

Dokur-Gryskiewicz, N. (1979) A Study of Adaptation of Turkish Migrant Workers to Living and Working in the United Kingdom, Unpublished PhD Thesis, Birbeck College, London.

Döndüren, Hamdi (1977) *Delilleriyle İslam hukuku*. Konya: İslam Hukuku Külliyati Yayınları.

Donnan, Hastings (1988) *Marriage among Muslims: Preference and choice in northern Pakistan*. Delhi: Hindustan Publishing Corporation.

Donnelly, Jack (1989) *The concept of human rights*. London: Routledge.

Donohue, John J. and John L. Esposito (1982) (eds) *Islam in transition. Muslim perspectives*. New York. Oxford: Oxford UP.

Dossetto, Felice and Gerd Nonneman (1996) 'Islam in Belgium and the Netherlands: Towards a typology of 'transplanted' Islam'. In: Gerd Nonneman et al (eds) *Muslim communities in Europe*. Reading: Ithaca Press. 187-217.

Dossetto, Felice and Yves Conrad Cedil (1996) *Muslims in Western Europe: An annotated bibliography*. Paris: L'Harmattan.

Douzinas, Costas et al (1991) *Postmodern jurisprudence: The law of text in the texts of law*. London and New York: Routledge.

Duben, Alan (1985) 'Turkish families and household in historical perspective'. In: N. 10 *Journal of Family History*. 75-97.

Duben, Alan and Cem Behar (1991) *Istanbul households: Marriage, family and fertility, 1880-1940*. Cambridge: Cambridge UP.

Duben, Alan and Cem Behar (1996) *Istanbul haneleri: Evlilik, aile ve dogurganlik, 1880-1940*. Istanbul: İletişim.

Dupret, Baudoin (1999) 'Legal pluralism, normative plurality, and the Arab world'. In: Dupret, Baudoin, Maurits Berger and Laila al-Zwaini (eds) (1999) *Legal pluralism in the Arab world*. The Hague: Kluwer Law International. 29-40.

Dupret, Baudoin, Maurits Berger and Laila al-Zwaini (eds) (1999) *Legal pluralism in the Arab world*. The Hague: Kluwer Law International.

Durkheim, E. (1961) *The elementary forms of the religious life*. New York: Collier.

Dworkin, Ronald (1977) *Taking rights seriously*. London: Duckworth.

Dworkin, Ronald (1985) *A matter of principle*. Cambridge, MA: Harvard Univeristy Press.

Dworkin, Ronald (1986) *Law's empire*. London: Fontana.

Dwyer, Claire and Astrid Meyer (1995) 'The institutionalization of Islam in the Netherlands and in the UK: The case of Islamic schools'. In: V. 21 N. 1 *New Community*. 37-54.

Dwyer, Daisy Hilse (ed) (1990) *Law and Islam in the Middle East*. New York et al: Bergin

& Garvey Publishers.
Eade, John, Tim Vamplew and Ceri Peach (1996) 'The Bangladeshis: the encapsulated community'. In: Ceri Peach (ed.) *Ethnicity in the 1991 census. Volume two. The ethnic minority populations of Great Britain*. London: HMSO. 150-160.
Ebrahim, Sheikh (1992) *The constitution of the Islamic Republic of Pakistan*. Lahore: P. L. D. Publishers.
Ebuzziya Tevfik (1974) *Yeni Osmanlılar tarihi*. Istanbul: Kervan Yayıncılık.
Edgeworth, B. (1986) 'Legal positivism and the philosophy of language: A critique of H. L. A. Hart's 'Descriptive sociology''. In: V. 6 *Legal Studies*. 115-139.
Edwards, Susan S. M. (1996) *Sex and gender in the legal process*. London: Blackstone.
Ehrlich, Eugen (1913) *Grundlegung der Soziologie des Rechts*. Berlin: Duncker & Humblot.
Ehrlich, Eugen (1922) 'The sociology of law'. In: V. 36 *Harvard Law Review*. 130-145.
Ehrlich, Eugen (1936) *Fundamental principles of the sociology of law*. Cambridge, MA: Harvard UP.
Ehrmann, Henry W. (1976) *Comparative legal cultures*. Englewood Cliffs, N. J.: Prentice-Hall.
Eickelman, Dale F. (1982) 'The study of Islam in local contexts'. In: Richard C. Martin (ed) *Islam in local contexts*. Leiden: E. J. Brill. 1-16.
Eickelman, Dale F. (1998) 'Inside the Islamic reformation'. In: V. 22 N. 1 *Wilson Quarterl*. 80-89.
Eisenstadt, S. N. (1971) 'Some reflections on political sociology and the experience of modernizing societies'. In: A. R. Desai (ed) *Essays on modernization of underdeveloped societies*. Bombay: Thacker & Co. 175-194.
Eisenstadt, Samuel Noah (1966) *Modernization: Protest and change*. New Jersey: Englewood Cliffs.
Eisenstadt, Samuel Noah (1968) *Comparative perspectives on social change*. Boston: Little Brown and Company.
Eisenstadt, Samuel Noah (1973) *Tradition, change, and modernity*. New York: John Wiley & Sons.
El Alami, Dawoud S. (1992) *The marriage contract in Islamic law*. London: Graham & Trotman.
Eldem, Edhem (1991) (ed) *Premier recontre internationale sur l'Empire Ottoman a la Turquie moderne*. Istanbul.Paris: ISIS.
Ellis, Jean (1991) 'Local goverment and community needs: A case study of Muslims in Coventry'. In: V. 17 N. 3 *New Community*. 359-376.
Elmacı, Nuran (1994) 'Polygamy: Çok-eşli evlilikler'. In: Necla Arat (ed) *Türkiye'de kadın olmak*. Istanbul: Say. 79-123.
El-Manssoury (1989) 'Muslims in Europe: The lost tribe of Islam?' In: V. 10 N. 1 *Journal of Institute of Muslim Minority Affairs*. 63-84.
Engel, David M. (1984) 'The oven bird's song: Insiders, outsiders, and personal injuries in an American community'. In: V. 18 N. 4 *Law and Society Review*. 551-582.
Engel, David M. (1987) 'Law, time, and community'. In: V. 21 N. 4 *Law and Society Review*. 605-637.
Engineer, Ashgar Ali (1980) *The Islamic state*. Delhi: Vikas.
Engineer, Ashgar Ali (1985) *Islam and Muslims: A critical reassessment*. Jaipur: Printwell Publishers.
Engineer, Ashgar Ali (1990) 'Islam, status of women and social change'. In: V. 21 N. 3 *Islam and the Modern Age*. 180-199.
Entzinger, Han (1994) 'A future for the Dutch 'ethnic minorities' model?'. In: Bernard

Lewis and Dominique Schnapper (eds) *Muslims in Europe*. London. New York: Pinter. 19-38.

Epstein, T. Scarlett and Rosemary A. Watts (1981) (eds) *The endless day. Some case material on Asian rural women*. Oxford et al: Pergamon Press.

Erder, Leila (1981) 'The women of Turkey: A demographic overview'. In: Nermin Abadan-Unat (ed) *Women in Turkish Society*. Leiden: E. J. Brill. 41-58.

Erder, Türköz (1984a) (ed) *Türkiye'de ailenin değişimi: Toplumbilimsel incelemeler*. Ankara: Türk Sosyal Bilimler Derneği.

Erder, Türköz (1984b) (ed) *Türkiye'de ailenin değişimi: Yasal açıdan incelemeler*. Ankara: Türk Sosyal Bilimler Derneği.

Erder, Türköz (1985) (ed) *Family in Turkish society. Sociological and legal studies*. Ankara: Turkish Social Science Association.

Eren, Ali (1995) *Islamda evlilik ve aile eğitimi*. Istanbul: Çetin.

Eren, Nuri (1963) *Turkey today and tomorrow, an experiment in Westernisation*. New York: Praeger.

Ergil, Doğu (2000) 'Identity crises and political instability in Turkey'. In: V. 54 N. 1 *Journal of International Affairs*. 43-60.

Erikson, Thomas Hylland (1993) *Ethnicity and nationalism. Anthropological perspectives*. London. Boulder, Co: Pluto Press.

Ertürk, Yakin (1990) 'Doğu Anadolu'da modernleşme ve kırsal kadın'. In: Şirin Tekeli (ed) *Kadın bakış açısından 1980'ler Türkiyesinde kadınlar*. Istanbul: İletişim. 183-194.

Eryılmaz, Bilal (1990) *Osmanlı devletinde gayri-Muslim tebanın yönetimi*. Istanbul: Risale.

Eryılmaz, Bilal (1992) *Tanzimat ve yönetimde modernleşme*. Istanbul: İşaret Yayınları.

Esposito, John L. (1976) 'Muslim family law reform: Towards an Islamic methodology'. In: V. 15 N. 1 *Islamic Studies*. 19-51.

Esposito, John L. (1977) 'Muslim family law reform in Pakistan'. In: V. 4 Part 2 *Journal of Malaysian and Comparative Law*. 293-310.

Esposito, John L. (1980a) 'Pakistan: Quest for Islamic identity'. In: John L. Esposito (ed) *Islam and development*. Syracuse: Syracuse UP. 139-162.

Esposito, John L. (1980b) 'Perspectives on Islamic law reform: The case of Pakistan'. In: V. 13 N. 2 *New York University Journal of International Law and Politics*. 217-245.

Esposito, John L. (1982a) 'Islamization: Religion and politics in Pakistan'. In: V. 72 *The Muslim World*. 197-223.

Esposito, John L. (1982b) *Women in Muslim family law*. New York: Syracuse UP.

Esposito, John L. (1986) 'Islam, Ideology and Politics in Pakistan'. In: Myron Weiner and Ali Banuazizi (eds) *The State, Religion, and Ethnic Politics*. Syracuse, NY: Syracuse University Press.

Esposito, John L. (1988) *Islam: The Straight Path*. Oxford: Oxford UP.

Esposito, John L. (1998) *Islam: The Straight Path*. 3rd ed. New York/Oxford: Oxford UP.

Esposito, John L. (2001) *Women in Muslim family law*. 2nd edition with Natana J. DeLong-Bas. New York: Syracuse UP.

Esposito, John L. and John O. Voll (1996) *Islam and democracy*. New York et al: Oxford UP.

Evan, William M. (1965) 'Law as an instrument of social change'. In: Alvin W. Gouldner and S. M. Miller (eds) *Applied sociology. Opportunities and problems*. New York: Free Press. 285-293.

Evans, D. (1988) *International families and the law*. Bristol: Jordan & Sons.

Ewing, Katherine P. (1988) (ed) *Shari'at and ambiguity in South Asian Islam*. Delhi et al: Oxford UP.

Fadl, K. A. E. (1994) 'Islamic law and Muslim minorities: The juristic discourse on Muslim minorities from the 2nd/8th to the 11th/17th centuries'. In: V. 1 N. 2 *Islamic Law and Society*. 141-187.

Farani M. (1986) *Manual of family laws in Pakistan*. Lahore: Lahore Law Times Publications.

Farani, M. (1994) *Manual of family laws in Pakistan*. Reprint. Lahore: Lahore Law Times Publications.

Faruki, Kemal A. (1987) *Islamic jurisprudence*. Islamabad: Islamic Book Foundation.

Fayerabend, Paul (1995) 'Anything goes'. In: W. T. Anderson (ed) *The truth about the truth: De-confusing and re-constructing the postmodern world*. New York: G. Putnam's Sons. 199-203.

Fenton, John Y. (1988) *Transplanting religious traditions: Asian Indians in America*. New York et al: Praeger.

Feroze, Muhammad Rashid (1962) 'Family laws of the Turkish republic'. In: N. 1 *Journal of Islamic Studies*. 131-147.

Field, Simon (1984) *The attitudes of ethnic minorities: A home office research and planning unit report*. London: HMSO.

Fındıkoğlu, Z. F. (1956) 'Special aspects of the Turkish reception of law'. In: N. 5 *Annales Faculté de la droit d'Istanbul*. Istanbul: Fakülteler Matbaası. 155-165.

Fındıkoğlu, Z. F. (1957) 'A Turkish sociologist's view'. In: V. 9 N. 1 *Unesco International Social Science Bulletin*. 13-20.

Findley, Carter (1980) *Bureaucratic reform in the Ottoman Empire*. Princeton: Princeton UP.

Firdous, Rehana (1990) *Discussions of polygamy and divorce by Muslim modernists in South Asia, with special reference to their treatment of Qur'an and Sunna*. London: SOAS (Unpublished PhD thesis).

Fischer, Michael and Mehdi Abedi (1990) *Debating Muslims: Cultural dialogues in postmodernity and tradition*. Madison: The University of Wisconsin Press.

Fişek, Hicri (1985) 'Introduction'. In: Türköz Erder (ed) *Family in Turkish society. Sociological and legal studies*. Ankara: Turkish Social Science Association. 287-298.

Fiske, Jo-Anne (1996) 'Introduction'. In: René Kuppe and Richard Rotz (eds) *Law and anthropology*. V. 8. The Hague: Martinus Nijhoff Publishers. vii-xiii.

Fitzpatrick, Peter (1980) *Law and state in Papua New Guinea*. London: Academic Press.

Fitzpatrick, Peter (1983a) 'Law, plurality and underdevelopment'. In: David Sugarman (ed) *Legality, ideology and the state*. London et al: Academic Press. 159-182.

Fitzpatrick, Peter (1983b) 'Marxism and legal pluralism'. In: V. 1 N. 2 *Australian Journal of Law and Society*. 45-59.

Fitzpatrick, Peter (1984) 'Law and societies'. In: V. 22 N. 1 *Osgoode Hall Law Journal*. 115-138.

Fitzpatrick, Peter (1986) 'Custom, law and resistance'. In: Peter Sack and Elizabeth Minchin (ed) *Legal pluralism. Proceedings of the Canberra Law Workshop VII*. Canberra: Research School of Social Sciences, (Australian National University). 63-82.

Fitzpatrick, Peter (1992a) *The mythology of modern law*. London. New York: Routledge.

Fitzpatrick, Peter (1992b) 'The impossibility of popular justice'. In: V. 1 *Social and Legal Studies*. 199-215.

Fitzpatrick, Peter (1995a) 'Being social in socio-legal studies'. In: V. 22 N. 1 *Journal of Law and Society*. 105-112.

Fitzpatrick, Peter (1995b) *Nationalism, racism and the rule of law*. Aldershot et al: Dartmouth.

Fitzpatrick, Peter and A. Hunt (eds) (1987) *Critical legal studies*. Oxford: Blackwell.

Fitzpatrick, Peter and Alfred Ruegg (1988) 'Book review: 'Without the law': Administrative

justice and legal pluralism in nineteenth century England by H. W. Arthurs'. In: N. 27 *Journal of Legal Pluralism*. 135-143.
Fitzpatrick, Peter et al (1993) (ed) *Law in the information society*. London: Pluto.
Foblets, Marie-Claire (1994) 'Community justice amongst immigrant family members in France and Belgium'. In: René Kuppe and Richard Rotz (eds) *Law and anthropology*. Dordrecht: Martinus Nijhoff Publishers. 371-385.
Foblets, Marie-Claire (1999) 'Conflicts of law in cross-cultural family disputes in Europe today. Who will reorient conflicts law?' In: Marie-Claire Foblets and Fons Strijbosch (eds.) *Relations familiales interculturelles/Cross cultural family relations*. Oñati: International Institute for the Sociology of Law, pp. 27-45.
Forer, Norman (1979) 'The imposed wardship of American Indian tribes: A case study of the Praire Band Potawatomi'. In: Sandra B. Burman and Barbara E. Harrell-Bond (eds) *The imposition of law*. New York: Academic Press. 89-114.
Foster, H. (1985) (ed) *Postmodern culture*. London: Pluto.
Foucault, Michel (1979) *History of sexuality, V. I: An introduction*. London: Allen Lane.
Foucault, Michel (1986) *The care of the self: The history of sexuality*. New York: Vintage Books.
Foucault, Michel (1987) *Söylemin düzeni*. Istanbul: Hil Y.
Foucault, Michel (1988) *Madness and civilization: A history of insanity in the age of reason*. New York: Vintage Books.
Foucault, Michel (1992) *Ders özetleri*. Istanbul: Yapi Kredi Y.
Foucault, Michel (1994) *Dostluga dair*. Istanbul: Hil Y.
Frank, Jerome (1930) *Law and the modern mind*. New York: Brenatano's.
Fransman, Laurie (1986) 'Family settlement cases: a denial of statutory rights'. In: V. 1 N. 1 [April 1986] *Immigration and Nationality Law and Practice*. 5-15.
Fransman, Laurie (1989) *British nationality law*. London: Fourmat.
Frey, Frederick W. (1965) *The Turkish political élite*. Cambridge, MA: MIT Press.
Friedman, L. M. (1969) 'Legal culture and social development'. In: V. 4 *Law and Society Review*. 29-44.
Friedman, L. M. (1977) *Law and society: An introduction*. Englewood Cliffs: Prentice Hall.
Friedmann, Wolfgang (1959) *Law in a changing society*. Baltimore: Stevens & Sons.
Friedmann, Wolfgang (1972) *Law in a changing society*. 2nd ed. Harmondsworth: Penguin.
Galanter, Marc (1966) 'The modernization of law'. In: Myron Weiner (ed) *Modernization*. New York. London: Basic Books. 153-165.
Galanter, Marc (1974) 'Why the 'haves' come out ahead: Speculations on the limits of legal change'. In: V. 9 *Law and Society Review*. 99-160.
Galanter, Marc (1981) 'Justice in many rooms: Courts, private ordering, and indigenous law'. In: V. 19 N. 1 *Journal of Legal Pluralism and Unofficial Law*. 1-47.
Galanter, Marc (1985) 'Indigenous law and official law in the contemporary United States'. In: G. R. Woodman and A. Allott (eds) *People's law and state law. The Bellagio papers*. Dordrecht: Foris Publications. 67-70.
Gandhi, J. S. (1989) (eds) *Law and social change*. Jaipur: Rawat Publications.
Gankovsky, Y. V. (1971) *The peoples of Pakistan: An ethnic history*. Lahore: People's Publishing House.
Gardner, James A. (1980) *Legal imperialism: American lawyers and foreign aid in Latin America*. Madison: University of Wisconsin Press.
Gardner, Katy (1995) *Global migrants, local lives. Travel and transformation in rural Bangladesh*. Oxford: Clarendon.
Gardner, Katy and Abdus Shukur (1994) '"I'm Bengali, I'm Asian, and I'm living here": The changing identity of British Bengalis'. In: Roger Ballard (ed) *Desh pardesh: The*

*South Asian experience in Britain*. London: Hurst & Co. 142-164.

Gardner, Katy and Dany Lewis (1996) *Anthropology, development and the post-modern challenge*. London: Pluto Press.

Garner, Roberta Ash (1956) *Social change*. Chicago: Harvard UP.

Geertz, Clifford (1968) *Islam observed*. New Haven, CT: Yale UP.

Geertz, Clifford (1973) *Interpretation of cultures*. New York: Basic Books.

Geertz, Clifford (1983) *Local knowledge: Further essays in interpretive anthropology*. New York: Basic Books.

Geertz, Clifford et al (1979) *Meaning and order in Moroccan society*. New York: Cambridge UP.

Gellner, Ernest (1992a) *Postmodernism, reason and religion*. London/New York: Routledge.

Gellner, Ernest (1992b) *Uluslar ve ulusçuluk*. Istanbul: Insan Yayınları.

Gellner, Ernest (1994) *Postmodernizm, Islam ve us*. Ankara: Ümit Y.

Gerber, Naim (1994) *State, society and law in Islam: Ottoman law in comparative perspective*. New York: State University of New York Press.

Gerholm, T. and Y. G. Lithman (1988) (eds) *New Islamic presence in Western Europe*. London: Mansell.

Ghayasuddin M. (1986) (ed) *The impact of nationalism on the Muslim world*. London: The Open Press. Al-Hoda Publishers.

Gibs, J. P. (1982) 'Law as a means of social control'. In: J. P. Gibbs (ed) *Social control: Views from the social sciences*. Beverly Hills: Sage. 83-113.

Giddens, Anthony (1982) *Profiles and critiques in social theory*. London: Macmillan.

Giddens, Anthony (1990) *The consequences of modernity*. Cambridge: The Polity Press.

Gilani, Riazul Hasan (1982) *The reconstruction of legal thought in Islam*. Lahore: Idara Tarjuman al *Qur'an*.

Gilani, Riazul Hasan (1990) 'A note on Islamic family law and Islamization in Pakistan'. In: Chibli Mallat and Jane Connors (eds) *Islamic family law*. London. Dordrecht. Boston: Graham & Trotman. 340-346.

Gilissen, John (1971a) 'Introduction × l'—tude compar—e du pluralisme juridique'. In: John Gilissen (ed) *Le pluralisme juridique*. Brussels: Universit— de Bruxelles. 7-17.

Gilissen, John (1971b) (ed) *Le pluralisme juridique*. Brussels: Universit— de Bruxelles.

Gill, Sean et al (1994) (eds) *Religion in Europe: Contemporary perspectives*. Kampen: Kok Pharos.

Glasner, Peter E. (1977) *The sociology of secularization: A critique of a concept*. London: Routledge & Kegan Paul.

Gledhill, Alan (1957) *Pakistan: The development of its laws and constitution*. London: Stevens and Sons.

Glenn, H. Patrick (1987) 'Reception and reconciliation of laws'. In: Peter Sack et al (eds) *Rechtstheorie: Monistic or pluralistic legal culture*. Berlin: Duncker & Humblot. 209-214.

Gluckman, Max (1965) *Politics, law and ritual in tribal society*. Chicago: Aldine.

Gökalp, Ziya (1959) *Turkish nationalism and Western civilisation*. New York: Columbia UP.

Gökalp, Ziya (1987) *Türkçülügün esaslari*. Istanbul: Inkılap Kitabevi.

Gökçe, B. (1991) *Gecekondularda aileler arası geleneksel dayanışmanın çağdas organizasyonlara dönüşümü*. Istanbul: Sosyoloji Derneği.

Golden, Aviva (1996) *Everyday law*. 2nd ed. Glasgow: Harper Collins.

Goldziher, I (1981) *Introduction to Islamic theology and law*. Princeton: Princeton UP.

Göle, Nilüfer (1994) *Modern mahrem*. Istanbul: Metis.

Göle, Nilufer (1996) 'Authoritarian Secularism and Islamist Politics: The Case of Turkey'. In: Augustus Richard Norton (ed) *Civil Society in the Middle East*. Leiden: E.J. Brill. 19-39.

Gordon, David (1988) *Foreign divorces: English law and practice*. Aldershot: Avebury.

Gordon, Robert (1986) 'Law and Ideology'. In V. 3 N. 1 *Tikkun*. 16.

Gotthard, J. (1964) *Türkiye'de imam nikahı*. Ankara: A. Ü. Hukuk Fakültesi Yay.

Goulbourne, Harry (1991) 'Varieties of pluralism: The notion of a pluralist post-imperial Britain'. In: V. 17 N. 2 *New Community*. 211-227.

Gouldner, Alvin W. and S. M. Miller (1965) (eds) *Applied sociology. Opportunities and problems*. New York: Free Press. 285-293.

Government of Pakistan Ministry of Education (1998) *National education policy, 1998-2010*. Islamabad: GPME.

Grace, Clive and Philip Wilkinson (eds) (1978) *Sociological inquiry and legal phenomena*. London: Collier Macmillan.

Greenawalt, Kent (1974) 'Some related limits of law'. In: J. Roland Pennock and John W. Chapman (eds) *The limits of law*. New York: Lieber-Atherton. 76-89.

Greenfeld, Liah (1992) *Nationalism: Five roads to modernity*. Cambridge: Harvard UP.

Greenhouse, Carol J. (1982) 'Nature is to culture as praying is to suing: Legal pluralism in an American suburb'. In: V. 20 *Journal of Legal Pluralism*. 17-35.

Greenhouse, Carol J. and Fons Strijbosch (1993) 'Legal pluralism in industrialized societies'. In: N. 33 *Journal of Legal Pluralism*. 1-9.

Griffiths, John (1985a) 'Introduction'. In: Gordon R. Woodman and A. Allott (eds) *People's law and state law. The Bellagio papers*. Dordrecht: Foris Publications. 13-20.

Griffiths, John (1985b) 'Four laws of interaction in circumstances of legal pluralism: First steps towards an explanatory theory'. In: Gordon R. Woodman and A. Allott (eds) *People's law and state law. The Bellagio papers*. Dordrecht: Foris Publications. 217-227.

Griffiths, John (1986a) 'What is legal pluralism?'. In: V. 24 *Journal of Legal Pluralism and Unofficial Law*. 1-56.

Griffiths, John (1986b) 'Recent anthropology of law in the Netherlands and its historical background'. In: Keebet von Benda-Beckmann and Fons Strijbosch (eds) *Anthropology of law in the Netherlands. Essays on legal pluralism*. Dortrecht. Cinnaminson: Foris. 11-66.

Groot, A. H. de (1995) 'Modernist attitudes in Ottoman official Islam (1856-1918)'. In: C. van Dijk and A. H. de Groot (eds) *State and Islam*. Leiden: Research School CNWS. 51-63.

Grunebaum, Gustave E. von (1955) (ed) *Unity and variety in Muslim civilisation*. Chicago: Chicago UP.

Gülalp, Haldun (1999) 'Political Islam in Turkey: The rise and fall of the Refah Party'. In: V. 89 N. 1 *The Muslim World*. 22-41.

Gülen, Fethullah (1995) *Fasıldan Fasıla I*. Izmir: Nil.

Gulliver, P. H. (1978) (ed) *Cross-examinations: Essays in memory of Max Gluckman*. Leiden: E. J. Brill.

Günenç, Halil (1990a) *Günümüz meselelerine fetvalar. V. I.* Istanbul: İlim.

Günenç, Halil (1990b) *Günümüz meselelerine fetvalar. V. II.* Istanbul: İlim.

Gupta, Kiran (1992) 'Polygamy- Law reform in modern Muslim states: A study in comparative law'. In: V. 12 N. 2 *Islamic and Comparative Law Review*. 114-154.

Güriz, Adnan (1966) 'Sources of Turkish law'. In: Tuğrul Ansay and Don Wallace Jr. (eds) *Introduction to Turkish law*. Ankara: Güzel Istanbul Matbaası. 1-22.

Güriz, Adnan (1984) 'Türk medeni kanununun aileyi ilgilendiren hükümlerinde gerekli görülen değişiklikler'. In: Türköz Erder (ed) *Türkiye'de ailenin değişimi: Yasal açıdan incelemeler*. Ankara: Türk Sosyal Bilimler Derneği. 140-152.

Güriz, Adnan (1996) 'Sources of Turkish law'. In: Tuğrul Ansay and Don Wallace, Jr. (eds) *Introduction to Turkish law*. The Hague et al: Kluwer Law International. 1-18.

Gürkan, Ülker (1967) *Hukuki realizm akimi*. Ankara: AUHFY.

Gürpınar, Serhat and Seref Malkoç (1994) 'Anayasa-uzlaşma belgesi önerisi: Yeni bir Medine vesikası taslağı üzerine tartışma'. In: N. 7 *Bilgi ve Hikmet*. 169-172.

Gurr, Ted Robert (1993) *Minorities at risk: A global view of ethnopolitical conflicts*. Washington, D. C.: US Institute of Peace Studies.

Gurvitch, Georges (1947) *Sociology of law*. London: Routledge and Kegan Paul.

Güvenç, Bozkurt (1976) *Siyasal ve kültürel değisme*. Ankara: Hacettepe Üniversitesi Yayınları.

Habermas, Jürgen (1974) *Theory and practice*. London: Heinemann.

Habermas, Jürgen (1976) *Legitimization crisis*. London: Heinemann.

Habermas, Jürgen (1979) *Communication and evolution of society*. London: Heinemann.

Haddad, Yvonne Yazbeck and Jane Idleman Smith (1994) (eds) *Muslim communities in North America*. New York: State University of New York Press.

Hahani-Hopkins, Vered and Nick Hopkins (2002) '"Representing" British Muslims: the strategic dimension to identity construction'. In: V. 25 N. 2 *Ethnic and Racial Studies*. 288-309.

Hale, William (1976) (ed) *Aspects of modern Turkey*. London: Bowker.

Hale, William (1981) *The political and economic development of Turkey*. London: Croom Helm.

Halevy, Eva Etzioni (1993) *The élite connection: Problems and potential of Western democracy*. Cambridge: Polity Press.

Halim, Shaikh Abdul (1987) *Muslim family laws*. Lahore: Law Publishing Co.

Hall, S. et al (1992) (eds) *Modernity and its futures*. London: Polity Press. Open University.

Hallaq, Wael B. (1984) 'Was the gate of ijtihad closed?'. In: V. 16 N. 1. *International Journal of Middle East Studies*. 3-41.

Hallaq, Wael B. (1986) 'On the Origins of the Controversy about the Existence of Mujtahids and the Gate of Ijtihâd'. In: V. 63 *Studia Islamica*. 129-41.

Hallaq, Wael B. (1987) 'The development of logical structure in Sunni legal theory'. In: V. 64 *Der Islam*. 42-67.

Hallaq, Wael B. (1996) '"Ifta" and ijtihad in Sunni legal theory: A developmental account'. In: Muhammad Khalid Masud et al (eds) *Islamic legal interpretation: Muftis and their fatwas*. Cambridge, MA and London, England: Harvard University Press. 33-43.

Hallaq, Wael B. (1997) *A history of Islamic legal theories: An introduction to Sunni usul al-fiqh*. Cambridge: Cambridge University Press.

Hallaq, Wael B. (2001) *Authority, continuity and change in Islamic law*. Cambridge: Cambridge University Press.

Halliday, Fred and Hamza Alavi (1988) *State and ideology in the Middle East and Pakistan*. London: Macmillan Education Ltd.

Hamilton, Carolyn (1995) *Family, law and religion*. London: Sweet & Maxwell.

Hamson, C. J. (1956) 'Preliminary report'. In: N. 5 *Annales Facult— de la droit d'Istanbul*. Istanbul: Fakülteler Matbaası. 3-10.

Handler, Joel F. (1978) *Social movements and the legal system: A theory of law reform and social change*. New York: Academic Press.

Hanioğlu, M. Şükrü (1985) *Osmanlı İttihad ve Terakki Cemiyeti ve Jön Türklük*. Istanbul: İletişim Yayınları.

Haq, Ferhat (1996) 'Women, Islams and the state in Pakistan'. In: V. 86 N. 2 *The Muslim*

*World*. 158-175.
Haq, M. Fazlul (1990) 'Polygamy in Islam: Misinterpreted and ill-judged'. In: *Kerala Law Times*, Journal Section. 14-18.
Haqq, A. et al (1995) *The Islamic will: A practical guide to being prepared for your death and writing your will according to the Shari'a of Islam and English law*. London: Dar al-Taqwa.
Haque, Ziaul (1983) 'Pakistan and Islamic ideology'. In: Hassan Gardezi and Jamil Rashid (eds) *Pakistan: The roots of dictatorship*. London: Zed Press. 367-383.
Harper, Charles (1993) *Explaining social change*. Englewood Cliffs: Prentice Hall.
Harrington, C. and B. Yngvesson (1990) 'Interpretive sociolegal research'. In: V. 15 N. 1 *Law and Social Inquiry*. 135-148.
Harrington, Christie (1985) *Shadow justice: The ideology and institutionalisation of alternatives to court*. Westport: Greenwood Press.
Harrison, Selig S. (1994) 'Ethnicity and the political stalemate in Pakistan'. In: Myron Weiner and Ali Banuazizi (eds) *The politics of social transformation in Afghanistan, Iran, and Pakistan*. New York: Syracuse UP. 267-298.
Hart, H. L. A. (1961) *The concept of law*. Oxford: Clarendon Press.
Hart, H. L. A. (1983a) 'Positivism and the separation of law and morals'. In: H. L. A. Hart (ed) *Essays in jurisprudence and philosophy*. Oxford: Clarendon Press. 49-87.
Hart, H. L. A. (1983b) (ed) *Essays in jurisprudence and philosophy*. Oxford: Clarendon Press.
Hart, H. L. A. (1994) *The concept of law*. 2nd ed. Oxford: Clarendon Press.
Hassan, Hussain Hamid (1997) *An introduction to the study of Islamic law*. Islamabad: International Islamic University.
Hassan, Ihab (1985) 'The culture of postmodernism'. In: V. 7 N. 2-3 *Theory, Culture and Society*. 191-233.
Hastings, Donnan (1988) *Marriage among Muslims*. Leiden: E. J. Brill.
Hatemi, Hüseyin (1993) 'Evlilik dışı birlikte yaşama üzerine'. In: N. 99 *Kadın ve Aile*. 50.
Hatemi, Hüsrev (1991) *Türk Aydını: Dünü ve bugünü*. Istanbul: Isaret Yayınlari.
Hayes, Mary and Catherine Williams (1995) *Family law. Principles, policy and practice*. London et al: Butterworths.
Heckmann, Friedrich (1994) 'Nation, nation-state and policy towards ethnic minorities'. In: Bernard Lewis and Dominique Schnapper (eds) *Muslims in Europe*. London. New York: Pinter. 116-129.
Heelas, Paul (1995) *The new age. Religion, culture and society in the age of postmodernity*. Oxford: Blackwell.
Helweg, Arthur Wesley (1979) *Sikhs in England: The development of a migrant community*. Delhi et al: Oxford UP.
Helweg, Arthur Wesley (1986) *Sikhs in England: The development of a migrant community*. 2nd ed. Delhi et al: Oxford UP.
Henry, Stuart (1983) *Private justice: Towards integrated theorising in the sociology of law*. London: Routledge & Kegan Paul.
Henry, Stuart (1985) 'Community justice, capitalist society, and human agency: The dialectics of collective law in the cooperative'. In: V. 19 N. 2 *Law and Society Review*. 303-327.
Heper, Metin (1976) 'Political modernisation as reflected in bureaucratic change: The Turkish bureaucracy and a 'historical bureaucratic empire' tradition'. In: N. 7 *International Journal of Middle East Studies*. 507- 521.
Heper, Metin (1981) 'Islam, polity and society in Turkey: A Middle Eastern perspective'. In: V. 3 *The Middle East Journal*. 345-363.

Heper, Metin (1985) *The state tradition in Turkey*. Hull: The Ethoen Press.
Heper, Metin (1994) *Historical dictionary of Turkey*. London. New Jersey: The Scarecrow Press.
Heper, Metin et al (eds) (1993) *Turkey and the West, changing political and cultural identities*. London. New York: I. B. Tauris & C.
Hepple, Bob and Erika M. Szyszczak (eds) (1993) *Discrimination: The limits of law*. London: Mansell.
Heyd, Uriel (1950) *Foundations of Turkish nationalism*. London: Luzac.
Heyd, Uriel (1954) *Language reform in modern Turkey*. Jerusalem: Israel Oriental Society.
Heyd, Uriel (1968) *Revival of Islam in Turkey*. Jerusalem: The Hebrew University & The Magnes Press.
Higgins, Rosalyn (1978) 'Rights can be wrong'. In: V. 6 N. 3 *New Community*. 230-257.
Hillman, Eugene (1975) *Polygamy reconsidered: African plural marriage and the Christian churches*. Marylenoll: Orbis Books.
Hinchcliffe, Doreen (1970) 'Polygamy in traditional and contemporary Islamic law'. In: V. 1 N. 3 *Islam and the Modern Age*. 13-35.
Hiro, Dilip (1991) *Black British, white British: A history of race relations in Britain*. London: Grafton Books.
Hirst, Paul (1979) *On law and ideology*. London: Oxford UP.
Hobbes, Thomas (1996) *Leviathan (1651)*. Ed. by J. C. A. Gaskin. Oxford: Oxford UP.
Hodkinson, Keith (1984) *Muslim family law. A sourcebook*. London. Canberra: Croom Helm.
Hoebel, E. Adamson (1954) *The law of primitive man: A study in comparative legal dynamics*. Cambridge, MA: Harvard UP.
Hoebel, E. Adamson (1965) 'Fundamental cultural postulates and judicial law making in Pakistan'. In: V. 67 N. 6 *American Anthropologist*. 43-56.
Hoebel, E. Adamson (1971) 'Concept, reality and method in the study of primitive law'. In: A. R. Desai (ed) *Essays on modernization of underdeveloped societies*. Bombay: Thacker & Co. 500-513.
Hoffman, Murad (1993) *Islam: The alternative*. Reading: Garnet Publishing.
Hoggett, Brenda M. and David Pearl (1987) *The family law and society*. London et al: Butterworths.
Hoggett, Brenda M. and David Pearl (1991) *The family law and society*. 3rd ed. London et al: Butterworths.
Holden, P. (1983) (ed) *Women's religious experience*. London: Croom Helm.
Hollinger, Robert (1994) *Postmodernism and the social sciences: A thematic approach*. California: Sage Publications.
Holmes, Colin (1991) *A tolerant country? Immigrants, refugees and minorities in Britain*. London and Boston: Faber and Faber.
Honig, Richard (1935) *Hukuk felsefesi*. Istanbul: Burhaneddin Matbaası.
Hooker, M. B. (1975) *Legal pluralism*. Oxford: Clarendon Press.
Hooker, M. B. (1984) *Islamic law in South-East Asia*. Oxford. New York: Oxford UP.
Horowitz, Donald L. (1994a) 'Islamic reform, legal change. Part I'. In: V. 42 N. 2 *The American Journal of Comparative Law*. 233-283.
Horowitz, Donald L. (1994b) Islamic reform, legal change. Part II. In: V. 42 N. 3 *The American Journal of Comparative Law*. 543-580.
Horton, John (1993) *Liberalism, multiculturalism and toleration*. New York: St. Martin's Press.
Horwitz, A. V. (1990) *The logic of social control*. New York: Plenum Press.
Hourani, Albert (1968) 'Ottoman reform and the politics of notables'. In: William R. Polk

and Richard L. Chambers (ed) *Beginning of modernization in the Middle East*. 41-68.

Houtte, J. van (1989) 'The socio-legal approach to the institutions of family law: Different paradigms'. In: J. S. Gandhi (ed) *Law and social change*. Jaipur: Rawat Publications. 116- 127.

Hubinger, Václav (1996) (ed) *Grasping the changing world: Anthropological concepts in the postmodern era*. London. New York: Routledge.

Hudson, M. O. (1927) 'Law reform in Turkey'. In: V. 13 *American Bar Association Journal*. 5-8.

HUNEE (Hacettepe Üniversitesi Nüfus Etüdleri Enstitüsü) (1989) *Türkiye nüfus ve sağlık araştırması*. Ankara: Ministry of Health and HUNEE.

HUNEE (Hacettepe Üniversitesi Nüfus Etüdleri Enstitüsü) (1993) *Türkiye nüfus ve sağlık araştırması*. Ankara: Ministry of Health and HUNEE.

Hunt, Alan (1990) 'The big fear: Law confronts postmodernism'. In: V. 35 *McGill Law Journal*. 507-540.

Hunt, Alan (1992a) 'Foucault's expulsion of law: Toward a retrieval'. In: V. 17 N. 1 *Law and Social Inquiry*. 1-38.

Hunt, Alan (1992b) 'Law and the condensation of power'. In: V. 17 N. 1 *Law and Social Inquiry*. 57-62.

Hunt, Alan (1993) *Explorations in law and society: Toward a constitutive theory of law*. London. New York: Routledge and Kegan Paul.

Huntington, S. P. ve I. J. Dominguez (1971) *Siyasal gelisme*. Ankara: Siyasal Ilimler Der. Y.

Huntington, Samuel P. (1993) 'The clash of civilisations?' In: V. 72 N. 3 *Foreign Affairs*. 22-49.

Husain, A. (1992) *Islamic fundamentalism. The sociology of faith and action*. Leicester: Volcano.

Husain, Wahed (1977) *Administration of justice during the Muslim rule in India*. Delhi: Idarah-i-Adabiyat-i-Delli.

Husband, Charles (1994) 'The political context of Muslim communities' political participation in British society'. In: Bernard Lewis and Dominique Schnapper (eds) *Muslims in Europe*. London. New York: Pinter. 79-97.

Huseyin, M. Muhammed (1986) *Modernizmin İslam dünyasina girişi*. Istanbul: İnsan Yayınları.

Hussain, Aftab (1987) *Status of women in Islam*. Lahore: Law Publishing Co.

Hussain, Asaf (1985) 'Islam and political integration of Pakistan'. In: Raphael Israeli (ed) *The crescent in the East. Islam in Asia major*. New Delhi: Saletbook Service Syndicate. 63-78.

Hussain, Freda (1984) (ed) *Muslim women*. London: Croom Helm.

Hussain, Mir Zohair (1994) 'Islam in Pakistan under Bhutto and Zia-ul-Haq'. In: Hussin Muttalib and Taj ul-Islam Hashmi (eds) *Islam, Muslims and the Modern State: Case-studies of Muslims in thirteen countries*. London: St. Martin's Press. 47-79.

Hussain, Syed Jaffer (1965) 'Legal modernism in Islam: Polygamy and repudiation'. In: V. 7 *Journal of the Indian Law Institute*. 384-398.

Hutnik, Nimmi (1986) 'Ethnic minority identification and social adaptation'. In: V. 9 N. 2 *Ethnic and Racial Studies*. 150-167.

Hutnik, Nimmi (1991) *Ethnic minority identity. A social psychological perspective*. Oxford: Clarendon Press.

Hyman, Anthony et al (1988) *Pakistan. Zia and after...* London: Asia Publishing House.

Hyman, Herbert and Paul Sheatsley (1964) 'Attitude toward desegregation'. N. 211 *Scientific American*. 16.

İlyasoğlu, Aynur (1993) *Örtülü kimlik*. Istanbul: Metis.
İnalcık, Halil (1964) 'Turkey: The nature of traditional society'. In: E. Ward and Dankwart A. Rustow (ed) *Political modernization in Japan and Turkey*. Princeton: Princeton UP. 42-63.
İnsel, Ahmet (1995) *Türkiye toplumunun bunalımı*. Istanbul: Birikim Yayınları.
Iqbal, Muhammad (1960) *The reconstruction of religious thought in Islam*. Lahore: Ashraf Press.
Irwin, Altman and Joseph Ginat (1996) *Polygamous families in contemporary society*. New York: Cambridge UP.
Irwin, John L. (1994) *Modern Britain: An introduction*. 3rd ed. London. New York: Routledge.
Ishaq, Ibn (1968) *The life of Muhammad*. Karachi: Oxford UP.
Ishaque, Khalid M. (1978a) *Islamic law in the modern world*. Karachi: Pakistan Feature Service.
Ishaque, Khalid M. (1978b) 'Islamization of laws in Pakistan. Problems and prospects'. In: V. 1 N. 3 *The Bulletin of Christian Institutions of Islamic Studies*. 24-29.
Islahi, Abdul Azim (1999) 'Prerequisites for *ijtihad*: A Reappraisal'. http://islamic-finance.net/research/*ijtihad*-islahi.html.
Islamic Council of Europe (1980) *Muslim communities in non-Muslim states*. London: ICE.
Islamic Shari'a Council (1995) *The Islamic Shari'a Council: An introduction*. London: ISC.
Israeli, Raphael (1985) (ed) *The crescent in the East. Islam in Asia major*. New Delhi: Saletbook Service Syndicate.
Iwuji, Emeka (1983) *Marriage form in Nigeria*. Rome: Tipolitografia.
Jackson, David (1999) *Immigration: law and practice*. 2nd ed. London et al: Sweet and Maxwell.
Jacobson, Jessica (1997a) 'Perceptions of Britishness'. In: V. 3 N. 2 *Nations and Nationalism*. 181-199.
Jacobson, Jessica (1997b) 'Religion and ethnicity: Dual and alternative sources of identity among young British Pakistanis'. In: V. 20 N. 2 *Ethnic and Racial Studies*. 26-45.
Jaeschke, Gotthard (1964) *Türkiye'de imam nikahı*. Tr. by Ahmet Mumcu. Ankara: Ankara Universitesi Yayınları.
Jaeschke, Gotthard (1971) *Yeni Türkiye'de İslamlık*. Ankara: Bilgi Yayınevi.
Jaeschke, Gotthard (1992) *Türkiye'de yeni İslamlık*. Ankara: Bilgi Yayınevi.
Jain, Kiran B. (1990-91) 'Polygamy in *Shastric* law – a study in comparison with *Shari'ah* rules'. In: Vs. X & XI *Islamic and Comparative Law Quarterly*. 169-186.
Jalal, Ayesha (1991) 'The convenience of subservience: Women and the state in Pakistan'. In: Deniz Kandiyoti (ed) *Women, Islam and the state*. Basingstoke: Macmillan. 77-114.
Jalibi, Jameel (1996) *Pakistan: The identity of culture*. 2nd ed. Karachi: Royal Book Company.
Jamal, J. Nasir (1986) *The Islamic law of personal status*. London: Graham and Trotman.
Jamal, J. Nasir (1990) *The Islamic law of personal status*. 2nd ed. London et al: Graham & Trotman.
Jamal, J. Nasir (1994) *The status of women under Islamic law and under modern Islamic legislation*. 2nd ed. London et al: Graham & Trotman.
Jameson, Frederic (1991) *Postmodernism, or the cultural logic of the late capitalism*. Durham, NC: Duke UP.
Jansen, Johannes J. G. (1994) 'Islam and civil rights in the Netherlands'. In: Bernard Lewis and Dominique Schnapper (eds) *Muslims in Europe*. London. New York: Pinter. 39-53.
Jeffery, P. (1976) *Migrants and refugees: Muslim and Christian Pakistani families in Bristol*. Cambridge: Cambridge UP.

Jencks, Charles (1989) *What is post-modernism?* 3rd ed. London: Academy Editions.

Johnson, Mark R. D. (1993) 'A question of ethnic origin in the 1991 Census'. In: V. 19 N. 2 *New Community*. 281-289.

Joly, Danièle (1989) *Reluctant hosts: Europe and its refugees*. Aldershot: Avebury.

Joly, Danièle (1995) *Britannia's crescent: Making a place for Muslims in British society*. Aldershot et al: Avebury.

Jones, P. R. and S. Shah (1980) 'Arranged marriages: A sample survey of the Asian case'. In: V. 8 N. 3 *New Community*. 339-343.

Jones, Richard and Gnanapala Welhengama (2000) *Ethnic minorities in English law*. Group for Ethnic Minority Studies, School of Oriental and African Studies; Stoke on Trent: Trentham.

Jones, Trevor (1993) *Britain's ethnic minorities. An analysis of the labour force survey*. London: Policy Studies Institute.

Jonhstone, P. (1981) 'Christians and Muslims in Britain'. In: V. 7 *Islamochristiana*. 167-199.

Jorgensen, S. (1986) 'What is law?'. In: Peter Sack and Elizabeth Minchin (eds) *Legal pluralism. Proceedings of the Canberra Law Workshop VII*. Canberra: Research School of Social Sciences, (Australian National University). 17-31.

Juss, Satvinder S. (1997) *Discretion and deviation in the administration of immigration control*. London: Sweet and Maxwell.

Kabbani, Rana (1995) 'Family matters'. In: Michael King (ed) *God's law versus state law: The construction of Islamic identity in Western Europe*. London: Grey Seal. 44-48.

Kadioglu, Ayse (1998) 'Republican epistemology and Islamic discourses in Turkey in the 1990s'. In: V. 88 N. 1 *The Muslim World*. 1-21.

Kagitcibasi, Cigdem (1975) 'Modernity and the role of women in Turkey'. In: N. 3 *Bogaziçi University Journal*. 83-93.

Kagitcibasi, Cigdem (1976) (ed) *Sex roles, family and community in Turkey*. Indiana: Indiana UP.

Kagitcibasi, Cigdem (1983) (ed) *Sex roles, family and community in Turkey*. Reprint. Indiana: Indiana UP.

Kalam, M. A. (1993) 'Ethnicity and Urduization amongst Pakistanis in Bradford'. London: SOAS. 1-25.

Kalaycıoğlu, Ersin and Ali Yaşar Sarıbay (1986b) (eds) *Türk siyasal hayatının gelişimi*. Istanbul: Beta.

Kalaycıoğlu, Ersin and Ali Yaşar Sarıbay (1986a) (eds) 'Modernleşme arayışı ve siyasal değişme'. In: Ersin Kalaycıoglu and Ali Yaşar Sarıbay (eds) *Türk siyasal hayatının gelişimi*. Istanbul: Beta. 9-30.

Kandiyoti, Deniz (1977) 'Sex roles and social changes. A comparative appraisal of Turkey's women'. In: V. 3 *Signs*. 57-73.

Kandiyoti, Deniz (1984) 'Aile yapısında değişme ve süreklilik: Karşılaştırmalı bir yaklaşım'. In: Türköz Erder (ed) *Türkiye'de ailenin değişimi: Toplumbilimsel incelemeler*. Ankara: Türk Sosyal Bilimler Derneği. 15-33.

Kandiyoti, Deniz (1991a) 'Introduction'. In: Deniz Kandiyoti (ed) *Women, Islam and the state*. London: Macmillan. 1-21.

Kandiyoti, Deniz (1991b) (ed) *Women, Islam and the state*. London: Macmillan.

Kandiyoti, Deniz (1991c) 'End of empire: Islam, nationalism and women in Turkey'. In: Deniz Kandiyoti (ed) *Islam and the state*. London: Macmillan. 22-47.

Kandiyoti, Deniz (1997) *Cariyeler, bacılar, yurttaşlar. Kimlikler ve toplumsal dönüşümler*. Istanbul: Metis.

Kangas, Urpo (1987) 'On studying the reception of legal ideas and their impact on the legal world view'. In: Peter Sack et al (eds) *Rechstheorie: Monistic or pluralistic legal culture*. N. 12. Berlin: Duncker & Humblot. 223-234.

Kannan, C. T. (1978) *Cultural adaptation of Asian immigrants: First and second generation*. London: Author.

Kanyadago, Peter M. (1991) *Evangelizing polygamous families. Canonical and African approaches*. Eldoret, Kenya: AMECEA Gaba Publications.

Kara, İsmail (1994) *İslamcıların siyasi görüşleri*. Istanbul: İz Yayıncılık.

Karadavi, Yusuf (1997) *Islam hukuku*. Istanbul: Marifet.

Karam, Azza M. (1995) 'Book review: The Islamization of the law in Pakistan, Rubya Mehdi'. In: N. 35 *Journal of Legal Pluralism*. 155-158.

Karaman, Hayreddin (1985a) 'İslam dünyasında yeni içtihad teşebbüsleri'. In: *Uluslararası Birinci İslam Araştırmaları Sempozyumu*. Izmir: Dokuz Eylül İlahiyat Fakültesi.

Karaman, Hayreddin (1985b) *İslam hukukunda içtihad*. Ankara: Diyanet İşleri Başkanlığı Yayınları.

Karaman, Hayreddin (1992) *Yeni gelişmeler karşısında İslam hukuku*. Istanbul: Nesil.

Karaman, Hayreddin (1993) *Anahatlarıyla İslam hukuku*. V. I. Istanbul: Ensar.

Karaman, Hayreddin (1996) *İslamın ışığında günümüz meseleleri*. Istanbul: Yeni Şafak.

Karaman, Hayreddin (1999) *İslam hukuk tarihi*. Istanbul: İz.

Karatepe, Şükrü (1993) *Darbeler, anayasalar ve modernleşme*. Istanbul: İz Yayıncılık.

Karlan, Dalmar and İlhan Arsel (1957) *Civil litigation in Turkey*. Ankara: Ajans-Türk Press.

Karlığa, Bekir (2001) 'Şimdiki Ramazanlar daha bilinçli yaşanıyor', *Daily Zaman*. 30 November 2001.

Karpat, Kemal (1996) *Türk demokrasi tarihi*. Istanbul: Afa.

Kastaryano, Riva (1990) 'Muslim migrants in France and Germany: Law and policy in family and group identity'. In: Chibli Mallat and Jane Connors (eds) *Islamic family law*. London. Dordrecht. Boston: Graham & Trotman. 167-180.

Kaushnik, Surendra Nath (1993) *Politics of Islamization in Pakistan. A study of Zia regime*. New Delhi: South Asian Publishers.

Kautsky, John H. (1972) *The political consequences of modernization*. New York: John Wiley and Sons.

Kaye, Ronald (1993) 'The politics of religious slaughter of animals: Strategies for ethno-religious political action'. In: V. 19 N. 2 *New Community*. 235-250.

Kaygı, Abdullah (1992) *Türk düşüncesinde çağdaşlaşma*. Ankara: Gündoğan Yayınları.

Kazamias, Andreas M. (1966) *Education and the quest for modernity in Turkey*. Chicago: University of Chicago Press.

Kazancıgil, A. (1991) 'Democracy in Muslim lands: Turkey in comparative perspective'. In: N. 43 *International Social Science Journal*. 343-360.

Kazancıgil, Ali (1986) 'Türkiye'de modern devletin oluşumu ve Kemalizm'. In: Ersin Kalaycıoğlu and Ali Yaşar Sarıbay (eds) *Türk siyasal hayatının gelişimi*. Istanbul: Beta. 171-188.

Kazancıgil, Ali and Ergun Özbudun (1981) (eds) *Atatürk: Founder of a modern state*. London: Hurst and Co.

Kazmi, Fareed (1987) *Human rights: Myth and reality*. New Delhi: Intellectual Publishing House.

Keddie, Nikki R. and B. Baron (1991) (eds) *Woman in the Middle Eastern history*. New Haven: Yale University Pres.

Kekes, John (1996) *The morality of pluralism*. Berkeley: University of California Press.

Kelly, J. M. (1992) *A short history of Western legal theory*. Oxford: Clarendon Press.

Kelly, Patricia (1998) 'Muslim Canadians, immigration policy and community development in the 1991 census'. In: V. 9 N. 1 *Islam and Christian-Muslim Relations*. 83-102.

Kelsen, Hans (1945) *General theory of law and state*. Tr. by A. Wedberg. Cambridge, MA: Harvard UP.

Kelsen, Hans (1967) *Pure theory of law*. Berkeley, LA: University of California Press.

Kennedy, Charles (1988) 'Islamisation in Pakistan: Implementation of the Hodood Ordinances'. In: V. 18 N. 3 *Asian Survey*. 307-316.

Kennedy, Charles (1992) 'Repugnancy to Islam- who decides? Islam and legal reform in Pakistan'. In: V. 41 *International and Comparative Law Quarterly*. 769-787.

Kennedy, Charles (1996a) 'The status of women in Pakistan'. In: V. 2 N. 1 *Journal of Islamic Studies*. 45-55.

Kennedy, Charles (1996b) *Islamizations of laws and economy*. Islamabad: Institute of Policy Studies.

Kennedy, Duncan and Karl E. Klare (1984) 'A bibliography of critical legal studies'. In: V. 94 N. 2 *Yale Law Journal*. 461-490.

Kepel, Gilles (1995a) *Allah'ın batısında*. Istanbul: Metis.

Kepel, Gilles (1995b) 'Foreword. Between society and community: Muslims in Britain and France'. In: Danièle Joly *Britannia's crescent: Making a place for Muslims in British society*. Aldershot et al: Avebury. ix-xxiii.

Kerimoğlu, Yusuf (1989a) *Fıkhi meseleler*. V. I. Istanbul: Ölçü.

Kerimoğlu, Yusuf (1989b) *Fıkhi meseleler*. V. II. Istanbul: Ölçü.

Kerr, D. et al (1992) (eds) *Religion, state and ethnic groups*. Aldershot: Dartmouth.

Kettani, M. Ali (1986) *Muslim minorities in the world today*. London: Mansell.

Kettani, M. Ali (1990) 'Muslims in non-Muslim societies: challenges and opportunities'. In: V. 11 N. 2 *Journal of Institute of Muslim Minority Affairs*. 226-233.

Kettani, M. Ali (1996) 'Challenges to the organization of Muslim communities in Western Europe: The political dimension'. In: W. A. R. Shadid and P. S. van Koningsveld (eds) *Political participation and identities of Muslims in non-Muslim states*. Kampen: Kok Pharos Publishing. 14-35.

Keyder, Çağlar (1993) *Türkiye'de devlet ve sınıflar*. Istanbul: İletişim.

Khadduri, Majid (1961) *Islamic jurisprudence: Shafi'i's risala*. Baltimore: Johns Hopkins UP.

Khadduri, Majid (1978) 'Marriage in Islamic law: The modernist viewpoints'. V. 26 *The American Journal of Comparative Law*. 213-218.

Khan, Mazhar ul Haq (1972) *Purdah and polygamy*. Pakistan: Nashiran-e, Ilm-o-Taraqiyet.

Khan, Mustafa Ali (1989) 'Islamic polygamy - a blessing in disguise'. In: N. 1 *Kerala Law Times*, Journal Section. 47-58.

Khan, Mustafa Ali (1996) *Islamic jurisprudence: Islamic laws in the modern world*. London: Avon Books.

Khan, Nighat Said (1992) *Voices within: Dialogues with women on Islam*. Lahore: ASR.

Khan, Rashid Ahmad (1993) *Islamic jurisprudence*. Lahore: Mansoor Book House.

Khan, Verity Saifullah (1976a) 'Pakistani women in Britain'. In: V. 5 Ns. 1-2 *New Community*. 99-108.

Khan, Verity Saifullah (1976b) 'Pakistanis in Britain'. In: V. 5 N. 3 *New Community*. 222-229.

Khan, Verity Saifullah (1979) (ed) *Minority families in Britain: Support and stress*. London. Basingstoke: Macmillan.

Khanam, Firdous (n. d.) *Attitudes of men and women towards polygamy*. Lahore: Author.

Kidder, Robert L (1983) *Connecting law and society*. Englewood Cliffs: Prentice Hall.

Kidder, Robert L. (1979) 'Towards an integrated theory of imposed law'. In: Sandra B. Burman and Barbara E. Harrell- Bond (eds) *The imposition of law*. New York: Academic Press. 289-306.

Kıllıoğlu, İsmail (1988) *Ahlak-hukuk ilişkisi*. Istanbul: MUIF Yayınları.
King, Martin Luther (1969) 'A letter from Birmingham city jail'. In: H. A. Bedau (ed) *Civil disobedience*. New York: Pegasus. 72-89.
King, Michael (1993) 'The truth about autopoiesis'. In: V. 20 *Journal of Law and Society*. 218-236.
King, Michael (ed) (1995a) *God's law versus state law: The construction of Islamic identity in Western Europe*. London: Grey Seal.
King, Michael (1995b) 'Introduction'. In: Michael King (ed) *God's law versus state law: The construction of Islamic identity in Western Europe*. London: Grey Seal. 1-15.
King, Michael (1995c) 'The Muslim identity in a secular world'. In: Michael King (ed) *God's law versus state law: The construction of Islamic identity in Western Europe*. London: Grey Seal. 91-114.
King, Michael and Anton Schütz (1994) 'The ambitious modesty of Niklas Luhmann'. In: V. 21 N. 3 *Journal of Law and Society*. 261-287.
King, R. (1982) 'The Changing Distribution of Cypriots in London'. In: V. 19 N. 65 *Etudes Migrations*. 93-120.
Kinross, Lord (1964a) *A biograph of Mustafa Kemal, father of modern Turkey*. New York: Quill.
Kinross, Lord (1964b) *Atatürk: The rebirth of a nation*. London: Weidenfeld and Nicolson.
Klautke, Heinz (1995) 'Religion and secularization: Introductory remarks from a Western-Christian perspective'. In: Tarek Mitri (ed) *Religion, law and society: A Christian-Muslim discussion*. Geneva. Kampen: WCC Publications. Kok Pharos. 86-91.
Klein, Heinz Gunther and Renate Nestvogel (1986) *Women in Pakistan*. Eschborn: Deutsche Gesellschaft für Technische Zusammenarbeit.
Knott, Kim (1992) *The changing character of the religions of the ethnic minorities of Asian origin in Britain: Final report of a Leverhulme Project*. Community religions project research papers. Leeds: The University of Leeds, Department of Theology and Religious Studies.
Knott, Kim (1994) 'Women and religion in post-war Britain'. In: Gerald Parsons (ed) *The growth of religious diversity: Britain from 1945*. Volume II. London: Routledge. The Open UP. 199-230.
Knott, Kim and S. Khokher (1993) 'The religious and ethnic identity among young Muslim women in Bradford'. In: V. 19 N. 4 *New Community*. 593-610.
Köker, Levent (1990) *Modernleşme, Kemalizm ve demokrasi*. Istanbul: İletişim.
Köker, Levent (1994) *Modernleşme, Kemalizm ve demokrasi*. 2nd impression. Istanbul: İletişim.
Kolars, John F. (1963) *Tradition, season, and change in a Turkish village*. Chicago: University of Chicago Press.
Kömeçoğlu, Uğur (1997) *A sociologically interpretive approach to the Fethullah Gülen community movement*. Istanbul: Bosphorus University.
Kömeçoğlu, Uğur (2000) 'Kutsal ile kamusal: Fethullah Gülen cemaat hareketi'. In Nilüfer Göle (ed) *İslamın kamusal yüzleri*. Istanbul: Metis.
Kongar, Emre (1976) *Türkiye'nin toplumsal yapısı*. Ankara: Cem.
Kongar, Emre (1985) *Toplumsal değişme kuramları ve Türkiye gerçeği*. Istanbul: Remzi Kitabevi.
Kongar, Emre (1986) 'Turkey's cultural transformation'. In Günsel Renda and C. Max Kortepeter (eds) *The transformation of Turkish culture, the Atatürk legacy*. Princeton, NY: Kingston Press. 19-68. http://www.kongar.org/aen_tr.php.
Kongar, Emre (1992) *İmparatorluktan günümüze Turkiye'nin toplumsal yapısı*. 6th ed. Istanbul: Remzi Kitabevi.

Koningsveld, P. S. van (1996) 'Islamic policies of the Western colonial powers: Their relevance in the European Union in the post-colonial era'. *The Centre of South Asian Studies Annual Lecture*. 6 November. London: SOAS.

Korkmaz, Alaaddin (1994) *Ziya Gökalp: Aksiyonu, meşrutiyet ve cumhuriyet üzerindeki tesirleri*. Istanbul: Milli Eğitim Bakanlığı Yayınları.

Korson, J. Henry (1975) 'Modernization, social change and the family in Pakistan'. In: W. H. Wriggins (ed) *Pakistan in transition*. Islamabad: University of Islamabad.

Korten, David C. (1976) *Planned change in a traditional society*. New York: Praeger Publishers.

Kozlowski, Gregory C. (1998) 'Islamic law in contemporary South Asia'. In: V. 41 *Current Affairs*. 68-88.

Kritzeck, James and R. Bayley Winder (1960) (eds) *The world of Islam*. London: Macmillan.

Kruger, Hilmar (1991) 'Aile hukuku sorunları Osmanlı İslam geleneği'. Tr. by Necla Giritlioğlu. In: Behlül Dikeçligil and Ahmet Çiğdem (ed) *Aile yazıları*. Ankara: T. C. B. Aile Araştırma Kurumu Başkanlığı. 203-215.

Kubalı, H. N. (1957) 'Modernization and secularization as determining factors in reception in Turkey'. In: V. 9 N. 1 *International Social Science Bulletin*. 65-69.

Kucukcan, Talip (1999) *Politics of Ethnicity, Identity and Religion: Turkish Muslims in Britain*, Aldershot: Ashgate.

Küçükömer, İdris (1994) *Düzenin yabancılaşması*. Istanbul: Bağlam Yayınları.

Kulcsar, Kalman (1987) *Modernization and law. Theses and thoughts*. Budapest: Hungarian Academy of Sciences.

Kulcsar, Kalman (1989) 'Law and social change'. In: J. S. Gandhi (ed) *Law and social change*. Jaipur: Rawat. 24-50.

Kumari, Jayawardena (1994) *Feminism and nationalism in the third world*. London. New Jersey: Zed Books.

Kümbetoğlu, Belkis (1997) 'Aile, evlilik, nikah: Farklılaşan kavramlar'. In: N. 73 *Toplum ve Bilim*. 111-126.

Kuppe, René and Richard Putz (1996) (eds) *Law and anthropology*. V. 8. The Hague: Martinus Nijhoff.

Kuran, Ercüment (1968) 'The impact of nationalism on the Turkish élite in the nineteenth century'. In: William R. Polk and Richard L. Chambers (ed) *Beginning of modernization in the Middle East*. Chicago: University of Chicago Press. 109-117.

Kurin, Richard (1986) 'Islamization: A view from the countryside'. In: Anita M. Weiss (ed) *Islamic reassertion in Pakistan*. Syracuse: Syracuse UP. 115-128.

Kurnaz, Şefika (1991) *Cumhuriyet öncesinde Türk Kadını, 1839-1923*. Ankara: T. C. B. Aile Araştırma Kurumu.

Kurnaz, Şefika (1992) *Cumhuriyet öncesinde Türk kadını, 1839-1923*. 2nd ed. Istanbul: MEBY.

Kurucan, Ahmet (1998) *Yeni bir fikhi açı*. Izmir: Işık.

Kurzman, Charles (1998) *Liberal Islam: A sourcebook*. New York/Oxford: Oxford University Press.

Kushner, David (1977) *The rise of Turkish nationalism, 1876-1908*. London: Frank Cass.

Kusum (1987) 'Divorce by mutual consent'. In: V. 29 N. 1 *JILI*. 110-114.

Kymlicka, Will (1995a) *Multicultural citizenship. A liberal theory of minority rights*. Oxford: Clarendon Press.

Kymlicka, Will (1995b) (ed) *The rights of minority cultures*. Oxford: Oxford UP.

Ladbury, S. (1979), 'Turkish Cypriots in London, Economy, Society and Culture', Unpublished PhD Thesis, SOAS (School of African and Oriental Studies), London.

Ladeur, Karl-Heinz (1997) 'Postmodern constitutional theory: A prospect for the self-organising society'. In: V. 60 N. 5 *The Modern Law Review*. 617-629.

Landau, Jacob M. (1974) *Radical politics in modern Turkey*. Leiden: E. J. Brill.

Langer, Suzanne (1942) *Philosophy in a new key*. Cambridge, MA: Harvard UP.

Lapidus, Ira M. (1996) *Modernizme geçiş sürecinde İslam dünyasi*. Tr. by Safa Üstün. Istanbul: IFAV.

Latifi, Danial (1973) 'Rationalism and Muslim law'. In: V. 4 N. 4 *Islam and the Modern Age*. 43-70.

Law Commission (1972) *Family law. Report on polygamous marriages*. London: HMSO.

Law Commission (1973) *Report on solemnisation of marriage*. Law Commission Report N. 53. London: HMSO.

Law Commission (1982) *Polygamous marriages, capacity to contract a polygamous marriage and the concept of the potentially polygamous marriage*. Law Commission Working Paper N. 83. London: HMSO.

Law Commission (1985) *Private international law: polygamous marriages – capacity to contract a polygamous marriage and related issues*. Law Commission Report N. 146, Scottish Law Commission Report N. 96. London: HMSO.

Lawrence, Bruce B. (1989) *Defenders of God: The fundamentalist revolt against the modern age*. New York: Harper & Row.

Lawrence, Daniel (1974) *Black migrants: White natives. A study of race relations in Nottingham*. London: Cambridge UP.

Layish, Aharon (1975) *Woman and Islamic law in a non-Muslim state*. Jerusalem: Israel Universities Press.

Lazarus-Black, Mindie and Susan Hirsch (eds) (1994) *Contested states: Law, hegemony and resistance*. New York: Routledge.

Legrand, Pierre (1996) 'How to compare now?' In: V. 16 N. 2 *Legal Studies*. 232-242.

Lerner, Daniel (1958) *The passing traditional society*. Glencoe: The Free Press.

Levine, Ned (1973) 'Old culture- new culture: A study of migrants in Ankara, Turkey'. In: N. 51 *Social Forces*. 355-368.

Levine, Ned (1983) 'Social change and family crisis- the nature of Turkish divorce'. In: Çiğdem Kagıtçıbaşı (ed) *Sex roles, family and community in Turkey*. Bloomington: Indiana UP. 323-347.

Lewis, Bernard (1966) *The emergence of modern Turkey*. London: Oxford UP.

Lewis, Bernard (1968) *The emergence of modern Turkey*. 2nd ed. Oxford: Oxford UP.

Lewis, Bernard (1992) 'Legal and historical reflections on the position of Muslim populations under non-Muslim rule'. In: V. 13 N. 2 *Journal of the Institute for Muslim Minority Affairs*. 1-16.

Lewis, Bernard (1994) 'Legal and historical reflections on the position of Muslim populations under non-Muslim rule'. In: Bernard Lewis and Dominique Schnapper (eds) *Muslims in Europe*. London. New York: Pinter. 1-18.

Lewis, Bernard and Dominique Schnapper (eds) (1994) *Muslims in Europe*. London. New York: Pinter.

Lewis, Philip (1994a) *Islamic Britain: Religion, politics and identity among Muslims*. London: I. B. Tauris.

Lewis, Philip (1994b) 'Being Muslim and being British: The dynamics of Islamic reconstruction in Bradford'. In: Roger Ballard (ed) *Desh pardesh: The South Asian experience in Britain*. London: Hurst & Co. 58-87.

Libson, Gideon (1997) 'On the development of custom as a source of law in Islamic law...'. In: V. 4 N. 2 *Islamic Law and Society*. 131-155.

Lipstein, K. (1956) 'The reception of western law in Turkey'. In: N. 5 *Annales de la droit*

*d'Istanbul*. Istanbul: Fakülteler Matbaası. 11-27.
Llewellyn, K. N. and E. Adamson Hoebel (1941) *The Cheyenne way*. Norman, Oklahoma: Oklahoma UP.
Llewellyn, Karl (1962) *Jurisprudence: Realism in theory and practice*. Chicago: University of Chicago Press.
Lord Lloyd of Hampstead (1979) *Introduction to juriprudence*. 4th ed. London: Stevens & Sons.
Ludington, Nicholas S. (1984) *Turkish Islam and the secular state*. Washington D. C.: American Institute for Islamic Affairs.
Luhmann, Niklas (1992) 'Operational closure and structural coupling: The differentiation of the legal system'. In: N. 13 *Cardozo Law Review*. 1419-1441.
Lynch, James (1990) 'Cultural pluralism, structural pluralism and the United Kingdom'. In: CRE *Britain: A Plural Society*. 29-43.
Lyotard, Jean François (1984) (La condition postmoderne) *The postmodern condition: A report on knowledge*. Tr. by Geoff Bennington and Brian Massumi. Manchester: Manchester UP.
Lyotard, Jean François (1990) *Postmodern durum: Postmodernizm*. Istanbul: Ara Y.
Lyotard, Jean François (1993) *The postmodern explained*. Minneapolis: University of Minnesota Press.
Macdonald, Ian A. and Nicholas J. Blake (1991) *Immigration law and practice in the United Kingdom*. 3rd ed.London et al: Butterworths.
MacEwen, Martin (1994) 'Anti-discrimination law in Great Britain'. In: V. 20 N. 3 *New Community*. 353-370.
MacFarlane, L. J. (1975) *The theory and practice of human rights*. London: Maurice Temple Smith.
Madan, T. N. (1995) (ed) *Muslim communities of South Asia: Culture, society, and power*. New Delhi: Manohar.
Magnarella, Paul J. (1973) 'The reception of Swiss family law in Turkey'. In: V. 46 N. 2 *Anthropological Quarterly*. 100-116.
Magnarella, Paul J. (1974) *Tradition and change in a Turkish town*. New York: John Wiley and Sons.
Magnarella, Paul J. (1988) 'Kanun ve aile (Law and family). Assessing the effects of Atatürk's efforts to transform the moral basis of Turkish life through the implementation of European legal codes'. In: N. 6 *The World and I*. 502-513.
Mahmood, Nadeem Shaukat (1982) *Muslim family laws*. Lahore: Islamic Publications.
Mahmood, Nadeem Shaukat (1989) *Muslim family laws*. 11th ed. Lahore: Legal Research Centre.
Mahmood, Nadeem Shaukat (1993) *Principles and digest of Muslim law*. 4th ed. Lahore: Legal Research Centre.
Mahmood, Tahir (1972) *Family law reform in the Muslim world*. Bombay: N. M. Tripathi Pvt.
Mahmood, Tahir (1993) 'Constitutional ideal of uniform civil code- Is Muslim personal law a stumbling block?'. In: V. 2 N. 2 *Religion and Law Review*. 166-174.
Maidment, S. (1974) 'The legal effect of religious divorces'. In: V. 37 *The Modern Law Times Journal*. 611-626.
Malinowski, Bronislaw (1926) *Crime and custom in savage society*. London: Routledge and Kegan Paul.
Malinowski, Bronislaw (1945) *The dynamics of culture change*. New Haven: Yale UP.
Malinowski, Bronislaw (1959) *Crime and custom in savage society*. Reprint. Paterson, NJ: Littlefield, Adams.

Malinowski, Bronislaw (1960) *A scientific theory of culture and other essays*. Oxford: Oxford UP.

Mallat, Chibli (1993) *The renewal of Islamic law*. Cambridge: Cambridge UP.

Mallat, Chibli and Jane Connors (1990) (eds) *Islamic family law*. London. Dordrecht. Boston: Graham & Trotman.

Man, Singh Das (1991) (ed) *The family in the Muslim world*. New Delhi: M. D. Publications.

Mandaville, Peter (1999) 'Digital Islam: Changing boundaries of religious knowledge?', at http://isim. leidenuniv.nl/newsletter/2/isim/1. html.

Mardin, Şerif (1961) 'Some explanatory notes on the origins of the Mecelle'. In: V. 51 N. 3 *The Muslim World*. 274-279.

Mardin, Şerif (1962) *The genesis of Young Ottoman thought. A study in the modernization of Turkish political ideas*. Princeton: Princeton UP.

Mardin, Şerif (1966) 'Opposition and control in Turkey'. In: V. 1 N. 3 *Government and Opposition*. 375-387.

Mardin, Şerif (1969a) 'Power, civil society, and culture in the Ottoman Empire'. In: N. 6 *Comparative Studies in Society and History*. 258-281.

Mardin, Şerif (1969b) *Religion as ideology*. Ankara: Hacettepe University Publications.

Mardin, Şerif (1971) 'Ideology and religion in the Turkish revolution'. In: N. 2 *International Journal of Middle Eastern Studies*. 197-211.

Mardin, Şerif (1973) 'Center-periphery relations: A key to Turkish politics'. In: V. 102 N. 1 *Daedalus*. 169-190.

Mardin, Şerif (1981) 'Religion and secularism in Turkey'. In: Ali Kazancıgil and Ergün Özbudun (1981) (eds) *Atatürk: Founder of a modern state*. London: Hurst and Co. 191-219.

Mardin, Şerif (1982) 'Turkey: Islam and westernization'. In: Carlo Caldorola (ed) *Religions and societies: Asia and the Middle East*. Berlin et al: Mouton Publishers. 171-198.

Mardin, Şerif (1986) 'Tanzimattan sonra asiri batililasma'. In: Ersin Kalaycıoğlu and Ali Yaşar Sarıbay (eds) *Türk siyasal hayatının gelişimi*. Istanbul: Beta. 31-68.

Mardin, Şerif (1989) *Religion and social change in modern Turkey: The case of Bediuzzaman Said Nursi*. Albany: State University of New York Press.

Mardin, Şerif (1992a) *Jön Türklerin siyasi fikirleri*. Istanbul: İletişim.

Mardin, Şerif (1992b) *Türkiye'de din ve siyaset*. Istanbul: İletişim.

Mardin, Şerif (1992c) *Bediüzzaman Said Nursi olayi: Modern Türkiye'de din ve toplumsal değişim*. Istanbul: İletişim.

Mardin, Şerif (1992d) *Türk modernleşmesi*. Istanbul: İletişim.

Mardin, Şerif (1992e) *Din ve ideoloji*. Istanbul: İletişim.

Mardin, Şerif (1995) 'Nurculuk'. In John L. Esposito (ed), *The Oxford Encyclopedia of the Modern Islamic World*. V. 3. New York: Oxford University Press. 256.

Marger, Martin (1991) *Race and ethnic relations: American and global perspectives*. Belmont: Wodsworth Publishing.

Martin, Richard C. (ed) (1982) *Islam in local contexts*. Leiden: E. J. Brill.

Marty, M. and R. Appleby (eds) (1991) *Fundamentalisms observed*. Chicago: The University of Chicago Press.

Mason, David (1995) *Race and ethnicity in Britain*. Oxford: Oxford UP.

Massell, Gregory (1968) 'Law as an instrument of revolutionary change in a traditional milieu: The case of Soviet Central Asia'. In: V. 2 N. 2 *Law and Society Review*. 179-228.

Mastura, Michael O. (1985) 'The status of Muslim personal law in selected non-Muslim countries'. In: V. 6 *Journal of the Institute of Muslim Minority Affairs*. 114-126.

Masud, Muhammad Khalid (1989) 'Being Muslim in a non-Muslim polity: Three alternate models'. In: V. 10 N. 1 *Journal of Institute of Muslim Minority Affairs*. 118-128.

Masud, Muhammad Khalid (1995) *Shatibi's philosophy of Islamic law*. Islamabad: Islamic Research Institute, International Islamic University.

Maududi, S. Abul A'la (1955) *The Islamic law and constitution*. Tr by Khurshid Ahmad. Lahore: Islamic Publications.

Maududi, S. Abul A'la (1960) *The Islamic law and constitution*. 2nd ed. Tr by Khurshid Ahmad. Lahore: Islamic Publications.

Maududi, S. Abul A'la (1972) *Purdah and the status of women in Islam*. Lahore: Islamic Publications.

Maududi, S. Abul A'la (1975) *Fundamentals of Islam*. Lahore: Islamic Publications.

Maududi, S. Abul A'la (1981) 'Islamic and western laws on divorce- a comparative historical perspective'. In: V. 1 *Islamic and Comparative Law Quarterly*. 17-23.

Mauss, M. (1906) 'Les variations saissonieres des societes esquimaux; —tude de morphologie social'. In: V. 9 *Anne Sociologigue*. 39-132.

Mayss, Abla (2000) 'Recognition of foreign divorces: Unwarrantable ethnocentrism'. In: John Murphy (ed) *Ethnic minorities, their families and the law*. Oxford, UK & Portland, OR: Hart. 51-70.

McAdoo, Hariette Pipes (ed) (1993) *Family ethnicity: Strength in diversity*. London: Sage.

McBride, William Leon (1974) 'An overview of future possibilities: Law unlimited?' In: J. Roland Pennock and John W. Chapman (eds) *The limits of law*. New York: Lieber-Atherton. 28-38.

McCarthy, Justin (1997) *The Ottoman Turks – An Introductory History to 1923*. London and New York: Longman.

McDermott, Mustafa Yusuf and Menazir Ahsan (1980) *The Muslim guide: For teachers, employers, community workers and social administrators in Britain*. Leicester: The Islamic Foundation.

McDonough, Shalia (1995) 'Typologies of religion and state'. In: Tarek Mitri (ed) *Religion, law and society: A Christian-Muslim discussion*. Geneva. Kampen: WCC Publications. Kok Pharos. 1-10.

McLachlan, Campbell Alan (1988) *State recognition of customary law in the South Pacific*. London: UCL (Unpublished PhD thesis).

McLellan, Janet and Anthony H. Richmond (1994) 'Multiculturalism in crisis: A postmodern perspective on Canada'. In: V. 17 N. 4 *Ethnic and Racial Studies*. 662-683.

McLoughlin, Sean (1996) 'In the name of the umma: Globalisation, 'race' and Muslim identity politics in Bradford'. In: W. A. R. Shadid and P. S. van Koningsveld (eds) *Political participation and identities of Muslims in non-Muslim states*. Kampen: Kok Pharos Publishing. 206-228.

Mehdi, Rubya (1994) *The Islamization of the law in Pakistan*. Richmond: Curzon Press.

Menski, Werner (1993) 'Asian laws in Britain and the question of adaptation to a new legal order: Asian laws in Britain?' In: Milton Israel and N. K. Wagle (eds.) *Ethnicity, identity, migration: the South Asian context*. Toronto: Centre for South Asian Studies, University of Toronto. 238-268.

Menski, Werner F. (1987) 'Legal pluralism in Hindu marriage'. In: R. Burhart (ed) *Hinduism in Great Britain: The perpetuation of religion in an alien cultural milieu*. London. New York: Tavistock: 180-200.

Menski, Werner F. (1988a) 'English family law and ethnic laws in Britain'. In: N. 1 *Kerala Law Times*, Journal Section. 56-66.

Menski, Werner F. (1988b) 'Uniformity of laws in India and England'. In: V. 7 N. 11 *Journal of Law and Society* (Peshawar). 11-26.

Menski, Werner F. (1990a) 'The reform of Islamic family law and a uniform civil code for India'. In: Chibli Mallat and Jane Connors (eds) *Islamic family law*. London. Dordrecht. Boston: Graham & Trotman. 253-293.

Menski, Werner F. (1990b) 'Uniform civil code in India: A false model for development?'. In: N. 2 *Kerala Law Times*. 3-10.

Menski, Werner F. (1990c) 'Comparative legal training in action: A reluctant defence of polygamy'. In: N. 1 *Kerala Law Times*, Journal Section. 50-69.

Menski, Werner F. (1991a) 'Change and continuity in Hindu marriage rituals'. In: S. Y. Killingley (ed) *Hindu ritual and society*. New Castle: Grevatt and Grevatt. 32-51.

Menski, Werner F. (1991b) 'Crocodile tears and Muslim polygamy in India'. In: N. 2 *Kerala Law Times*, Journal Section. 20-24.

Menski, Werner F. (1993a) 'Asians in Britain and the question of adaptation to a new legal order: Asian laws in Britain'. In: Milton Israel and Narendra Wagle (eds) *Ethnicity, identity, migration: The South Asian context*. Toronto: University of Toronto. 238-268.

Menski, Werner F. (1993b) *Angrezi shariat: Plural arrangements in family law by Muslims in Britain*. London: SOAS (Unpublished paper). 1-10.

Menski, Werner F. (1996) *Law, religion and South Asians*. London: SOAS (Unpublished paper). 1-33.

Menski, Werner F. (1997a) *Ethnicity, discrimination and human rights*. London: SOAS (Unpublished paper). 1-10.

Menski, Werner F. (1997b) *Concluding analysis: Possibilities and limits of promoting ethnic/racial equality and human rights. Or: What is a Brazilian, anyway?* London: SOAS (Unpublished paper). 1-9.

Menski, Werner F. (1997c) 'South Asian Muslim law today: An overview'. In: V. 9 N. 1 Sharqiyyât. 16-36.

Menski, Werner F. (1999) 'South Asian women in Britain, family integrity and the primary purpose rule'. In: Rohit Barot, Harriet Bradley and Steve Fenton (eds.) *Ethnicity, gender and social change*. Basingstoke: Macmillan and New York: St. Martin's Press. 81-98.

Menski, Werner F. (2000) *Comparative law in a global context. The legal systems of Asia and Africa*. London: Platinium.

Menski, Werner F. (2001) *Modern Indian family law*. Richmond, Surrey: Curzon.

Menski, Werner F. and Prakash Shah (1996) *Cross-cultural conflicts of marriage and divorce involving South Asians in Britain*. London: SOAS (Unpublished paper). 1-11. In: Strijbosch, Fons and Mari-Claire Foblets (eds) *Cross-cultural family relations. Reports of a socio-legal seminar*. Onati: International Institute for the Sociology of Law. 167-184.

Mernissi, Fatima (1975) *Beyond the veil: Male-female dynamics in a modern Muslim society*. New York: John Wiley.

Merry, Sally Engle (1988) 'Legal pluralism'. In: V. 22 N. 5 *Law and Society Review*. 869-896.

Merry, Sally Engle (1992) 'Popular justice and the ideology of social transformation'. In: V. 1 *Social and Legal Studies*. 161-176.

Merry, Sally Engle (1995) 'Resistance and cultural power of law: 1994 presidential address'. In: V. 29 *Law and Society Review*. 11-24.

Merry, Sally Engle and Neal Milner (1993) (eds) *The possibility of popular justice: A case study of community mediation in the United States*. Ann Arbor: University of Michigan Press.

Mert, Nuray (1994) *Laiklik tartışmasına kavramsal bir bakış*. Istanbul: Bağlam.

Messick, Brinkley (1996) 'Media Muftis: Radio *Fatwa*s in Yemen'. In: Muhammad Khalid Masud et al (eds), *Islamic Legal Interpretation: Muftis and Their Fatwas*. Cambridge,

MA and London, England: Harvard University Press. 310-320.

Meyer, Leonard B. (1967) *Music, the arts, and ideas*. Chicago: The University of Chicago Press.

Miller, Ruth A. (2000) 'The Ottoman and Islamic Substratum of Turkey's Swiss Civil Code'. In V. 11 N. 3 *Oxford Journal of Islamic Studies*. 335-361.

Mills, Wright C. (1956) *The power élite*. New York: Oxford UP.

Milne, A. J. M. (1986) *Human rights and human diversity*. London: Macmillan.

Milovanovic, Dragan (1992) *Postmodern law and disorder: Psychoanalytic semiotics, chaos and juridic exegeses*. Illinois: Deborah Charles Publications.

Minai, Naila (1981) *Women in Islam*. London: John Murray.

Minda, Gary (1995) *Postmodern legal movements: Law and jurisprudence at century's end*. New York. London: New York UP.

Ministry of Planning and Development Government of Pakistan (1998) *Pakistan 2010. A vision for knowledge-led, just, tolerant, enterprising and prosperous society*. Islamabad: MPDGP.

Minority Rights Group (1991) *Minorities and autonomy in Western Europe*. London: MRG.

Mir-Hosseini, Ziba (1993) *Marriage on trial. A study of Islamic family law*. London: Tauris.

Mirza, Kauser (1989) *The silent cry: Second generation Bradford Muslim women speak*. Muslims in Europe Research Papers, 43. Birmingham: The Centre for the Study of Islam and Christian-Muslim Relations.

Mitri, Tarek (1995) (ed) *Religion, law and society: A Christian-Muslim discussion*. Geneva. Kampen: WCC Publications. Kok Pharos.

Modood, Tariq (1986) 'Religious anger and minority rights'. In: V. 60 N. 3 *Political Quarterly*. 280-284.

Modood, Tariq (1992) *Not easy being British. Colour, culture and citizenship*. Stoke-on-Trent: Runnymede Trust and Trentham Books.

Modood, Tariq (1993) 'Muslim views on religious identity and racial equality'. In: V. 19 N. 3 *New Community*. 513-519.

Modood, Tariq (1994) *Racial equality. Colour, culture and justice*. London: Institute for Public Policy Research.

Modood, Tariq and Pnina Werbner (eds) (1996) *The politics of multiculturalism in the new Europe: Racism, identity, community*. London: Zed.

Modood, Tariq et al (1997) *Ethnic minorities in Britain*. London: PSI.

Mole, Nuala (1987) *Immigration: family entry and settlement*. Bristol: Jordan and Sons.

Montgomery, Jonathan (1992) 'Legislating for a multi-faith society: Some problems of special treatment'. In: Bob Hepple and Erika M. Ssyszczak (eds) *Discrimination. The limits of law*. London. New York: Mansell. 193-213.

Moore, Sally Falk (1973) 'Law and social change: The semi-autonomous social field as an appropriate subject of study'. In: V. 7 N. 4 *Law and Society Review*. 719-746.

Moore, Sally Falk (1978) *Law as process: An anthropological approach*. London et al: Routledge and Kegan Paul.

Moosa, Ebrahim (1999) 'Language of change in Islamic law: Redefining death in modernity'. In: V. 38 N. 3 *Journal for Islamic Studies*. Reprinted. RS. Khare (ed) *Perspectives on Islamic law and justice*. Lanham et al: Rowman & Littlefield. 161-197.

Morris, H.F. (1972) 'Indirect rule and the law of marriage'. In: H.F. Morris and James S. Read: *Indirect rule and the search for justice. Essays in East African legal history*. Oxford: Clarendon. 213-250.

Morrison, Wayne L. (1982) *John Austin*. London: Edward Arnold.

Morrison, Wayne L. (1997) *Jurisprudence: From the Greeks to post-modernism*. London: Cavendish Publishing House.

Morse, Bradford W. (1988) 'Indigenous law and state legal systems: Conflict and compatibility'. In: Bradford W. Morse and G. R. Woodman (eds) *Indigenous law and the state.* Dordrecht: Foris Publications. 101-120

Morse, Bradford W. and G. R. Woodman (eds) (1988) *Indigenous law and the state.* Dordrecht: Foris Publications.

Mullard, Chris (1973) *Black Britain*. London: Allen and Unwin.

Mumtaz, Khawar and Farida Shaheed (1987) *Women of Pakistan. Two steps forward, one step back?* London and New Jersey: Zed Books.

Murad, Abdal-Hakim (1999) 'The Problem of Anti-*madhhab*ism', at http://Sunna.org/fiqh/antimadhhabism.htm.

Murphy, Ronalda (1995) 'Postmodern pride: Mary Joe Frug's manifesto'. In: V. 19 N. 4 *Law and Social Inquiry*. 1079-1105.

Muslehuddin, Mohammad (1975) *Islamic jurisprudence and the rule of necessity and need.* Islamabad: Islamic Research Institute.

Muslim Institute (1990) *The Muslim manifesto: A strategy for survival.* London: The Muslim Institute.

Muslim, Abdul Gafur (1996) 'Islamization of law in Pakistan: Problems and prospects'. In: H. S. Bhatia (ed) *Studies in Islamic law, religion and society*. New Delhi: Deep & Deep. 145-155.

Mustafa Baktir (1998) 'Bediuzzaman's views on *ijtihad*', at http://www.nesil.com.tr.

Muttalib, Hussin and Taj ul-Islam Hashmi (1994) (eds) *Islam, Muslims and the modern state: Case-studies of Muslims in thirteen countries*. London: St. Martin's Press.

Nader, Laura (1965) 'The anthropological study of law'. In: V. 67 N. 6 *American Anthropologist*. 3-32.

Nader, Laura (1969) (ed) *Law in culture and society*. Chicago: Aldine.

Nader, Laura and D. Metzger (1963) 'Conflict resolution in two Mexican communities'. In: V. 65 N. 3 *American Anthropologist*. 584-592.

Nader, Laura and Harry F. Todd Jr. (eds) (1978) *The disputing process: Law in ten societies*. New York: Columbia UP.

Nadwi, Syed Hasan Ali (1983) *Muslims in the West. The message and mission*. Leicester: The Islamic Foundation.

Najam, Muhammed and Malik Aziz-ur-Rehman (1997) *Complete digest on Mahomedan law*. Lahore: Khyber Law Publishers.

Nasr, Sayyid Vali Reza Nasr (1994) *The vanguard of the Islamic revolution: The Jamaat-i-Islami of Pakistan*. Berkeley: The University of California Press.

Nasr, Seyyed Hossein (1994) *Traditional Islam in the modern world*. London. New York: Kegan Paul.

Nasr, Syed Vali R. (2000) 'The rise of sunni militancy in Pakistan: The changing role of Islamism and the ulama in society and politics'. In: V. 34 N. 1 *Modern Asian Studies*. 139-180.

Nauck, Bernard (1994) 'Changes in Turkish migrant families in Germany'. In: Bernard Lewis and Dominique Schnapper (eds) *Muslims in Europe*. London. New York: Pinter. 130-147.

Nelken, David (1984) 'Law in action or living law? Back to the beginning in sociology of law'. In: V. 4 *Legal Studies*. 157-174.

Nesbitt, Eleanor (1995) 'Panjabis in Britain: Cultural history and cultural choices'. In: V. 15 N. 2 *South Asia Research*. 221-240.

Niazi, Kausar (1976) *Modern challenge to Muslim families*. Lahore: M. Ansari.

Nielsen, Jørgen S. (1984) *Muslim immigration and settlement in Britain*. Research Papers, Muslims in Europe. N. 30-31. Birmingham: Selly Oak Colleges.

Nielsen, Jørgen S. (1981) (ed) *Islam in English law and administration*. A symposium. Birmingham: Selly Oak Colleges.

Nielsen, Jørgen S. (1983) (ed) *Muslim children present their faith*. Muslims in Europe Research Papers, 9. Birmingham: CSIC-MR.

Nielsen, Jørgen S. (1985a) 'Muslims in Britain: Searching for an identity?'. In: V. 13 N. 3 *New Community*. 384-394.

Nielsen, Jørgen S. (1985b) 'Muslim family law and multi-cultural Britain'. In: N. 14 *Newsletter of the Centre for the Study of Islam and Christian-Muslim Relations*. Birmingham: Selly Oak Colleges. 15-18.

Nielsen, Jørgen S. (1987a) 'Muslims in Britain: Searching for an identity'. In: V. 13 N. 3 *New Community*. 384-394.

Nielsen, Jørgen S. (1987b) *Muslims in Western Europe*. Edinburgh: Edinburgh UP.

Nielsen, Jørgen S. (1988) 'Muslims in Britain and local authority responses'. In: T. Gerholm and Y. G. Lithman (eds) *New Islamic presence in Western Europe*. London: Mansell. 53-77.

Nielsen, Jørgen S. (1989) 'Islamic communities in Britain'. In: Paul Badham (ed) *Religion, state, and society in modern Britain*. Lewiston et al: The Edwin Mellen Press. 225-241.

Nielsen, Jørgen S. (1991a) 'Muslim organizations in Europe: Integration or isolation?'. In: W. A. Shadid and P. S. van Koningsveld (eds) *The integration of Islam and Hinduism in Western Europe*. Kampen: Kok Pharos Publishing. 43-59.

Nielsen, Jørgen S. (1991b) 'A Muslim agenda for Britain: Some reflections'. In: V. 17 N. 3 *New Community*. 467-475.

Nielsen, Jørgen S. (1992a) *Muslims in Western Europe*. Edinburgh: Edinburgh UP.

Nielsen, Jørgen S. (1992b) 'Islam and Islamic law in the United Kingdom'. In: *Recht van de Islam 10. Recht in West-Europa*. Maastricht: RIMO. 92-99.

Nielsen, Jørgen S. (1992c) (ed) *Religion and citizenship in Europe and the Arab world*. London: Grey Seal.

Nielsen, Jørgen S. (1992d) *Islam, Muslims, and British local and central government*. CSIC Papers N. 6 Birmingham: CSIC-MR.

Nielsen, Jørgen S. (1993a) *Emerging claims of Muslim populations in matters of family law in Europe*. CSIC Papers N. 10 Birmingham: CSIC-MR.

Nielsen, Jørgen S. (1993b) 'State, religion and laicité: The Western European experience'. In: Gé Speelman et al (ed) *Muslims and Christians in Europe: Breaking new ground*. Kampen: Kok Pharos. 90-99.

Nielsen, Jørgen S. (1995a) *Muslims in Western Europe*. 2nd ed. Edinburgh: Edinburgh UP.

Nielsen, Jørgen S. (1995b) '*Shari'ah*, change and plural societies'. In: Tarek Mitri (ed) *Religion, law and society: A Christian-Muslim discussion*. Geneva. Kampen: WCC Publications. Kok Pharos. 27-32.

Nielsen, Jørgen S. (1995c) 'State, religion and laïcitè. The Western European experience. In: Tarek Mitri (ed) *Religion, law and society: A Christian-Muslim discussion*. Geneva. Kampen: WCC Publications. Kok Pharos. 100-110.

Nina, D. and S. Stavrou (1993) *Research on perceptions of justice*. Working Paper 9. Centre for Social and Development Studies. Durban: University of Natal.

Nina, Daniel and Pamela Jane Schwikkard (1996) 'The 'soft vengeance' of the people: Popular justice, community justice and legal pluralism in South Africa'. In: N. 36 *Journal of Legal Pluralism*. 69-87.

Niyazi, Mehmet (1990) *İslam devlet felsefesi*. Istanbul: Ötüken.

Nolan, Mary (1994) *Visions of modernity*. New York: Oxford U. P.

Nonneman, Gerd et al (1996) (eds) *Muslim communities in Europe*. Reading: Ithaca Press.

Nursi, Said (1997) *Words II*. Izmir: Kaynak.

Nyazee, Imran Ahsan Khan (n. d.) *Theories of Islamic law. The methodology of Ijtihad.* Islamabad: Islamic Research Institute and International Institute of Islamic Thought.

O'Donnel, Guillermo A. (1973) *Modernization and bureaucratic- authoritarianism.* Berkeley: Institute of International Studies University of California.

Oakley, Robin (1979) 'The Cypriot Migration to Britain'. In: V. S. Khan (ed) *Minority Families in Britain.* London: Macmillan. 13-34.

Oakley, Robin (1995) *Background paper on ethnic minority family patterns.* 2nd draft. London: Ethnic Minorities Advisory Committee Judicial Studies Board.

Ocak, Ahmet Yaşar (1995) 'Türk Müslümanlığı: Çözüm bekleyen tarihsel ve aktüel bir kimlik problemi'. In: N. 33 *Türkiye Günlüğü.* 34-40.

Ogburn, William F. (1964) *Social change.* Gloucester: Peter Smith.

Öğün, Süleyman Seyfi (1995) *Modernleşme, milliyetçilik ve Türkiye.* Istanbul: Bağlam.

Öktem, Niyazi (1995) *Devlet ve hukuk felsefesi akimlari.* 2nd ed. Istanbul: Der.

Omvedt, Gail (1971) ''Modernization' theories: The ideology of empire?'. In: A. R. Desai (ed) *Essays on modernization of underdeveloped societies.* Bombay: Thacker & Co. 119-137.

Onar, Sıddık Sami (1955) 'The Majalla'. In: Majid Khadduri and Herbert J. Liebesny (eds) *Law in the Middle East.* Washington DC: The Middle East Institute. 292-308.

Önger, Beria (1967) *Kadınların kurtuluşu.* Istanbul: Kurtuluş.

Ortaylı, İlber (1984) 'Osmanlı toplumunda aile'. In: Türköz Erder (ed) *Türkiye'de ailenin değişimi: Toplumbilimsel incelemeler.* Ankara: Türk Sosyal Bilimler Derneği. 79-89.

Ortaylı, İlber (1986) 'Osmanlı devletinde laiklik hareketi üzerine'. In: Ersin Kalaycıoğlu and Ali Yaşar Sarıbay (eds) *Türk siyasal hayatının gelişimi.* Istanbul: Beta. 159-170.

Ortaylı, İlber (1992) 'Osmanlılarda aile'. In: *Sosyo-külturel değisme sürecinde Türk ailesi.* 434-467. In: BAAK *Sosyo-kültürel değişme sürecinde Türk ailesi.* Ankara: B Aile Araştırma Kurumu. 456-480.

Örücü Esin (1994) 'Hukukta kadın ve son gelişmeler'. In: Necla Arat (ed) *Türkiye'de kadın olmak.* Istanbul: Say. 21-42.

Örücü, Esin (2002) 'Turkish law', LSAA Lecture given at SOAS, University of London, 16 January 2002.

Osmond, John (1988) *The divided kingdom.* London: Constable.

Ostrorog, Count Leon (1927) *The Angora reform.* London: University of London Press.

Owen, David (1992) *Ethnic minorities in Great Britain: Settlement patterns.* Coventry: University of Warwick.

Owen, David (1993) *Country of birth: Settlement patterns.* Coventry: University of Warwick.

Özay, Mehmet (1990) *Islamic identity and development. Studies of the Islamic periphery.* London. New York: Routledge.

Özbilgen, Tarık (1971) *Eleştirel hukuk sosyolojisi dersleri.* Istanbul: IUHF Yayınları.

Özcan, Yusuf (2001) *Gençlik ve evlilik rehberi.* Istanbul: Semerkand.

Özek, Çetin (1962) *Türkiye'de laiklik.* Istanbul: Baha.

Özgen, Eralp (1984) 'Erken evlenme, başlık, kadın kaçırma'. In: Türköz Erder (ed) *Türkiye'de ailenin değişimi: Yasal açıdan incelemeler.* Ankara: Türk Sosyal Bilimler Derneği. 27-66.

Özgen, Eralp (1985) 'Early marriage, brideprice and abduction of women'. In: Türköz Erder (ed) *Family in Turkish society. Sociological and legal studies.* Ankara: Turkish Social Science Association. 313-349.

Özsoy, Osman (1997) *Interview with Gülen*, Haber Kritik, STV, 29 March 1997.

Öztemiz, Mutay (1997) *Cumhuriyet döneminde devletin din politikaları.* Istanbul: Pencere.

Palley, Claire et al (1991) (eds) *Minorities and autonomy in Western Europe.* London:

Minority Rights Group.

Parekh, Bhikhu (1990) 'Britain and social logic of pluralism'. In: CRE *Britain: A plural society. Report of a seminar*. London: Commission for Racial Equality. 58-76.

Parker-Jenkins, Marie (1995) *Children of Islam*. Stoke-on-Trent: Trentham Books.

Parla, Taha (1993) *Ziya Gökalp, Kemalizm ve Türkiye'de korporatizm*. Istanbul: İletişim Yayınları.

Parla, Taha (1994) *Türkiye'de siyasi kültürün resmi kaynakları: Atatürk'ün nutku*. Istanbul: İletişim Yayınları.

Parsons, Gerald (1993) (ed) *The growth of religious diversity: Britain from 1945*. V. I. London: Routledge. The Open UP.

Parsons, Gerald (1994) (ed) *The growth of religious diversity: Britain from 1945*. V. II. London: Routledge. The Open UP.

Patel, Rashida (1979) *Women and law in Pakistan*. Karachi: Faiza Publishers.

Patel, Rashida (1986) *Islamization of laws in Pakistan?* Karachi: Faiza Publishers.

Patel, Rashida (1991) *Socio-economic political status and women and law in Pakistan*. Karachi: Faiza Publishers.

Patridge, P. H. (1961) 'Ehrlich's sociology of law'. In: N. 39 *Australasian Journal of Philosophy*. 201-222.

Patry, Robert (1970) 'Les systemes d'unit— ou d'autonomie en droit priv—'. In: *Medeni Kanunun 50. yılı sempozyumu. Tebliğler*. Istanbul: Fakülteler Matbaası. 37-58.

Patterson, D. M. (1992) 'Postmodernism.Feminism.Law'. In: V. 77 *Cornell Law Review*. 254-317.

Patterson, D. M. (1994) (ed) *Postmodernism and law*. New York: New York UP.

Peach, Ceri (1990) 'The Muslim population of Great Britain'. In: V. 13 N. 3 *Ethnic and Racial Studies*. 414-419.

Peach, Ceri (1996a) (ed) *Ethnicity in the 1991 Census*. London: HMSO.

Peach, Ceri (1996b) (ed) *Ethnicity in the 1991 Census. V. 2: The ethnic minority populations of Great Britain*. London: HMSO.

Peach, Ceri and Gunther Glebe (1995) 'Muslim minorities in Western Europe'. In: V. 18 N. 1 *Ethnic and Racial Studies*. 26-45.

Pearl, David (1969) 'Family law in Pakistan'. In: V. 9 *Journal of Family Law*. 165-189.

Pearl, David (1971a) 'Arranged marriages'. In: V. 29 *Cambridge Law Journal*. 206-207.

Pearl, David (1971b) 'The impact of the Muslim Family Laws Ordinance (1961) in Quetta (Baluchistan) Pakistan'. In: V. 13 *JILI*. 561-569.

Pearl, David (1972) 'Muslim marriages in English law'. In: V. 30 N. 2 *Cambridge Law Journal*. 120-143.

Pearl, David (1972-3) 'Immigrant marriages- some social problems'. In: V. 2 N. 1 *New Community*. 67-73.

Pearl, David (1976) 'The legal rights of Muslim women in India, Pakistan and Bangladesh'. In: V. 5 N. 1-2 *New Community*. 68-74.

Pearl, David (1979) *A textbook on Muslim law*. London: Croom Helm.

Pearl, David (1980) 'Legal decisions affecting ethnic minorities and discrimination'. In: V. 8 Ns. 1-2 *New Community*. 146-153.

Pearl, David (1981) 'Islam in English family law'. In: J. S. Nielsen (ed) *Islam in English law and administration. A symposium*. Birmingham: Selly Oak Colleges. 6-10.

Pearl, David (1986) *Family law and the immigrant communities*. Bristol: Jordan & Sons.

Pearl, David (1987a) 'South Asian immigrant communities and English family law: 1971-1987'. In: V. 14 Ns. 1-2 *New Community*. 161-169.

Pearl, David (1987b) *A textbook on Muslim personal law*. 2nd ed. London: Croom Helm.

Pearl, David (1990) 'Three decades of executive, legislative and judicial amendments to

Islamic family law in Pakistan'. In: Chibli Mallat and Jane Connors (eds) *Islamic family law*. London: Graham & Trotman. 321-337.

Pearl, David (1995) 'The application of Islamic law in the English courts'. In: E. Cotran and Chibli Mallat (eds) *Yearbook of Islamic and Middle Eastern law*. London et al: Kluwer International. 3-11.

Pearl, David and Werner F. Menski (1998) *Muslim family law*. 3rd ed. London: Sweet & Maxwell.

Pennock, J. Roland and John W. Chapman (1974) (eds) *The limits of law*. New York: Lieber-Atherton.

Percy, Walker (1976) *The message in the bottle*. New York: Farrar, Strauss and Giroux.

Peristiany, J. G. (1976) (ed) *Mediterrenean family structures*. Cambridge: Cambridge UP.

Pierce, Leslie (1993) *The imperial harem. Women and sovereignty in the Ottoman Empire*. New York. Oxford: Oxford: Oxford UP.

Piscatori, James S. (1991) *Islam in a world of nation-states*. Cambridge et al: Cambridge UP. Royal Institute of International Affairs.

Podgorecki, Adam (1974) *Law and society*. London. Boston: Routledge & Kegan Paul.

Podgorecki, Adam (1985) 'Intuitive law versus folk law'. In: Gordon R. Woodman and A. Allott (eds) *People's law and state law. The Bellagio papers*. Dordrecht: Foris Publications. 71-72.

Polis, Adamantia and Peter Schwab (1979a) 'Human rights: A Western concept with limited applicability'. In: Adamantia Polis and Peter Schwab (1979b) *Human rights, cultural and ideological perspectives*. New York: Praeger. 1-19.

Polis, Adamantia and Peter Schwab (1979b) *Human rights, cultural and ideological perspectives*. New York: Praeger.

Polk, William R. and Richard L. Chambers (1968) (ed) *Beginning of modernization in the Middle East*.

Pope, Nicole (1998) 'An Ottoman Empire of the Mind', at http://www.turkeyupdate.com/merv.htm.

Pospisil, Leopold (1967) 'Legal levels and multiplicity of legal systems in human societies'. In: V. 2 N. 1 *Journal of Conflict Resolution*. 2-26.

Pospisil, Leopold (1971) *Anthropology of law: A comparative theory*. New York et al: Harper and Row.

Pospisil, Leopold (1978) 'The structure of society and its multiple legal systems'. In: P. H. Gulliver (ed) *Cross-examinations: Essays in memory of Max Gluckman*. Leiden: E. J. Brill. 96-109.

Poulter, Sebastian M. (1986) *English law and ethnic minority customs*. London: Butterworths.

Poulter, Sebastian M. (1987) 'Ethnic minority customs, English law and human rights'. In: V. 36 *International and Comparative Law Quarterly*. 589-615.

Poulter, Sebastian M. (1989a) 'The significance of ethnic minority customs and traditions in English criminal law'. In: V. 16 N. 1 *New Community*. 121-128.

Poulter, Sebastian M. (1989b) 'Divorce reform in a multicultural society'. In: V. 19 *Family Law*. 99-101.

Poulter, Sebastian M. (1990a) 'Cultural pluralism and its limits: A legal perspective'. In: CRE *Britain: A plural society. Report of a seminar*. London: Commission for Racial Equality. 3-28.

Poulter, Sebastian M. (1990b) 'The claim to a separate Islamic system of personal law for British Muslims'. In: Chibli Mallat and Jane Connors (eds) *Islamic family law*. London. Dordrecht. Boston: Graham & Trotman. 147-166.

Poulter, Sebastian M. (1990c) *Asian traditions and English law*. Stoke-on-Trent:

Runnymede Trust and Trentham Books.

Poulter, Sebastian M. (1992) 'The Muslim community and English law'. In: V. 3 N. 2 *Islam and Christian-Muslim Relations*. 259-273.

Poulter, Sebastian M. (1993) 'The limits of legal, cultural and religious pluralism'. In: Bob Hepple and Erika M. Ssyszczak (eds) *Discrimination: The limits of law*. London. New York: Mansell. 172-192.

Poulter, Sebastian M. (1994) 'Minority rights'. In: Gerald Chambers and Christopher McGrudden (eds) *Individual rights and the law in Britain*. Oxford: Clarendon Press. 457-489.

Poulter, Sebastian M. (1995) 'Multiculturalism and human rights for Muslim families in English law'. In: Michael King (ed) *God's law versus state law: The construction of Islamic identity in Western Europe*. London: Grey Seal. 81-87.

Poulter, Sebastian M. (1997) 'Muslim headscarves in school: Contrasting legal approaches in England and France'. In: V. 17 N. 1 *Oxford Journal of Legal Studies*. 43-74.

Poulter, Sebastian M. (1998) *Ethnicity, Law and Human Rights: The English Experience*. Oxford: Oxford UP.

Pye, Lucian and Sidney Verba (1965) (eds) *Political culture and political development*. Princeton: Princeton UP.

Quddus, Muhammed A. (1981) *Pakistan: A case study of a plural society*. Calcutta: Minerva.

Qureshi, M. A. (1992) *Muslim law of marriage, divorce and maintenance*. New Delhi: Deep & Deep.

Qureshi, Muhammed Ibrahim (1993) *World Muslim minorities*. Islamabad: World Muslim Congress.

Rabinow, Paul (1975) *Symbolic domination: Cultural form and historical change in Morocco*. Chicago: University of Chicago Press.

Rabinow, Paul (1977) *Reflections on fieldwork in Morocco*. Berkeley: University of California Press.

Rachedi, Nadia (1994) 'Élites of Maghrebin extraction in France'. In: Bernard Lewis and Dominique Schnapper (eds) *Muslims in Europe*. London. New York: Pinter. 67-78.

Radcliffe-Brown, A. R. (1952) *Structure and function in primitive society*. New York: Free Press.

Rahman, Fazlur (1966) 'The controversy over the Muslim family law'. In: Donald Eugene Smith (ed) *South Asian politics and religion*. Princeton: Princeton UP. 414-427.

Rahman, Fazlur (1971) 'The ideological experience of Pakistan'. In: V. 2 N. 4 *Islam and the Modern Age*. 1-20.

Rahman, Fazlur (1979) *Islam*. 2nd ed. Chicago. London: University of Chicago Press.

Rahman, Fazlur (1993) *Islam*. Tr. by Mehmet Dağ and Mehmet Aydın. 3rd ed. Ankara: Selçuk.

Rahman, S. A. (1967) *The Mejelle. A translation of Majallahel-Ahkam-i Adliya and a complete code on Islamic civil law*. Tr. by B. A. L. Tyser. Lahore: PLD Publishers.

Ramsaur, E. E. (1957) *The Young Turks: Prelude to the revolution of 1908*. Princeton: Princeton UP.

Ranger, T. et al (1995) (eds) *Culture, identity and politics. Ethnic minorities in Britain*. Aldershot: Avebury.

Rapoport, R. N. et al (1982) *Families in Britain*. London et al: Routledge & Kegan Paul.

Rashid, Abdur (1987) *The Islamization of law in Pakistan with special reference to the status of women*. London: SOAS (Unpublished PhD thesis).

Ratcliffe, P. (1981) *Racism and reaction: A profile of Handsworth*. London: Routledge and Kegan Paul.

Ratcliffe, Peter (1994a) ''Race' in Britain: Theory, methods and substance'. In: Peter Ratcliffe (ed) *'Race', ethnicity and nation: International perspective on social conflict.* London: UCL Press.

Ratcliffe, Peter (ed) (1994b) *'Race', ethnicity and nation: International perspective on social conflict.* London: UCL Press.

Rath, Jan et al (1991) 'The recognition and institutionalization of Islam in Belgium, Great Britain and the Netherlands'. In: V. 18 N. 1 *New Community.* 101-114.

Rattansi, Ali and Sallie Westwood (eds) (1994) *Racism, modernity and identity.* Cambridge: Polity Press.

Rawls, John (1977) 'A theory of civil disobedience'. In: R. M. Dworkin (ed) *The philosophy of law.* London: Oxford UP. 89-111.

Raz, Joseph (1984) 'Legal principles and limits of law'. In: Marshall Cohen (ed) *Ronald Dworkin and contemporary jurisprudence.* London: Duckworth. 73-87.

Raza, Mohammed S. (1991) *Islam in Britain: Past, present and the future.* Leicester: Volcano Press.

Raza, Mohammed S. (1993) *Islam in Britain: Past, present and the future.* 2nd revised ed. Leicester: Volcano Press.

Reed, Alan (1996) 'Extra-judicial divorces since Berkovits'. In: V. 26 *Family Law.* 100-103.

Renner, Karl (1949) *The institution of private law and their social functions.* London: Routledge & Kegan Paul.

Renteln, Alison Dundes (1990) *International human rights. Universalism versus relativism.* Newbury Park, London and New Delhi: Sage.

Renteln, Alison Dundes and Alan Dundes (1994) (eds) *Folk law: Essays in the theory and practice of lex non scripta.* New York. London: Garland Publishing.

Reza-ur-Rahim, Muhammed (1976) 'A reconstruction of the procedure of divorce according to the holy Qur'an'. In: V. 7 N. 2 *Islam and the Modern Age.* 5-14.

Rheinstein, Max (1956) 'Types of reception'. In: N. 5 *Annales Faculté de la droit d'Istanbul.* Istanbul: Fakülteler Matbaası. 31-40.

Richmond, Anthony H. (1988) *Immigration and ethnic conflict.* London: Macmillan.

Rida, Rashid (1974) *Islam'da birlik ve fıkıh mezhebleri.* Tr. by Ahmed Hamdi Akseki. Ankara: DIB.

Rippin, Andrew (1993) *Muslims: Their religious beliefs and practices.* V. 2: The contemporary period. London. New York: Routledge.

Roberts, Robert (1978) *The social laws of the Qur'an.* New Delhi: Cosmo Publications.

Robilliard, St. John (1984) *Religion and the law: Religious liberty in modern English law.* Manchester: Manchester UP.

Robinson, Francis (1988) *Varieties of South Asian Islam.* Research Papers of Ethnic Relations. N. 8. Coventry: University of Warwick.

Rosen, Lawrence (1984) *Bargaining for reality: The construction of social relations in a Muslim community.* Chicago: University of Chicago Press.

Rosen, Lawrence (1989) *The anthropology of justice: Law as culture in Islamic society.* Cambridge: Cambridge UP.

Rosen, Lawrence (1995a) 'Islamic concepts of justice'. In: Michael King (ed) *God's law versus state law: The construction of Islamic identity in Western Europe.* London: Grey Seal. 62-72.

Rosen, Lawrence (1995b) 'European Islam and the state'. In: Michael King (ed) *God's law versus state law: The construction of Islamic identity in Western Europe.* London: Grey Seal. 88-90.

Rosenau, Pauline Marie (1992) *Postmodernism and the social sciences: Insights, inroads, and intrusions*. Princeton: Princeton UP.

Rosenthal, Erwin I. J. (1965) *Islam in the modern national state*. Cambridge: Cambridge UP.

Ross, Alf (1958) *On law and justice*. London: Stevens & Sons Limited.

Ross, Edward A. (1932) *Social control: A survey of the foundations of order*. New York: Macmillan.

Rousseau, Jean Jacques (1987) *The social contract*. Chicago: Encyclopedia Britannica.

Rousseau, Jean Jacques (1992) *Toplum anlasmasi*. Istanbul: M. E. B. Yayınları.

Roy, Oliver (1994a) *The failure of political Islam*. London: I. B. Tauris.

Roy, Olivier (1994b) 'Islam in France: Religion, ethnic community or social ghetto?'. In: Bernard Lewis and Dominique Schnapper (eds) *Muslims in Europe*. London. New York: Pinter. 54-66.

Runnymede Trust (1997) *Islamaphobia*. London: Runnymede Trust.

Rustow, Dankwart (1965) 'Turkey: The modernity of tradition'. In: Lucian W. Pye and Sidney Verba (eds) *Political culture and political development*. Princeton: Princeton UP. 171-198.

Sa'ban, Zekiyuddin (1996) *Islam hukuk ilminin esasları (Usul'ul fikh)*. Tr. by I. Kafi Dönmez. Ankara: Türkiye Diyanet Vakfi Yayınları.

Sachdeva, Sanjiv (1993) *The primary purpose rule in British immigration law*. Group for Ethnic Minority Studies, School of Oriental and African Studies. Stoke on Trent: Trentham.

Sack, Peter (1986) 'Legal pluralism: Introductory comments'. In: Peter Sack and Elizabeth Minchin (eds) *Legal pluralism. Proceedings of the Canberra Law Workshop VII*. Canberra: Research School of Social Sciences, (Australian National University). 1-16.

Sack, Peter et al (eds) (1999) *Rechstheorie: Monistic or pluralistic legal culture*. N. 12. Berlin: Duncker & Humblot.

Sacks, J. (1991) *The persistence of faith*. London: Weidenfeld and Nicolson.

Sadowski, Yahya (1999) 'Book Review: Turkey Unveiled: Nicole and Hugh Pope,' at http://www. turkeyupdate. com/tunveil.htm.

Saeed, Javaid (1994) *Islam and modernization: A comparative analysis of Pakistan, Egypt, and Turkey*. Westport, Connecticut. London: Praeger.

Sahgal, G. and N. Yuval-Davis (1992a) (eds) *Refusing holy orders: Women and fundamentalism in Britain*. London: Virago.

Sahgal, G. and N. Yuval-Davis (1992b) 'Fundamentalism, multiculturalism and women in Britain'. In: G. Sahgal and N. Yuval-Davis (eds) *Refusing holy orders: Women and fundamentalism in Britain*. London: Virago. 1-25.

Şahinkaya, Rezan (1983) *Diyarbakır ili merkez köylerinde aile strüktürü*. Ankara Üniversitesi: Ziraat Fakültesi Yayınları.

Saif, Walid (1995) '*Shari'ah* and modernity'. In: Tarek Mitri (ed) *Religion, law and society: A Christian-Muslim discussion*. Geneva. Kampen: WCC Publications. Kok Pharos. 11-19.

Saifi, Samar Fatima (1980) *A study of the status of women in Islamic law and society with special reference to Pakistan*. Durham: University of Durham (Unpublished PhD thesis).

Sajo, Andras (1995) 'On old and new battles: Obstacles to the rule of law in Eastern Europe'. In: V. 22 N. 1 *Journal of Law and Society*. 97-103.

Salvadori, Cynthia (1989) *Through open doors. A view of Asian cultures in Kenya*. Nairobi: Kenway Publications. Revd. 2nd ed.

Santos, Boaventura de Sousa (1977) 'The law of the oppressed: The construction and reproduction of legality in Pasagarda'. In: V. 12 *Law and Society Review*. 5-126.

Santos, Boaventura de Sousa (1987) 'Law: A map of misreading. Toward a postmodern conception of law'. In: V. 14 N. 3 *Journal of Law and Society*. 279-302.
Santos, Bouventura de Sousa (1992) 'State, law and community in the world system: An introduction'. In: V. 1 *Social and Legal Studies*. 131-142.
Santos, Bouventura de Sousa (1995a) 'Three metaphors for a new conception of law. The frontier, the baroque, and the south'. In: V. 29 N. 4 *Law and Society Review*. 569-584.
Santos, Bouventura de Sousa (1995b) *Toward a new commonsense: Law, science and politics in the paradigmatic transition*. New York: Routledge.
Sarat, Austin (1990) ''...The law is over': Power, resistance and the legal consciousness of the welfare poor'. In: V. 2 *Yale Journal of Law and the Humanities*. 343-379.
Sarat, Austin (1994) 'A prophesy of possibility: Metaphorical expolarations of postmodern legal subjectivity'. In: V. 29 *Law and Society Review*. 615-630.
Sarıbay, Ali Yaşar (1986) 'Kemalist ideolojide modernleşmenin anlamı: Sosyo-ekonomik bir çözümleme denemesi'. In: Ersin Kalaycıoğlu and Ali Yaşar Sarıbay (eds) *Türk siyasal hayatının gelişimi*. Istanbul: Beta. 189-204.
Sarıbay, Ali Yaşar (1994) *Postmodernite, sivil toplum ve Islam*. Istanbul: İletişim.
Sarwar, G. (1994) *British Muslims and schools*. London: Muslim Educational Trust.
Sawer, Geoffrey (1965) *Law in society*. Oxford: Clarendon Press.
Scantlebury, Elizabeth (1995) 'Muslims in Manchester: The depiction of a religious community'. In: V. 21 N. 3 *New Community*. 425-435.
Scarman, Lord (1978) 'Minority rights in a plural society'. In: V. 6 N. 3 *New Community*. 248-252.
Schacht, Joseph (1950) *Origins of Muhammadan jurisprudence*. Oxford: Oxford UP.
Schacht, Joseph (1955) 'The law'. In: Gustave E. von Grunebaum (ed) *Unity and variety in Muslim civilisation*. Chicago: Chicago UP. 74-87.
Schacht, Joseph (1959) 'Islamic law in contemporary states'. In: V. 8 *American Journal of Comparative Law*. 133-147.
Schacht, Joseph (1964) *An introduction to Islamic law*. Oxford: Clarendon Press.
Schmale, Wolfgang (1993) (ed) *Human rights and cultural diversity*. Goldbeach: Keip Publishing.
Schnapper, Dominique (1994) 'Muslim communities, ethnic minorities and citizens'. In: Bernard Lewis and Dominique Schnapper (eds) *Muslims in Europe*. London. New York: Pinter. 148-160.
Schur, Edwin M. (1968) *Law and society. A sociological view*. New York: Random House.
Schuz, Rhona (1996) 'Divorce and ethnic minorities'. In: Michael Freeman (ed) *Divorce: Where next?* Aldershot: Dartmouth. 131-157.
Seidman, Robert Benjamin (1978) *The state, law and development*. London: Croom Helm.
Seidman, Robert Benjamin and Ann Seidman (1994) *State law and development process. Problem solving and institutional change in the third world*. Basingtoke: Macmillan.
Seidman, S. and D. G. Wagner (1992) *Postmodernism and social theory*. Oxford: Basil Blackwell.
Şener, Esat (1984) 'Cumhuriyet Türkiyesinde içtihadların ışığında aile yapısının değişimi'. In: Türköz Erder (ed) *Türkiye'de ailenin değişimi: Yasal açıdan incelemeler*. Ankara: Türk Sosyal Bilimler Derneği. 119-138.
Şener, Esat (1985) 'Change in the family as reflected in the jurisprudence of the Republican era'. In: Türköz Erder (ed) *Family in Turkish society. Sociological and legal studies*. Ankara: Turkish Social Science Association. 401-416.
Shadid, W. A. R. and P. S. van Koningsveld (1991a) 'Blaming the system or blaming the victim? Structural barriers facing Muslims in Western Europe'. In: W. A. Shadid and P. S. van Koningsveld (eds) *The integration of Islam and Hinduism in Western Europe*.

Kampen: Kok Pharos Publishing. 2-21.

Shadid, W. A. R. and P. S. van Koningsveld (1991b) 'Institutionalisation and integration of Islam in The Netherlands'. In: W. A. Shadid and P. S. van Koningsveld (eds) *The integration of Islam and Hinduism in Western Europe*. Kampen: Kok Pharos Publishing. 89-121.

Shadid, W. A. R. and P. S. van Koningsveld (1991c) 'Integration and change: Some future prospects'. In: W. A. Shadid and P. S. van Koningsveld (eds) *The integration of Islam and Hinduism in Western Europe*. Kampen: Kok Pharos Publishing. 228-239.

Shadid, W. A. R. and P. S. van Koningsveld (1996a) (eds) *Political participation and identities of Muslims in non-Muslim states*. Kampen: Kok Pharos Publishing.

Shadid, W. A. R. and P. S. van Koningsveld (1996b) 'Political participation: The Muslim perspective'. In: W. A. R. Shadid and P. S. van Koningsveld (eds) *Political participation and identities of Muslims in non-Muslim states*. Kampen: Kok Pharos Publishing. 2-13.

Shah, Nasim Hasan (1992a) *Islamization of law in Pakistan*. Islamabad: *Shariah* Academy, International Islamic University.

Shah, Nasim Hasan (1992b) *The Objectives Resolution and its impact on the administration of justice in Pakistan*. Islamabad: *Shariah* Academy, International Islamic University.

Shah, Nasim Hasan (1995) 'Islamisation of law in Pakistan'. In: *PLD Journal Section*. 37-53.

Shah, Nasra M. (1986) (ed) *Pakistani women: A socio-economic and demographic profile*. Islamabad. Honolulu: Pakistan Institute of Development Economics and East-West Institute.

Shah, Prakash (1994) 'Legal pluralism- British law and possibilities with Muslim ethnic minorities'. In: Ns. 66-67 *Retfoerd*. 18-33.

Shaham, Ron (1995) 'Custom, Islamic law, and statuary legislation: Marriage registration and minimum age at marriage in the Egyptian *Shari'a* courts'. In: V. 2 N. 3 *Islamic Law and Society*. 258-281.

Shah-Kazemi, Sonia Nûrîn (2001) *Untying the knot. Muslim women, divorce and the Shariah*. London: Nuffield Foundation.

Shaikh, Farzana (1992) *Islam and Islamic groups*. London: Longman Current Affairs. CIRCA.

Shankland, David (1999) *Islam and society in Turkey*. Huntingdon: The Eothen Press.

Sharif, R. (1985) *Interviews with young women of Pakistani origin*. Muslims in Europe Research Papers, 27. Birmingham: Centre for the Study of Islam and Christian-Muslim Relations.

Shaw, Alison (1988) *A Pakistani community in Britain*. Oxford: Basil Blackwell.

Shaw, Alison (1994) 'The Pakistani community in Oxford'. In: Roger Ballard (ed) *Desh pardesh: The South Asian experience in Britain*. London: Hurst & Co. 35-57.

Shaw, Stanford (1976) *History of the Ottoman Empire and modern Turkey. Volume I: Empire of the Gazis: The rise and decline*. Cambridge: Cambridge UP.

Shaw, Stanford J. and Ezel Kural Shaw (1977) *Reform, revolution, and republic: The rise of modern Turkey. History of Ottoman Empire and modern Turkey*. Cambridge: Cambridge UP.

Sherwani, Riaz R. (1988) 'Comment on Abdur Rahman Doi: Duties and responsibilities in non-Muslim states: A point of view'. In: V. 9 N. 1 *Journal of Institute of Muslim Minority Affairs*. 186-189.

Shils, Edward (1972) 'Tradition'. In: A. R. Desai (ed) *Essays on modernization of underdeveloped societies*. 2nd ed. New York: Humanities Press. 1-39.

Shils, Edward (1975) *Center and periphery: Essays in macrosociology*. Chicago: The

University of Chicago Press.

Siddiqi, Muhammad Iqbal (1984) *The family laws of Islam*. Lahore: Kazi Publications.

Siddiqi, Zakia A. and Anwar Jahan Zubari (1993) *Muslim women: Problems and prospects*. New Delhi: MD Publications.

Siddiqui, Kalim (1986) 'Nationalism in the light of the *Qur'an* and the *Sunna*'. In: M. Ghayasuddin (ed) *The impact of nationalism on the Muslim world*. London: The Open Press. Al-Hoda Publishers. 23-33.

Silbey, Susan (1992) 'Making a place for cultural analyses of law'. In: V. 17 N. 1 *Law and Social Inquiry*. 39-48.

Simmel, George (1956) *Conflict and the web of group affiliations*. Glencoe, Illinois: The Free Press.

Simon, Jonathan (1992) '"In another kind of wood": Michel Foucault and socio-legal studies'. In: V. 17 N. 1 *Law and Social Inquiry*. 1-38.

Simon, Jonathan (1995) 'Ballad of a thin man: Socio-legal studies in a time of postmodern crisis'. In: V. 29 N. 4 *Law and Society Review*. 631-637.

Simons, Jon (1995) *Foucault and the political*. London: Routledge.

Sinai, Robert (1971) 'Modernization and the poverty of the social sciences'. In: A. R. Desai (ed) *Essays on modernization of underdeveloped societies*. Bombay: Thacker & Co. 40-52.

Smart, Barry (1992) *Modern conditions, postmodern controversies*. London: Routledge.

Smart, Barry (1993) *Postmodernity*. London: Routledge.

Smart, Ninian (1989) 'Church, party and the state'. In: Paul Badham (ed) *Religion, state, and society in modern Britain*. Lewiston et al: The Edwin Mellen Press. 381-393.

Smith, Anthony D. (1986) *The ethnic origin of nations*. Oxford: Basil Blackwell.

Smith, Anthony D. (1989) *The ethnic revival in the modern world*. Cambridge: Cambridge UP.

Smith, Anthony D. (1991) *National identity*. Harmondsworth: Penguin Books.

Smith, Anthony D. (1995) *Nations and nationalism in a global era*. Cambridge: Polity Press.

Smith, Donald Eugene (1966) (ed) *South Asian politics and religion*. Princeton: Princeton UP.

Smith, Graham (1996) (eds) *Federalism: The multi-ethnic challenge*. London: Longman.

Smith, Huston (1995) 'Postmodernism and the world's religions'. In: W. T. Anderson (ed) *The truth about the truth: De-confusing and re-constructing the postmodern world*. New York: G. Putnam's Sons. 209-214.

Smith, M. G. (1974) *Corporations and society*. London: Duckworth.

Sollors, Werner (1995) 'The idea of ethnicity'. In: W. T. Anderson (ed) *The truth about the truth: De-confusing and re-constructing the postmodern world*. New York: G. Putnam's Sons. 58-65.

Sonyel, Salahi R. (1988) *The Silent Minority, Turkish Muslim Children In British Schools*, Cambridge: The Islamic Academy.

Speelman, Gé (1991) (ed) *Religion and state in Europe: Two seminar reports*. CSIC Papers N. 4. Birmingham: CSIC-MR.

Speelman, Gé (1995) 'Muslim minorities and *Shari'ah* in Europe'. In: Tarek Mitri (ed) *Religion, law and society: A Christian-Muslim discussion*. Geneva. Kampen: WCC Publications. Kok Pharos. 70-77.

Speelman, Gé et al (1993) (ed) *Muslims and Christians in Europe: Breaking new ground*. Kampen: Kok Pharos.

Spencer, Sarah (1995) *Migrants, refugees and the boundaries of citizenship*. London: IPPR.

Starr, J. & J. Collier (1989) *History and power in the study of law*. Ithaca: Cornell

University Press.

Starr, June (1978) *Dispute and settlement in rural Turkey: An ethnography of law*. Leiden: E. J. Brill.

Starr, June (1980) 'First thoughts on Western law in Islam: Its effects on family life in Aegean Turkey'. In: N. 4 *American Legal Studies Forum*. 23-31.

Starr, June (1985) 'Folk law in official courts of Turkey'. In: G. R. Woodman and A. Allott (eds) *People's law and state law. The Bellagio papers*. Dordrecht: Foris Publications. 123-141.

Starr, June (1989) 'The role of Turkish secular law in changing the lives of rural Muslim women, 1950-1970'. In: V. 23 N. 3 *Law and Society Review*. 497-523.

Starr, June (1990) 'Islam and the struggle over state law in Turkey'. In: Daisy Hilse Dwyer (ed) *Law and Islam in the Middle East*. New York et al: Bergin & Garvey Publishers. 77-96.

Starr, June (1992) *Law as metaphor: From Islamic courts to the palace of justice*. New York: State University of New York Press.

Starr, June and Jane F. Collier (1987) 'Historical studies of legal change'. In: V. 28 *Current Anthropology*. 367-372.

Starr, June and Jonathan Pool (1974) 'The impact of a legal revolution in rural Turkey'. In: V. 8 N. 4 *Law and Society Review*. 533-560.

State Institute of Statistics Prime Ministry Republic of Turkey (1993) *Marriage statistics: 1991*. Ankara: SIS.

State Institute of Statistics Prime Ministry Republic of Turkey (1995) *Women in statistics: 1927-1992*. Ankara: SIS.

State Institute of Statistics Prime Ministry Republic of Turkey (1996) *Marriage statistics: 1994*. Ankara: SIS.

State Institute of Statistics Prime Ministry Republic of Turkey (1997a) *Marriage statistics*. Ankara: SIS.

State Institute of Statistics Prime Ministry Republic of Turkey (1997b) *Divorce statistics*. Ankara: SIS.

State Planning Organization (1989) *Türk aile yapısı özel ihtisas komisyonu raporu*. Ankara: DPT.

State Planning Organization (1992) *Türk aile araştırması*. Ankara: DPT.

Statistics Division (1976) *Labour Force Survey 1974-75*. Islamabad: Ministry of Finance, Planning and Economic Affairs, Government of Pakistan.

Stirling, Paul (1957) 'Land, marriage, and the law in Turkish villages'. In: N. 9 *International Social Science Bulletin*. 21-33.

Stirling, Paul (1965) *Turkish village*. London: Weidenfeld and Nicolson.

Stokes, Martin (1994) 'Turkish arabesk and the city: Urban popular culture as spatial practice'. In: Akbar S. Ahmed and Hastings Donnan (eds) *Islam, globalization and postmodernity*. London: Routledge. 21-37.

Stone, Lawrence (1990) *Road to divorce*. Oxford: Oxford UP.

Subaşı, Necdet (1995) 'Günümüz Türkiye'sinde dinin halk katındaki görüntüleri'. In: N. 34 *Türkiye Günlüğü*. 57-62.

Sugarman, David (1983a) 'Law, economy and the state in England, 1750-1914: Some major issues'. In: David Sugarman (ed) *Legality, ideology and the state*. London et al: Academic Press. 213-266.

Sugarman, David (1983b) (ed) *Legality, ideology and the state*. London et al: Academic Press.

Summers, Robert S. (1971) *More essays in legal philosophy*. Berkeley, LA: University of California Press.

Summers, Robert S. (1982) *Instrumentalism and American legal theory*. Ithaca: Cornell UP.

Summers, Robert. S. (1977) 'Naive instrumentalism and the law'. In: P. M. S. Hacker and J. Raz (eds) *Law, morality, and society*. Oxford: Clarendon Press. 119-131.

Sumner, Colin (1979) *Reading ideologies: An investigation into the theory of ideology and law*. New York: Academic Press.

Sumner, William G. (1906) *Folkways: A study of the sociological importance of usages, manners, customs, mores, and morals*. Boston: Ginn.

Sunar, Ilkay (1974) *State and society in the politics of Turkey's development*. Ankara: Ankara Üniversitesi Siyasal Bilgiler Fakültesi Yayınları.

Sunar, Ilkay (1985) *Düşün ve toplum*. Istanbul: Birey ve Toplum Yayınları.

Surtry, Muhammed Ibrahim H. I. (1991) 'The *Shari'ah* family courts in Britain and the protection of women's rights in Muslim family law with special reference to the dissolution of marriage at the instance of the wife'. In: V. 9 N. 1 *Muslim Education Quarterly*. 59-68.

Synder, F. (1981a) 'Anthropology, dispute processes and law: A critical introduction'. In: V. 8 *British Journal of Law and Society*. 141-180.

Szyliowicz, Joseph (1973) *Education and the modernization in the Middle East*. Ithaca: Cornell UP.

Szyliowicz, Joseph (1975) 'Élites and modernisation in Turkey'. In: Frank Tachau (ed) *Political élites and political development in the Middle East*. New York: Schenkmen. 23-68.

Talay, Birsen (1994) *The changes in Turkish family structure between the years 1923-1935*. Istanbul: Boğaziçi University (Unpublished MA thesis).

Tamanaha, Brian Z. (1993) 'The folly of the 'social scientific' concept of legal pluralism'. In: V. 20 N. 2 *Journal of Law and Society*. 192-217.

Tamanaha, Brian Z. (1997) *Realistic sociolegal theory: Pragmatism and social theory of law*. Oxford: Clarendon Press.

Tanzilur-Rahman (1989) *Islamization of Pakistan law*. Karachi: Hamdard Academy.

Tanzilur-Rahman (1997) *Muslim Family Laws Ordinance: Islamic and social survey*. Karachi: Royal Book Company.

Tapper, Nancy (1985) 'Changing wedding rituals in a Turkish town'. In: V. 9 *Turkish Studies*. 305-312.

Tapper, Richard (1994) (ed) *Islam in modern Turkey: Religion, politics and literature in a secular state*. London. New York: I. B. Tauris.

Taşkıran, Tezer (1976) *Women in Turkey*. Istanbul: Redhouse.

Tay, Alice Erh-Soon (1986) 'Legal culture and legal pluralism in common law, customary law, and Chinese law'. In: V. 26 N. 2 *Hong Kong Law Journal*. 194-209.

Taylan, Necip (1989) *Gazzali'nin düşünce sisteminin temelleri*. Istanbul: MUIF Vakfı Yayınları.

Taylan, Necip (1991) *Anahatlarıyla Islam felsefesi*. 3rd impression. Istanbul: Ensar.

Taylor, Charles (1994) (ed) *Multiculturalism: Examining the politics of recognition*. New Jersey: Princeton UP.

Taylor, Charles (1995) *Modernliğin sıkıntıları*. Istanbul: Ayrıntı Yayınları.

Taylor, J. H. (1976) *The half-way generation: A study of Asian youths in Newcastle upon Tyne*. Windsor: NFER.

TDV (Türkiye Diyanet Vakfı) (1999) *Günümüz Meselelerine Fetvalar* (*Fatwa*s on contemporary problems). Ankara: TDV.

Tekeli, Şirin (1990) (ed) *Kadın bakış açısından 1980'ler Türkiye'sinde kadın*. Istanbul: İletişim.

Tekeli, Şirin and Meryem Koray (1991) *Devlet, kadın ve siyaset*. Istanbul: Türkiye Sosyal,

Ekonomik, Siyasal Araştırmalar Vakfı.

Tekinay, Selahattin Sulhi (1971) *Türk aile hukuku*. Istanbul: Fakülteler Matbaası.

Tekinay, Selahattin Sulhi (1976) 'Evlilik dışı nesep meselelerine toplu bir bakış'. In: AUHF *Medeni Kanunun 50. yılı: Bilimsel hafta, 15-17 Nisan 1976*. Ankara: AUHF Yayınları. 83-96.

Tester, Keith (1993) *The life and times of postmodernity*. London: Routledge.

Teubner, Gunther (1992) 'The two faces of janus: Rethinking legal pluralism'. In: N. 13 *Cardozo Law Review*. 1443-1462.

Teubner, Gunther (1993) *Law as an autopoietic system*. Oxford UK. Cambridge USA: Blackwell.

Teubner, Gunther (ed) (1988) *Autopoietic law: A new approach to law and society*. Berlin: W. de Gruyter.

Therborn, Göran (1978) *What does the ruling class do when it rules?* London: NLB.

Thornberry, Patrick (1991) *Minorities and human rights law*. London: Minority Rights Group.

Tie, Warwick (1999) *Legal pluralism: Toward a multicultural conception of law*. Dartmouth: Ashgate.

Timur, Hifzi (1956a) 'The place of Islamic law in Turkish law reform'. In: N. 5 *Annales Faculté de la droit d'Istanbul*. Istanbul: Fakülteler Matbaası. 75-80.

Timur, Hıfzı (1956b) 'Views on the transition in Turkey from Islamic law to a western legal set-up'. In: N. 5 *Annales Faculté de la droit d'Istanbul*. Istanbul: Fakülteler Matbaası. 81-88.

Timur, Hıfzı (1957) 'Civil marriage in Turkey: Difficulties, cause and remedies'. V. 9 *International Social Studies Bulletin*. 34-36.

Timur, Serim (1972) *Türkiye'de aile yapısı*. Ankara: Hacettepe University Publications.

Timur, Serim (1981) 'Determinants of family structure in Turkey'. In: Nermin Abadan-Unat (ed) *Türk toplumunda kadın*. Ankara: Turkish Social Science Association. 59-73.

Tönnies, Ferdinand (1955) *Community and association (Gemeinschaft and Gesellschaft)*. London: Routledge & Kegan Paul.

Topçuoğlu, Abdullah and Yasin Aktay (ed) (1996) *Postmodernizm ve Islam. Küreselleşme ve oryantalizm*. Ankara: Vadi.

Toprak, Binnaz (1981) *Islam and political development in Turkey*. Leiden: E. J. Brill.

Toprak, Binnaz (1982) 'Türk kadını ve din'. In: Nermin Abadan-Unat (ed) *Türk toplumunda kadın*. Ankara: Turkish Social Science Association. 361-373.

Toprak, Binnaz (1986) 'Türkiye'de dinin denetim işlevi'. In: Ersin Kalaycıoğlu and Ali Yaşar Sarıbay (eds) *Türk siyasal hayatının gelişimi*. Istanbul: Beta. 359-368.

Toprak, Binnaz (1995) 'Islam and the secular state in Turkey'. In: Çiğdem Balım et al (eds) *Turkey: Political, social and economic challenges in the 1990s*. Leiden et al: E. J. Brill. 90-96.

Toroslu, Nevzat (1984) 'Ailenin korunması yönünden ceza kanununda yapılması gereken değişiklikler'. In: Türköz Erder (ed) *Türkiye'de ailenin değişimi: Yasal açıdan incelemeler*. Ankara: Türk Sosyal Bilimler Derneği. 153-163.

Tosun, Resul (2001) 'Çok eşlilik', *Daily Yeni Şafak*. 12 February 2001.

Toulmin, Stephen (1990) *Cosmopolis: The hidden agenda of modernity*. New York: Free Press.

Touraine, Alain (1992) *Modernliğin eleştirisi*. Istanbul: Yapı Kredi Yayınları.

Trimberger, Ellen Kay (1978) *Revolution from above: Military bureaucrats and development in Japan, Turkey, Egypt, and Peru*. New Brunswick, NJ: Transaction Books.

TRT (The Runnymede Trust and the Radical Statistics Race Group) (1980) *Britain's black population*. London: Heinemann.

Trubek, D. M. (1972) 'Toward a social theory of law. An essay on the study of law and development'. In: V. 82 N. 1 *The Yale Law Journal*. 1-50.

Tunçay, Mete (1981) *Türkiye Cumhuriyetinde tek parti yönetiminin kurulması*. Ankara: Yurt Yayınları.

Tunçay, Mete (1992) *T. C. 'nde tek parti yönetiminin kurulmasi (1923-1931)*. 3rd ed. Istanbul: Cem Yayınevi.

Turkel, Gerald (1990) 'Michel Foucault: Law, power, and knowledge'. In: V. 17 N. 1 *Journal of Law and Society*. 170-193.

Türköne, Mümtaz'er (1994a) *Modernleşme, laiklik ve demokrasi*. Istanbul: Ark Yayınları.

Türköne, Mümtaz'er (1994b) *Siyasi ideoloji olarak İslamcılığın doğuşu*. Istanbul: İletişim Yayınları.

Turner, B. S. (1990) *Theories of modernity and postmodernity*. London: Sage.

Turner, B. S. (1994) *Orientalism, postmodernism and globalism*. London: Routledge.

Ünal, Ali and Alphonse Williams (2001) *Advocate of Dialogue: Fethullah Gülen*. Fairfax, VA: The Fountain.

Unger, Roberto (1976) *Law in modern society*. New York: Free Press.

Unger, Roberto (1986) *Critical legal studies movement*. Cambridge, MA: Harvard UP.

Union of Muslim Organizations of the United Kingdom and Eire (1983) *Why Muslim family law for British Muslims?* London: UMO.

United Kingdom Action Committee of Islamic Affairs (1993) *Muslims and the law in multi-faith Britain. Need for reform. Memorandum submitted by the UKACIA*. London: UKACIA.

Üşür, Serpil (1992) 'Islamcı kadınların yaşam alanı: Tepkisel indirgemecilik mi?'. In: Necla Arat (ed) *Türkiye'de kadın olgusu*. Istanbul: Say. 131-149.

Utas, Bo (1988) *Women in Islamic societies. Social attitudes and historical perspectives*. Reprint. London. Malmo?: Curzon Press.

Vago, Steven (1988) *Law and society*. 2nd ed. Englewood Cliffs: Prentice Hall.

Vanderlinden, Jacques (1971) 'Le pluralisme juridique: Essai de synthese'. John Gilissen (ed) *Le pluralisme juridique*. Brussels: Universite de Bruxelles. 19-56.

Vanderlinden, Jacques (1989) 'Return to legal pluralism: Twenty years later'. In: N. 28 *Journal of Legal Pluralism*. 149-157.

Varga, Csaba (1992) *Comparative legal cultures*. Aldershot: Dartmouth.

Vatikiotis, P. S. (1987) *Islam and the state*. London. New York: Routledge.

Vattimo, Giovanni (1991) *The end of modernity: Nihilism and hermeneutics in post-modern culture*. Baltimore: The Johns Hopkins UP.

Veer, Peter van der (1995) (ed) *Nation and migration: Politics of space in the South Asian diaspora*. Philadelphia: University of Pennsylvania Press.

Vefa (1990) (ed) *Islam'da evlilik ve aile*. Istanbul: Vefa.

Velidedeoğlu, Hıfzı Veldet (1957) 'The reception of the Swiss Civil Code in Turkey'. N. 9 *International Social Science Bulletin*. 60-65.

Velidedeoğlu, Hıfzı Veldet (1968) *Türk kadınınn eski ve yeni hukuktaki ve gerçek hayattaki durumu*. Izmir: Izmir Eğitim Enstitüsü Yayınları.

Verma, Gajendra K. (1990) 'Pluralism: Some theoretical and practical considerations'. In: CRE *Britain: A plural society. Report of a seminar*. London: CRE. 44-57.

Vertovec, Steven (1993) *Annotated bibliography of academic publications regarding Islam and Muslims in the United Kingdom, 1985-1992*. Coventry: University of Warwick, CRER.

Vertovec, Steven (1996) 'Muslims, the state, and the public sphere in Britain'. In: Gerd Nonneman et al (eds) *Muslim communities in Europe*. Reading: Ithaca Press. 169-186.

Vikor, Knut S. (1999) 'The Development of *ijtihad* and Islamic Reform' at www.hf-fak.uib.no/institutter/smi/paj/Vikor.html.

Vincenzi, Chirstopher and David Marrington (1992) *Immigration law. The Rules explained*. London: Sweet and Maxwell.

Voll, John Obert (1999) 'Renewal and Reformation in the Mid-twentieth Century: Bediuzzaman Said Nursi and Religion in the 1950s' In: V. 89 Ns. 3-4 *The Muslim World*. 248.

Vries, Pieter de (1996) 'The multiple faces of the ideology of intervention: A story of administrators' fantasies and implementors' anxieties'. In: N. 36 *Journal of Legal Pluralism*. 89-110.

Vyas, Yash et al (1994) (eds) *Law and development in the Third World*. Nairobi: Faculty of Law, University of Nairobi.

Waardenburg, J. (1978) 'Official and popular religion in Islam'. In: V. 15 *Social Compass*. 315-341.

Waardenburg, J. (1991) 'Muslim associations and official bodies in some European countries'. In: W. A. R. Shadid and P. S. van Koningsveld (eds) *The integration of Islam and Hinduism in Western Europe*. Kampen: Kok Pharos Publishing. 24-42.

Wagner, Roy (1995) 'The idea of culture'. In: W. T. Anderson (ed) *The truth about the truth: De-confusing and re-constructing the postmodern world*. New York: G. Putnam's Sons. 53-57.

Wahhab, Iqbal (1989) *Muslims in Britain. Profile of a community*. London: Runnymede Trust.

Wakil, S. Parvez (1991) 'Marriage and the family in Pakistan'. In: Man Singh Das (ed) *The family in the Muslim world*. New Delhi: M. D. Publications. 42-77.

Wallis, Sue (1976) 'Pakistanis in Britain'. In: V. 4 N. 1 *New Community*. 105-115.

Ward, Robert and Dankwart Rustow (1964) (eds) *Political modernization of Japan and Turkey*. Princeton: Princeton UP.

Watson, Alan (1974) *Legal transplants*. Edinburgh: Scottish Academic Press.

Watson, Alan (1976) 'Legal transplants and law reform'. In: V. 92 *The Law Quarterly Review*. 70-85.

Watson, Alan (1977) *Society and legal change*. Edinburgh: Scottish Academic Press.

Watson, Alan (1993) *Legal transplants*. 2nd ed. Edinburgh: Scottish Academic Press.

Watson, Alan (1995) 'From legal transplants to legal formats'. In: V. 43 N. 3 *The American Journal of Comparative Law*. 469-476.

Watson, Alan (1996) 'Aspects of reception of law'. In: V. 44 N. 2 *The American Journal of Comparative Law*. 335-351.

Watson, Helen (1994) 'Women and the veil: Personal responses to global process'. In: Akbar S. Ahmed and Hastings Donnan (eds) *Islam, globalization and postmodernity*. London: Routledge. 141-159.

Watson, J. L. (1977) (ed) *Between two cultures: Migrant and minorities in Britain*. Oxford: Basil Blackwell.

Watt, W. M. (1988) *Islamic fundamentalism and modernity*. London: Routledge.

Weber, M. 1978. *Economy and society*. Berkeley : University of California Press.

Weber, Max (1954) *On law in economy and society*. Tr. by Edward Shils and Max Rheinstein. New York: Simon & Schuster.

Weber, Max (1958) *The Protestant ethic and spirit of capitalism*. Tr. by Talcott Parsons. New York: Scribner's.

Weber, Max (1967) *Law in economy and society*. New York: Simon and Schuster.

Weber, Max (1993) *Sosyoloji yazıları*. Istanbul: Hürriyet Vakfi Yayınlari.

Weiker, Walter F. (1968) 'The Ottoman bureaucracy: Modernisation and reform'. In: V. 13

N. 3 *Administrative Sciences Quarterly*. 451-470.

Weiker, Walter F. (1981) *The modernization of Turkey: From Atatürk to the present day*. New York. London: Holmes & Meier Publishers.

Weiner, Myron (1966) (ed) *Modernization*. New York. London: Basic Books.

Weiner, Myron (1971) 'Political problems of modernizing pre-industrial societies'. In: A. R. Desai (ed) *Essays on modernization of underdeveloped societies*. Bombay: Thacker & Co. 166-174.

Weiner, Myron and Ali Banuazizi (1994) (eds) *The politics of social transformation in Afghanistan, Iran, and Pakistan*. New York: Syracuse UP. 412-444.

Weinstein, Michael A. (1974) 'A binary theory of the limits of law'. In: J. Roland Pennock and John W. Chapman (eds) *The limits of law*. New York: Lieber-Atherton. 102-114.

Weiss, Anita M. (1986a) 'The historical debate on Islam and the state in South Asia'. In: Anita M. Weiss (ed) *Islamic reassertion in Pakistan*. Syracuse: Syracuse UP. 1-20.

Weiss, Anita M. (1986b) (ed) *Islamic reassertion in Pakistan*. Syracuse: Syracuse UP.

Weiss, Anita M. (1986c) 'Implications of the Islamization program for women' In: Anita M. Weiss (ed) *Islamic reassertion in Pakistan*. Syracuse: Syracuse UP. 97-113.

Weiss, Anita M. (1990) 'Benazir Bhutto and the future of women in Pakistan'. In: V. 30 N. 5 *Asian Survey*. 433-445.

Weiss, Anita M. (1994a) 'Challenges of Muslim women in a postmodern world'. In: Akbar S. Ahmed and Hastings Donnan (eds) *Islam, globalization and postmodernity*. London: Routledge. 127-140.

Weiss, Anita M. (1994b) 'The consequences of state policies for women in Pakistan'. In: Myron Weiner and Ali Banuazizi (eds) *The politics of social transformation in Afghanistan, Iran, and Pakistan*. New York: Syracuse UP. 412-444.

Weiss, Bernard G. (1978) 'Interpretation in Islamic law: The theory of *ijtihad*'. In: V. 26 *The American Journal of Comparative Law*. 199-212.

Weiss, Bernard G. (1998) *The spirit of Islamic law*. Athens and London: The University of Georgia Press.

Weissbourd, Bernard and Elizabeth Mertz (1985) 'Rule-centrism versus legal creativity: The skewing of legal ideology through language'. V. 19 N. 4 *Law and Society Review*. 623-660.

Werbner, Pnina (1979) 'Avoiding the ghetto: Pakistani migrants and settlement shifts in Manchester'. In: V. 7 N. 3 *New Community*. 376-389.

Werbner, Pnina (1986) 'The virgin and the clown: Ritual elaboration in Pakistani migrants' weddings'. In: V. 21 *Man*. 227-250.

Werbner, Pnina (1991a) 'Shattered bridges: The dialectics of progress and alienation among British Muslims'. In: V. 17 N. 3 *New Community*. 331-346.

Werbner, Pnina (1991b) 'The fiction of unity in ethnic politics: Aspects of representation and the state among British Pakistanis'. In: Pnina Werbner and M. Anwar (eds) *Black and ethnic leadership in Britain: The cultural dimensions of political action*. London: Routledge. 113-145.

Werbner, Pnina (1994a) 'Diaspora and millennium: British Pakistani global-local fabulations of the Gulf War'. In: Ahmed Akbar S. and Hastings Donnan (eds) *Islam, globalization and postmodernity*. London: Routledge. 213-236.

Werbner, Pnina (1994b) 'Islamic radicalism and the Gulf War: Lay preachers and political dissent among British Pakistanis'. In: Bernard Lewis and Dominique Schnapper (eds) *Muslims in Europe*. London. New York: Pinter. 98-115.

Werbner, Pnina (1995) 'The ranking of brotherhoods: The dialectics of Muslim caste among overseas Pakistanis'. In: T. N. Madan (ed) *Muslim communities of South Asia: Culture, society, and power*. New Delhi: Manohar Book Review Literary Trust. 103-144.

Werbner, Pnina (1996) 'Public spaces, public voices, gender, feminism, and aspects of British Muslim participation in the public sphere'. In: W. A. R. Shadid and P. S. van Koningsveld (eds) *Political participation and identities of Muslims in non-Muslim states*. Kampen: Kok Pharos Publishing. 53-70.

Werbner, Pnina and M. Anwar (ed) (1991) *Black and ethnic leadership in Britain: The cultural dimensions of political action*. London: Routledge. 113-145.

Wertheim, W. F. (1971) 'The way towards 'modernity''. In: A. R. Desai (ed) *Essays on modernization of underdeveloped societies*. Bombay: Thacker & Co. 76-94.

White, Elizabeth H. (1978) 'Legal reform as an indicator of women's status in Muslim nations'. In: Louis Beck and Nikki Keddie (eds) *Women in the Muslim world*. Cambridge, Massachusetts. London: Harvard UP. 52-68.

White, Stephen K. (1991) *Political theory and postmodernism*. Cambridge: Cambridge UP.

Wigmore, J. H. (1926/1927) 'The new regime of law in the Turkish Republic'. V. 21 *Illinois Law Review*. 83-87.

Wilkinson, I. (1988) *Muslim belief and practices in a non-Muslim country: A study of Rochdale*. Muslims in Europe Research Papers, 9. Birmingham: CSIC-MR.

Williams, H. P. (1982) *The role of adjudicatory law in divorce proceedings in Turkey*. Tufts: Tufts University (Unpublished PhD dissertation).

Williams, Ivy (1925) (ed) *The Swiss Civil Code*. Oxford: Oxford UP.

Williams, N. (1987) *Two laws: Managing disputes in a contemporary aboriginal community*. Canberra.

Wilson, A. (1978) *Finding a voice: Asian women in Britain*. London: Virago.

Wilson, R. (2000) 'Reconciliation and revenge in post-apartheid South Africa'. In: V. 41 *Current Anthropology*.157-185.

Wilson, R. (ed.) (1997) *Human rights: Culture and context*. London: Pluto Press.

Wolffe, John (1994) 'Fragmented universality: Islam and Muslims'. In: Gerald Parsons (ed) *The growth of religious diversity: Britain 1945*. London: Routledge. The Open UP. 133-172.

Woodman, Gordon R. (1983) 'Review Essay: The limits of "the limits of law"'. In: V. 21 *Journal of Legal Pluralism*. 129-146.

Woodman, Gordon R. (1985) 'Introduction'. In: G. R. Woodman and A. Allott (eds) *People's law and state law. The Bellagio papers*. Dordrecht: Foris Publications. 277-280.

Woodman, Gordon R. (1988a) 'How state courts create customary laws in Ghana and Nigeria'. In: Bradford W. Morse and Gordon R. Woodman (eds) *Indigenous law and the state*. Dordrecht: Foris Publications. 181-220.

Woodman, Gordon R. (1988b) 'Book review: Peter Sack and Elizabeth Minchin (1986) (eds) *Legal pluralism. Proceedings of the Canberra Law Workshop VII*. Canberra: Law Department, Research School of Social Sciences, Australian National University'. In: N. 27 *Journal of Legal Pluralism*. 173-177.

Woodman, Gordon R. (1992) 'Book review: Masaji Chiba *Legal pluralism*'. In: N. 32 *Journal of Legal Pluralism*. 141-148.

Woodman, Gordon R. (1995) 'Book review: Folk law: Essays in the theory and practice of lex non scripta. New York. London: Garland Publishing (1994) by Alison Dundes Renteln and Alan Dundes'. In: N. 35 *Journal of Legal Pluralism*. 167-172.

Woodman, Gordon R. and Antony Allott (1985) (eds) *People's law and state law. The Bellagio papers*. Dordrecht: Foris Publications.

Woodsmall, Frances (1936) *Moslem women enter a new world*. London: Publications of the American University of Beirut.

Woodsmall, Frances (1983) *Women in the changing Islamic system*. 2nd impression. Delhi:

Bimla Publishing.

Wriggins, W. H. (1979) (ed) *Pakistan in transition*. Islamabad: University of Islamabad.

Yamani, Mai (1996) (ed) *Feminism and Islam: Legal and literary perspective*. Berkshire: Ithaca Press.

Yates, C. (1993) *Religion, family and the law*. London: Sage.

Yavuz, Hakan (1999a) 'The assassination of collective memory: The case of Turkey'. In: V. 89 Ns. 3-4 *The Muslim World*. 195.

Yavuz, Hakan (1999b) 'Towards an Islamic liberalism?: The Nurcu movement and Fethullah Gülen'. In V. 19 N. 1 *The Middle East Journal*. 599.

Yavuz, Hakan (1999c) 'Societal search for a new contract: Fethullah Gülen, Virtue party and the Kurds'. In: V. 19 N. 1. *SAIS Review*.

Yavuz, Hakan (2000) 'Cleansing Islam from the Public Sphere'. In: Fall 2000 *Journal of International Affairs*.

Yazıcıoğlu, Hulusi (1993) *Bir din politikasi olarak laiklik*. Istanbul: IFAV.

Yıldırak, Nurettin (1992) *Köy kadınlarının sosyo-ekonomik ve kültürel konumları*. Istanbul: Friedrich Ebert Vakfı.

Yıldırım, Ergun (1995) *Türkiye'nin modernleşmesi ve Islam*. Istanbul: Insan.

Yılmaz, Aytekin (1995) *Modernden postmoderne siyasal arayışlar*. Ankara: Vadi.

Yilmaz, Ihsan (1999) *Dynamic legal pluralism and the reconstruction of unofficial Muslim laws in England, Turkey and Pakistan*. Unpublished PhD thesis. London: School of Oriental and African Studies.

Yılmaz, Ihsan (2000a) 'Changing Turkish-Muslim discourses on modernity, West and dialogue'. The Congress of The International Association of Middle East Studies (IAMES). Freie Universitat Berlin, Germany. 5-7 October 2000.

Yılmaz, Ihsan (2000b) 'Interview with Fethullah Gülen', 27 March 2000, New York, The United States of America (unpublished).

Yılmaz, Ihsan (2000c) 'Muslim Law in Britain, Reflections in the Socio-Legal Sphere and Differential Legal Treatment', V. 20 N. 2 *Journal of Muslim Minority Affairs*. 353-360.

Yılmaz, Ihsan (2000d) 'Interview with Cemal Uşşak', 3 September 2000, Istanbul, Turkey (unpublished).

Yılmaz, Ihsan (2000e) 'Interview with Yusuf Kalkan', 16 August 2000, Ankara, Turkey (unpublished).

Yilmaz, Ihsan (2000f) 'Interview with Abdullah Aymaz', 3 September 2000, Istanbul, Turkey (unpublished).

Yılmaz, Ihsan (2000g) 'Interview with Harun Tokak', 1 September 2000, Istanbul, Turkey (unpublished).

Yılmaz, Ihsan (2001a) 'Is having a personal law system a solution? Towards a supra-modern law', V. 20 *Journal for Islamic Studies*. 98-122.

Yılmaz, Ihsan (2001b) 'Legal Pluralism in Turkey: Persistence of Muslim laws'. In: V. 7 Ns. 1-2 *International Journal of Turkish Studies*. 110-124.

Yılmaz, Ihsan (2001c) 'Law as chameleon: The question of incorporation of Muslim personal law into the English law' in: V. 21 N. 2 *Journal of Muslim Minority Affairs*. 297-308.

Yılmaz, Ihsan (2002a) 'Secular law and the emergence of unofficial Islamic law in Turkey'. In: V. 56 N. 1 *The Middle East Journal*. 113-131.

Yılmaz, Ihsan (2002b) 'Tavırlarla içtihad ve tecdid: Gülen ve Gülen hareketi', translated by Cemal Uşşak, in Cemal Uşşak (ed) *Küresel barışa doğru*, Istanbul: Gazeteciler ve Yazarlar Vakfı. 27-54.

Yılmaz, Ihsan (2002c) 'Dynamic legal pluralism in England: The challenge of postmodern Muslim legality to legal modernity'. In: V. 28 N. 2 *Journal of Ethnic and Migration*

*Studies*. 343-354.

Yılmaz, Ihsan (2003a) 'Muslim alternative dispute resolution and neo-*Ijtihad* in England'. In: V. 1. N. 5 *Alternatives: Turkish Journal of International Relations*, at http://www.alternativesjournal.net.

Yılmaz, Ihsan (2003b) '*Ijtihad* and *tajdid* by conduct: Gülen and his movement'. In: John Esposito and Hakan Yavuz (eds) *Turkish Islam and the secular state: The Gülen movement*. New York: Syracuse University Press. 208-237.

Yılmaz, Ihsan (2003c) 'Non-recognition of post-modern Turkish socio-legal reality and predicament of women'. In: V. 30 N. 1 *British Journal of Middle Eastern Studies*. 25-41.

Yılmaz, Ihsan (2003d) 'Turkey in London, Diaspora Turks and the Turkish Foreign Policy'. In: U. Ozdag, Y. Kalafat and M. S. Erol (eds) *Turkish Geopolitics in the 21st Century*. V. 2. (in Turkish). Ankara: ASAM. 227-240.

Yılmaz, Ihsan (2004) 'Marriage Solemnization among Turks in Britain: Emergence of the Hybrid Anglo-Muslim Turkish Law'. In: V. 24 N.1 *Journal of Muslim Minority Affairs*. 57-66.

Yılmaz, Ihsan (forthcoming) 'Inter-*madhhab* surfing, neo-*Ijtihad*, and faith-based movement leaders'. In: Frank Vogel, Peri Bearman and Ruud Peters (eds) *The Islamic School of Law: Evolution, Devolution and Progress*. Cambridge, MA: Harvard University Press.

Yngvesson, Barbara (1993) *Virtuous citizens, disruptive subjects*. New York: Routledge.

Zander, Michael (1989) *The law making process*. 3rd ed. London: Weidenfeld and Nicolson.

Zevkliler, Aydın (1984) 'Evliliğin sona ermesi ve kadının malvarlığı'. In: Türköz Erder (ed) *Türkiye'de ailenin değişimi: Yasal açıdan incelemeler*. Ankara: Türk Sosyal Bilimler Derneği. 79-107.

Zevkliler, Aydın (1985) 'Dissolution of marriage and the estate of the woman'. In: Türköz Erder (ed) *Family in Turkish society. Sociological and legal studies*. Ankara: Turkish Social Science Association. 365-388.

Zevkliler, Aydın (1995) *Medeni hukuk*. Istanbul: Savaş.

Ziadeh, Farhat J. (1960) 'Urf and law in Islam'. In: James Kritzeck and R. Bayley Winder (eds) *The world of Islam*. London: Macmillan. 60-67.

Ziadeh, Khalid (1995) 'On the urgency of *ijtihad*'. In: Tarek Mitri (ed) *Religion, law and society: A Christian-Muslim discussion*. Geneva. Kampen: WCC Publications. Kok Pharos. 48-50.

Zinn, Howard (1968) *Civil disobedience and democracy*. New York: Random House.

Zuhayli, Vehbe (1997) *Islam fikhı ansiklopedisi* (Encycopediea of Islamic *Fiqh*). 1-10. Istanbul: Zaman.

Zwahlen, Mary (1981) *Le divorce en Turquie: Contribution à l'étude de la réception du code civil Suisse*. Genéve: Librarie Droz.

# Index